Epistolary Courtiership and
Dramatic Letters

Edinburgh Critical Studies in Renaissance Culture

Series Editors: Lorna Hutson, Katherine Ibbett, Joe Moshenska and Kathryn Murphy

Titles available in the series

Visit the Edinburgh Critical Studies in Renaissance Culture website at www.edinburghuniversitypress.com/series/ECSRC

Epistolary Courtiership and Dramatic Letters

Thomas Overbury and the Jacobean Playhouse

Jackie Watson

EDINBURGH
University Press

Edinburgh University Press is one of the leading university presses in the UK. We publish academic books and journals in our selected subject areas across the humanities and social sciences, combining cutting-edge scholarship with high editorial and production values to produce academic works of lasting importance. For more information visit our website: edinburghuniversitypress.com

Edinburgh University Press Ltd
13 Infirmary Street
Edinburgh EH1 1LT

First printed in hardback by Edinburgh University Press 2024

Typeset in 10.5/13 Adobe Sabon by
Cheshire Typesetting Ltd, Cuddington, Cheshire

A CIP record for this book is available from the British Library

ISBN 978 1 4744 8337 7 (hardback)
ISBN 978 1 4744 8338 4 (paperback)
ISBN 978 1 4744 8339 1 (webready PDF)
ISBN 978 1 4744 8340 7 (epub)

Contents

Acknowledgements

There are many people who enable a book to be written, in many different ways. As this book emerged from the research for my PhD thesis, gratitude extends back over several years . . .

In terms of work space, resources and handling queries, I thank the staff in the Bodleian's Upper Reading Room. I've also benefited from the help of those in the British Library Manuscripts Room and in the National Archive.

I completed my doctoral work at Birkbeck, University of London, and in particular I thank Sue Wiseman for years of support and guidance as I returned to research later in life. Without her belief in me, this book simply wouldn't have been possible. Discussions, conferences and research events with my peers at Birkbeck, including Simon Smith, Rebecca Tomlin, Sue Jones, Judith Hudson and Linda Grant, also contributed a great deal to my work in many ways. I lament the changes in government policy recently that make places like Birkbeck less accessible to future generations of students; it's a very special place.

Ideas from, and sections of, this book have made their way into papers for many conferences over the years. Firstly, I thank all those who contributed to the conference that Darren Royston and I organised at Birkbeck and Middle Temple in 2013, and those at Middle Temple who made it possible; that was a real stimulus to the work here. I also thank Rachel Holmes and Toria Johnson for 'Bonds, Lies, and Circumstances' in St Andrews where my work on letters first emerged blinking into the light. Writing for the Forum special issue after this led to really helpful comment from the two editors. Simon Smith and Emma Whipday's 'Players and Playgoing' conference at Queen's College, Oxford, and writing for the volume emerging from that was also helpful. Most recently, Chloe Fairbanks and Catherine Jenkinson's hugely enjoyable 'On Location' conference at Lady Margaret Hall, Oxford, was an opportunity to air some of the finished writing on Overbury's letters.

Meeting fellow scholars at conferences over the years has led to so many productive conversations that have found their way into my work, often unacknowledged, over the writing of this book; I thank them here.

PhD examiners are important people and I am very grateful to mine; Lucy Munro and Michelle O'Callaghan gave really good advice at that time. Since then, Michelle and Emma Rhatigan have joined me in setting up the Mapping Inns online network, which has allowed me to hear and talk to some amazing scholars in the early modern Inns of Court field. It's been a great way to continue work as an independent scholar, providing a sense of community in what can otherwise be a lonely situation.

Living in Oxford over the last few years has enabled me to access the CEMS Early Modern Literature seminar convened by Lorna Hutson, Katie Murphy, Joe Moshenska and Emma Smith. I thank all of them, their students, and the many wonderful speakers at the seminar, for continuing to widen my thinking after my PhD research was complete.

As well as all those who have heard and commented on parts of this book 'live' at conferences, I would particularly like to thank Simon Smith and Emma Whipday for reading chapters. On top of their heavy workloads, I really appreciate it.

It almost goes without saying that I also thank firstly Michelle Houston and more recently Emily Sharp, Elizabeth Fraser, Fiona Conn and the rest of the team at Edinburgh University Press for their practical help and their faith in me when this almost didn't reach the press! Cathy Falconer was an amazing copy editor! As editors of the Edinburgh Critical Studies in Renaissance Culture series, Katherine Ibbett, Joe Moshenska and Katie Murphy have given very helpful feedback for which I thank them, and I owe a particularly large debt of gratitude to Lorna Hutson, who has given a great deal of friendly support over the last few difficult years, and without whom this book would never have been published. Reading it will show what an inspiration her work has been.

I want, too, to thank Katherine Duncan-Jones for her inspiration, conversation and friendship over many years. She is, unfortunately, no longer able to read this book, but her teaching at Somerville lies behind my love of early modern literature.

Friends are so very important, and, as well as some of those mentioned above, I'd like to thank Lesley Maddox, who supported me through the years of PhD research, and all those special people who have kept me sane through the time I've been writing the book. They know who they are!

Series Editor's Preface

Edinburgh Critical Studies in Renaissance Culture may, as a series title, provoke some surprise. On the one hand, the choice of the word 'culture' (rather than, say, 'literature') suggests that writers in this series subscribe to the now widespread assumption that the 'literary' is not isolable, as a mode of signifying, from other signifying practices that make up what we call 'culture'. On the other hand, most of the critical work in English literary studies of the period 1500–1700 which endorses this idea has rejected the older identification of the period as 'the Renaissance', with its implicit homage to the myth of essential and universal Man coming to stand (in all his sovereign individuality) at the centre of a new world picture. In other words, the term 'culture' in the place of 'literature' leads us to expect the words 'early modern' in the place of 'Renaissance'. Why, then, 'Edinburgh Critical Studies in *Renaissance Culture*'?

The answer to that question lies at the heart of what distinguishes this critical series and defines its parameters. As Terence Cave has argued, the term 'early modern', though admirably egalitarian in conception, has had the unfortunate effect of essentialising the modern, that is, of positing 'the advent of a once-and-for-all modernity' which is the deictic 'here and now' from which we look back.[1] The phrase 'early modern', that is to say, forecloses the possibility of other modernities, other futures that might have arisen, narrowing the scope of what we may learn from the past by construing it as a narrative leading inevitably to Western modernity, to 'us'. *Edinburgh Critical Studies in Renaissance Culture* aims rather to shift the emphasis from a story of progress – early modern to modern – to a series of critical encounters and conversations with the past, which may reveal to us some surprising alternatives buried within texts familiarly construed as episodes on the way to certain identifying features of our endlessly fascinating modernity. In keeping

[1] Terence Cave, 'Locating the Early Modern', *Paragraph* 29.1 (2006), pp. 12–26 (p. 14).

with one aspect of the etymology of 'Renaissance' or 'Rinascimento' as 'rebirth', moreover, this series features books that explore and interpret anew elements of the critical encounter between writers of the period 1500–1700 and texts of Greco-Roman literature, rhetoric, politics, law, oeconomics, *eros* and friendship.

The term 'culture', then, indicates a licence to study and scrutinise objects other than literary ones, and to be more inclusive about both the forms and the material and political stakes of making meaning both in the past and in the present. 'Culture' permits a realisation of the benefits to be reaped after two decades of interdisciplinary enrichment in the arts. No longer are historians naïve about textual criticism, about rhetoric, literary theory or about readerships; likewise, literary critics trained in close reading now also turn easily to court archives, to legal texts, and to the historians' debates about the languages of political and religious thought. Social historians look at printed pamphlets with an eye for narrative structure; literary critics look at court records with awareness of the problems of authority, mediation and institutional procedure. Within these developments, modes of research that became unfashionable and discredited in the 1980s – for example, studies in classical or vernacular 'source texts', or studies of literary 'influence' across linguistic, confessional and geographical boundaries – have acquired a new critical edge and relevance as the convergence of the disciplines enables the unfolding of new cultural histories (that is to say, what was once studied merely as 'literary influence' may now be studied as a fraught cultural encounter). The term 'Renaissance' thus retains the relevance of the idea of consciousness and critique within these textual engagements of past and present, and, while it foregrounds the Western European experience, is intended to provoke comparativist study of wider global perspectives rather than to promote the 'universality' of a local, if far-reaching, historical phenomenon. Finally, as traditional pedagogic boundaries between 'Medieval' and 'Renaissance' are being called into question by cross-disciplinary work emphasising the 'reformation' of social and cultural forms, so this series, while foregrounding the encounter with the classical past, is self-conscious about the ways in which that past is assimilated to the projects of Reformation and Counter-Reformation, spiritual, political and domestic, that finally transformed Christendom into Europe.

Individual books in this series vary in methodology and approach, sometimes blending the sensitivity of close literary analysis with incisive, informed and urgent theoretical argument, at other times offering critiques of grand narratives of the period by their work in manuscript transmission, or in the archives of legal, social and architectural history, or by social histories of gender and childhood. What all these books have in common, however, is the capacity to offer compelling, well-documented and lucidly written critical accounts of how writers and thinkers in the period 1500–1700 reshaped, transformed and critiqued the texts and practices of their world, prompting new perspectives on what we think we have learned from them.

Lorna Hutson, Katherine Ibbett,
Joe Moshenska and Kathryn Murphy

A Note on Letter Transcriptions

In letters I have transcribed from manuscript sources, I have expanded names throughout (so Thom: is written as Thomas, and so on), and I have written in full words that are commonly contracted in early modern writing, such as Lordship, your, which, letters, etc.

I have also regularised spelling in the following ways:

- I have removed e from the ends of words where they are used irregularly and modern spelling would not use them (e.g. Queene becomes Queen)
- I have changed u/v and i/j to match modern spelling
- I have modernised the use of then and than to ensure clarity

I have retained other early modern orthographic variants.

As in many early modern sources, the syntax can be difficult for a modern reader, but I have resisted the temptation to rephrase sentences as it is intended that the letters transcribed here should form a base for further research. I have made some changes to sentence punctuation to enable clearer understanding, though I have not modernised all punctuation, or expanded marks such as the ampersand.

Letters from published collections maintain the spelling and punctuation in that source.

For the supportive women
who have made this book possible.

Introduction
'Common Secrets, Common Dangers': The Origins of a 'Tragical' Courtier

'In good faith, these two made plays of all the world beside themselves; but though it were a play then, it hath proved tragical since.'[1]

On 25 May 1616, a series of trials for the murder of Sir Thomas Overbury came close to an end. Francis Bacon, prosecuting counsel, brought evidence against the Earl of Somerset. Robert Carr before his ennoblement, the earl was accused of poisoning a man who had been his best friend. Thought by many at the royal court to have had a culpable closeness with this same man, he was here in court being accused by Bacon of killing him: not actually because he opposed Carr's marriage to Frances Howard, the usual reason given for the rift between them. Instead, Bacon makes dark allusions to Overbury knowing 'secrets of state' or even 'secrets of nature' that, if exposed, would have ruined Carr; 'he therefore dealt violently with him,' the prosecutor tells the court of Somerset's peers with his customary rhetorical flourish, 'to make him desist with menaces of discovery and the like'.[2] The nobleman was, Bacon persuades the jury, guilty of a 'stream of hatred [against Overbury] of a more deep nature' than simply that resulting from jealousy over a woman.

Bacon's prosecution continues, using a persuasive form of evidence: the epistolary hand of the murdered man against the man accused of killing him. Oddly, the first letter Bacon cites as evidence against Somerset is not extant amongst the papers remaining from the trial, but Overbury is supposed to have written:

---

[1] *A Complete Collection of State Trials and Proceedings for High Treason and Other Crimes and Misdemeanours from the Earliest Period to the Year 1783, with Notes and Other Illustrations, Compiled by T. B. Howell, Esq.*, Vol. II (London: T. C. Hansard, 1816), p. 981.
[2] Howell, *State Trials*, p. 974.

Is this the fruit of my care and love to you? Be these the fruits of common secrets, common dangers? As a man, you cannot suffer me to lie in this misery; yet your behaviour betrays you.[3]

The 'common secrets, common dangers', shared between men who have given 'care and love' to one another, give further evidence of the main motive Bacon argues to have lain behind the murder: the collusion between the king's favourite and the favourite's favourite that meant that Overbury 'knew more of the secrets of state, than the council-table did' because he 'perused [. . .], copied [. . .], registered [. . .], [and] made table-talk' of all the letters sent from ambassadors and intelligenc- ers abroad.[4] A victim Bacon clearly dislikes intensely, who is – apart from not having murdered a man – as guilty as the accused, Thomas Overbury is on trial here too.

A second letter, in Overbury's hand and still remaining in the British Library archive, is used as further evidence of the souring relationship between these unnaturally close men. This time, Bacon seems to add in a line to this letter that isn't there in the original manuscript. Overbury is quoted as writing, 'I was caught in the trap, persuading me that it was a plot of mine enemies to send me beyond sea; and urging me not to accept it, assuring me to free me from any long trouble', seeming to refer to the public reason why he was imprisoned in April 1613. The king had asked him to undertake a diplomatic posting abroad, and Overbury refused. It sounds a foolish thing to have done, and it is understandable that the king would wish to punish such behaviour. But a close prisoner in the Tower for five months? Indeed, as Bacon comments in the trial, getting Overbury made a close prisoner 'but for a contempt' 'was by the device and means of my lord of Somerset, who denied his father to see him, denied his servants that offered to be shut up close prisoners with him, and in effect made him close prisoner to all his friends, and exposed to all his enemies'.[5]

Looking at this trial record opens many of the key ideas behind this book. Francis Bacon's prosecution asks us to consider early modern legal process and evidence giving. It asks that we consider the role of letters in Jacobean society: the issue of who reads them, and how they can be used as evidence against their writer or recipient. Bacon's use of rhetoric to persuade the noble jury of Carr's guilt gives an example of how language guides the hearers' inferences about motive, means, opportunity and the like. Both men were, after all, not natural aristocrats, he seems to tell the

---

[3] Howell, *State Trials*, p. 979.
[4] Howell, *State Trials*, p. 973.
[5] Howell, *State Trials*, p. 977.

lords in the courtroom, and their behaviour was not what many of them might expect of courtiers. Their relationship was close and the closeness, at that level of political power, was a threat to the realm. The king had been deceived by both of them, and his authority misused. To all of these issues, we will return.

This book aims to look again at the story of Thomas Overbury. I want to think about him, not as a murder victim, but as a politician: a successful politician, who gained influence at the court of James VI and I, though he was to lose that influence very suddenly and in a rather sensational way. I should like to examine why that rise and fall might have happened, by looking not at who aimed to kill him, but at his own behaviour and how his contemporaries viewed his professional life at court. Establishing what was important for the success of a Jacobean courtier, and how this compared with the ways men achieved success in the previous reign, leads me to propose that the nature and mechanisms of courtiership shifted profoundly from the court of Elizabeth to that of her successor. James's gender, his personality and his Scottishness contributed to his demand for a different kind of service from the men who surrounded him, though this shift in the nature of courtiership was based on roots in the earlier reign. So, this book aims to revise the modern view of Thomas Overbury and to present him as a man who rose at that court initially because of his ability to meet the expectations of the new king; he became a new kind of courtier.

Key evidence allowing me to assess the nature of courtiership lies in letters: both his own and those of the men who surrounded him at the Jacobean court. The first half of this book, therefore, focuses in three chapters on epistolary evidence of Thomas Overbury's rise at court, his short period of influence, and his subsequent sudden decline. I shall begin in this Introduction, then, with an exploration of the critical context for this work, before moving on to introduce the key areas of focus emerging from that exploration of the letters in the first three chapters.

Much scholarly work has been done in recent years on early modern epistolarity, and I am clearly indebted to the work of researchers such as Gary Schneider and James Daybell on letters as social and material texts.[6] Seeing letters as embedded in social networks, not merely as

---

[6] Key texts that underlie ideas on epistolarity through the first half of this book are Gary Schneider's *The Culture of Epistolarity: Vernacular Letters and Letter Writing in Early Modern England, 1500–1700* (Newark: University of Delaware Press, 2005) and James Daybell's *The Material Letter in Early Modern England: Manuscript Letters and*

exchanges of ideas and feeling between two individuals, is key here. Thinking about the ways in which letter writing opened up the writers to potential danger lies behind a lot of my work on letters between Thomas Overbury and his great friend, Robert Carr: a danger obvious from the preceding account of how these letters were used as evidence in the murder trials. Similarly, Schneider's analysis of the common tropes of early modern letter writing to counteract the instinctive distrust of the content of letters, partly a reaction to the contemporary valorisation of oral communication, has been very useful when exploring how the letters I examine engage with their reader.

I am equally interested to see letters not merely in their social and material context, but as the outcome of humanist education and legal training. As my title suggests, the book's argument is that letters are in many key ways like drama. Written between men who shared many of the experiences of a humanist education, the kind of letters that I look at here rely on formative rhetorical skills learnt in the schoolroom, at university and at the Inns of Court: training that Francis Bacon too benefited from. In this way, the writing of letters is stimulated by the same learning that scholarship has shown to lie behind the writing of drama, and the book aims to demonstrate that, in terms of style and impact on their readers, the letters I examine are productively read in this context.

The work of many scholars in this field has shown the importance of early modern theories of rhetoric, and of how men in the late sixteenth and early seventeenth centuries learnt to develop arguments, propose ideas, influence their audiences and create emotion. Recent influential studies by Colin Burrow, Kathy Eden and Lorna Hutson have made those of us working with early modern texts think about issues of classical influence and reception, and how a knowledge of classical writers translated into *imitatio*, speaking and writing in an effective and affective way.[7] Men with a humanist education were familiar with the content and style of classical texts, and were trained not only to reproduce elements of that in their own work but to embody classical writers they admired. Letters produced by these men had a practical purpose; individuals who aspired to power built their relationships and gained preferment through these means. The persuasive qualities of such

---

the *Culture and Practices of Letter-Writing, 1512–1635* (London: Palgrave Macmillan, 2012).

[7] I am here thinking of texts such as Colin Burrow's *Imitating Authors: Plato to Futurity* (Oxford: Oxford University Press, 2019), Kathy Eden's *Rhetorical Renaissance: The Mistress Art and Her Masterworks* (Chicago: University of Chicago Press, 2022), and Lorna Hutson's *The Invention of Suspicion* (Oxford: Oxford University Press, 2007) and *Circumstantial Shakespeare* (Oxford: Oxford University Press, 2015).

letters secured positions of influence and the wealth consequent on such positions.

In *Imitating Authors*, Colin Burrow gives an overview of sixteenth-century ideas about the essence of *imitatio*. Examining the debate between Gianfrancesco Pico and Pietro Bembo, for instance, he compares their ideas on whether a modern producer of text should pick and choose between elements of different authors as Pico suggested. Noting that each author has their own *elocutio* (choice of words), *inventio* (way of discovering matter to an audience) and disposition (way of ordering elements in discourse), Pico argued that each individual author is inimitable and instead one should pick more eclectically between them. Bembo responded that it was more effective to pick just one author and to transfer 'the likeness of another person's style into your own writing'.[8] The debate influenced texts by Philipp Melanchthon, read widely at the end of the sixteenth century, such as his commentary on Cicero's *De Oratore* (1525) and the two books of his *Rhetorices* (1531). Melanchthon encourages readers to see what a writer does as a 'series of habitual ways of structuring form, or of patterns of structuration', and in his posthumously published book on Book X of Quintilian's *Institutio Oratoria*, printed in 1570, he talked of imitators holding 'an idea' of Cicero in their minds and imitating the *forma* or character of the author concerned, rather than just words and phrases, or even just structure.[9] The writings of Melanchthon, and his pupil Johannes Sturm, were highly influential on the work of educationalists at the end of the century, with publications such as Ascham's *The Scholemaster* (1570) and popular schoolroom texts by Erasmus and Mantuan reliant upon their ideas. These texts, Burrow notes, 'were the core of a slow-burning stylistic and rhetorical revolution'.[10]

This debate in the last decades of the sixteenth century led Thomas Overbury's contemporaries to focus on the development of effective style at the very time when he was at school and university. Born in 1581, Overbury moved from rural Warwickshire to The Queen's College in Oxford, and thence to Middle Temple, registered as entering the Inn in July 1597. His education, like that of the contemporaries this book also discusses, was reliant on humanist learning methods. Burrow elsewhere comments on the facility of playwrights to produce such effective work for the stage because of the practice of the schoolroom that they, like Overbury, had experienced, and their subsequent ability

---

[8] Burrow, *Imitating Authors*, p. 210.
[9] Burrow, *Imitating Authors*, p. 213; p. 216.
[10] Burrow, *Imitating Authors*, p. 226.

to generate engaging and convincing speeches.[11] I argue that many of the letters I examine here are effective in their own situation due in part to the writers' grasp of dramatic impact: based on the very same educational training that led to work for the stage. The seminal work of Lorna Hutson in the field of forensic rhetoric, looking at the use of the topics of circumstance to produce *enargeia* and to create emotion in playhouse audiences, and to guide the inferences they make, has been extremely useful in my examination of the effectiveness of the letters I work with.[12] Her exploration in *The Invention of Suspicion* of the impact on dramatic writing of a pervasive understanding of classical works on rhetoric, popularly by Cicero and Quintilian, shows how audience inference and response to character and situation are driven by the use of circumstantial detail. In the first half of this book I argue that this process, driving the inference of a listener or a reader, works similarly in the reception of letters.

New ideas on *imitatio* and the prevalence of rhetoric in the context of schooling developed in a practical context because Elizabethans considered they could lead to success in public life. Speaking and acting decorously are key facets of advice literature on the subject, from Castiglione's *Book of the Courtier* onwards, and learning from classical models how to persuade orally and in writing was clearly connected to this. The connection between performance on stage and effective performance in the legal courtroom is the subject of Julie Stone Peters' recent work, *Law as Performance*, and she demonstrates persuasively how ancient and medieval ideas developed into the practice of the early modern Inns and in contemporary legal trials.[13] Most of the letter writers I examine in the first half of this book have an education that encompasses the law, and the centrality to legal learning of forensic rhetoric means that the letters I examine are responsive to this.

The construction of legal argument, of a dramatic speech, or of a letter, therefore, uses techniques which Aristotle considered produc-

---

[11] Colin Burrow, *Shakespeare and Classical Antiquity* (Oxford: Oxford University Press, 2013), pp. 42–3. For further discussion of techniques such as *prosopopoeia* see Chapter 2, p. 61 and note.

[12] For instance, in *The Invention of Suspicion*, p. 206, Hutson comments on the process whereby 'we infer probable motives in such a way as to "invent" distinctions and subtly distinctive relationships between dramatic characters. Mimetic "reading" of this kind (which is not just a textual experience, but includes the interpretative hearing and seeing of a performance by theatre audiences) accounts for much of the sophisticated pleasure and comparative naturalism of neoclassical drama (including its Shakespearean development).'

[13] Julie Stone Peters, *Law as Performance: Theatricality, Spectatorship, and the Making of Law in Ancient, Medieval, and Early Modern Europe* (Oxford: Oxford University Press, 2022), *passim*.

tive of artificial proof. As Kathy Eden explains in her work on the Aristotelian tradition, one of the earliest and most influential of Western authorities on the construction of argument explored the power of different types of evidence:

> Early in the *Rhetoric*, Aristotle distinguishes between two kinds of proof (*pisteis*): one is *entechnos* or artificial and belongs properly to the art of rhetoric; the other is *atechnos* or inartificial and is not properly part of the rhetorical art. The inartificial proofs (*atechnoi pisteis*), according to Aristotle, include witness testimony, slave testimony extracted under torture, oaths, laws, oracles, written documents, and so on.[14]

A letter, as a written document, according to Aristotle's taxonomy should be *atechnos*. In the *Rhetoric* his preference is for artificial proof, as it is more responsive to the intention of the accused or a witness in a trial; this should, he argues, produce a more reliable judgement of action. Yet, a letter too can rely on the rhetorical strategies of an oral argument in a courtroom, and reveal intention. On stage, as I've argued elsewhere, the *atechnos* proof of a letter can have the influence of the *entechnos* through being summarised in a particular way by a character, leading to specific audience inferences.[15] In the courtroom too this can be seen to happen, not least in the murder trial this Introduction began with. Some of the letters I will consider in the first part of my book here remain accessible today simply because they were transcribed as evidence for the trial of the Earl and Countess of Somerset, and were used by Francis Bacon in his highly rhetorical courtroom speeches. Even if the rhetorically informed content of the letter itself is not actually to be defined as artificial proof, then, in its oral interpretation, it becomes part of the actor or lawyer's rhetoric. However, I would argue that a letter can convey intention and guide inference in the same way as a legal speech, and the first half of my book explores how the letters surrounding Overbury's rise, power and fall do just this.

In the examination of letters and events in the opening half of this book, then, three key areas of focus emerge that are important to the ideas of courtiership that the book as a whole considers. Firstly, the evidence I examine leads to an exploration of social mobility, and the part played in that by humanist education.[16] As Lynn Enterline reminds

---

[14] Kathy Eden, *Poetic and Legal Fiction in the Aristotelian Tradition* (Princeton: Princeton University Press, 1986), p. 12.
[15] Jackie Watson, '"My lodging is so near the Star Chamber that my pens shake in my hand": Letters, Truth and Lawyers' Fears', in *Forum for Modern Language Studies* special issue, 'In Pursuit of Truth: Law and Emotion in Early Modern Europe' (January 2018), p. 54.
[16] See Chapter 1, pp. 33–5 below.

us in her influential book on the schooling of this period, 'Tudor schoolmasters explicitly designed [. . .] lessons to "train" their boys "up" the social ladder'.[17] Many of the men whose letters I reference in the book, including Overbury, come from comfortable families, of 'the middling sort'. They are not aristocratic, and without talent, hard work and, I argue, the necessary training, and the preferment consequent on these, they would not gain a place in the royal court. The political success of these men relied on the education they had at all levels and, for most of them, their connections to the Inns of Court.

Secondly, another feature of life shared by Overbury and most of the men writing letters that I examine here is homosociality.[18] The importance of male friendship, and male space, to the success of many courtiers is exemplified in an examination of the life of Thomas Overbury, whose friendship with Robert Carr is key to his position at court. As we've seen already, Cicero's work on rhetoric is influential on men's education and verbal training, but another Ciceronian influence significant in this focus on male friendship is *De Amicitia*. Through this widely read classical exemplum, and work inspired by it, developed the understanding that male bonds were not just vital practically to worldly success, but also affective and emotional supports. Friendships between letter writers and their recipients often echoed the close relationship between Overbury and Carr; many of the men writing shared the homosocial context of life at university, at the Inns, and at large parts of James's royal court. The inspiring of affective bonds with potential patrons was the core of an ambitious man's success.

Finally, the first half of the book also considers the relationship between royal power and common law.[19] Legal historians such as Alan Cromartie have proposed that the rising significance of common law in post-Reformation England saw 'the emergence of a mode of government that both expanded and constrained the powers of the monarch'.[20] In fact, '[t]he country's legalistic Reformation', he proposes, 'helped to encourage the belief that English common law was in a strict sense omnicompetent, that is, was capable of finding answers to every social and political question'.[21] A perceived movement from a more confessional idea of justice, seeing the revelation of this as religious mystery,

---

[17] Lynn Enterline, *Shakespeare's Schoolroom: Rhetoric, Discipline, Emotion* (Philadelphia: University of Pennsylvania Press, 2012), p. 6.
[18] See Chapter 2, pp. 51–6 below.
[19] See Chapter 3, pp. 99–102 below.
[20] Alan Cromartie, *The Constitutionalist Revolution: An Essay on the History of England, 1450–1642* (Cambridge: Cambridge University Press, 2006), p. 3.
[21] Cromartie, *The Constitutionalist Revolution*, p. 3.

to the growing importance of the English jury trial, with all the consequences for a more communal idea of justice, has been developed in
recent books by Penelope Geng and Judith Hudson.[22] In their work,
the English jury is part of a wider community of evidence seeking and
judgement making, leading to a more collective judgement and punishment system than is traditionally seen as existing on the continent. The
need to persuade a jury in legal procedure lies of course behind work
such as Lorna Hutson's on the need for persuasive evidence giving, and
contributes to the legal fiction of a constitutional English common law
that the royal prerogative was often positioned against. A rising fear of
absolutism emerging under the Stuart monarchy, coming in part from
James's perception of his own power, led to a debate about the king's
legal authority. Focusing on that Jacobean tension between common
law and royal prerogative, this book goes on to examine perceptions of
advisors, looking at ideas about courtly favourites and abuse of power,
and, contrastingly, lawyers and royal counsellors who represent the
commonweal.

A key argument of this book, that expectations of courtiership
shifted from the reign of Elizabeth to that of James, relies on a conjunction of these three themes. All these ideas were present in some form
in Elizabethan culture, but developed and acted together in Jacobean
England to change wider perceptions of the nature of the royal court,
and to develop an increasing sense of corruption. Talented men rising
socially through humanist education and using male friendship to secure
preferment is not a new situation and was a growing feature of Tudor
England. Those men being vulnerable to royal authority, with equitable
judgement being made as a result of prerogative power, is not, either, a
totally new feature of James's reign. But what developed particularly in
the early years of the seventeenth century was a sense of decline in moral
standards at court and a growing characterisation of its corruption.

The interest in Roman history that often lay behind discussions of
corrupt kingship and abuse of power, again, was not a new feature in
Jacobean England. Interest in the narratives of Tacitus and Suetonius,
and their descriptions of imperial Rome, began to resonate with the
Protestant group that surrounded Sir Philip Sidney, and later the second
Earl of Essex, under Elizabeth, and became something of a touchstone
of oppositional ideas. One of the translators of Tacitus, Sir Henry
Savile, was, like other university classicists such as Henry Cuffe, con-

---

[22] Penelope Geng, *Communal Justice in Shakespeare's England: Drama, Law and
Emotion* (Toronto: University of Toronto Press, 2021), and Judith Hudson, *Crime and
Consequence in Early Modern Literature and Law* (Edinburgh: Edinburgh University
Press, 2022).

nected with Essex in the run-up to his 1601 rebellion, but they suffered to differing degrees as a consequence.[23] Cambridge historian John Hayward's *The First Part of the Reign of Henry IIII* was a product of shifting ideas of historiography in the latter years of Elizabeth's reign, and a book for which he was famously punished by the queen, who saw his account of the deposition of the childless Richard II after a revolt in Ireland as a comment on the succession crisis of the late 1590s.[24] Interest in Neostoicism and Roman history, along with new ideas of the purpose of historical writing, were elements of a courtly counter-culture in the Sidney/Essex circle, and after the execution of Essex and the death of Elizabeth I, members of this circle moved to surround the new Protestant hope, Prince Henry; ideas of courtly reform and opposition to the corruption of power in Jacobean England found a home there until his death in 1612. Interest in Tacitus did not begin as a way of opposing monarchy, but as Malcolm Smuts comments, 'A Tacitean language then developed primarily in association with the issues that dominated court politics, such as the relationship between religion and foreign policy, the proper role of aristocratic warriors in national affairs, and the impact of war and peace on the moral fibre of the nation.'[25] Comparison of the English monarchy to Roman models became part of the subsequent focus on the relationship between king and commons, and out of this political discourse grew the fear of the court favourite: a man whose position at court lay in the wishes of the monarch rather than right of birth.[26] Where the ambitious young men of earlier regimes may have seen preferment in the hands of the aristocracy, others, such as the young Thomas Overbury, turned initially for patronage to men such as Robert Cecil, and later, as I've suggested above, he relied on his

---

[23] Cuffe was hanged for his part in the rebellion, but, after a brief imprisonment, Savile was released.

[24] See S. L. Goldberg's groundbreaking study looking at shifting ideas of history in this period, 'John Hayward, Politic Historian', *The Review of English Studies*, n.s., Vol. 6, No. 23 (July 1955), pp. 233–44. His work is developed by Alan T. Bradford, 'Stuart Absolutism and the "Utility" of Tacitus', *Huntington Library Quarterly*, Vol. 46, No. 2 (Spring 1983), pp. 127–55, and Malcolm Smuts in 'Court-Centred Politics and the Uses of Roman Historians, c.1590–1630', in *Culture and Politics in Early Stuart England*, ed. by Kevin Sharpe and Peter Lake (London: Macmillan, 1994), pp. 21–43.

[25] Smuts, 'Court-Centred Politics', p. 40.

[26] As Alastair Bellany notes, in his consideration of the nature of the Overbury scandal to Jacobeans, '[t]he Tacitean critique of court life was accompanied during the 1590s by critiques of the *regnum Cecilianum* generated from the archaic codes and values of traditional English honour culture' (*The Politics of Court Scandal: News Culture and the Overbury Affair* (Cambridge: Cambridge University Press, 2002), p. 140). This mixture of Roman history and English social hierarchy also led to judgements of James's court favourites, and of Overbury himself.

closeness to Robert Carr, whose own power relied on the affection of the king.

My exploration of the epistolary evidence surrounding Overbury's career, in this political context and in the contemporary legal context, thus allows me to draw conclusions about likely reader response to these letters. As scholars working on rhetoric have argued, audiences in a playhouse made inferences about a character's motivation and feelings based on the circumstantial detail presented in the language of the play. I argue here that the readers of a letter made the same kind of judgement, and were driven by the detail provided by the writer to make assessments of the action and motivation specifically of Thomas Overbury. As for an audience in a theatre, rhetorical evidence allows readers of letters to act in a similar way to a member of a jury in a legal trial. This combination of understanding of the mechanics of a rhetorical education, familiarity with contemporary legal procedure, and grasp of the early Jacobean political moment enables me, in the first half of this book, to present new ideas on the reception of the courtier Thomas Overbury by his peers, and, from this, to draw conclusions about the changing nature of courtiership in the period.

It is perhaps useful at this point to give a fuller understanding of Thomas Overbury's life leading up to the period under discussion here. Neither landed nor titled, but part of the lesser gentry from yeoman stock, Overbury was a member of a rising class of Protestant men, educated to make his mark on the world. Born in 1581 in Compton Scorpion (or Scorfen), near Ilmington in Warwickshire, he was the son of Nicholas Overbury, a man who clearly had ambitions for the family. Sending his sons to be expensively educated at Oxford, Nicholas ensured that they could go on to consolidate these family aspirations. All three, Thomas, Giles and Walter, then followed their father to the Inns of Court. Nicholas was admitted to Middle Temple on 2 May 1574, was called to the bar apparently around July 1582, and led an active legal life.[27] Records of his activities at the Inn become patchier between February 1585 and the summer of 1596, during which time his business seems to have taken him out of London. In 1598 he bought the manor of

[27] See the *Minutes of parliament of the Middle temple, tr. and ed. by C. T. Martin, with an inquiry into the origin and early history of the inn, by J. Hutchinson*, Vol. I (London: Middle Temple, 1904), p. 252. Nicholas Overbury is named one of the three men *likely* to be called by the Reader, Mr Hannam, in 1582, though the date when he is actually called is not recorded.

Bourton-on-the-Hill from John Palmer, to whom he was related through marriage, as well as an interest in the manor of Compton Scorpion (where Thomas had been born) from a Henry Maynard.[28] Nicholas became a Reader at Middle Temple in 1600 and finally its Treasurer in 1610.[29] This last honour, as well as his becoming MP for Gloucester and gaining a knighthood, came only after his eldest son rose to a courtly position that seems to have helped his father's advancement.[30] Though his father was clearly respected in the legal world and an increasingly successful man, Thomas was, as we shall see, self-motivated and force-ful. Unlike his father, much of whose success was provincial, Thomas aimed for influence close to the throne. Thus, encouraged by his father and equipped with a suitable background, he demonstrated his own ambition.

This relied upon a suitable university education. There were many examples of men from non-aristocratic backgrounds, whose families had only been part of the gentry for a generation or two, or were from merchant or artisanal stock, who throve this way and Thomas was part of a wider societal shift. A more theoretical consideration of the relation-ship between education and social class weighs the cultural capital that such an upbringing gives. In his exploration of early modern educational experience as a transition from boyhood to manhood, Alan Stewart cites Pierre Bourdieu's theory that the educative process is one which marks out different social groups: a process which Bourdieu calls 'acts of con-secration' or 'acts of institution'. Further developing this idea through modifying Arnold van Gennep's work on rites of passage, Bourdieu explains that such a rite 'separate[s] those who have undergone it, not from those who have not yet undergone it, but from those who will not undergo it in any sense'. It 'thereby institute[s] a lasting difference between those to whom the rite pertains and those to whom it does not pertain'.[31] In this context, Overbury was educated in a system that sepa-

---

[28] See John Considine's *ODNB* entry on Thomas Overbury, which mentions acquisition of the Bourton-on-the-Hill manor (see https://www.oxforddnb.com for all references to the *ODNB*). The transfer of Compton Scorpion is recorded in Victoria County History of Warwickshire; see State Papers Online, http://www.british-history.ac.uk/report.aspx ?compid=57077&strquery=Overbury (accessed 15 October 2010).

[29] *Minutes of parliament*, Vol. I, p. 198. On 27 June of the same year, Nicholas Overbury is recorded as joining Mr Swayne's chamber (p. 202), though he was in chambers with a quick succession of men over his first few years, as Mr Swayne quickly surrendered his place (p. 207), then his successor, Mr Holbech, died and was replaced by Mr Robert Rosyer (p. 211). See also Arthur Robert Ingpen, KC, *The Middle Temple Bench Book* (London: Chiswick Press, 1912), p. 168.

[30] Nicholas Overbury was MP for Gloucester from 1604 to 1611. He was knighted in 1621, fourteen years after his son.

[31] Alan Stewart, *Close Readers: Humanism and Sodomy in Early Modern England*

rated out aspirant young men from those who did not attend university or the Inns of Court. He was part of an educative system that fostered courtly ambition: one which both empowered those who experienced it to compete for court preferment, and expected that they should do so.

Thomas's entry to The Queen's College, Oxford, thus gave him the first element of the cultural capital required for entry to that elite group of men who could access courtly success. His matriculation at fourteen may have demonstrated that he was already showing signs of being intelligent; his brothers did not go up until they were seventeen and eighteen years old, and, although he was by no means unique in his entry at this age, it is below average. According to the nineteenth-century editor of what were then supposed to be Thomas's works, Edward F. Rimbault, 'through the aid of a good tutor and severe discipline, he made rapid progress in philosophy and logic' and, through his intellect, embarked on his rising path.[32] Equally, though, his entry at fourteen could have been further evidence of his father's ambition for his eldest son, and the differential could simply reflect more pragmatic, financial challenges in funding three young men at university.

The choice of college is perhaps of some significance in Thomas's future decisions and affiliations. As the first of his immediate family to access a university education, at Queen's in the late 1590s he was immersed in a college strongly Puritan in its outlook. Although it is impossible to tell whether his family chose Queen's because of its religious sympathies, it is likely that the young Thomas was influenced by them.

In order to establish early influences on Thomas, it is productive to look at those who taught at Queen's. The college was ably led by Henry Robinson, who had turned the college around after his election as Provost in 1581: an election which relied on the assistance of Francis Walsingham. Queen's was thus gaining in reputation. Monumental brasses at the college and at the cathedral in Carlisle, where Robinson was later to be bishop, celebrate his achievements and state that 'invenit destructum, reliquit extructum et instructum'; that is, he had found the

---

(Princeton: Princeton University Press, 1997), p. 101; Pierre Bourdieu, *Ce que parler veut dire: l'économie des échanges linguistiques,* trans. by Gino Raymond and Matthew Adamson, ed. by John B. Thompson, as *Language and Symbolic Power* (Cambridge: Polity, 1991), p. 117, which cites Arnold van Gennep, *Les rites de passage,* trans. by Monika B. Vizedom and Gabrielle L. Caffee as *The Rites of Passage* (Chicago: University of Chicago Press, 1960).

[32] *The Miscellaneous Works in Prose and Verse of Sir Thomas Overbury, Knt,* ed. by Edward F. Rimbault (London: John Russell Smith, 1856), p. xxvi. Since then, attribution of many of these writings has been contested.

college run down, and had left it built up, physically and spiritually.[33] As well as ensuring that the place was on a secure financial footing, Robinson set the religious tone. As Bishop of Carlisle in 1599 he would go on to do all he could to support those who opposed Catholicism and what they perceived as Catholic tendencies within the Anglican Church, writing to Robert Cecil complaining of the number of recusants in his diocese; his strongly Protestant attitudes were also visible in Oxford.[34] This is seen in the appointments made to the fellowship under his leadership, which saw the arrival of influential and charismatic men, residing and working at Queen's while Thomas was a student.

Fellows included William Hynde, who was elected in 1595 as Thomas matriculated and is described by the college historian as a 'ringleader of non-conformists'; Bernard Robinson, whose preaching in 1591 led to his suspension for 'being Calvinistical'; and John Aglionby, who later took part in the project to create the Authorised Version of the Bible.[35] One of Robinson's most influential moves while in Oxford was to support John Rainolds in his migration from Corpus Christi to Queen's in 1586.[36] Originally from a Catholic family, Rainolds converted in the late 1560s and was considered reliable enough in his faith to be tutor to Richard Hooker. Indeed, he became a champion of Protestantism. Working alongside other fellows from Queen's, Rainolds was later to take a leading part in the Hampton Court Conference and was influential in the work on the Authorised Version of the Bible. He was a powerful speaker and he was under the patronage of powerful Protestant courtiers throughout: first, the Earl of Leicester and Francis Walsingham, and, later, the Earl of Essex, who inherited the mantle of protector of Protestantism. Rainolds was, for instance, selected by Walsingham early in the 1580s to defeat prominent Jesuits in public debate and his special lectureship in controversial theology was paid for initially by Walsingham, and after his death by his then son-in-law, Essex. It appears that Rainolds was a determined and sometimes difficult man to work with. Resigning his twenty-three-year Fellowship at Corpus after irreconcilable differences over the college presidency, he moved to Queen's as a place of refuge.

As Rainolds took an active role in teaching, it is likely that Thomas was in the audience for his very popular lectures. Part of this popularity

---

[33] J. R. Magrath, *The Queen's College* (Oxford: Clarendon Press, 1921), p. 212.
[34] See Margaret Clark's *ODNB* entry for Henry Robinson.
[35] Magrath, *The Queen's College*, pp. 216–17.
[36] Magrath, *The Queen's College*, p. 220, gives the date 1586; Mordechai Feingold's *ODNB* entry on John Rainolds clarifies that the lectureship was endowed in 1586, but that Rainolds moved to Queen's in 1588.

may be explained by his evidently charismatic personality, and an early enjoyment of acting could well have helped develop the performative skills he relied upon in later life. The Oxford antiquary Miles Windsor recalls Rainolds' role in *Palamon and Arcite*, written by Richard Edwards, Master of the Children of the Chapel Royal. The play was performed at Christ Church in 1566, while Rainolds was still a student, and it provoked royal approval:

> The Queen laughed full heartily afterward at some of the players [. . .] and gave unto John Rainolds, a scholar of Corpus Christi College which was a player in the same play, eight old angels in reward.[37]

For schoolboys reared in a humanist tradition, dramatic performance was a key part of their training. Hence, what we might see as the irony of a Puritan-leaning and later anti-theatrical theologian having begun his public life as a student actor must have been one to which many such men at this period were subject. Yet whether Rainolds' histrionic talent was at the root of his attraction as a lecturer or not, he certainly continued to be an influence on Oxford and on Queen's through the 1590s. Despite Elizabeth's early enjoyment of his dramatic performance, she was concerned that his Puritan ideas were sometimes ahead of the Elizabethan settlement, and refused to support his promotion and consequent return to Corpus, instead making him Dean of Lincoln in 1593.[38] Rainolds continued, though, to live and work in Oxford; he took part in tuition at Queen's until, at the point when Thomas left the college in 1598, he finally gained the Presidency of Corpus Christi.[39]

As we can see illustrated amongst the ambitious university men of Queen's, political culture in Elizabethan England demanded the acquisition of patronage. Walsingham's support for Henry Robinson, as well as his adoption of John Rainolds as his champion against the Jesuits, meant that both men gained status and the means to continue their academic and religious work. The patronage of the Earl of Essex after Walsingham's death allowed Rainolds influence. Thomas thus witnessed as a student one of the key mechanisms of power in the late Elizabethan regime. Both his Protestant beliefs and his understanding of preferment, the most common means of achieving greatness in late sixteenth-century England, have their roots in his life before he reached London.

---

[37] John R. Elliott et al., eds, *Records of Early English Drama: Oxford*, 2 vols. (Toronto: University of Toronto Press, 2004), Vol. I, pp. 131–3.
[38] Though he continued to obfuscate and was only actually installed five years later, in 1598 (see Feingold's *ODNB* entry on Rainolds).
[39] Magrath, *The Queen's College*, p. 220.

Social mobility in the political culture of late Elizabethan England was most often secured by men who took the path from Oxford or Cambridge to the Inns of Court: men aiming to achieve, or consolidate, the status of gentleman. Thomas Overbury was in this respect typical and he became a member of his father's Inn, the Middle Temple, joining an increasingly large number of young men, as the effect of humanist educational development was felt in London, as well as in Oxford and Cambridge.[40] Philip J. Finkelpearl notes that, 'by the end of the century, there were said to be 1,040 men in residence (1,703 including those in the Inns of Chancery)' and this constituted 'a thirty percent increase in attendance' at the Inns since the 1570s.[41] His analysis of the numbers in Thomas's time indicates the rising power and influence of Innsmen. Approximately half were university graduates, and this represents a growing proportion, reflecting the increasing number of men, like Thomas, who were the first generation of their family to attend university. Although his father was already a gentleman, he was of the lesser gentry, with origins in the yeoman class, and several late Elizabethan writers comment on the mobility of the sons of this particular group. As William Harrison tells his readers in his *Historical Description*, appendant to Holinshed's *Chronicles*:

> many of them are able and do buy the lands of unthrifty gentlemen, and often sending their sons to the schools, to the universities, and the inns of court, or otherwise leaving them sufficient lands whereupon they may live without labour, do make them by these means to become gentlemen.[42]

Thomas Wilson, like Harrison, comments on this social shift, but without Harrison's objective tone. He condemns those who are 'not contented with their states of their fathers to be counted yeomen [. . .] but must skipp into his velvett breches and silken dublett and, getting to be admitted into some Inn of Court or Chancery, must ever after thinke skorne to be called any other then gentlemen'.[43] Citing this quotation from Wilson in her examination of audiences at the nearby theatre at

---

[40] H. A. C. Sturgess, *Register of admissions to the Honourable Society of the Middle Temple, from the fifteenth century to the year 1944*, 3 vols. (London: Published for the Honourable Society of the Middle Temple by Butterworth, 1949). This records that he was admitted on 30 July 1597 (Vol. I, p. 72), though he is usually described as entering in 1598 (as in Considine's *ODNB* entry for Overbury).

[41] Philip J. Finkelpearl, *John Marston of the Middle Temple: An Elizabethan Dramatist in His Social Setting* (Cambridge, MA: Harvard University Press, 1969), p. 5.

[42] William Harrison, *An Historical Description of the Iland of Britaine*, printed in Ralph Holinshed's *Chronicles* (London, 1587), p. 163, ll. 32–9.

[43] *The State of England Anno Dom. 1600 by Thomas Wilson*, ed. by F. J. Fisher, in *The Camden Miscellany*, Vol. XVI (London: Royal Historical Society, 1936), p. 19.

Blackfriars, Lucy Munro demonstrates how difficult it became to define rank in such a socially mobile environment. '[A]spirant children of yeomen, tradesmen and professionals, and anxious gentry', she notes, were 'the section of society' that

> was the most nebulous of social categories, since it was increasingly difficult to ascertain which features defined a gentleman. Most frequently mentioned as reliable indicators are the possession of external rank or office, money and an education, and, most vague of all, the 'appearance' of a gentleman.[44]

At least in part, this difficulty is the result of the number of young men in a similar position to that of Thomas. As those with a university education, an Inns of Court training, and other skills which gave this gentlemanly 'appearance' grew in number, the older established definitions of what it meant to be of such a rank were less easy to maintain.

At the Inns of Court in the final years of Elizabeth's reign, Thomas and many of the men in residence alongside him were typical in grasping the potential for social mobility. A final piece of Finkelpearl's evidence sets Thomas's presence at Middle Temple in context and establishes another series of links which a young man could use to his advantage. Though men from a range of counties were to be found at all four Inns, each had larger numbers from certain parts of the kingdom and Finkelpearl comments that, 'of such concentrations, the most extreme occurred in the Middle Temple'. As well as members from the south and west generally, it was 'the favorite Inn for Warwickshire: thirty-one admitted between 1587 and 1603, while the three other Inns admitted a total of twenty'.[45] In so many ways, then, Thomas Overbury typified his London contemporaries; his education, his county of origin and his family connection all explained his presence at Middle Temple and gave him a network of connections with his peers. Amongst those was his father. Nicholas Overbury was often in residence alongside his son, and features regularly during this period in the Inn's parliament records. As Finkelpearl comments, 'it was not unusual for a lawyer-father to have as his chambermate his own son: such was the case with John Marston, the dramatist, whose father was one of the Benchers of the Middle Temple'.[46] This was the case with Thomas too who, approximately two years after his entry to the Inn, was admitted to the chamber of his father and Mr John Ashcombe.[47]

---

[44] Lucy Munro, *Children of the Queen's Revels* (Cambridge: Cambridge University Press, 2005), p. 66.
[45] Finkelpearl, *John Marston of the Middle Temple*, p. 7.
[46] Finkelpearl, *John Marston of the Middle Temple*, p. 6.
[47] On 6 June 1600, according to the *Minutes of parliament*, Vol. I, p. 406.

Beyond his filial ties, Thomas found himself contemporary with others who were to become famous in legal, political and literary terms. This coterie included John Marston, and also John Hoskins, Benjamin Rudyerd, Richard Martin, John Davies and John Manningham. All of these, bar Manningham, had been junior members of Middle Temple for some time.[48] Richard Martin was a man whose rhetorical brilliance was to be shown most publicly when in 1604 he was chosen to deliver an oration at Stamford Hill, on the new monarch's entry into London. Martin shared an Oxford background with Marston and Wykehamists John Hoskins, Benjamin Rudyerd and John Davies, though not all had graduated. While Marston studied at Brasenose, and others had been at New College, John Davies had, as Thomas, been a student at Queen's, albeit some ten years earlier. The act of being bound with another man at the Inns was, alongside school, university, family or regional connections, influential on the building of social groupings there. It meant, as antiquary William Dugdale explained, 'two others formerly admitted of the House, enter into Bond with him, as his sureties, to observe the Orders, and dischardge the duties of the House'.[49] The circle of Middle Templars, as Finkelpearl notes, '[t]o a remarkable degree [. . .] pursued the same course in life, shared the same tastes and preferences, and often tended to act in very similar ways'. Their later path in life was very similar too as 'all became lawyers, most of them highly distinguished ones. None of them had much money; consequently they had to acquire a profession'.[50] They had begun from the same kind of roots as Thomas, and the homosocial environment in which they flourished continued to support and influence the Innsmen who followed them.

In the first half of this book, then, I look at Thomas Overbury's life as he leaves Middle Temple. I have made the choice to refer to him throughout this section as Thomas. This is a deliberate attempt to encourage the reader to see him, not as a victim of others' actions,

[48] John Marston was admitted to Middle Temple in 1592, though he probably didn't take up residence until he had graduated from Oxford in 1594; John Hoskins entered Middle Temple in 1593; Benjamin Rudyerd in 1590; Richard Martin in 1590; and John Davies in 1588.

[49] William Dugdale, *The Histories and Antiquities of the Four Inns of Court* (London, 1780), p. 102. Thomas Overbury was bound with his father, according to the *Minutes of parliament*, Vol. I, p. 376. There is a second name, deleted in the printed version. Subsequently, on 30 January 1601, both Mr William Uvedale, of Wickham, Hants, and his brother, Richard, are bound with Thomas, as well as with each other, and on 5 February 1601, Robert Barkeley, of Worcester, is bound with Thomas and Mr Austin (or Augustine) Nyccolles (p. 410).

[50] Finkelpearl, *John Marston of the Middle Temple*, pp. 46–7. See also Sean Kelsey's *ODNB* entry for Sir John Davies, and Wilfrid Prest's for John Hoskins.

as most previous books have done, but as the protagonist in his own drama. Whether we approve of his choices, or think he was wise to have made them; whether we feel we would have liked him if we had met him, or can see the appeal he had for his friends; this book aims to encourage readers to think about him as the character at the centre of the stage.

As I mention above, my book is written in two halves. The first three chapters focus, respectively, on the rise, the power and the fall of Thomas, with edited versions of the letters cited in the chapter following each. The second half of the book moves to drama, looking at three plays, contemporary with the time covered in the first chapters, that exemplify the representation of courtiership on stage.

In the first half of the book, then, I use letters as a way to examine the political, social and legal context in which Thomas lived. The first chapter begins with his trip to Edinburgh while he is still a student at Middle Temple – technically before the period the book focuses on, but indicative of the ambition for professional success that I go on to discuss in key letters dating from 1609. These are written by Thomas to Robert Cecil as the young man aims to gain status and, it appears, to work for the Lord Secretary. Though Thomas has already appeared to be rising at court, made a server by the king and knighted in 1608, he writes a series of letters to Cecil that show his ability to write persuasively, to meet the requirements of such letters in the period, and appear to show his aspiration lying in the area of government bureaucracy, ambassadorial work, or intelligencing abroad. The chapter shows how social mobility in the period is enabled by the training provided in a humanist education, and how Thomas uses his facility with language to build his political career. Thus, it explores the first of the areas the book as a whole argues are elements of successful courtiership.

The second chapter moves to 1611–12, and focuses on Thomas's growing political power. I examine here two sequences of letters, one, in 1611, showing speculation about his political potential and the events leading up to his expulsion from court at the queen's request; the second from his political zenith, amidst the battle to replace Robert Cecil as Secretary in 1612. Thomas's conflict with Queen Anna exposes a weakness in his position, but he is, at this point, supported by many at court, and he returns to grow ever more influential over the succeeding months, largely due to his friendship with Robert Carr. The second group of letters also rely on this friendship, as Henry Neville and Ralph

Winwood aim to secure Thomas's support, and through him that of Robert Carr, in their bid for the king's preferment. Perceptions of male friendship, and its context within contemporary ideas about *amicitia* and sodomy, underlie this chapter: the second of the key areas connected with political success at the Jacobean court. Topographically, Thomas has moved now from Edinburgh in Chapter 1, where I argue he first showed real ambition to rise in Jacobean society, to Royston, where the king's hunting lodge formed an alternative court when James escaped the capital with his male entourage. In Chapter 2, Thomas is at its homosocial centre.

Thomas's sudden and rapid political decline in 1613, and the months from his arrest in April until his death in September, are the subject of the third chapter: the last of the first half of the book. The letters here are a mixture of those written by courtly commentators, with more or less objectivity, and the deeply personal, often dictatorial, letters written by Thomas to Carr from the location symbolic of this stage in his career: the Tower. The chapter looks at the king's legal authority and how, when Thomas offends him, James makes the courtier a close prisoner without legal redress. I explore in more detail here the king's relationship with common law, how royal prerogative was viewed as a threat to historically English values, and how courtly counsel relates to the potential threat of absolute power.

Following these chapters on the political career of Thomas Overbury, raising key issues of courtiership in this period, the second half of the book moves on to the stage. I look at plays from the period under discussion here, between 1609 and 1613, that show the wider dissemination of these issues. Chapter 4 continues the discussion of common law and the royal prerogative, and the potential for a king moving towards absolutism, by focusing on the role of Camillo, Leontes' counsellor, in Shakespeare's *The Winter's Tale*. This leads on to a discussion in Chapter 5 of the need for homosocial skill and a flexible morality to secure social mobility in Webster's *The Duchess of Malfi*. Finally, in Chapter 6, I consider two plays by Chapman, *Bussy D'Ambois* and *The Revenge of Bussy D'Ambois*. The plays in the previous two chapters were written in the period under discussion in the book. My argument in the final chapter is that Chapman's revisions of the earlier play, written originally for performance around 1604 and first published in 1607, along with the writing of the sequel in 1610, demonstrate effectively the thesis of this book as a whole. The two plays, one pre-dating Overbury's court career, and the other written in the midst of it, show shifting ideas about what it means to work at the king's court. Focused too on social mobility, the practical and personal need for homosocial friendship, and tension between law and monarchy, Chapman's plays show clearly a reflection on stage of the shifting nature of courtiership that I argue Thomas Overbury's career exemplifies.

Chapter 1

The Path to Power at the Jacobean Court: Overbury's Rise

> Who would rely upon these miserable dependences, in expectation to be advanced tomorrow?
>
> *The Duchess of Malfi*, 1.1.56–7

Thomas Overbury's rise at the Jacobean court can, in retrospect, be seen to have its origins not only in the late Elizabethan education covered in this book's Introduction, but in the apparently serendipitous advantage emerging from a 'voyage of pleasure'. Thomas's father, Nicholas, later dictated his memories of this time to his grandson, Nicolas Oldisworth of Borton, and told him, as the third in a rather random list of recollections:

> when Sir THOMAS OVERBURY was a little past 20 years old, he and John Guilby, his father's chief clerk, were sent (upon a voyage of pleasure) to Edinburgh, with 60*li* between them. There Thomas mett with Sir William Cornwallis, one who knew him in Queen's college at Oxford. Sir William commended him to diverse, & among the rest to Robin Carr, then page to the earl of Dunbarre: so they two came along to England together, & were great friends.[1]

In a short space, his father accounts for the later success his son is to achieve at the court of James VI and I. With the benefit of hindsight, it is clear that this meeting with Robert Carr (or Kerr) was to be the political making of Thomas.[2] Interestingly, he was 'sent' to the court of the Scottish king (begging the question, 'by whom?') as the Essex Rebellion and its aftermath stirred up London, keeping the young man well away from the potential attractions of the earl's party. Building on the homo-

---

[1] BL Add. MS 15476, fol. 92ᵛ.

[2] Nicholas is not quite right in his recollection that the two men travelled down to London together. It was not until 1603, on the new king's accession, that Carr journeyed south.

social training of his university and Inns of Court education, Thomas immediately made his connections count. His university friendship with Sir William Cornwallis led to his new acquaintance with 'diverse' others, including Carr: a well-born, but still rather lowly, page in the household of Sir George Home, Lord Treasurer of Scotland and soon to be the Earl of Dunbar. This particular friendship would prove the most important of his life, and its basis lay in Thomas's ability to work effectively in a homosocial environment.

The Scottish court was a very different place from that of the elderly queen Thomas had left behind in London. The structures of power were different, and closer to those established by the French that were influential on Edinburgh as a result of 'the auld alliance' and the time spent by James's mother, Mary Queen of Scots, at the French court. The Scottish court aimed to manage access to the king, rather than to ensure that a royal distance was kept from their courtiers, as Tudor monarchs had preferred in England. Even the physical layout of the buildings demonstrated this dynamic. As scholar of court history Neil Cuddy explains:

> The planning of the Scottish palace tells its own story. The sequence of rooms consisted of the Hall or Guard Hall, Presence Chamber and Bedchamber. Beyond lay a Cabinet; then a door leading to the queen's Chamber. The whole suite functioned as the royal lodging: James worked in his Cabinet; slept in his Chamber and dined in his Presence, chatting informally as he did so with the waiters at his table and lookers-on alike.[3]

Another visitor to James's court in 1601 while the Essex Rebellion took place was Thomas's fellow student at Oxford and Middle Temple, Henry Wotton. In his case continental, and now Scottish, travels also distanced him from the dangerous earl, whose secretary he had been not many months before. The reason for Wotton's presence in Edinburgh sounds like the plot of an early modern play. In the guise of an Italian merchant, Ottavio Baldi, he brought the Scottish king a secret message from Ferdinand I, Grand Duke of Tuscany, warning James of a potential poison plot and bearing a box of antidotes as a token of the Italian duke's good will. We are told by Sir Isaak Walton, Wotton's later biographer, that he was welcomed and his true identity concealed by the king during his stay. He wrote to his Italian friends of the nature of the Scottish court. 'Fra gli suoi domestici et gentilhuomini di Camera si mostra molto famigliare,' he writes, noting the king's familiarity

---

3 Neil Cuddy, 'The Revival of the Entourage: The Bedchamber of James I, 1603–1625', in *The English Court: From the Wars of the Roses to the Civil War*, ed. by David Starkey et al. (London: Longman, 1987), pp. 173–225 (p. 178).

with the Gentlemen of his Bedchamber.[4] Discussing how difficult it is, in such a relatively small court, to remain unknown, he notes how everyone around James will question someone new on why they are at court, and what they want. Their 'gran zelo verso lor Padrone' is clear, and the king's safety is clearly maintained, but nonetheless this was a court with relatively open access to the monarch and was thus quite different to English palaces.[5] This was a difference which Thomas too must have noticed on his visit in 1601, and foreknowledge may have given him an advantage three years later in his quest for promotion after James's arrival in London as the king of England. Thomas's familiarity with the demands of homosocial life must have helped, as he worked later for preferment at the new Jacobean court. Two central aspects of Jacobean courtiership – homosociality and the quest for social mobility – are thus already combined in his early career.

Whereas physical proximity to Elizabeth in her private courtly space was mediated by female attendants, access to the body of the Scottish king enabled male power. The different system of rule in Scotland meant that men with an official post in the royal Bedchamber had a more intimate and personal influence over James and in this context they could work effectively for preferment. Physical closeness between men was, of course, a normal part of early modern life at many levels. Thomas's friend Sir William Cornwallis, who met the younger man in Scotland in 1601, was an intimate of John Donne and, as Donne's biographer notes, their friendship was so close, it no longer required niceties:

> Sir William Cornwallis, the friend who urged Donne to 'come to my den' whenever he had a spare hour, wrote telling Donne that they would have to stop saying they love each other. 'Often have I tolde thee I love thee,' he said, but 'our love is now of some Continuance'; those words were no longer even necessary.[6]

The reference to his 'den' is typical of the creation of private male spaces within early modern households – ambiguous spaces discussed by Alan Stewart in a chapter entitled 'Epistemologies of the Early Modern Closet'. He notes that these rooms are 'not designed to function as a place of individual withdrawal, but as a secret non-public transactive space between two men behind a locked door', and it is within this pervasive homosocial, quasi-erotic context that Thomas's friendship

---

[4] 'He shows himself to be most familiar amongst his servants and gentlemen of the Bedchamber' (author's translation). See *The Life and Letters of Sir Henry Wotton*, ed. by Logan Pearsall Smith, 2 vols. (Oxford: Clarendon Press, 1907), Vol. I, p. 315.

[5] He comments here on their 'great zeal for their Patron' (author's translation).

[6] John Stubbs, *Donne: The Reformed Soul* (London: Penguin, 2007), p. 187.

with Carr must be positioned.[7] There will be more discussion of the *amicitia* underlying this kind of male friendship in Chapter 2. This first, though, explores Thomas's first steps on the path to power. Beginning in the Middle Temple, then looking at his early success at James's English court, we move to letters he writes on a journey to the continent.

Legal Learning and Beyond: Thomas at Middle Temple

Yet Thomas's next steps on the road to courtiership were not taken with Carr. Leaving Edinburgh and returning to London, the aspirant courtier also returned to the Middle Temple, where, as we saw in the Introduction, young men were trained both in the law and in the skills needed for social mobility. Perhaps inevitably then, it is in the homosocial context of the Inns that we find evidence of Thomas in 1602–3. This is the fifteen-month period covered by a rather famous 'diary' written by his contemporary Innsman, John Manningham. Manningham's text is not so much a diary as we would think of it but rather a common-place book, recording the substance of sermons he attended, some key events at the Inns and in London, and, importantly from our point of view, the comments of his contemporaries. Thomas Overbury was one such, quoted several times in the months covered by the extant volume. Through Manningham's often dry records we begin to see the acerbic wit, the transgression and the impertinence of the clever young man who was his friend. One entry records a joke at the expense of fellow Innsman Sir John Davies. The much-maligned author of an account of the celestial nature of dance (a poem called *Orchestra*) was the target of a great deal of such mockery at the Inn – not least, perhaps, because he appears from the Inn's records to have been a regular transgressor of the rules and liable to erupt into anger and violence.[8] Appropriately enough for one whose interest is in dance, the quip recorded in Manningham's *Diary* focuses on John Davies' physique: 'John Davys goes waddling

---

[7] Stewart, *Close Readers*, p. 171.

[8] John Davies had a record of Christmas rule breaking. The Middle Temple parliament minutes record that in 1590–1, along with several others, he had 'broke the ordinance by making outcries, forcibly breaking open chambers in the night and levying money as the Lord of Misrule's rent', for which he was fined £20 (*Minutes of parliament*, Vol. I, p. 318). By the end of the 1597–8 revels, Davies is recorded, again by the Inn's parliament, as attacking his erstwhile friend, Richard Martin, in hall: 'Taking from under his gown a stick, which is commonly called "a Bastianado", he struck Martyn on the head with it till it broke, and then running to the bottom of the Hall he took his servant's sword out of his hand, shook it over his own head [. . .] and ran down to the water steps and jumped into a boat. He is expelled, never to return' (ibid., pp. 379–80).

with his arse out behinde as though he were about to make every one he meetes a wall to pisse against.'[9] Though the comment could, Manningham admits, have been made by either the young Thomas Overbury or another Innsman, Benjamin Rudyerd, it is easy to believe that the offensive remark could have originated from the former: a man later renowned for his insolence.

Other entries in Manningham's *Diary* have Thomas making jokes at the expense of Ben Jonson, mocking bishops, and criticising contemporary political leaders. He clearly knew Jonson, and his comment is recorded that the playwright 'lives upon one Townsend and scornes the world' (p. 130). He will continue to be linked with Jonson, and this familiarity provides evidence of his connection with literary circles.[10] Another comment, on the Bishop of London, reveals the strongly Protestant sympathies that characterised Thomas as a student at the Queen's College in Oxford. He is recorded as commenting idealistically that 'He would not have the bishops to have anie temporalities, or temporall jurisdicion, but live upon tithes, and nothing but preach' (p. 169). Of political life, as well as of religion, the Innsman Thomas is outspoken. He is noted as saying, 'Sir Rob. Cecile followed the E of Ess[ex's] death not with a good mynde' (p. 169), showing familiarity with the high-ranking courtier, as well as an interest in the aftermath of the Essex Rebellion. Indeed, this apparent insight into Cecil's attitudes might suggest that Thomas was acquainted with the Secretary of State, and some historians have suggested that he may have been working for Cecil even as a student at Middle Temple. Chester Dunning notes that 'Cecil had been impressed enough with Overbury's talents to take him into his own service [. . .] preparing him for a career in government' and it is possible that his trip to Scotland in 1601 was much more political than a mere 'voyage of pleasure'.[11] This assumption of an early connec-

---

[9] *Diary of John Manningham of the Middle Temple and of Bradbourne, Kent, Barrister-at-Law, 1602–3*, ed. by John Bruce, Esq. (London: J. B. Nichols and Sons, 1868), p. 168. Further page references to this edition are marked in the text.

[10] His connection with the group meeting at the Mitre in Bread Street is suggested by Anthony Arlidge in *Shakespeare and the Prince of Love: The Feast of Misrule in the Middle Temple* (London: Giles de la Mare, 2000), p. 75, though he is absent from the group when their composition is explored more substantially by Michelle O'Callaghan, *The English Wits: Literature and Sociability in Early Modern England* (Cambridge: Cambridge University Press, 2007), pp. 3–4.

[11] Chester Dunning, 'The Fall of Sir Thomas Overbury and the Embassy to Russia in 1613', *Sixteenth Century Journal*, Vol. 22, No. 4 (Winter 1991), pp. 695–704 (p. 697). Earlier writers on the Overbury scandal, William McElwee and Beatrice White, both write of Thomas's career starting with Cecil. See McElwee, *The Murder of Sir Thomas Overbury* (Oxford: Oxford University Press, 1952), p. 14, who says he was 'used largely to carry letters between Sir Robert Cecil and King James' on his return to London, and

tion is regularly seen in writing on Thomas. In his introductory description of the man's life, for example, his nineteenth-century editor writes that 'by the entreaty of my Lord Treasurer, Sir Robert Cecil, [Thomas was] preferred to honour, and found favour extraordinary'.[12] However far we can assume this kind of connection, though, Thomas's epigrammatic and satirical comments are regularly recorded in the *Diary*, and it is clear that he became a part of the atmosphere of wit and sharp satire dominant in the late Elizabethan Middle Temple. His aspiration for social mobility was, at the Inn, linked firmly to his male friendships and acquaintances. Yet his political career was not to develop through his Inn; instead, he would have to negotiate the even more challenging environment of James's new Jacobean court.

Choosing a Different Direction

As he left Middle Temple, Thomas would have contemplated paths that were traditional to the aspirational courtier and had helped those before him to secure social mobility at the Tudor courts. We might consider the rather nostalgic comments on such mobility and preferment in Elizabethan England made later in the seventeenth century by the Earl of Newcastle:

> In Queen Elizabeths dayes a gentle man would put his younger son, to the universety, then to the Ins of Courte, to have a smakering in the Lawe, afterwardes to wayte of an Embasador, afterwardes, to bee his secretary, Then to be Lefte as Agente, or resedent, behind him, then sent of many forrayne Imployments, – & after some 30 years Breeding, to bee made a Clarke of the Signett, or a Clarke of the Counsell, – itt may be afterwards, Secretary of state, – this was not onely breeding, but a breed of statesmen, fitt to serve the greateste monarke in the world.[13]

This was the common path to courtiership, Newcastle tells Charles II, before the arrival of 'the great Favoritts' of the Jacobean period, who 'Justled outt this Breed of stattesmen'. Clearly his advice to Charles

White, *The Cast of Ravens: The Strange Case of Sir Thomas Overbury* (London: John Murray, 1965), p. 7, who notes less specifically that 'Robert Cecil was aware of his potentialities'.

[12] Rimbault, *The Miscellaneous Works [. . .] of Sir Thomas Overbury*, p. xxvi. We cannot take at face value these early works on Thomas's life, though, as Rimbault avers, in seeming conflict with this assumption, that in 1602–3, 'Overbury was probably unknown at Court' (p. xxxii).

[13] William Cavendish, Earl of Newcastle, *Ideology and Politics on the Eve of the Restoration: Newcastle's Advice to Charles II*, ed. by Thomas P. Slaughter (Philadelphia: American Philosophical Society, 1984), pp. 57–8.

is conservative and has a specific purpose in the Restoration, but his account of the usual career path in Elizabethan England is reinforced by an examination of the routes taken by several of Thomas's slightly older contemporaries. Henry Wotton, as ambassador to Venice, finds his influence through diplomacy; Sir Henry Neville, whom we shall see in Chapter 2 begging Thomas Overbury for his support as he works to become Lord Secretary after Cecil's death, is first the French ambassador; and Ralph Winwood, who becomes Secretary of State in 1614 and whose work in that role is to lead to the prosecutions for Thomas's murder, is firstly secretary to Sir Henry Neville in Paris, before becoming James's representative in The Hague. As Elizabeth's reign ended, intelligent men earned political authority through work as secretaries and diplomats, and used postings abroad to prove their worth.

After the death of Elizabeth, James's accession appeared to provide more scope for young men in Thomas's position to thrive, as the new king's arrival in London in 1604 changed the landscape of English court life. The emerging Jacobean court in England was to echo the power structures of that James left behind in Edinburgh, and again to see the dominance of the Gentlemen of the Bedchamber. To the chagrin of several commentators south of the border, it was a Bedchamber largely populated by Scottish lords. But that did not mean there was no place for an attractive and talented young Englishman who had already shown his interest by visiting the Scottish capital, and whose skill in building male friendships was already established.

In his memories of his son's early success, Nicholas Overbury gives an account of the king's recognition of Thomas's potential:

> when Sir Thomas was made sewer to the king, his Majesty walking in the privy garden shewed him to the Queen, saying, Look you, this is my new sewer; and queen Anne answered Tis a prety yong fellow.[14]

Acquiring the position of 'sewer', or server, to the king is by no means as minor as it might appear.[15] Though retrospective and partial, his father's comment is interesting in several ways to anyone concerned with Thomas's subsequent career. The appointment placed him in a prime position of access to James from early in the new reign. Although the date of the appointment is not given in the record of his father's memories, a gift of silver given to Thomas by the King of Denmark in the summer of 1606 suggests that, by that point, he was at court and

---

[14] BL Add. MS 15476, fol. 92ᵛ.

[15] The *OED* (2a) notes that a sewer was 'an attendant at a meal who superintended the arrangement of the table, the seating of the guests, and the tasting and serving of the dishes'.

under the eye of the charismatic visiting monarch.[16] It is likely that he was already a server, and thus one of those whom, on his visit to the Scottish capital, Wotton had noted were privileged to talk to James and his associates during meals. James's propensity for promoting those around him that he initially tested in a more menial position suggests that Thomas was on track for further success.

This success seemed to be coming. In September 1607 he gained the lease on a saltworks in Worcester, and was a rising man. His knighthood was bestowed in June 1608 and sometime at the end of that year, or in early 1609, Thomas was given further wealth, with the reversion of the treasurership of the chamber, 'a position valued in 1613 at £2000'. The Overbury family too continued to gain honours. By the end of 1609 his brothers Giles and Walter were given a life grant of the office of registering assurances on ships or goods in the Royal Exchange.[17] All of these have been argued to be the result of his relationship with Robert Carr, and this is possible. Carr had come to London as a very minor and insignificant part of the new king's entourage, but a fall at the 1607 Accession Day tilts threw him into contact with James and the king personally nursed him back to health. From that point on, Carr received a steady stream of honours and advancement. Whether it was Carr's influence or the result of his personal charm, in 1606–9 Thomas too seemed to be a courtier on the rise.

An Intelligencer: Thomas's Letters from France

Yet the next time we find evidence of Thomas he is not in London, but in France.[18] He is in the company of Francis Rous, a fellow Middle Templar, yet again suggesting that he has made the most of the homosocial network the Inns provided. A letter written by Rous in May

[16] Details of Christian's visit with James to Theobald's can be seen in a letter from Sir John Harington, printed in *The Progresses, Processions, and Magnificent Festivities, of King James the First, His Royal Consort, Family, and Court*, by John Nichols, 4 vols. (London: J. B. Nichols, 1828), Vol. II, pp. 73–5. The letter is to William Barlow, tutor to Prince Henry. Thomas's likely involvement in this visit leads us to wonder what Christian's silver was actually for. Perhaps he shared James's penchant for attractive young men, or Thomas played a part in the masquing.

[17] All of these gifts are recorded in John Considine's *ODNB* entry on Overbury.

[18] His stream of rewards at the court come just before this trip to France. The assumption of some commentators is that his journey abroad is in response to an argument with Queen Anna; for instance Donald Beecher comments that 'Overbury was knighted in the summer of 1608 in Greenwich, but spent much of 1609 abroad under a cloud, allegedly for having annoyed Queen Anne'; see the introduction to his edition of *Overbury's Characters* (Ottawa: Dovehouse Editions, 2003), p. 20.

1609, and the postscript added by Thomas, shows that the two men were travelling together and had plans to return together to England in the August.[19] Both, at this stage, offer their future services to Thomas Edmondes, ambassador in Brussels, through a letter to his secretary, William Trumbull. Further evidence of Thomas's influential European connections is seen in the friendship he seems to have with the French ambassador, George Carew. A surviving letter from Carew shares gossip on the French court, and, although he is about twenty-five years older than Thomas, the fact that he is a fellow Middle Templar might account for its friendly tone and apparent openness.[20] Thomas has shown signs already of being a successful courtier, but by 1609 he seems to be looking at a traditional career built up through diplomacy. There has to be a reason for his travels at this point. One account suggests that his journey to France was a result of 'discontents' at court: 'having obtained some favour in Court beforetimes, because of some discontents, [he] got licence to travel'.[21] But for many aspirant courtiers, as we have seen, experience abroad was a natural part of the quest for courtly advancement and we do not need to read temporary disgrace or his own discontent into his decision to go to France. Whatever the reason, he now spent time at the French court, considering effective ways to rule a country and developing diplomatic skills.

As well as gaining these wider benefits, Thomas seems to have joined other aspirant young men who wished to travel abroad and agreed to become an intelligencer.[22] His choice of correspondent in the succeeding months of 1609 was a much more powerful man than William Trumbull. He writes at least three letters from France to Sir Robert Cecil, and establishing a relationship with the Lord Secretary would undoubtedly advance his position.[23] The tentativeness of the first letter

---

[19] See Letter 2, p. 40.

[20] See Letter 6, p. 48.

[21] 'The Secret History of the Reign of James', printed in *The Autobiography and Correspondence of Sir Simonds D'Ewes*, ed. by James Orchard Halliwell, 2 vols. (London: Richard Bentley, 1845), Vol. II, p. 335. This seems to be the same text as *Truth Brought to Light and Discouered by Time or a Discourse and Historicall Narration of the first XIIII Yeares of King Iames Reigne* (London: Richard Cotes for Michael Sparke, 1651). Chapter 6 concerns Thomas's rise, which is subsequent to the death of Cecil, but no prior relationship between Cecil and Thomas is mentioned.

[22] See Will Tosh, *Male Friendship and Testimonies of Love in Shakespeare's England* (Basingstoke: Palgrave Macmillan, 2016), p. 10: 'As continental travel became more popular among elite young men in the sixteenth century, permission to depart increasingly came with a condition: well-connected travellers were expected to send home intelligence from foreign countries.'

[23] Autograph letters from Thomas to Cecil (created Earl of Salisbury in May 1605) are transcribed below as Letters 3, 5 and 7, pp. 42, 44 and 49.

perhaps suggests he hadn't been working for Cecil eight years earlier, but their professional relationship develops effectively over this summer. In these three extant letters, he offers information and asks for patronage, while professing love and service to the established and powerful court figure.

In his study of epistolary function, exploring the conventions, purposes and anxieties of early modern letter writing, Gary Schneider demonstrates that in this period letters were vital in establishing the connectedness of their writers; news exchange was one of the prime functions of both personal and political letters.[24] Yet, despite its professional function and its likely wider readership, Schneider argues that the kind of letter Thomas writes to Cecil should also appear to be personal. These three letters from France exemplify the effective, and affective, style he describes. The skill Thomas shows in these early letters reveals his education; writing to other men in this polished and engaging way is what men of his middling class, with ambitions to work in the bureaucracy of the court, are trained to do. The letters demonstrate his social aspiration and reveal the homosocial environment within which he hopes to thrive. The language of men's letter writing at this period often blurs the boundaries of what we might today consider professional and personal spheres of life. Political and administrative writers exploit the expressions and figures of more intimate letters in establishing their political affiliations, and Schneider comments on 'the type of emotion-laden rhetoric that regularly mediated political negotiation in early modern England, but was most often associated with the familiar letter'.[25] He adds, the 'rhetoric of love and friendship was indeed an expected component of court intercourse, one of the social modes of courtiership'. If he is to succeed in his quest for Cecil's patronage, Thomas must show that he can gather relevant information and then convey it to his superior in an appropriate manner.

Cecil's careful preservation of these apparently personal missives from his correspondents, though, suggests another key feature of early modern epistolarity; information transmitted was used and shared in a professional context, and thus Thomas's accounts of the French court would have been read by others in the Secretary's trust. James Daybell's consideration of the 'social materiality' of letters encourages readers to consider early modern letters in this context: to examine 'the social and cultural practice of manuscripts and the material conditions and contexts in which they were produced, disseminated and consumed'.[26] It is

---

[24] Schneider, *The Culture of Epistolarity*, pp. 22–3.
[25] Schneider, *The Culture of Epistolarity*, pp. 101–2.
[26] Daybell, *The Material Letter*, p. 11.

thus clear that Thomas's letters were intended to form part of a wider discussion of foreign affairs and French court life, and were not simply a personal interaction with Cecil. The different hand that adds '12 July 1609 Paris Sr Thomas Overbury to my Lord' to the second of Thomas's letters, and the other that writes, at the end of the third, '28 July 1609 Sr Thomas Overbury to my Lord from Paris', give a glimpse of this wider circle surrounding Cecil and force us to broaden the readership of the apparently personal letters.

Thomas's first surviving letter, dated 2 June, opens with sentiments and expressions both appropriate and typical in this kind of epistolary exchange:

> I had long ere this given your Lordship notyce of such occurrents as have descended to my knowledg, had not I mistrusted that my intelligence could present you with nothing that could scape on[e] of these two misfortunes eyther of being late or uncertaine, but at length mere despayre of having any other occasion to manifest my betrothd devotion made me venture, and the rather uppon confidence that, this being my end, my affection should excuse my matter.[27]

Introducing himself as Cecil's lowly servant, to whom news 'descend[s]', he employs a self-deprecatory tone which establishes the hierarchy. In contrast to some of his later writings, where Thomas gives plentiful evidence of the insolence of which he was often accused, these early letters show his understanding of the expected quasi-Petrarchan conventions. He creates the persona of the despairing lover, whose 'betrothd devotion' is at the mercy of the beloved recipient, and who 'venture[s]' despite his fear of rejection. His 'affection' will excuse his 'matter', either his poor style or the paucity of his news. Indeed, Thomas makes the common claim of 'having no news worth writing but writing nonetheless' and thus gives Cecil an accepted 'signal of loyalty and duty'.[28] In reality though, to continue in Gary Schneider's terms, he is very aware that 'the reportage of news was an important responsibility of the client, as a testimony of social duty, shared interest, or mutual enterprise'. He may claim to have no news, but he finds many points of interest about French courtiers to engage Cecil's attention. In this way examining these letters brings together all three issues this book argues to be key to an exploration of courtiership in this period, as they encourage an exploration of the extent of the royal prerogative in an ideal state. As in Manningham's *Diary*, Thomas is again showing his confidence in exploring the behaviour, the rights and the responsibilities of the power-

---

[27] Letter 3, p. 42.
[28] Schneider, *The Culture of Epistolarity*, p. 61.

ful. The main aim of the letters to Cecil, though, is to secure Thomas's social mobility, and how they are written shows that they function effectively in their homosocial environment.

To make his communication acceptable to its recipient, it has to be written in the expected style, and Thomas will have learnt about how to speak and to write persuasively from his schooldays onwards. Schneider notes that 'early modern epistolary theory grew out of classical rhetorical theory, primarily theories of oratory', and Chapter 2 will examine more theoretically the use of classical ideas of rhetoric and the creation of emotion in letters written about Thomas's courtly career.[29] His own letters to Cecil work hard to convey a personal tone: one of affection for their recipient. He clearly hopes that they will be received as an appropriate tribute and will build the relationship on which his future preferment rests. To Daybell's 'social materiality' is added a consideration of the significance of 'material rhetorics' in letters: the non-verbal aspects of epistolary communication that conveyed so much about the relationship between writer and recipient.[30] The signature of Thomas's first letter, for instance, comes after a half-page gap, and a great deal of paper is thus 'wasted'. The respect demonstrated through this profligacy with an expensive material adds to the affective language of this letter and to its 'hope' for future contact with the Lord Secretary.

After the hope of the first letter, the second, on 12 July, opens with the writer's 'gratitude'; the desired response from Cecil has clearly been an encouraging one. Thomas is ready to build further:

> The favours I have receavd from your Lordship dubbled by the manner of them do inflame me to seek all means to do you servyce, gratitude being to me a stronger motive than hope, but finding none let me entreat your Lordship to accept acknowledgment as a sign of <u>thanckfullnes</u> though no part of it.[31]

Again, the language is affective; the writer is 'inflame[d]' by Cecil's response. But as well as setting the appropriate connection between the two, Thomas makes sure his letter demonstrates his utility. To achieve its purpose and prove that Cecil's correspondent is worthy of preferment, a letter must display his ability to provide useful and reliable information. The possession of inside information is a familiar method of establishing a claim upon a potential patron, and, as Fritz Levy has established, '[c]laiming inside knowledge was the way to be noticed; indeed for many [aspirant courtiers], news replaced (or at least supplemented) clothes as the new social marker, the way of distinguishing

---

[29] Schneider, *The Culture of Epistolarity*, p. 18.
[30] Daybell, *The Material Letter*, p. 11.
[31] Letter 5, p. 44.

themselves from the hordes pressing on them from below'.[32] In his first letter, Thomas had shown his fear of sending ill-timed or unreliable information, reflecting a contemporary anxiety about the potentially untrustworthy or even deceptive nature of letters. The second quickly moves on to the quality of the information he has to impart: 'The last action of note here was Vendosms marriage which I only of the English being at shall therefore relate to your <u>Lordship</u> more particularly.' The exclusivity of this news is emphasised as he stresses that he 'only of the English' was there and therefore he is able to 'relate' the information to his recipient 'particularly'. His implication is that other intelligence gatherers at court will not have this information and therefore only Cecil will receive it. The writer suggests his personal appeal, which led him to be invited to such an exclusive gathering. Equally, eyewitness testimony lends veracity to the substance of the letter, and the potential for deceit is lessened. The fear of letters deceiving a reader is a common thread through writing of this period, and a variety of strategies such as these are used to emphasise the honesty of the writer.[33]

Once he has established his credentials, Thomas's second letter is particularly keen to impress Cecil with the quality of the information he will acquire from his servant. It concludes with information from the French court, showing the writer's grasp of the prevailing political context and demonstrating the reliability and exclusivity of his sources:

> The Duke of Sully to perfitt and exceed his other publick works hath long threatened the buylding of a navy and of late to that purpose was about to undertake a journey to survey all the Ports toward Spain, but yesterday I receavde news from Court, that that journey was at least differd if not broken of[f]. I have here sent your Lordship a paper which I receavd from Court during the tyme that I wrote this letter, [. . .]

In making it clear that he 'receavd [news] from Court', Thomas reveals his own intelligence-gathering network, which, if Cecil desires, will be at the senior courtier's disposal. There is manuscript evidence of this network not only in letters written from Carew to Thomas, but also in those to Thomas from French writers during his sojourn in Paris; a letter, for example, is extant from a Monsieur Montmartin in May, and another from an affectionate correspondent at Fontainebleau in early

---

[32] Fritz Levy, 'The Decorum of News', in *News, Newspapers, and Society in Early Modern Britain*, ed. by Joad Raymond (London: Frank Cass, 1999), pp. 12–38 (p. 17).
[33] See Schneider, *The Culture of Epistolarity*, p. 17: 'letters were considered potentially deceptive cultural forms and systems of letter exchange as potentially treacherous transmission mechanisms', and 'letters often mediated [. . .] anxieties and dilemmas [. . .] by employing epistolary strategies that attempted to authenticate the emotion, sincerity, and veracity of correspondents'.

June.[34] The writer's portrayal of himself as a centre of information in this second letter to Cecil is not a fiction, and the Secretary sees something useful in the younger man.

The third of Thomas's letters is dated 28 July and the mere two-week gap here suggests Cecil's interest in developing this source. It is clear from the opening to this third letter that the Secretary's reply has been encouraging:

> I have receavd your gracious letter which gives me assurance of your Lordships acceptance of my servyce and love, which happines I value according to that difference of the Roman which sayd mallem Caesaris iudicium quam Antonii beneficium. Neyther shall that favour ever beget in me a confidence to be importunate but rather an alacrity to deserve.[35]

Although Thomas still maintains his desire to please Cecil, the tone has begun to shift and the use of coded Latin reference attempts to show a shared understanding between two educated men.[36] His classical education, with the rhetorical training of university and Middle Temple, lies behind the balanced clauses in the final sentence, where his 'confidence to be importunate' is replaced with the more appealing 'alacrity to deserve'. Now, in this third communication with Cecil, the excesses of Petrarchan affection have been replaced by a more pragmatic declaration of modest fidelity, love and humility echoed in the letter's closing sentences:

> For my self by reason of the importunity of some domestick affayrs I shall return in August to England, but before that [. . .] I intend to make a journey to Orleans to see my Lord of Cranborne that your Lordship may know that not only your self are the object of my faythfullnes and love but even all that may be called yours. And so till then I humbly take my leave.

There is neat flattery and intelligence in Thomas's plan to visit Lord Cranbourne, Cecil's son, as he returns to England; it provides him with news to relay to the Secretary in person and increases the bond between them.

These three letters from 1609, as well as revealing Thomas's developing relationship with Cecil, his courtly skills and his aspiration for patronage,

---

[34] Letter 1, p. 39, Monsieur Montmartin to Thomas, May 1609; that to Thomas from Fontainebleau on 3 June is Letter 4, p. 44. Both letters are in French and, together with the easy familiarity of his progress at the French court at this time, they give the lie to Thomas's later claim to have no language skills when he refuses the ambassadorship (see pp. 48 and 105).

[35] Letter 7, p. 49.

[36] The imperfect subjunctive of 'mallem' ('I should prefer') suggests that this reference is in some way contrasting the judgement of Caesar with the 'kindness' of another, represented as 'Antony'. If the compliment is to work, it appears that Caesar may be Cecil, though it is possible that (as on later occasions) Cecil is mediating with James on Thomas's behalf. (In later letters with coded names, 'Julius' does indeed refer to the king.)

also show his personal commentary on the activities of the French court and reveal clues to the young man's political attitudes. Further evidence of these can be seen in the record of what he had learnt on his journey, circulated in manuscript and eventually published posthumously in 1626 as *Sir Thomas Overbury His Observations in his Travailes upon the State of the XVII Provinces as they stood Anno Dom. 1609*. Although dismissed by modern critics as 'unspectacular', the *Observations* show glimpses of his attitude to royal prerogative through his comments on the French monarchy at the end of the Wars of Religion.[37] He writes, for instance, about the supreme power of the French king (in 1609, Henri IV) and the lack of parliamentary power in France:

> The King [...] enioying what Lewis the II. did gain, hath the entire Soueraigntie in himselfe, because hee can make the Parliament doe what he please, or else doe what he please without them.[38]

Though the years leading up to the reign of Henri IV, and in particular the power of the Catholic League during the previous reign, would explain the desire of a French king to maintain his power over potentially threatening noblemen, Overbury's analysis of the French state confirms that here lies the only possible challenge to royal absolutism, as they form 'the onely entire Body there, which participate with the Prerogatiues of the Crowne'. As a result of the nobility's potential to disrupt royal power, the unhappy consequence is that

> the King is ready to support inferiour persons against them, and is glad to see them waste one another by Contention in Law, for feare they grow rich, because hee fore sees, that as the Nobilitie onely can doe him service, so they onely misapplyed can doe him harme. (pp. 15–16)

The published text shows clearly the potential for abuse underlying absolutist royal power. Thomas's letters to Cecil show his quick grasp of the political situation on the ground, and the king's need to assert his authority over his lords. In his first letter to Cecil, he notes that 'The journey of Provence is broken of[f], having bene intended by the King chiefly to abate the Duke of Guyses power there, of whom he hath bene informed of late that for every two Gentlemen that he hath there the Duke hath two & twenty [...]'.[39] He is quick to note the events of the

---

[37] John Considine, *ODNB* entry on Overbury.

[38] Thomas Overbury, *Sir Thomas Overbury His Observations in his Travailes upon the State of the XVII Provinces as they stood Anno Dom. 1609, the Treatie of Peace being then on foot* (London: Bernard Alsop for John Parker, 1626), p. 14. Further references are in the text.

[39] Letter 3, p. 42.

French court, and to interpret the king's motives: in this case, to undermine a powerful Lord, who has threatened the power of royalty in the
past, and whose support in this region is much larger than that of the
monarch. Equally, the French king cannot allow challenges from his
nobility in matters of the heart. Thomas appears rather to enjoy telling
Cecil about the Princess of Condé and her attractions. 'Monsieur Le
Grand (the King and who have even had the luck to be rivalls) having
had the start of the King in this love to the said Princess would not give
over his suyte uppon the Kings entreaty,' he informs Cecil. He relates
the king's response when Le Grand would 'not come from Paris where
she was uppon the Kings sending for', explaining that 'he was in disgrace for three or four days but is now recovering'. Knowing the current
petty jealousies of the French court allows Cecil to manoeuvre in his
relations with those in power, and readily acting as one of his gossips,
Thomas conveys them. The text which was to become the published
version of his journey shows a more critical view of the French system
than this gossip alone suggests, and the criticism is that of one with legal
training.

Thomas's assessment of the pleasure the king gains from the nobility's
'Contention in Law' demonstrates to this Middle Templar some of the
problems inherent in the French legal system:

> the King there, not only makes Peace and Warres, Calls and dissolues
> Parliaments, Pardoneth, naturalizeth, Innobleth, Names the value of Money,
> Presseth to the Warre; but euen makes Lawes, and imposes Taxes at his
> pleasure: And all this he doth alone: for as for that forme that his Edicts must
> be authorized by the next Court of Parliament, that is, the next Court of
> soueraigne Iustice; first the Presidents thereof are to be chosen by him, and to
> bee put out by him; and secondly, when they concurre not with the King, he
> passeth any thing without them. (p. 12)

With his legal background, and perhaps envisaging readers of his notes
as being similarly Inns of Court men, Thomas emphasises the impact
of parliamentary weakness on national legislation. The king has total
control over new laws and Thomas explains the impact this royal power
has, producing limited access to justice, as well as slow and expensive
legal cases (p. 18).

Thomas's later published comments on the French system reveal his
fear of a royal prerogative unchecked by the relative parliamentary
and legal independence he sees in England, and it is in this context
we must see the alliances he is to make over the next years, once he
gains a measure of courtly influence. It may even go some way towards
explaining his later confrontation with James. There are hints here
of the kind of conversations to which he must have been party as an

Innsman, and similarities with those fellow Templars who were to make combative parliamentary speeches: speeches such as those of John Hoskins in the Commons' disputations over royal finance of the following year.

In conclusion, then, the three letters sent by Thomas to Robert Cecil in 1609, together with the evidence of his *Observations*, reveal the aspirant courtier's attitudes to key issues of Jacobean political culture. James's emphasis on the importance of the royal prerogative may well have worried him. Thomas, once returned to England and established in a position of greater power, will ally himself with those at the English court who oppose the unrestrained power of the king: those, such as the Earl of Southampton and Sir Henry Neville, who wish the monarchy to find agreement with parliament and to work with them.

In terms of Thomas's own career, the letters to Cecil show the kind of skills that led to preferment and social mobility; he is a persuasive wordsmith and observer of political events, able to build the kind of effective working relationships with men that were so necessary to an ambitious young man. These letters of 1609 suggest, perhaps, that at this point Thomas planned to broaden his experience in Europe and pursue a well-trodden route to court position. With Cecil's patronage, he could have developed a career akin to those of contemporaries such as Wotton, Neville and Winwood: a career of diplomatic service that, for the talented, could eventually lead back to position and status at the English court. Thomas, though, had gained a measure of success already under the new Jacobean regime and knew the lure of the Bedchamber and the king's personal circle.

Thus, the chapter finishes with Thomas demonstrating the potential for social mobility in the culture within which he lived, and reaching the centre of Jacobean power: not the Privy Council of Elizabeth, difficult to access for those outside the established group and slow to change, but the Jacobean Bedchamber and the opportunities it presented for more quickly gained success that were to prove tempting to this young man. He clearly had the abilities that would enable him, in the ensuing months, to work effectively as secretary to his friend, Robert Carr, and, through this, to continue to build up his status and political influence. But what kind of relationship was he developing with the man now accepted as the king's favourite?

Appendix 1: Letters, 1609

Letter 1

May 1609: Monsieur Montmartin to Overbury[40]

The Duke of Nemours, who died six days ago in Savoy, made the Duke of Mayne his heir. This is a fine inheritance.

In Parliament two major reforming edicts are being passed, recorded by M. de Sully, and received at the Counsel to ban the wearing of foreign fabrics of gold, silver and tinselled with precious metals, silk finery, and all sorts of embroidery, particularly coming from Milan, punishable by the confiscation of all the possessions of the sellers and heavy fines for those who wear them; an absolute prohibition to all merchants and mercers from selling anything on credit to the nobility on pain of losing the money they have lent and in the case that they hide the obligation, a heavy fine to the merchant, in order that the nobility reduces the excessive spending that consumes their money – a ban on wearing silk stockings except for lords and gentleman of good family –

Another edict against all kinds of jewels with a ban on wearing, selling or pawning anything, under pain of heavy fines and a general ban on bringing any gold coins to the gambling table, and that everything that

---

[40] The letter is a transcription of NA SP 78/55/101. In French the letter reads:

Le Duc de Nemours depuis six jours mort en Sauoye a fait Le Duc du Mayne son heritier. La succession est belle.

Il se passe a la cour de parlement deux grands edits de reformat minutes par Monsieur de Sully et receux au Conseil Lon [unclear], pour la defence des Estoffes etrangeres du port d'habis dor dargent et Clinolant [taken to be 'clinquant'], parures de soye sur soyes et toutes sortes de broderyes sur tout venantes de Milan, sur peines de confiscations des biens de ceux qui les debitent et grosses amandes pour ceux qui les portent, une pro-hibition absolue a tous marchands et merciers de ne vendre rien a credit a la noblesse sur peine de perdre leur debte et au cas que les obligations en soyent deguisees grosse amende au marchant affin que la noblesse cuite les depences excessives qui la degarnis-sent d'argent – defence de porter bas de soye excepte pour seigneurs et gentishommes de bonne maison –

Une autre edit contre toutes sortes de pierreries avec defence de rien porter vendre ny engager, sous la punition de grosses amandes une defence generale de porter aucunes pieces dor sur le jeu et que tout ce qui se joura doibt estre en argent monaye.

Le gain qui se fera en or sera restituables au perdant et amende imposee au gaigneur, defence a tous joueurs de jouer a credit ou sur gages ou sur manquement et toute debte de jeu, non soluables – avec grands profits aux delateurs.

Yours to honor and serve you, [in English in the original letter]
Montmartin

will be gambled must be in silver money, the gain which is made in gold will be given back to the loser, and a fine imposed on the winner; a ban on all gamblers playing on credit, and on bets, on failed payments and on all gambling debts, that cannot be resolved – with great profits to those who denounce them.

Yours to honour and serve you,
Montmartin

Letter 2

19 May 1609: Francis Rous to William Trumbull (with postscript by Overbury)[41]

Because our time in France draws so near an end as it will not allow much more traffic of letters, and I am desirous that our acquaintance so well preserved hitherto, may not now at parting unhandsomely break off in an abruptness, but being still correspondent may remain fit to be continued on future occasions, I write these at this time the *Vale* and period to the rest. I might make excuses for venturing so much upon a friendship whereto I had no right but by the kind and free offer of itself; and so likewise for exchanging words for things: but that I hope the same good disposition, which drew and encouraged me thereto, will also sufficiently excuse and justify me to itself. My readiness to be used in the same kind when occasion may serve, is some approbation to myself, and were there need of it, I could also offer it to you. But how-soever if it must be a fault, I think it is a reasonable good one for a man of an honest intent to be somewhat dissolute after honest acquaintance.

---

[41] The letter is printed in *Report on the Manuscripts of the Marquess of Downshire, preserved at Easthampstead Park, Berks* (London: His Majesty's Stationery Office, 1936), Vol. II, pp. 102–3. Francis Rous was the same age as Overbury, he was his contemporary in Oxford (studying at Broadgates Hall between July 1593 and January 1597), and he entered Middle Temple on 5 May 1601 (see Colin Burrow's article on Rous in the *ODNB*). In Letter 2, Rous and Overbury write from Paris to William Trumbull, one of two secretaries working for Sir Thomas Edmondes, ambassador in Brussels. The second of these secretaries is Jean Beaulieu. In May 1609 Trumbull is in London, as he leaves Brussels annually to visit England at this time and this particular year he was in London from April to early June (p. vi). Rous appears to remain in, or return to, Paris in service to Edmondes, as he referred to in a letter from Beaulieu to Trumbull on 4 October 1609. Rous writes to Edmondes in London 'to recommend in his place Sir Geo. Carew's chaplain, Mr Taylor, who is reputed very sufficient in his profession, having given great satisfaction to all the English' (p. 156).

I must need before I leave tell you my news, not for the novelty or the over-certain knowledge of it, but because I am glad to write it – that your lord is to remove into France.[42] If it fall out otherwise, yet hereby you may perceive my affection, out of which also I entreat you to remember my service to my Lord.

Our continuance in France is to reach to the end of July, and in August I hope we shall be in England, whither I mean also to transport my present well wishing to you. I pray commend me to Mr Floyd.[43]

[Thomas adds a postscript]

I pray you let us hear what you know of Baynam and Blunt, and the rest of our English upon this peace.[44]

In the State House at Antwerp I saw the names of the Dukes of Burgundy and their wives, being writ by their pictures down to this present Archduke. Being straitened in time I could not write them out. I ask you to take the pains to send me an entire note of them as they are in Mr. Rous his next letter from you.[45] I would be glad to serve my lord in any use for England in August. Thomas Overbury.

[42] The rumour that Rous reports to Trumbull here – that Edmondes is to become ambassador in Paris – is borne out by events. Trumbull is left behind to manage affairs in Brussels, without the official title of ambassador.

[43] This is perhaps a reference to Thomas Lloyd (also called Floyd) who was part of the circle around William Trumbull and Sir Thomas Edmondes in 1609. See Sonia P. Anderson's 'The Elder William Trumbull: A Biographical Sketch' for *The Electronic British Library Journal* (1993), available at http://www.bl.uk/eblj/1993articles/article9 .html (accessed 9 August 2017).

[44] 'Baynam' may be Sir Edmund Baynham (b.1577) who entered Middle Temple in 1595, and perhaps met Overbury there. He left the Inn to join the Earl of Essex in Ireland, and was knighted there on 24 September 1599. A year later he was part of 'the cursed crew' arrested for disorder at the Mermaid Tavern. Having been tried for that offence in the Star Chamber, and in 1603 imprisoned in the Marshalsea for speeches against James VI of Scotland (as he was at that point), Baynham was associated with the Gunpowder Plot in 1605. He was never to return to England again, and lived in a variety of places on the continent. See *The House of Commons 1558–1603*, ed. by P. W. Hasler, Vol. I (London: Her Majesty's Stationery Office, 1981), p. 408; Hasler's article on Baynham is amongst the House of Commons' Members' Biographies online at http://www.historyofparlia mentonline.org/volume/1558-1603/member/baynham-edmund-1577 (accessed 9 August 2017). It is unclear who is referred to as 'Blunt'.

[45] Thomas's request for a copy of the family line of the dukes of Burgundy suggests that he sees Trumbull as a social equal. He is happy to serve Edmondes, but is quite blunt in his request from the younger man, only a few years older than he was, suggesting no need to employ affective modes in writing to him. Compare later letters from Trumbull to Thomas, written when the latter has more influence at court: Letters 27 and 35.

Letter 3

2 June 1609: Overbury to Salisbury[46]

Most honorable

I had long ere this given your Lordship notyce of such occurrents as have descended to my knowledg, had not I mistrusted that my intelligence could present you with nothing that could scape on[e] of these two misfortunes eyther of being late or uncertaine, but at length mere despayre of having any other occasion to manifest my betrothd devotion made me venture, and the rather uppon confidence that, this being my end, my affection should excuse my matter. Monsieur D'Esdiguieres is sent for and coming to Court.[47] The cause of it is thought to be a designe of the Kings to break the contract beetwixt Crequis daughter his grandchild, and Suillys sonne,[48] and that donne to sett a foot again the prevented match of Sullys son and Vendomes sister, against which they say the Duke of Suilly being resolute is like to runne a great hazard of his fortune.[49] The journey of Provence is broken of[f], having bene intended by the King chiefly to abate the Duke of Guyses power there, of whom he hath bene informed of late that for every two Gentlemen that he hath there the Duke hath two & twenty and that concurring with the title of the house of Lorraine to that County may prove dangerous especially he of all other Governors having no Lieftenant.[50] The match

---

[46] The letter is a transcription of NA SP 78/55/99. Thomas's presence in Paris in June–July 1609 puts him in the city at a busy time. In the late summer of 1609, the English ambassador to France, George Carew, was recalled, and, after some delay, replaced in 1610 by a former ambassador, Thomas Edmondes. It is clear from Letter 6 below that Thomas was well acquainted with Carew, a man some twenty-five years his senior, but a fellow Middle Templar. Much of the content of Thomas's letter to Cecil here is similar to that sent at the same time by Carew, as ambassador (compare, for instance, Carew's letter to Cecil sent a day before Thomas's in SP 78/55, fol. 95).

[47] François de Bonne, duc de Lesdiguières (1543–1626), became Marshal of France under Henri IV. He is part of the Créquy family.

[48] Maximilien de Béthune, duc de Sully, was one of the most powerful of Henri's courtiers. He began to discuss marrying his son, François, to the daughter of Charles de Blanchefort, the marquis de Créquy, in 1608.

[49] Vendôme's sister is Catherine Henriette de Vendôme, the legitimised daughter of Henri IV and his mistress (later his second wife), Gabrielle D'Estrées. According to Sully's memoir, Henri himself proposed this match, and it meant rejecting a proposed alliance with Lesdiguières. Sully – a firm Protestant – opposed the match as it meant his son converting to Catholicism. See Pierre-Mathurin de L'Ecluse de Loges, *Memoirs of Maximilien de Bethune, Duke of Sully, Prime Minister of Henry the Great: Newly Translated from the French Edition of M. de L'Ecluse de Loges*, 5 vols. (Edinburgh: Alex Lowrie, 1805), Vol. IV, pp. 259–60.

[50] Before the accession of Henri IV, the Guise family had been at the forefront in the Wars of Religion, and led the Catholic League, set up to eradicate Protestantism in France. Though the duc de Guise, Henri I, had made peace with the king after his acces-

betwixt the Constables son and the daughter of Chemille thryves very ill hitherto for the affection of the partyes.[51] St. Luc having concurd with M. de Espernon in the last plot uppon Rochell,[52] came presently to sue to M. de Suilly for his brother to have bene Guidon of the Queens company, but was therefore denyde it by M. de Suilly who is Lieftenant of that company and th[missing text]hich escheated by Giteys death was [missing text] his 2 brothers upon the first beginning [missing text] oue to this new Princess of Condé the house of Memorency took advantage to sue for the Count of Auvergnes pardon, but could not be heard. Monsieur Le Grand (the King and who have even had the luck to be rivalls) having had the start of the King in this love to the said Princess would not give over his suyte uppon the Kings entreaty and not come from Paris where she was uppon the Kings sending for, whereuppon he was in disgrace for three or four days but is now recovering.[53] The fault that I have committed in interrupting your Lordships affairs thus long I will seek to amend by ever making good this protestation of being allways

[half a page gap]

your Lordships most faithful servant

[Signature torn off]

sion, this powerful family was always a potential enemy. The letter reflects concern at any extension to their power base.

[51] The Constable of France was Henri I de Montmorency. His son, Henri II, was godson of the king and married Jeanne de Scépeaux (daughter of Guy de Scépeaux, the seigneur de Chemille) in 1609. The marriage was annulled shortly afterwards; as Thomas suggests here, this was not a love match.

[52] Timoléon d'Epinay was seigneur, then marquis, de Saint-Luc.

[53] Although the letter is a little confused with regard to the princesse de Condé (as Thomas's signature has been torn off on the reverse and some words are therefore missing), it is clearly a reference to Charlotte de Montmorency. She was married to Henri II de Bourbon in 1609 and became princess as a result. King Henri IV was only one of the men who admired her, as she was a renowned court beauty, and Thomas's letter reflects the competition for her affections. Here the king is seen to be the rival of Roger de Saint-Lary, duc de Bellegarde, 'Monsieur Le Grand', or the Grand Ecuyer de France (roughly equivalent to the English Master of the Horse).

Letter 4

3 June 1609: Fontainebleau to Overbury[54]

[. . .] the news of the Court if you send your man to fetch him. He is today or will be tomorrow in Paris, and by many promises that I have received from him here, he has given me his faith and his right hand that he will serve you with more faithfulness than we have words [to express]. Take my honour in trust and put it under the seal and stamp of the affection that you bear for me and you will judge for both of us that these are inviolable things such as I unfold before God and in your hands, that I will be to the death –

Fontainebleau, the 3 June

Letter 5

12 July 1609: Overbury to Salisbury[55]

Most honorable

The favours I have receavd from your Lordship dubbled by the manner of them do inflame me to seek all means to do you servyce, gratitude being to me a stronger motive than hope, but finding none let me entreat your Lordship to accept acknowledgment as a sign of <u>thanckfullnes</u> though no part of it. The last action of note here was Vendosms marriage which I only of the English being at shall therefore relate to your <u>Lordship</u> more particularly.[56] The substance of the marriage was performed last Monday very privatly, the ceremony on the morrow, the King <u>leading</u>

---

[54] The letter is a transcription of NA SP 78/55/94. The French reads:

[. . .] les nouvelles de la Cour si vous envoyes vostre homme lequerir il est aujourdhuy ou sera demain a Paris, et par beaucoup de veues que j'ay icy eu de luy, il ma donné sa foy et sa dextre quil vous serviroit avec plus de fidelité que nous navons de paroles prenez mon honneur en depost et le mettez sous le seel et le cachet de l'affection que vous me portez et vous jugerez de part et dautre que ce sont choses inviolables comme je depose devant dieu et entre vos mains q[ue] je seray jusques de la mort –

Fontainbleau, le 3 Juin

This is a small paper, cut from a large sheet and addressed to Thomas on the reverse. It seems to be the final part of a longer letter.

[55] The letter is a transcription of NA SP 78/55/126–7.

[56] César, duc de Vendôme, was the legitimised elder son of Henri IV and his mistress (later his second wife), Gabrielle D'Estrées. Vendôme married Françoise, daughter of Philippe-Emmanuel de Lorraine, duc de Mercoeur.

the Bryde to Church by the leaft arm, and Monsieur Le Grand by the right. The Church solemnities ended supper began; the table was as they call it a la Potence.[57] Those that sat were these, and in this Order. The Bride, the King, the Queen, the eldre Princess of Condé,[58] the younger, the Princess of County, the Countess of Soissons,[59] Mademoiselle de Vendosme,[60] the Dutchesses of <u>Guise</u>,[61] of <u>Luxembourg</u>, of Rohan,[62] of Suilly.[63] There were of the same quality that sat not Madame de Mercoeur, the mother [of the bride], and Madame d'Angolesme.[64] For the Princes <u>they</u> all servd the King, the Count Soissons going before the meat as Grand Maistre. After supper they dauncd only solemn measures, amongst which the King dauncd the Suisses march to do honour to that nation, and so the company dissolvde. On the morrow the King ranne at Ring and at nyght there was a Ballett. On Thursday the King promisd Tilting but the Prince of Condé carrying away his lady that morning took of[f] all the jollity of the Court, and beefore dinner the whole Company broke in pieces. Upon the marriage day the Dutches of Mercoeur presented her daughter with jewells to the value of four hundred thousand crowns more than ever she promisd her. The King was at first very glad of this addition, but after the jewells being surveyd it was found that they were all jewells belonging to the crown sent by Duke of Mercoeurs sister, Henry the thirds wife, to her brother during the warr. At the first sight thereof the King was much disturbde and sent for the Duke of Suilly, but after was appeasd because what he lost his child got. The Kings love continues still to the yong Princess and in the like vehemency, and all the Court seeks to be imployd, among other Monsieur Beumont undertook to do much in it, but afterward fayling it confirmed his former disgrace. Those that are the dayly sollicitors are the Counts

[57] This idiom refers to the shape of the table, with a cross table at the top. 'Potence' means 'gibbet', so the shape evoked that of the gallows.

[58] Charlotte Catherine de La Trémouille was the princesse de Condé until her husband's death in 1588, and was after that referred to as the Dowager Princess.

[59] The comte de Soissons, Charles de Bourbon, was first cousin to the king, and was married to Anne de Montafié, comtesse de Clermont-en-Beauvaisis.

[60] Younger sister of the duc de Vendôme, Catherine Henriette de Bourbon was known as Mademoiselle de Vendôme until her marriage in 1619.

[61] This is likely to be Catherine of Clèves, the dowager duchess of Guise, as her son, Charles, the current duke, did not marry until after 1609.

[62] This was Marguerite de Béthune, daughter of the duc de Sully, who was married to Henri II de Rohan.

[63] The second wife of the duc de Sully, who turned Protestant to marry him and bore him nine children, was Rachel de Cochefilet.

[64] This is likely to have been Charlotte de Montmorency, comtesse de Fleix, who was the daughter of Henri I de Montmorency, and the wife of Charles d'Angoulême.

of Cramail and Granmont,[65] and the old Princess her self is not unsuspected to be on[e] of the Kings best instrumentes, by whose means they say her daughter is brought so far as to hearken.[66] The Duke of Bullion and the Princess of Orange are both sent from Court as being thought adverse to that affayre and Bassompiere, her former sutour, because he was suspected to possess some part of her affection.[67] The Queen was at first well content with it, because it cast the Marquis of Vernueil into utter neglect,[68] but now she consumes herself because she thincks the Kings publick carriage of it reflects disgrace uppon her, which made her appear little at the marriage. Essars is now with child, but the King they say will not avow it.[69] The Count of Auvergne is permitted by reason of his sicknes to have a lodging out of the Bastyle but with a strait guard uppon him.[70] The Duke Epernons elder sonne being sickly is gone to the Baths. For his second, La Valette, he goes shortly to invest him in the governement of Messin.[71] As for the town of Mets, the King hath disposed of it. The new-made friendship betwixt the Count of Soissons and the Duke of Sully hath made the Duke colder than before toward the house of Guyse. The Duke of Guyse himself is now in Provence to receave his yearely present from that County [illegible] of Duells hath allready so fair prevaild, as that they have shewd theyr occasions and

---

[65] Adrien de Montluc, comte de Cramail, and Antoine II, comte de Gramont.

[66] This is a little confused. The matter being referred to appears to be the king's desire for a relationship with the young princesse de Condé, and the list of figures those who are trying to persuade her. But she is not the Dowager Princess's daughter. Indeed, Éléonore de Bourbon, the Dowager Princess's actual daughter, is princesse d'Orange, and one of those 'sent from court' (in the next sentence of the letter) as 'thought adverse to that affair'.

[67] Henri de La Tour d'Auvergne was duc de Buillon. For the princesse d'Orange see previous note. François de Bassompierre was a great favourite of the king, and prevented by him from his proposed marriage to Charlotte de Montmorency. When Charlotte married in 1609, and became princesse de Condé, this appears to have been a ploy by the king to prevent a love match with Bassompierre.

[68] This appears to be a reference to Catherine Henriette de Balzac d'Entragues, marquise de Verneuil, who had been Henri IV's mistress and borne him two sons. Angry that the king married Marie de Medici after the death of his second wife, Gabrielle D'Estrées, the marquise took part in a conspiracy against the king, but appears to have been back in favour by 1609. The queen was notoriously jealous of her and when Henri IV died the following year and she took over as regent, she exiled Catherine from court.

[69] Charlotte des Essarts, comtesse de Romorantin, was another of the king's mistresses, and she bore him a daughter, Marie Henriette, in 1609, who was legitimised.

[70] Charles de Valois, comte d'Auvergne, was the illegitimate son of Charles IX. Involved with the marquise de Verneuil in a conspiracy against the king, he was condemned to death, but this verdict was commuted to life imprisonment in the Bastille. He was imprisoned from 1605 to 1616.

[71] Jean-Louis de Nogaret, duc d'Epernon, powerful opponent of the Catholic League, had three sons. The eldest, Henri, duc de Candale, would have been eighteen in 1609. His second son, Bernard de Nogaret de La Valette, was a year younger.

demanded leavy and had it not bene for that the French say there had been forty quarrells the day of the marriage. Those of Biscay have lately made incursions uppon the Country of Bearne. Monsieur La Forse being governour gave notyce to the King of it, who bade him repayre the loss with advantage, and if need were he would come himself to help him.[72] The Duke of Sully to perfitt and exceed his other publick works hath long threatened the buylding of a navy and of late to that purpose was about to undertake a journey to survey all the Ports toward Spain, but yesterday I receavde news from Court, that that journey was at least differd if not broken of[f]. I have here sent your Lordship a paper which I receavd from Court during the tyme that I wrote this letter, and besyde the Censure of Pere Cotton uppon his Majestyes book, but me thincks tis so mild for a Jesuit as I ghess that he suspected it was demanded of him with intent to be delivered to some Huguenot.[73] Thus, craving pardon for having thus long disturbd your Lordships better affayrs, I rest with protestations of being ever

[half page gap]
Paris, 12 of July

Your Lordships to command

[signature torn off]

[72] Jacques Nompar de Caumont, duc de La Force, was governor of Béarn and viceroy of Navarre.

[73] Pierre Coton was a French Jesuit who became a friend of king Henri IV, and, by 1609, the confessor of his son, the Dauphin. After Henri's death in 1610, Coton was accused of having supported his murderer, Ravaillac, and Pierre du Moulin, a Huguenot minister who had been educated in England, was believed to be behind the writing of a satirical pamphlet, *Anti-Coton, in which it is proved that the Jesuits are guilty of parricide against Henri IV*. Du Moulin had been a defender of James's books in France. In 1609, King James issued an accompaniment to the second edition of his *An Apologie for the Oath of Allegiance*, a *Premonition to All most Mightie Monarches*, and sent Du Moulin a personal copy. Attacks on the king's books by Cardinal Bellarmine and by the French Dominican Nicolas Coëffeteau prompted Du Moulin to write an officially sanctioned reply to the latter, which appeared in 1610 in his *Defence of the Catholique Faith Contained in the Booke of [. . .] King James the First*. See Brian G. Armstrong and Vivienne Larminie's article on Du Moulin in *ODNB*.

Letter 6

21 July 1609: George Carew to Overbury[74]

[. . .] The king here ever since his new lover waxeth young & silly; every day running at ring, & beginneth now also to speak that men may chance see him in the head of an army of 40,000 men in Clenco:[75] and yet I doubt that all these great Demonstrations will turn into wind. But he is pitifully perplexed in that matter of his lover still, & looketh pretty anxious to draw the Prince of Condé to the Court who now standeth out.[76] One time he saith he gives him not his pension to spend in the country: another, that he is about an Edict of apparel, & would have the princes & princesses choose what they would have appropriated to themselves; & that therefore he would have the prince called hither to declare his opinion therein. But the best was that he told Madame de la Tremouille, that he would have come to the Court, that he might spend his time virtuously: & for his wife <u>I cannot really think well of her, but he is become so wicked, so wicked, that he doesn't pray at all to God</u>.[77]

---

[74] The letter is a transcription of BL Add. MS 4160, fol. 332, copied in the hand of Thomas Birch. The letter shows a close relationship between Thomas and the French ambassador, George Carew. The latter was twenty-five years older than Thomas, but both men were Middle Templars and could have met there. The homosocial network provided by the Inn could just as easily, though, have allowed Rous and Thomas to make the acquaintance of the ambassador on their arrival in Paris. Carew was recalled to London later that summer, and replaced by Sir Thomas Edmondes.

[75] The name of the place is obscure in Birch's manuscript.

[76] This refers to the king's desire for the princesse de Condé to return to court. Her husband carefully keeps her out of the king's reach by refusing to bring her there.

[77] This final sentence is written in French in the original letter: 'je ne puis bien penser d'elle vrayement; mais luy est devenu si méchant, si méchant, qu'il ne prie point Dieu'. The fact that Carew writes in French is further evidence that Thomas speaks French proficiently (along with Letters 2 and 4 above, and his ability to function so well as Cecil's informer at the French court). This will become relevant in Chapter 3, as one of the reasons he gives James I for declining his offer of a post as ambassador is his lack of language. If that ambassadorship had been to France (one of the posts suggested in correspondence at the time), then this would have been palpably ridiculous.

Letter 7

28 July 1609: Overbury to Salisbury[78]

Most honorable

I have receavd your gracious letter which gives me assurance of your Lordships acceptance of my servyce and love, which happines I value according to that difference of the Roman which sayd mallem Caesaris iudicium quam Antonii beneficium.[79] Neyther shall that favour ever beget in me a confidence to be importunate but rather an alacrity to deserve. The Count of Auvergne mends but is not yet returnd to the Bastyle.[80] During the extremity of his sicknes he refusd the help of all the Kings physitians, as he told them because he knew theyr servyce to him would not be pleasing to the King, but as on[e] of themselvs told me that he thought it was out of some suspicion of theyr honesty, and the same man related to me yesterday the sicknes two days since of the Countess of Moret, whose sole Physitian he is, at which the King was present at midnight four hours together.[81] At length she despayring of lyfe sayd to the King, 'Sire, to you I recommend my sonne'. Whereuppon the King wept and would not leave her till he saw her recovering. Her disease was the mother.[82] The King is yet so angry at Madame de Essars as he hath by expres messenger forbid her to come to ly in at Paris, but they which know him well say that notwithstanding all this she will by intreaty bring him at length to avow the child.[83] The Coronell Chastilion by reason of the memory of his ancestors and his owne hopefullnes hath much respect at Court.[84] The Prince of Condé makes

[78] The letter is a transcription of NA SP 78/55/144.

[79] I have been unable to trace the source of this quotation, though common knowledge of the Latin source, and their shared classical education, is likely to be used by Thomas here to form a bond between him and Cecil. See discussion of the passage above, on p. 35.

[80] See footnote 70 above.

[81] The citation of the source here, one of the king's physicians, adds weight to Thomas's narrative, showing both the likelihood of the story's veracity and the writer's web of connections. Jacqueline de Bueil, comtesse de Moret, was another mistress of Henri IV, to whom she had borne a son, Antoine, two years previously.

[82] Having 'the mother' as your disease implies that she was suffering from hysteria. *A briefe discourse of a disease called the Suffocation of the Mother*, a treatise written by physician Edward Jorden in 1603, is the first work in English on the subject. The Duchess of Malfi (2.1.113) tells the court that she is 'troubled with the mother', allowing Bosola in an aside to pun, and make a link to her increasingly visible pregnancy. References to *The Duchess of Malfi* are taken from the 4th edition of the New Mermaid edition of the play, edited by Brian Gibbons (London: A&C Black, 2001), and will usually be in the text.

[83] See footnote 69 above.

[84] 'Coronel Chastilion' (perhaps intended to be Colonel) probably refers to Gaspard III de Coligny, maréchal de Châtillon, whose ancestors included Gaspard and François, the Coligny brothers, renowned Huguenot leaders in the Wars of Religion.

much towards him, and the Duke of Sully useth him extraordinarily well notwithstanding the old quarrell betwixt him and the Duke of Rohan. Since the edict there hath been dayly demanded the combat, and some say here, that none being granted uppon such variety of occasions it will grow shortly scarse honorable to ask it, but me thincks the rigorous justyce they have done hitherto for any the least offence (as casting of Pensions and banishment from Court only for ill words) will shortly take away all occasions eyther to break the Edict or make use of it. To give countenance to my own letter I have here sent your Lordship one of a French Gentleman of the Kings chamber and a Protestant, which I received this night from St Germaine where the Court now is.[85] For my self by reason of the importunity of some domestick affayrs I shall return in August to England, but before that (if Mr Frimett or Doctor Lyster come not hither)[86] I intend to make a journey to Orleans to see my Lord of Cranborne that your Lordship may know that not only your self are the object of my faythfullnes and love but even all that may be called yours. And so till then I humbly take my leave. Paris the xxviii[th] of July.

Your Lordships to command

Thomas Overbury

[85] As in Letter 5 above, where he also encloses a letter he has received, Thomas's accompanying evidence here both adds weight to his own intelligence and shows that he is in the midst of his own intelligence-gathering network.

[86] It is unclear who the 'Mr Frimett' is that Thomas refers to here. There are two possible candidates for Dr Lister. Edward Lister and his younger brother, Matthew, were both physicians serving at the English court. The elder (born in 1557) served Elizabeth and James I, but his younger brother (born just ten years before Thomas in 1571) is perhaps the one referred to here. He served James VI and I (and later Charles I), and was to treat Robert Cecil during his final illness in 1612.

Secretary, Conduit and Minion: Overbury's Courtly Zenith

> I'll seat thee by my throne of state,
> And make thee rival in those governments
> That by thy secrecy thou liftst me to [. . .]
> *Tragedy of Hoffman*, 2.3.87–9

As Chapter 1 has established, Thomas Overbury's rise was enabled by a close friendship with Robert Carr, and the preferment that accompanied this at the Jacobean court. The homosociality of the court reflected other male communities at the Inns of Court, at the universities, even in the playhouses, and its importance was based on classical antecedents. It will be useful therefore to begin Chapter 2 with a more conceptual look at this kind of relationship in the early modern period, and in particular at how modern scholarship has come to understand its agency at the Jacobean court. This will then allow me in the rest of the chapter to look at the letters surrounding Thomas's rising success at court, and perceptions of the friendship with Carr that enabled this.

Scholars of the early modern have been interested for some decades now in the practice and cultural significance of male friendship. Influential in this area is the work of Eve Kosofsky Sedgwick, who argued in the 1980s that 'the structure of homosocial continuums is culturally contingent'; that is, that understanding of aspects of such a continuum (patronage, male friendship, sodomy and so on) shifts from period to period.[1] In exploring the likely perceptions of male relationships in early modern England, and noting the closeness of men emotionally and physically, as well as intellectually, she quite rightly problematises a continuum linking homosociality to homosexuality. She recognises that those living in the early years of the seventeenth century would see

---

[1] Eve Kosofsky Sedgwick, *Between Men: English Literature and Male Homosocial Desire* (New York: Columbia University Press, 1985), p. 5.

close relationships between men as normative and, in practical terms, contributive to happiness and future success; but, for the modern reader, outside the culture, it is a 'closeness between males, to which [we] find[] it difficult to perceive the boundaries'.[2] These boundaries also interested Alan Bray in his groundbreaking exploration of the changing nature of male friendship. In *The Friend* and the research leading up to this, a decade after Sedgwick, he examines what would and would not have been acceptable to Thomas's contemporaries.[3]

Bray proposes that perceptions of male intimacy began to shift at the end of the sixteenth century, during Thomas's lifetime, from essentially normative to potentially transgressive. Bray comments that at the end of the Elizabethan period this normality was seen in the practice of sharing a bed with another man: a common occurrence and not indicative of sexual relations between them. He concludes, 'beds are not only places where people sleep: they are also places where people talk. To be someone's "bedfellow" suggested one had influence.'[4] Men who had round-the-clock physical access to another were influential over them. Women of Elizabeth's circle would also have had influence, of course, used for the benefit of husbands, brothers and so on, but access to the body of James VI and I enabled direct male power; the men who wished to gain positions of power themselves could influence the king who was the source of that preferment. As we saw in Chapter 1, as well as the difference inherent in the change of gender of those influencing the monarch, there was a shift in the locus of power when James replaced Elizabeth that enabled individual favourites to consolidate their positions. As Gentleman of the Bedchamber, Carr was one of a small number of men who took turns to sleep in James's room at night, and this intimacy and personal power over someone in authority appears analogous to Thomas's influence over Carr.

Classically educated young men were, of course, familiar with the discussion of male friendship in Cicero's popular *De Amicitia*. Here the speaker, Laelius, discusses the qualities that mark out his friendship with Scipio. Throughout the treatise the moral quality of the relationship is stressed: 'friendship cannot exist except among good men'.[5] It is also exclusive, binding together only men of similar experiences, and

[2] Sedgwick, *Between Men*, p. 35.

[3] Alan Bray, *The Friend* (Chicago: University of Chicago Press, 2003).

[4] Alan Bray, 'Homosexuality and Male Friendship', in *Queering the Renaissance*, ed. by Jonathan Goldberg (Durham, NC: Duke University Press, 1994), pp. 40–61 (p. 42).

[5] Cicero, *De Amicitia*, from *De Senectute, De Amicitia, De Divinatione*, trans. by William Armistead Falconer for Loeb Classical Library, Vol. XX (Cambridge, MA: Harvard University Press, 1923), p. 128.

'the bonds of affection always united two persons only, or, at most, a few'.[6] The nature of such a relationship is, he tells us, above that of others:

> all other objects of desire are each [. . .] adapted to a single end — riches, for spending; influence, for honour; public office, for reputation; pleasures, for sensual enjoyment; and health, for freedom from pain and full use of the bodily functions; but friendship embraces innumerable ends; turn where you will it is ever at your side; no barrier shuts it out; it is never untimely and never in the way.[7]

Indeed, this kind of friendship between men, above all kinds of common relationships – even marriage – is, according to Cicero, uniquely close. The friend grows to be an *alter idem*: 'he who looks upon a true friend, looks, as it were, upon a sort of image of himself'.[8] The idealisation of relationships between men originating in Cicero's text pervades human-ist society and Alan Bray argues that until the latter part of the sixteenth century such friendships were common and ordinarily perceived as unthreatening to society. It was only when the ideal was disturbed, such as when the social status of the men involved was not equal, that such friendships became potentially disruptive.[9] In later work on the social context and the reception of the male favourite, Curtis Perry refers to friendship between men in the sixteenth century as part of 'the fabric of society itself'.[10] Indeed, in his exploration of the symbolic importance of poisoning, he argues that a crime undermining male friendship is trea-sonous as it is a betrayal of the natural order.

It is in the multivalence of such relationships that the challenge to modern interpretation lies; as Cicero noted in the quotation above, 'friendship embraces innumerable ends'. Early modern male friendship *could* be a pure, spiritual bond. Equally, though, it could become a physical relationship that transgressed socially accepted norms, and a relationship was particularly problematic when (as in Thomas's later relationship with Robert Carr) it was publicly discussed. In his analysis of sodomy lying beneath his recent work on character types, Mario DiGangi uses ideas from feminist and queer theory to explore the dif-ficulty in distinguishing between what was perceived as normative male friendship and that transgressing socially and morally acceptable behav-iour. He points out that '[t]he sodomite's habits of same-sex association

---

[6] Cicero, *De Amicitia*, p. 130.
[7] Cicero, *De Amicitia*, p. 133.
[8] Cicero, *De Amicitia*, p. 134.
[9] See Bray, 'Homosexuality and Male Friendship', *passim*.
[10] Curtis Perry, *Literature and Favoritism in Early Modern England* (Cambridge: Cambridge University Press, 2006), p. 104.

[. . .] might [. . .] be recognized as the same activities which constituted authorized masculine relations'.[11] The activities he lists, 'eating and drinking with male companions; participating in riotous camaraderie; nurturing same-sex friendships; sharing intimacies with bedfellows', were clearly what men in an early modern homosocial environment considered quotidian behaviour. Thus, sodomy can be seen as different only in degree from behaviour that was considered morally and legally acceptable. In this way, as DiGangi infers, 'the sodomite can serve both to establish definitions of orderly community (through representations of his practices as antithetical to social norms) and to destabilize those definitions (through unsettling revelations of the proximity of his "sodomitical" practices to those very norms)'; that is, the sodomite helps expose those boundaries that interested Sedgwick and Bray.

DiGangi's interpretation of the ambiguity that lies in these relationships between men, and his argument that this exposes a potential instability underlying the moral norms of urban life, is clearly connected to the earlier work of Alan Stewart. In the introduction to his perceptive critique of the relationship between male friendships and humanist thinking, Stewart notes that, beyond merely sexual behaviour, socially disruptive acts are often discussed in terms of sodomy. Echoing Bray's identification of a shift in the early seventeenth century, Stewart perceives a growing tendency to link male friendship and wider socially unacceptable behaviour; he declares his intention to 'contend that it is in anxiety about the generation of these new bonds between men that the question of sodomy, and its relationship to humanism, surfaces'.[12] If, as Eve Kosofsky Sedgwick noted, in such male friendships 'a reader from outside the culture finds it difficult to perceive the boundaries', it is difficult to see the boundary between the spiritual and the physical, or between the acceptable and the illicit.

However difficult those boundaries were to perceive, though, we can see that there *were* boundaries from the discussion in contemporary sources of what constituted licit behaviour between men. These limits are discussed by Montaigne in his essay 'On Friendship', translated into English by John Florio in 1603. As Cicero's Laelius had explained, these ideal friendships must be made between equals and Montaigne's

---

[11] Mario DiGangi, *Sexual Types: Embodiment, Agency, and Dramatic Character from Shakespeare to Shirley* (Philadelphia: University of Pennsylvania Press, 2011), p. 22. Using original work by Alan Bray in *Homosexuality in Renaissance England* (London: Gay Men's Press, 1982), DiGangi suggests that 'sodomy trials were so rare in the early modern period because it was so difficult for people to recognize the monstrous sodomite in the actual persons of their barbers or bakers'.

[12] Stewart, *Close Readers*, p. xiv.

famous declaration reveals just how ideal was that friendship he formed with Étienne de La Boétie. In Florio's translation Montaigne explains, 'If a man urged me to tell wherefore I loved him, I feele it can not be expressed, but by answering; Because it was he, because it was myself'.[13] He discusses how, in theory, this 'entire jouissance' which is available to men's minds should be available to their bodies too, forming perfect homosexual unions. However, there are no examples of this having been successful and 'ancient schooles' have thus rejected it. Furthermore this 'Greeke licence is justly abhorred by our customs'. This is mainly, he argues, because of the discrepancy in age the Greeks advise for such relationships between men, as forming such a bond would 'no more sufficiently answere the perfect union and agreement, which here we require'.[14] Montaigne's exploration of the limitations on the physicality of male relationships thus illustrates one way in which they can be problematic.

In this way the relationships between Thomas Overbury and Robert Carr, and between Carr and the king, were accepted by many as an inevitable feature of court life, but seen by some epistolary commentators on the court as transgressive. To illustrate how one such saw a blurred line between licit and illicit practices, one could look at Thomas Howard's letter of 1611 to his friend, John Harington. Writing in the period this chapter focuses on, Howard reports to the courtier, who is thinking of returning to the court after an absence of some years, that all is not as it was when Elizabeth was on the throne. Where she 'did talk of her subjects love and good affections, and in good truth she aimed well', James, he reports, 'talketh of his subjects fear and subjection'. His perception of love, it appears, revolves around Robert Carr: '[t]he Prince leaneth on his arm, pinches his cheek, smoothes his ruffled garment, and, when he looketh at Carr, directeth discourse to divers others'.[15] Howard's slightly tongue-in-cheek advice to Harington is to appear as the king wishes his favourite courtiers to dress, and to be 'well trimmed; get a new jerkin well borderd and not too short; the King saith, he liketh a flowing garment'.[16] Thomas Howard, who as Frances Howard's father is to play his role in the events of 1613, can see the ambiguity the king

---

[13] John Florio's translation of Montaigne's Essays, *The Essayes or Morall, Politike and Millitarie Discourses of Lo: Michaell de Montaigne, Knight of the noble Order of St Michaell, and one of the Gentlemen in Ordinary of the French king, Henry the third his Chamber* (London: Valentine Sims, 1603). Quotations are from 'The seaven and twentieth Chapter: Of Friendship', p. 91.

[14] Montaigne, *The Essayes*, p. 92.

[15] Sir John Harington, *Nugae Antiquae: Being a Miscellaneous Collection of Original Papers in Prose and Verse*, Vol. I (London: J. Wright, 1804), p. 392.

[16] Harington, *Nugae Antiquae*, p. 391.

is modelling in his relationships with other men. It will not, though, prevent Howard from using Carr for his own ends; this ambiguity accompanies influence, and power.

Carr and Thomas were resented by figures central to the Jacobean court, from the most powerful such as Queen Anna to those who depended on the influence of the pair for their position. We can often see how contemporary perceptions of Thomas's character were connected to the observers' attitudes to close male friendship.

It is in this context, then, that we see reactions to Thomas's growing influence at the Jacobean court. This chapter will now take as evidence two groups of letters from contemporary commentators and political actors, with little comment from Thomas himself; the first group dates from March, and then from May, 1611, and the second is a collection written through 1612. That he is now the subject of others' letters, rather than simply the producer of his own, shows that he is rising in the public eye; he is a young man gaining confidence and power, reliant on his bond with the royal favourite but, due to that relationship, increasingly able to work without appeasing others. This confidence or unapologetic decision making is, of course, often interpreted as insolence by those who resent his power: a power which they often see as greater than should be held by a man without a higher social status.

A Potential Diplomat

The first group of letters date to 1611, preceding a dispute between Thomas and the queen in May of that year. An early appearance of Thomas in these letters from intelligencers to their diplomatic masters is two months earlier, in the March. William Trumbull had been left to play the role of ambassador in Brussels over a year before, on the departure of Thomas Edmondes for the higher-ranking embassy in Paris. Trumbull had not been appointed full ambassador (indeed, he was not to be so, despite continuing in the post until 1625), and there was in early 1611 a fever of speculation about who would replace Edmondes. There were, it appeared, three key contenders in the running: Sir Henry Wotton, recently James's ambassador in Venice; Sir George Calvert, who worked at court and abroad for Robert Cecil; and Thomas Overbury. John Sandford, writing from London to Edmondes in Paris on 6 March, names all three men: 'The ambassador to be sent from hence is diversly spoken of: some say Sir Henry Wotton, lately arrived at court; some suspect Mr. George Calvert, who came to London on Sunday last; or late Sir Thomas Overbury, a great favourite of Sir Robert

Carr, hath been mentioned.'[17] Thomas, identified to Edmondes by his relationship with Carr, only needs the indefinite article at this point; he is not a man Sandford expects Edmondes to have heard of. Another London correspondent, William Devick, writing to William Trumbull in Brussels the next day, thinks only two of them are real contenders, and dismisses Wotton, who has recently returned in disgrace from his Venice posting.[18] Devick, close to Trumbull and aware of his difficult position after Edmondes' departure, comments, 'After compliments I should be glad if I could in requital [. . .] but send you word who were certainly designed to relieve you from your purgatory which yet I cannot do, but am in expectation thereof in brief, since we shall have your Amb: so soon here, which will enforce us to a resolution. The report runs upon one named Sir Thomas Overbury, a favourite of Sir Robert Carr's, or else Mr. Calvert who arrived here the 5th of this month from Paris.'[19] Thomas is first named here – he is certainly a serious contender for the ambassadorship in these expert intelligencers' minds – but he is still someone of whom the recipient is unlikely to have heard and still identified only by his close friendship with Carr. Although the letter writers of March 1611 couldn't know it, Thomas was forging a way to power that was to offer him more direct influence than being an ambassador would have done.

Between 1610 and 1612 political life and leadership in Jacobean England were changing, and Robert Carr was to be the main beneficiary. Some historians think that even before the final illness of Robert Cecil, Earl of Salisbury, his great power – a power that had survived regime change – was on the wane. In 1610 he had tried in the Great Contract to mediate between king and parliament, with a move that would have

---

[17] Letter 8, p. 74.

[18] Wotton had famously written in a friend's commonplace book what, in English, is a humorous punning comment on his chosen career: 'An ambassador is an honest man sent to lie abroad for the good of his country'. The pun on 'lie', also meaning to 'reside' in English, was lost completely as he wrote the phrase in Latin, where '*mentiendum*' does not have the same double meaning.

[19] Letter 9, p. 75. Several more letters are sent to Trumbull mentioning the subject. In London on 22 March 1611 (Letter 10), Edmondes' man, Samuel Calvert, agrees that 'some give out' that Thomas shall succeed to the Brussels post (see *Downshire III*, p. 44). Jean Beaulieu, who has worked alongside Trumbull under Edmondes in Brussels, and now works for him in Paris, writes to inform Trumbull of the contents of Sandford's letter (Letter 11, 27 March 1611: p. 76). On 29 March, Calvert has grown stronger in his belief that it will be Thomas, noting to Trumbull, 'Sir Thos. Overbury would like to go Ambassador to Brussels. My cousin, G. Calvert, is talked on, but is not ambitious' (Letter 12, p. 76). Edmondes himself has written to Trumbull on 9 March 1611, 'From England I hear that Mr. Calvert is to go Amb[r.] to Brussels' (*Downshire III*, p. 34). This is after Sandford's letter to him, sent on 6 March, and suggests that he dismisses Thomas and Wotton as contenders (see footnote to Letter 8).

guaranteed the king's financial supply in return for some moderation in James's use of his royal prerogative.[20] With the benefit of hindsight, of course, this kind of move would have helped alleviate the tension between monarch and parliament in the period where we can see that the seeds of the Civil War are being sown. But Cecil's attempts failed, and Neil Cuddy's is typical of one kind of historical view when he concludes that, 'By 1610 all this conspired to put a question mark over the continuance of Salisbury's ministry'.[21] James's desire to maintain the freedom of royal prerogative meant he was persuaded against the scheme by members of the Bedchamber, who, Cuddy continues, 'offered both an alternative (and more effective) route to the king, and possibly even the power-base for a new sort of regime'. This efficacy was surely the reason that Thomas seems to have decided not to follow the more traditional bureaucratic route that in Chapter 1 we saw opening up for him: a route offered by Cecil's patronage, and assumed by the writers of diplomatic intelligence in March 1611.

Another historical view has it that the influence of Cecil recovered after the 1610 failure, citing the continuing level of control he exerted in three key courtly positions: Secretary, Treasurer and Master of the Court of Wards. Pauline Croft summarises his continuing influence when she notes that 'by February 1611 the king had returned to his former practice of channelling virtually all privy council business through him. Salisbury the supreme bureaucrat was simply indispensable.'[22] Historians may not be able to agree on how much sway Cecil had through this time, but the balance of power certainly shifted towards the king's favourite when Cecil's illness became debilitating in late 1611. By this point, Robert Carr had become the most influential courtier in the kingdom and this changed the nature of royal counsel in England, with supremacy conclusively passing from the Privy Council to the man of the king's choosing. By this point, Jacobean courtiership is moving away

---

[20] See Chapter 3 for further discussion of James's personal power and contemporary attitudes to the royal prerogative.

[21] Cuddy, 'The Revival of the Entourage', p. 206.

[22] Pauline Croft, 'The Reputation of Robert Cecil: Libels, Political Opinion and Popular Awareness in the Early Seventeenth Century', *Transactions of the Royal Historical Society*, 6th series, No. 1 (1991), pp. 43–69 (p. 69). This perspective is certainly supported by the correspondence between the Venetian ambassador, Antonio Foscarini, and the Doge and Senate in Venice. Foscarini reports on 21 May 1612: 'The King avails himself also in parts of the earl of Northampton, and he has created Viscount Rochester of the Council, but notwithstanding all this he settles nothing without the advice of Salisbury, who, in spite of ill health and absence, governs everything' (*Calendar of State Papers and Manuscripts Relating to English Affairs, existing in the archives and collections of Venice and in other Libraries of Northern Italy*, Vol. XII, 1610–1613, ed. by Horatio F. Brown (London: His Majesty's Stationery Office, 1905), p. 356).

from its Elizabethan antecedents, and the context in which Thomas is rising is shifting.

As testimony to the royal favourite's growing influence, in March 1611 Thomas's long-standing friend was created Viscount Rochester and, two months later, installed as a Knight of the Garter. The letters of this same month, that we have just seen, show that Thomas was generally identified through his position as Carr's favourite; but although this was the route for Thomas's success at court, it was also the reason for his being vilified in some influential quarters. Though I refer here to 'the court', of course in Jacobean terms there were three distinct, though interrelated, court spaces – the king's, Queen Anna's and Prince Henry's. This, along with the rising influence of the favourites of the Bedchamber (and consequent declining influence of the Privy Council – and perhaps even of Cecil himself), delineates further the changing court context in which Thomas is working. All three Jacobean courts had physical spaces of their own, and courtiers, writers and so on moved between them; some of these individuals undoubtedly had a different status in different loci. Thomas's status was rising in the homosociality of the king's sphere, but in May 1611 he was to feel the queen's ire despite, or rather because of, the growing power of Carr.

Although as a Scottish Gentleman of the Bedchamber the new Viscount Rochester represented what many English courtiers had opposed, his power and influence were so great that most found they had to gain his favour if they wished for the king's support. But the queen felt keenly the power accorded by the king to his favourite and in May 1611 her jealousy of the increasingly powerful courtier led to an incident at Greenwich recorded by London correspondents for diplomats across Europe.

Conflict with Queen Anna

Still in his 'purgatory' and waiting to be relieved of his post in Brussels, William Trumbull heard of the events from a Mr Taverner. Details of this writer are scant, but typically, as we have seen so far, the men who supplied diplomatic intelligence were educated men of the middling sort, linked through their business with their correspondents, and part of their social circle. It is not unreasonable to assume that Mr Taverner had a humanist education, and was familiar with the guiding principles of classical rhetoric, as he writes the first extant letter giving a fuller picture of Thomas. He certainly guides his reader's inferences about the rising young courtier:

On Monday last Rochester and his dear Overbury, walking in the garden at Greenwich whither the queen's window openeth, she broke into a sudden and contemptible laughing at them. 'So,' saith she, 'they did at her,' which belief carried her so far that she went to the king with tears in her eyes and complained and besought him that she might have right of them, which he not seeming to be so sensible of as she hoped, she cast herself on her knees and besought him not to suffer her to be so scorned and despised of his grooms, though she were content to suffer it from him, with earnest protestation that if he would not right her, she would go back into Denmark. All this while the good king much afflicted walked up and down the chamber. 'Ah, woe is me, my queen will go from me, my Carr, my Carr.' But doing nothing to content her. [. . .] The conclusion was, she finding herself not able to supplant Carr, which she desireth of all things in the world, turned all her force against Overbury, against whom she hath so far prevailed that he is banished from the Court. But Rochester told the king if he would so far give credit to the rage of a jealous woman to banish a faithful and discreet servant for his friendship, which was the only fault the queen could impute unto him, for his part he was resolute to share with him in his fortune, banishment or whatsoever it were. So the business yet hangs. Overbury is from Court, here at his lodging by Whitehall, where Rochester and all men almost visit him and my ld. of Pembroke, too.[23]

The letter evokes clear literary stereotypes: the jealous wife, the pair of young male friends, and the enamoured and irresolute king. As James Daybell tells us, 'Renaissance letters were often written with the intention of being read out aloud and performance was integral to their presentation', and this seems to have been the case for Taverner's.[24] He certainly relishes the entertainment value of his tale and, using a typical epistolary strategy, ventriloquises his subjects. The king and queen's dialogue in direct and reported speech, as well as Carr's words in his friend's defence, all appear to give the oral evidence of its veracity: a strategy in successful early modern letter writing.[25] Taverner's background is likely to have involved learning about rhetoric through study of Cicero and Quintilian, and writing in a manner guided by classical exemplars was commonplace in Renaissance education (as we saw in the Introduction). Thus, Taverner's letter uses the familiar topics of rhetorical circumstance to guide his reader's response when describing the incident, and amongst many lists of these in the textbooks young men

---

[23] Letter 13, p. 77. See notes to that letter for discussion of who Mr Taverner may have been.

[24] Daybell, *The Material Letter*, p. 18.

[25] Schneider notes that 'early modern Europe tended to valorize speech and face-to-face interaction as a more reliable, trustworthy, and authentic mode of communication compared to written or printed modes' (*The Culture of Epistolarity*, p. 16), and this makes the adoption of spoken mode in written form a useful strategy to lessen the distrust of letters.

would have seen at the time is Quintilian's: 'motive, time, place, oppor-tunity, means, method and the like'.[26] Taverner refuses to let his reader sympathise with any of the protagonists in his tale, with arguments of proof showing their conflicting motives and methods. Anna's method of approaching the king, for instance, in tears and kneeling, is clearly designed to appeal to her husband's pity for her but reduces her status in the eyes of readers; his pacing 'up and down the chamber' is sugges-tive of his unkingly indecision as he chooses whose side to take in the dispute. Taverner is a sophisticated supplier of intelligence and an enter-taining correspondent, whose description of the royal household shows an awareness of theatrical, as well as rhetorical, convention. This letter demonstrates clearly the techniques that drama and epistolarity shared.

For anyone interested in Thomas's career, there are troubling issues, and it is as a direct consequence of being Carr's friend that he faces them. The queen's 'sudden and contemptible laughing' causes the altercation according to Taverner, and suggests a decided change in her attitude since she had described her husband's 'sewer' as 'a pretty yong fellow' five or six years earlier. It is clear, though, that Carr's friend is not the queen's primary target, and her motive, supplied by Taverner, is 'to sup-plant Carr, which she desireth of all things in the world'. Her declared motive to James, to 'have right of them', clearly aims to achieve this, and she calls upon the king's sense of justice; a particularly powerful argument as James saw himself as the royal embodiment of legal justice in his kingdom.[27] The choice of language in her plea to James 'not to suffer her to be so scorned and despised of his grooms, though she were content to suffer it from him' makes it sound as if Taverner were present and quoting the queen; either he was, and her verb choices actually *were* emotive, or, in an exercise in *prosopopoeia*, he is ventriloquising her and Taverner uses his own facility with language to compose lines that sound as if they might emerge from a noble but wronged heroine on the playhouse stage.[28] By her own words and Taverner's gloss on her

[26] Quintilian, *Institutio oratoria (The Orator's Education)*, ed. and trans. by Donald A. Russell for Loeb Classical Library, 5 vols. (Cambridge, MA: Harvard University Press, 2001), 5.10.23. See Lorna Hutson, *Circumstantial Shakespeare*: this list is quoted on p. 2, where Hutson explores the emotional effects of topics of circumstance on stage, as well as their role in the structure of argument.

[27] For the position of the law in the wider concept of the king's body natural and body politic, see Ernst H. Kantorowicz, *The King's Two Bodies* (Princeton: Princeton University Press, 1957), p. 143.

[28] Cf. Chapter 1, p. 49, where Thomas used this strategy of quoting key figures in his reports from the French court to reassure Cecil of his veracity. *Prosopopoeia* is a rhetori-cal device taught in humanist schoolrooms, where pupils give voice to classical characters from their reading in particular circumstances: clearly a skill transferable into the play-house. See Burrow, *Shakespeare and Classical Antiquity*, pp. 42–3, where he notes that

motive Thomas is not her target. One final troubling issue, then, is that the result of this royal altercation has him punished for returning the queen's laughter, while the new Viscount Rochester (equally guilty, but with the protection afforded to the king's favourite) is not; even at this stage, Thomas is a target because of his friendship with Carr, and in this letter he is presented as the means of the king appeasing the queen and appearing to punish the royal favourite.

Carr's reported reaction is interesting too. He clearly feels sufficiently secure in James's affections to challenge the queen, and to call her 'a jealous woman', reformulating her motive with impunity. He sets up as antithetical the 'jealous' Anna and Thomas, the 'faithful and discreet servant', whose love for Carr is his 'only fault'. If the queen is cast here as the villain, and Thomas the victim, then Robert Carr is the valiant knight: a latter-day Damon, whose own motive is established as selfless, offering to suffer on behalf of his Pythias.[29] As we shall see in the next chapter, this doughty defence of his 'favourite' is clearly what Thomas expects in 1613, as he writes from the Tower for his friend's help against another bout of the king's displeasure.

Another of the topics of circumstance significant in Taverner's telling of this story is place, and this links to the importance of multiple court settings established earlier. The palace setting for the initial offence is Greenwich, at this point the queen's space and home to her court.[30] The fact that the king's favourite and his friend are in the park at Greenwich must accentuate the offence for Anna. After the main 'court' business, the tears and the pacing, there is an alternative mise-en-scène created in Overbury's rooms near Whitehall at the end of the narrative. As Taverner concludes, 'Overbury is from Court, here at his lodging'; his use of the deictic 'here' again suggests his presence in the scene, once more adding veracity to the epistolary account. His ability to name those

'The skills of the early modern dramatist were multiple, but at their absolute centre lay the ability to put a case plausibly, to represent a debate from both sides, to mimic style and character, and to write as though from a particular character's situation and perspective. These were grammar-school skills [. . .]'

[29] In the Greek legend, retold by Cicero in *De Officiis*, Pythias is found guilty of treason by Dionysius I, tyrannical king of Syracuse. He accepts his guilt, but asks for time to settle his affairs before execution. The king takes up the offer of his close friend, Damon, to be hostage in his absence and, when Pythias returns to accept his fate, Dionysius is so surprised by their devoted friendship that he frees both men. The story is often used as an archetype of male friendship.

[30] See Leeds Barroll, *Anna of Denmark, Queen of England: A Cultural Biography* (Philadelphia: University of Pennsylvania Press, 2001), p. 39: 'it will be significant for our assessment of Anna's later activity that the palace at Greenwich, downriver from central London, would eventually become her abode as her court acquired a separate physical space – a local habitation and a name.'

who visit Thomas implies his first-hand knowledge as he again guides his reader's response, and if 'all men', even the Earl of Pembroke, are in the courtier's rooms, the king and queen appear almost isolated at Greenwich. Pembroke, it is worth noting, is one of the Protestant lords often seen in connection with Prince Henry's court, and not the obvious ally of Robert Carr's favourite. This evidence suggests Thomas's growing influence at court, even though it does at this point lead to his temporary banishment. I will argue later in this chapter that letters through 1612 develop this portrait of the man we might be otherwise tempted to think of as a victim: emphasising that, before his arrest, Thomas is a man with status and political influence.

Taverner's is not the opinion of all writers looking at Thomas at this time, and there are different views of the altercation with the queen. Another correspondent, Edward Cecil, tells Trumbull '[y]our servant will tell you of her Majesty's just offence taken at viscount Rochester, or rather Sir Thomas Overbury's uncivil demeanours towards her'.[31] As in Taverner's letter, Carr seems to be the initial target of the queen's anger, but Cecil reformulates this to focus the blame on the 'uncivil' Thomas. No longer a victim, he is now the churlish perpetrator of acts against the royal *amour propre*. Godfrey Goodman, whose *Court of King James I* presents the memories of a Royalist contemporary writing during the Civil War, gives the following account, different to that of Taverner in some interesting particulars:

> Upon this occasion, the Queen was looking out of her window into the garden, where Somerset and Overbury were walking; and when the Queen saw them, she said, 'There goes Somerset and his governor;' and a little after Overbury did laugh. The Queen conceiving that he had overheard her, thought that they had laughed at her; whereupon she complained, and Overbury was committed.[32]

In this version, the queen's insult of Carr comes first, and may have triggered the men's laughter. In a text sympathetic to the 'wise, discreet' king, and his favourite, again Thomas becomes the antagonist; Goodman characterises him as Carr's 'special friend [. . .] a very witty gentleman but truly very insolent'.[33] The queen's comment that Thomas is Carr's 'governor' echoes a later letter from John Chamberlain to Dudley Carleton, describing the 1613 arrest of Thomas, where he

---

[31] Letter 15, p. 78. Edward is nephew to Robert Cecil.
[32] John S. Brewer, ed., *The Court of King James the First*, Vol. I (London: Richard Bentley, 1839), p. 216. The text was written by Bishop Godfrey Goodman in the 1650s, but only published later. Robert Carr is referred to by his later title, the Earl of Somerset.
[33] Goodman, *The Court of King James the First*, p. 216.

says the king is afraid that courtiers will think 'Rochester ruled him and Overburie ruled Rochester'.[34] It appears to be a common conceit, and reflects either Thomas's high-handed manner with Carr, or the affection in which he is held, leading Carr to oppose him in nothing. Goodman conflates this offence against the queen with his being committed to the Tower two years later, and immediately moves from the events of May 1611 to Wotton's account of Thomas's arrest in April 1613. Another contemporary looking back on the Jacobean court from the 1650s is Arthur Wilson, a former member of the third Earl of Essex's staff and thus unsympathetic to Carr.[35] Wilson suggests that the queen's 'animosity' to Carr may be the result of 'the king's love and company [being] alienated from her, by this masculine conversation and intimacy', but he also proposes that it may be due to 'the man's [i.e. Carr's] insolence'.[36] Of Thomas, he simply comments on 'his creature Overbury being a little before his Commitment condemned for presumptuous walking with his hat on in her Palace Garden, she being in the window'. The cause of offence has shifted from inappropriate laughter to the inappropriate wearing of a hat, but Wilson's is here an accusation of what Leeds Barroll, in his recent biography of Anna of Denmark, dismissively calls 'Overbury's lack of appropriate political skills'.[37] Many of those writing with the benefit of hindsight see a pattern of royal disfavour but opinion differs greatly on how talented Thomas was as a politician – a question this chapter will address directly in the following section.

Clearly the queen's sense of injury was not quickly remedied, and even by September 1611 John More is writing to Brussels of the continuing feud.[38] The battleground has by this stage shifted to the 'contestation'

[34] Letter 39, p. 131. Overbury himself refers to such 'libells' in what is headed 'Letter X' from the Tower (printed here as Letter 61, p. 151).

[35] Essex was the first husband of Frances Howard, separated from her through the annulment granted in 1613. She then went on to marry Carr, with whom she had been in a relationship for some time.

[36] Arthur Wilson, *History of Great Britain: being the life and reign of King James the first, relating to what passed from his first access to the crown, till his death* (London: Richard Lownds, 1653), p. 79.

[37] Barroll, *Anna of Denmark*, p. 135. Despite the evidence throughout 1612 of Thomas's influence and his engagement in the factionalism surrounding the appointment of a new Secretary to the king, many writers argue that he had no political acumen. What is clear is that without him, after April 1613, Carr's attempts to sustain an active political role at court are much less successful.

[38] Letter 15, p. 78. John More was one of the 'family' of diplomats originally surrounding Sir Thomas Edmondes in Brussels and is the agent in London for Ralph Winwood. He writes to Trumbull, 'During this progress there hath been some contestation between their Maties about Sir Tho. Overbury's offence, and though her Ma^ty's displeasure be not yet much mitigated, Sir Thomas begins to approach the Court again, his great friend Rochester much labouring in his behalf.' Indeed 'that scandalous offence of the Queen at

between the king and queen, as the latter holds to her demand for her husband's support, which has not been forthcoming. Carr is not yet supreme, as over three months after the original events, James is still 'much labouring' against uxorial demands, but Thomas, the offender, is now approaching the court again, despite 'her Majesty's displeasure'. More's perceptive account tells Trumbull that the reason lies in 'his great friend['s]' support, and, again, we have to consider how mutually dependent the men were. Looking now at the third group of letters, epistolary evidence in 1612 and early 1613, before Thomas's arrest in April, allows us to draw conclusions both about Thomas's social status and political power, and about his close friendship with Robert Carr.

The Aftermath of Royal Disfavour

The incident with the queen in May 1611 plays an important part in our perception of Thomas's status at this point. He is perceived by the court as Robert Carr's favourite, and this enables his position. The queen seems to be isolated as the power Carr holds over the king becomes clear. Due to the patronage of Carr, Thomas is already growing to be a man of influence, and it was not only Carr who went to his side after the queen secured his banishment from court.[39] Yet already there are hints of the potentially insecure status he holds and some of the first suggestions of his later reputed insolence or political misjudgement. Until this point there has been little reference to his propensity to offend others; indeed, his letters of 1609 to Cecil, pleading as they did for patronage,

---

Greenwich' is still being referred to by Wotton on 22 April 1613 as having 'never but a palliated cure', and being part of the reason for his arrest (see Letter 38, p. 129).

[39] There may even have been a second incident similar to that in May 1611 a year later. See Courtney Erin Thomas, 'Politics and Culture at the Jacobean Court: The Role of Queen Anna of Denmark', *Quidditas: The Journal of the Rocky Mountain Medieval and Renaissance Association*, Vol. 29 (2009), pp. 64–107: 'In 1612, Anna discovered that Sir David Wood, a member of her household, had been obliged to pay Carr and Overbury £1200 to achieve the grant of a suit that he had presented to the King. The Queen was furious at their presumption and launched into a fresh series of complaints before James. As in 1611, James was reticent to act against Carr (whom he had recently made Viscount Rochester), but Overbury, sensing that he again would be singled out for punishment (a stint in the Tower was threatened) voluntarily retired from court and journeyed to the Continent for five months.' Thomas does not, though, cite her evidence for this account. Sir David Wood, mentioned here, is called 'boisterous and atheistical' by Nicholas Overbury (in BL Add MS 15476), and he is the man Frances Howard allegedly tried to persuade to kill Overbury, due to his having been an enemy before (cf. Considine's *ODNB* article). He gives evidence in the trial of Richard Weston, where he swears that he was crossed in a plan to make £2,200 by Thomas and Carr, was offered £1,000 by Howard to kill Thomas and refused (Howell, *State Trials*, p. 925).

suggested a useful ability to write effectively and to flatter. Yet later writers on Thomas's life have often concluded, even about his earlier court life, as Beatrice White does, that he 'was fully conscious of his power and took no trouble to conciliate those whom he considered negligible or to whom he was actively opposed'.[40]

The consequences of the Greenwich incident, as we have seen, continue into September 1611, and Thomas makes use of his relationship with Robert Cecil, writing to his former patron for assistance:

> My honorable Lord, as your Lordship was a judge of mine Innocence before so would I now crave that favour, that your Lordship would vouchsafe to be a witness of that submission both of myself & ~~that~~ cause to the Queen's mercy [. . .][41]

As well as demonstrating that he has not lost his ability to write with appropriate deference, the letter reveals much about Thomas's relationship with Cecil. He has had to call upon the Lord Secretary before in what he suggests were similar circumstances. What is also suggestive here is the discrepancy which can be inferred between his 'submission' and what he goes on to describe as the queen being 'not fully satisfied of the Integrity of my Intent'. A reader can imagine either that the talk of submission is merely a rhetorical means to an end, or that, when he intends to be submissive, there is something about his manner which does not convince the queen. In either of these senses, the letter may add weight to later descriptions of Thomas as insolent, or, at the very least, appearing so to the queen. On the other hand, he may simply appear so to a woman who is strategically and emotionally opposed to the man on whom Thomas relies for his position. She is unlikely to be 'satisfied' by his apology, however genuine.

Undoubtedly Cecil knew Thomas well, and was well placed to judge whether his submission was real or assumed. The Lord Secretary was able to help him in this case, and following his appearances near the court in the September, he was officially accepted back in the November.[42] Cecil's ability to assist his former 'most faithfull servant'

---

[40] White, *The Cast of Ravens*, p. 23. Many writers, as White does on p. 21, refer to Overbury as 'insolent and thrasonical' in terms of Francis Bacon's words at the trial of Somerset (*The Letters and the Life of Francis Bacon*, ed. by James Spedding, 7 vols. (London: Longmans, Green, Reader, and Dyer, 1861–74), Vol. V, p. 312) and those of later commentators who pick up on his accusations, rather than the words of contemporaries who worked with and observed the courtier.

[41] Letter 16, p. 79.

[42] In the queen's letter to Cecil, copied beneath Thomas's letter in BL Add. MS 4160, fol. 3 (Letter 16, p. 79), and presumably in response to Cecil's pleas on Thomas's behalf, she calls him 'that fellow' and shows little sign of appeasement.

was, however, coming to an end, and by the end of 1611, his health, which had never been strong, was failing. Even if one doesn't see it preceded by a year of decline in political influence, the physical decline of Cecil was now clear, and early in 1612 'government business nearly came to a standstill'.[43] Rumours about who should succeed Cecil as Secretary of State had begun at least six months earlier. Whether we accept the accusation of insolence or not, by 1611 Thomas's participation in this process showed him acting as an effective politician, perceived as such by those keen to gain preferment and able to manipulate and engage others when he so wished. Even through the period of the queen's resentment in 1611, there is evidence that Thomas retained that influence, as we can infer from his role in the preferment of Sir Henry Vane to the position of carver, a coveted Bedchamber post.[44] Thomas's ability to attain such a position for Vane suggests that he was, even at this point, able to work effectively on the king, probably through Carr though it is 'the friendship of Sir Thomas Overbury' that Vane credits with his success.

Nicholas Overbury, Thomas's father, in the memoir dictated to his nephew in 1637, recalls that even Sir Francis Bacon 'used to stoop and crouch' to gain Thomas's support in his request for preferment as Master of the Court of Wards, and the memory of this perhaps lies behind Bacon's lack of sympathy for either victim or alleged murderer as he leads the trial against Robert Carr in 1615.[45] Even he, though, is forced to admit the 'great interest and great friendship' Thomas had with Carr, 'both in his meaner fortunes and after'. Bacon notes that Thomas 'was a kind of oracle of direction unto him' and sneers that Thomas boasted about his effect: 'he took upon him, that the fortune, reputation, and understanding of [Carr] proceeded from his company and counsel'.[46] Although Bacon cannot resist taunting the by this stage murdered Thomas about his insolence, he would not have been able to comment on the courtier's power over his friend, just two years after his death, if this were not generally believed.

This ability to influence Carr, and, through the favourite, the king,

---

[43] See Pauline Croft's *ODNB* article on Robert Cecil.

[44] Vane recalls in a later memoir, 'I put myself into court, and bought a carver's place by means of the friendship of Sir Thomas Overbury, which cost me 5,000*l*.' See G. E. Aylmer, *The King's Servants* (London: Routledge & Kegan Paul, 1961), p. 85. This is the same preferment that loses Sir David Wood his money.

[45] Beatrice White, *The Cast of Ravens*, p. 21, quotes this as being from BL Add. MS 15476. See Howell, *State Trials*, p. 973, where Bacon, in Somerset's trial, talks of 'this excess [. . .] of friendship' and argues that Overbury should not have been trusted with state secrets.

[46] Bacon, *Letters and Life*, Vol. V, p. 312.

made Thomas a desirable connection for men seeking preferment in the vacuum left in April 1612 after Cecil's departure on what was to be his final journey to Bath. One of the contenders to become Secretary of State, Henry Neville, worked with his former secretary, Ralph Winwood (now English agent at The Hague), to form a Protestant opposition to the Howards' preferred candidate, Thomas Lake. They desired to work with Thomas, who had, in more than a year of influence at court, grown to be a thorn in the side of the crypto-Catholic Howard family.[47]

Thomas's influence at this point is shown retrospectively in a letter from an epistolary commentator very close to the king, Viscount Fenton. He writes to his kinsman, the Earl of Mar, outlining the two main factions at court and showing Thomas's connections and influence: 'our present steat is at this tyme in tuo factions, the Howards [. . .] the uther Southe[hamptoun] and Pem[brooke] with sume of the Lower Houss men that heirtofore hes bein drawin to follow my Lord of Ro[tchester] by the maines of Overberrye.'[48] The influence of Thomas, and his ability to help others gain positions they wish for, is seen as an established fact by such men as Levinus Munck. As early as October 1611 Munck, the long-time secretary to Robert Cecil and a clear authority close to power, is quoted by John More as saying that there are 'still (but especially were before Sir Thomas his disgrace with the Queen) more suitors following him than my Lord Treasurer'.[49] Indeed, according to More, Munck says that Thomas 'hath brought to pass many great and strange matters' by means of his friendship with Carr. These comments make clear Thomas's power, despite Anna's attempts against him, and explains why a man such as Neville will expend such efforts working to gain his support in 1612. More writes to Winwood before the latter decides to work with Sir Henry Neville, and he quotes Munck as saying 'I wonder from whence should grow so much discourse of Sir H. Nevill to be a Secretary of State, or at the least a Privy Councillor'; the 'discourse' appears to be news to More. His surprise is not flattering to Neville, and he shares a joke with Winwood, referring to Neville's 'unwieldy body'; indeed, More feels that the rumour of Neville's ambition is unlikely as 'he did not [. . .] speak in Parliament for the King's demands, but ranged himself with those [. . .] of a contrary faction to the Courtiers; which I think he would not have done, if he had aspired to any Court employment'. Neville is clearly linked to the Protestant faction men-

---

[47] Bacon notes in Carr's trial that Thomas 'had always professed hatred and opposition' against them (Howell, *State Trials*, p. 974).

[48] Letter 58, p. 149.

[49] Letter 17, p. 80. This adds weight to the view that Cecil's influence is declining by this point, as Carr's, and Thomas's, rise.

tioned by Fenton, and thus to the men who went to Thomas's rooms when he was banished from court in May 1611. An associate of the Earl of Southampton and a former supporter of the second Earl of Essex, deprived of his ambassadorship in France by the latter's arrest in 1601, Neville was also related by marriage to Sir Robert Killigrew, a man very close to Thomas and Carr (as we shall see in Chapter 3).

More's letter explains to Winwood that Neville 'doth seek for some advancement [...] through [Sir] Thomas Overbury, by means of Viscount Rochester'. Thomas's reputation for gaining the required outcomes for suitors through his influence with Carr is already established, and he is considered Neville's 'best instrument'.[50] However, More is rather surprised by Munck's report of Thomas's influence, and he implies that reliance on it may not be helpful to Neville:

> I marvelled much at Sir Thomas Overbury's greatness, and especially at his report of Sir H. Nevill; and indeed I think it may be some speech cast out rather to his hindrance than advancement.[51]

Despite More's incredulity, a few months later the substantive truth of the aspirant secretary's growing reliance on Thomas is clearly established.

After the death of Cecil in May 1612, the pursuit of the secretaryship grew even more heated. Winwood was by now working with Neville, and letters between the two, dating from the summer, show how much reliance they place on Thomas's influence. Two short, pragmatic missives from Neville explain why he will or will not be able to visit Winwood, who is on a short (and rare) visit to London at this point. The first suggests his dependence on Thomas's goodwill:

> I sent yesternight to Sir Tho. Overbury to know what time I might come to him this morning; and he made me answer that he went out of town early, but would return about 6 of clock in the evening, and prayed me to come to him then.[52]

The second short letter, sent the next day, reveals Neville's frustration, and that it is not unexpected:

> I feared that which happened: that Sir Tho. Overbury would not return yesterday till it was very late. Therefore I sent not [...] but this afternoon, about

---

[50] Letter 60, p. 151. Lorkin is, of course, describing what Neville has lost on Thomas's imprisonment.
[51] Letter 17, p. 80.
[52] Letter 21, p. 84.

two of clock, he will be with me, because I am not well, and cannot go to him. And he is desirous to meet you here, if you be returned from Court.[53]

Although the three men are working together for a common purpose, it is clear who is the lynchpin.

In a third letter in September, Neville describes two meetings with Thomas and gives an impression of the latter in action as the influential courtier. Winwood, now back in The Hague, is keen to know when he might be called back to London as this would help him further their ambitions. Both men are anxious to discover the king's plans, and in his account of the action he is taking to secure this information, Neville reports from Windsor, where the king has gone hunting, that '[t]his tumultuary and uncertain attendance upon the King's sports affords me little time to write'.[54] He is relieved to say that he has been able to see Thomas, whose support is still the means by which he plans they should achieve preferment. The clearly adept courtier 'renewed his protestations of all sincere meaning both on his part and his friends', and reassures Neville that 'he is in good hope of some speedy resolution'.

The picture this letter presents of Thomas is helpful in understanding the skills which have enabled his rise. Chapter 1 established his desire for social mobility and the rhetorical strengths he used to begin that journey. Here the younger man projects an appearance which may or may not reflect his genuine feeling, though Neville seems to believe in him. He reassures them of genuine concern and support, and his reference to his 'friends', or perhaps more likely his 'friend', shows the importance to his position of that friendship with Carr. Emphasising to his interlocutor that his connections are powerful means, of course, that his patronage is efficacious. The letter is an account of a skilled political operator, giving nothing and promising everything. Nothing in Neville's letter reveals a distrust of Thomas, and indeed, in letters which could be intercepted and read by those perhaps unsympathetic to his cause, this would have been foolish. However, there is the possibility that, even at this stage, the older man felt concern over the courtier's active dedication to their cause. Certainly, as we shall see shortly, when the plan seems to fall victim to Thomas's arrest less than a year later, Neville finds much fault with the courtier's action on his behalf. Even in September 2012, though, rumours were abroad which suggested that Thomas had a slightly different agenda to the one agreed with Neville. The appearance of support Neville describes may well be deceptive.

[53] Letter 22, p. 84.
[54] Letter 24, p. 85.

One man clearly intimidated by the power of courtiers, amongst Ralph Winwood's many correspondents at this time, was a cousin by the name of Sir Robert Naunton, a go-between for Winwood and at this point delivering his letters. Naunton is keen to come to the notice of Robert Carr, but, in lines which hint at how intimidated he is by the great lord and how hesitant to irritate him by importunity, he finally writes that he is pleased, instead, to have been recognised by his friend. With relief, he tells Winwood that he 'saluted Sir Thomas Overb[urie] *en passant*, which was sufficient to continue me in both their remembrance', and he asks that when Winwood 'write[s] to my Lord of Rochester, or to Sir Tho. Overbury' that 'if it please you to use me for delivery of your letter, it may happily occasion me some further overture [. . .]'.[55] Yet further news has reached Naunton which casts doubt on Thomas's veracity. An account of a friendly meeting between Neville and the king is followed by rumours circulating about the courtier's own ambitions:

[S]ome standers by are apt to conceive that the King mea[neth] to keep these places in suspense between himself and my Lord of Roch[este]r, as they we[re] after Sir Fr. Walsyngham's death; and that meanwhile Sir Tho. Overburie may fit himself with as good a probability to furnish the place in time, by the practice and experience he is now in [. . .]

There are clearly those at court who fear Thomas's growing influence.

The Influential Courtier

The letters discussed in this chapter, written when Thomas's political career seems set for the highest honours and when his influence was greatest, thus present an ambiguous portrait of the courtier. The altercation with the queen showed his potential to be a victim on Carr's behalf, and his application to Cecil for help demonstrated his reliance on his former patron despite his new ties to the new Viscount's rising power. Contemporary observers note his growing political influence, which appears to be power in itself. Men fear to offend him and they show pleasure in merely catching his eye at court. Important figures in the country's administration need him, and discuss how to retain his help once obtained. But there are also the hints of insolence and duplicity which will become a stronger strand of the discourse surrounding him as his political power diminishes and will dominate after his death. At the later trial of Carr for the murder of his friend, Sir Francis Bacon gave

---

[55] Letter 26, p. 87.

his view of Thomas's character, and the relationship between lord and secretary, at this point:

> Sir Thomas Overbury for a time was known to have had great interest and great friendship with my Lord of Somerset, both in his meaner fortunes and after; insomuch as he was a kind of oracle of direction unto him; and if you will believe his own vaunts (being of an insolent Thrasonical disposition), he took upon him, that the fortune, reputation, and understanding of this gentleman [. . .] proceeded from his company and counsel.[56]

One must not overplay early comments on Thomas's insolence. In 1611 and 1612 they are rare and Bacon, speaking after his death, is hardly an impartial source. But he had known both men personally, as had many of his listeners, and it is unlikely that he made an insolent, power-hungry figure out of a mild-mannered and submissive servant. Thomas's potential to appear insolent lies alongside his quick wits, his ability to build power, and his skilful manipulation of others, and it is perhaps a character trait which grows over his time in power. They also lie alongside his capacity for building male friendship, and it is this, particularly of course his friendship with Robert Carr, that enables this power in the first place.

Although most of the evidence in this chapter comes from court observers, and not from the courtier himself, Thomas's manner is shown in his own words to the two diplomats whose letter collections contain considerable evidence of the political situation in 1612: Winwood and Trumbull. A brief note to Winwood in October appears curt, issuing instructions for a course of action he expects to be carried out.[57] Thomas is, throughout this period, with the king, outside of London, as he moves between royal residences and engages in his passion for hunting. The letter to Winwood is from Royston, and the king's use of this small town as an alternative locus for his court began in the first year of his English reign. The residence there was conveniently close to other royal residences at Newmarket and Theobalds, but by 1612 it had developed from the small hunting lodge he had originally envisaged to allow him to escape from royal business and enjoy the hunt with some of his close associates. Instead, as he spent so much time in the place, the business of the king's court followed him to Hertfordshire and the property rented and owned by the king and his courtiers overwhelmed the small market town. James's gentlemen and their followers needed lodging, feeding and leisure of their own as they spent weeks at a time waiting on the king and pressing their own business. Thomas's presence at the centre of the court there, as in Newmarket and Windsor, demonstrates

---

[56] Howell, *State Trials*, p. 973.
[57] Letter 28, p. 90.

his centrality; though it frustrates Neville, who couldn't speak to him directly, his absence from London enables him to exert direct influence and to be of practical use to those he wished to have preferred. His note to Winwood gives instructions to the diplomat, plotting to build support for Carr, and showing his own status: 'I pray you fasten the Count upon my Lord; and if you please, you may name me to him.' He clearly expects his name to carry weight.

A month earlier, from Theobalds, Thomas tells Trumbull that he has presented to the king's favourite the diplomat's case for escaping his Brussels posting, and Carr has, in turn, taken it to the king. 'Be vigilant', Thomas instructs, 'and large in promises toward such as only offer their service and for such as perform the king will prove as bountiful, nor shall you want means to recompense merit'.[58] The experienced diplomat is likely to be already versed in how to acquire information and build his network, but Thomas gives a clear signal of his own importance, giving the impression that he is in a position to offer the king's bounty if Trumbull manages things as Thomas instructs. His Protestantism shines through his dislike of Brussels, and is likely to collude with Trumbull's own religious views: 'it behoves to look about you, for your residence is in the shop of wickedness'.[59]

Having turned away from the diplomatic career on which he seemed set in the years before 1611, Thomas had discovered a new source of personal influence and power. Through his friendship with Robert Carr, he gained more status than he might be expected to have had at this stage in his life, as demonstrated by the contrast between his position and that of older men who were in terms of birth, education and early experience comparable with him: men such as Wotton, Winwood, Neville and Trumbull. While others were seeking preferment, he was, by the end of 1612, in a position to help them gain it. The growing unease at Thomas's rise, and early comments hinting at his self-importance and his insolence, give a foretaste of the considerably more pejorative references which are to come in the letters of the following year.

Chapter 1 began with Thomas in Edinburgh, reaching the centre of Stuart power in Scotland, before James VI became king of England. The end of this chapter sees Thomas engaged in court business near the king, for example at his hunting lodge in Royston. His presence with the king, though geographically he is removed from London, shows that he is now at the centre of the homosocial English court. He is, despite

---

58 Letter 25, p. 86.
59 This shared Protestantism is also clear in other letters from Trumbull to Thomas, such as Letter 27.

Neville's persistence, difficult to access: a sign of how much in demand he is as an intermediary, someone able to influence those in power.

Appendix 2: Letters, 1611–12

Letter 8

6 March 1611: Rev. John Sanford to Sir Thomas Edmondes, from London[60]

The time of our departure for Spain drawing near, which is assigned about the 20th of March, and myself upon the point of taking my leave of those to whom for love or respect I owe this duty, I thought it fit to begin from your lordship, in whose honourable favours I have found the greatest place of my poor fortunes.

[. . .]

The ambassador to be sent from hence is diversly spoken of: some say Sir Henry Wotton, lately arrived at court; some suspect Mr. George Calvert, who came to London on Sunday last;[61] or late Sir Thomas Overbury, a great favourite of Sir Robert Car, hath been mentioned.

[60] The letter is printed in Thomas Birch's *The Court and Times of James I: Illustrated by Authentic and Confidential Letters from Various Public and Private Collections*, 2 vols. (London: Henry Colburn, 1849), Vol. I, pp. 105–8. The letter is dated 1610 in this volume, but this is probably an error leading from early modern dating of years; external evidence dates it to 1611 (for instance, the three Knights of the Garter mentioned in the letter 'fell', that is they died, in the first three months of 1611). John Sanford (or Sandford) resided in the household of Thomas Edmondes before he took up a post as chaplain to Sir John Digby, Earl of Bristol, who is appointed ambassador to Madrid in 1610. It is with the latter that he will make the journey to Spain that is the major subject of this letter (according to the *ODNB* article on Sir John Digby they arrived in Spain in June 1611). The correspondence between Sandford and Edmondes took place throughout the time of the embassy, from March 1610 to April 1613. Thomas Edmondes (see footnotes to Letters 2, 3 and 6 above) was a very experienced diplomat, whose postings had included several in France. He had been resident ambassador in Brussels until September 1609, when he had been moved back to London and had left his secretary, William Trumbull, behind him in Brussels. Edmondes was expected to replace George Carew (who retired in October 1609) as ambassador and return to Paris at that time, but in fact it was not until April 1610 that he actually went to France: a month after the sending of this letter. He was a good friend of Ralph Winwood and both were part of the circle of men of business who met at the Mermaid Tavern in the early years of James I's reign (this circle included several writers of letters in this volume, including John Sandford, Jean Beaulieu, Samuel Calvert and John Chamberlain). See Michelle O'Callaghan's article on the Patrons of the Mermaid Tavern in the *ODNB*). She refers to Sandford as Edmondes' 'witty chaplain'.
[61] It appears that Edmondes at least thinks George Calvert is likely to get the post as, in

Letter 9

7 March 1611: William Devick to William Trumbull[62]

After compliments I should be glad if I could in requital [. . .] but send you word who were certainly designed to relieve you from your purgatory which yet I cannot do, but am in expectation thereof in brief, since we shall have your Amb: so soon here, which will enforce us to a resolution.[63] The report runs upon one named Sir Thomas Overbury, a favourite of Sir Robert Carr's, or else Mr. Calvert who arrived here the 5th of this month from Paris.[64] [. . .]

Letter 10

22 March 1611 (Good Friday): Samuel Calvert to William Trumbull, from London[65]

[. . .] I wish you were secretary to those merchants in London [. . .] that you might take allowance of 200*l.* per an. and be free to yourself and enjoy your good friends rather than live ever in doubt and distrust.

a letter to Trumbull on 9 March 1611 (*Downshire III*, p. 34), he tells Trumbull, 'From England I hear that Mr. Calvert is to go Amb[r.] to Brussels. If so, it is to qualify him for better employment later.' He has either had information other than that in Sandford's letter, or he thinks Thomas and Wotton are less likely contenders. His comment on 'better employment' must have rankled with Trumbull, left doing the job, in the end, for another fourteen years.

[62] The letter is printed in *Downshire III*, pp. 31–2. William Devick was one of Sir Thomas Edmondes' team of servants, and brother-in-law to another, Jean Beaulieu. (See Anderson, 'The Elder William Trumbull', p. 119.)

[63] Trumbull's 'purgatory' is clearly his post in Brussels. He'd been left there on a 'temporary' basis in 1609 (and was to stay in the city, but not officially made ambassador, until 1625).

[64] The content of Devick's letter to Trumbull is very similar to that in Sandford's to Edmondes, suggesting that the rumours of possible ambassadors to Brussels are focused on Calvert and Thomas. As the men have recently met (Devick mentions their meeting above), perhaps discussion beforehand could explain the similarity in the contents of the letters. Wotton, mentioned by Sandford, interestingly, is not mentioned by Devick.

[65] The letter is printed in *Downshire III*, p. 44. Samuel Calvert looked after Sir Thomas Edmondes' business in England (along with John More) while Edmondes was acting for the monarch abroad. (See Anderson, 'The Elder William Trumbull', p. 119.) Michelle O'Callaghan, in her *ODNB* article on the 'Patrons of the Mermaid Tavern', comments that Samuel Calvert is 'clerk of the Virginia Company, brother of George Calvert, secretary to Robert Cecil'. Hence, he is writing here about the possible chances of a relative of his going to Brussels, which might explain the slightly ironic tone of the passive verb and Latin tag. (In Letter 12, Calvert writes to Trumbull again, calling George Calvert his cousin.)

How Geo. Calvert shall be disposed is yet *in nubibus*. Some give out Sir Thomas Overbury shall come to relieve you. [. . .]

Letter 11

27 March 1611: Jean Beaulieu to William Trumbull, from Paris[66]

[. . .] We are expecting Sir John Digby who is going Amb^r· to Spain, and with him we shall see our friend, Mr. Sanford, who lately sent us copies of a Spanish grammar which he hath written since our coming hither. For your parts, he writes that Sir H. Wotton, Sir Tho. Overbury and Mr. Calvert are spoke of [. . .]

Letter 12

29 March 1611: Samuel Calvert to William Trumbull, from London[67]

[. . .] 'When you are returned, you may find a change in Court, not the houses or mansions, but the men and manners both growing from worse to stark naught'.[68] Mr. More is back from the Hague. He grows rich and is worthy of it because he cares after it. On Monday the King's minion Sir Robert Carr was made Viscount Rochester.[69] Viscount Bindon and Sir Henry Lea are dead, and two Garters void. Sir J. Digby grows impatient till he have his new honour in Spain. Sir Thos. Overbury would like

[66] The letter is printed in *Downshire III*, pp. 46–7. Jean Beaulieu was secretary to Thomas Edmondes, along with William Trumbull, from the late 1590s. This letter shows how quickly news spreads amongst the group of friends and that Thomas Edmondes has shown Sandford's letter to Beaulieu.

[67] The letter is printed in *Downshire II*, pp. 272–3. It is thus located in 1610, though, like Letter 8 above, it is clearly referring to events in 1611, and has been wrongly positioned, seemingly due to the early modern dating of the year.

[68] The quotation (from Mr More?) shows a contemporary feeling that the court is in decline (cf. Ideas of courtly decline drawing on Roman history, pp. 207–9).

[69] This took place on 26 March 1611. The use of the term 'minion' for Carr, contrasting with the ennoblement to Viscount Rochester of which he speaks, suggests the lack of respect for Carr within this diplomatic circle.

to go Ambassador to Brussels.[70] My cousin, G. Calvert, is talked on, but is not ambitious.[71] He is now Clerk of the Council [. . .]

Letter 13

1 June 1611: Mr Taverner to William Trumbull[72]

[. . .] There have happened since my being here two irreconcilable quarrels and undeterminable. The first between our General Cecill and Captain Horwood, who have exchanged as much bitterness as rage and malice can think. [. . .] The other and greater hath been between the queen and my ld. of Rochester. On Monday last Rochester and his dear Overbury, walking in the garden at Greenwich whither the queen's window openeth, she broke into a sudden and contemptible laughing at them. 'So,' saith she, 'they did at her,' which belief carried her so far that she went to the king with tears in her eyes and complained and besought him that she might have right of them, which he not seeming to be so sensible of as she hoped, she cast herself on her knees and besought him not to suffer her to be so scorned and despised of his grooms, though she were content to suffer it from him, with earnest protestation that if he would not right her, she would go back into Denmark. All this while the good king much afflicted walked up and down the chamber. 'Ah, woe is me, my queen will go from me, my Carr, my Carr.' But doing nothing to content her. The next day she sent to the prince to Richmond to entreat him, and so to the lords in Whitehall to come to Greenwich to have the hearing of her cause, where on Wednesday it was cunningly urged by her and as confidently denied by them. The conclusion was, she finding herself not able to supplant Carr, which she desireth of all things in the world, turned all her force against Overbury, against whom she hath so far prevailed that he is banished from the Court. But Rochester told

---

[70] This letter is the first to give ambition to Thomas. While others say he is talked of for the post, Calvert states clearly that he would like it. This adds to the idea that his plan early in his career may be for a more traditional courtly route than that he ends up pursuing.

[71] Calvert has actually written about Trumbull's possible replacements only a week earlier, in Letter 10 above. In neither letter does he refer to Wotton.

[72] The letter is printed in *Downshire III*, pp. 82–3. It is unclear who Mr. Taverner is, though there is in the same volume an earlier letter to Trumbull from an R. Taverner in Flushing, who might be the same person. It seems most likely to be a Richard Taverner, who gained a BA from Magdalen College, Oxford, in 1597 and was admitted to Gray's Inn in 1599. He is reputed to have acted as second to Sir John Danvers in a duel. His younger brother, Edmund, another alumnus of Magdalen, was MP for Woodstock.

the king if he would so far give credit to the rage of a jealous woman to banish a faithful and discreet servant for his friendship, which was the only fault the queen could impute unto him, for his part he was resolute to share with him in his fortune, banishment or whatsoever it were. So the business yet hangs. Overbury is from Court, here at his lodging by Whitehall, where Rochester and all men almost visit him and my ld. of Pembroke, too. [. . .]

Letter 14

5 June 1611: John More to William Trumbull, from London[73]

[. . .] Your servant will tell you of her Mat$^{y's}$ just offence taken at viscount Rochester, or rather Sir Thomas Overbury's uncivil demeanours towards her.[74]

[. . .]

I send this by Mr. Monger who promiseth to 'lay aside his Cripplegate, and set the best leg forward'.

Letter 15

10 September 1611: John More to William Trumbull, from London[75]

[. . .] I came hither on Saturday from the country, where my wife is forcibly detained as a pledge for my return, which I am now to make. The King, Queen and Prince returning from the progress met at Hampton Court on Saturday. During this progress there hath been some contestation between their Maties about Sir Tho. Overbury's offence, and though her Ma$^{ty's}$ displeasure be not yet much mitigated, Sir Thomas begins to

---

[73] The letter is printed in *Downshire III*, pp. 84–6. John More, like Samuel Calvert, looked after Trumbull's business in London during his absences. See Anderson, 'The Elder William Trumbull', p. 119.

[74] The servant in question here, Mr Monger, carries the letter to Brussels. He is likely to be James Monger, a London merchant, who is mentioned in Michelle O'Callaghan's *ODNB* article on the Patrons of the Mermaid Tavern.

[75] The letter is printed in *Downshire III*, pp. 138–9.

approach the Court again, his great friend Rochester much labouring in his behalf. [. . .]

Letter 16

11 September 1611: Overbury to Salisbury[76]

11 Sept   My honorable Lord, as your Lordship was a judge of mine Innocence before so would I now crave that favour, that your Lordship would vouchsafe to be a witness of that submission both of myself & ~~that~~ cause to the Queen's mercy; which desire the rather, because, as I understand, her majesty is not fully satisfied of the Integrity of my Intent that way. and to that purpose if your Lordship will grant me access & audience I shall hold it as a great favour, & ever rest

Your Lordships to be commanded

London the 11th   T. Overbury
of September (*)

[In margin]
(*) Letter of Sir Thomas Somerset to Sir. Thomas Edmondes from Whitehall 8 Nov. 1611. 'Sir Thomas Overbury is received again into the Court'.

[Written beneath the letter from Thomas]

The Queen to the Earl of Salisbury

My Lord, The King hath told me, that he will advise with you & some other four or five of the Counsell of that fellow. I can say no more, either to make you understand the matter or my mind, than I said the other day. Only I recommend to your care how to publish the matter now both in Court & City, & how far I have reason in that respect. I refer the rest to this [illegible], & myself to your Love.

Anna R.

---

[76] The letter is a transcription of BL Add. MS 4160, fol. 3. Both letters on this page are copied in the hand of Thomas Birch, and the queen's letter is not dated.

Letter 17

29 October 1611: John More to Ralph Winwood, from London[77]

[. . .] Being the other day with Mr. Levinus [Munck], tal[king] of divers occurents, he fell suddenly from another matter to this speech: 'I wonder from whence should grow so much discourse of Sir H. Nevill to be a Secretary of State, or at the least a Privy Councillor.' I answered him (and that truly) that for my part I never heard any such discourse, neither did I see much reason to believe it; for, besides his unwieldy body and giving himself to a mere country life, he did not (like Sir Dudley Carleton) speak in Parliament for the King's demands, but ranged himself with those Patriots that were accounted of a contrary faction to the Courtiers; which I think he would not have done, if he had aspired to any Court employment.[78] He said that, all that notwithstanding, he doth seek for some advancement, and that through [Sir] Thomas Overbury, by means of Viscount Rochester, who of late (said he) hath brought to pass many great and strange matters, there being still (but especially were before Sir Thomas his disgrace with the Queen) more suitors following him than my Lord Treasurer.[79] I marvelled much at Sir Thomas Overbury's greatness, and especially at his report of Sir H. Nevill; and indeed I think it may be some speech cast out rather to his hindrance than advancement. The plot (he said) was, that Sir H. Nevill should undertake to deal with the Lower House, and then (so my Lord Treasurer would not intermeddle) there was no doubt but that better effects would come of the next Session (which is like to be in February next) than did come of the former. [. . .]

---

[77] The letter is printed in *Report on the Manuscripts of the Duke of Buccleuch and Queensberry, K. G., K. T., preserved at Montagu House, Whitehall*, Vol. I (London: Her Majesty's Stationery Office, 1899), pp. 101–2.

[78] Henry Neville has been one of those who spoke up in parliament in favour of the English, against the Scots who largely ran the Bedchamber. This letter suggests his political principle (or perhaps his naïveté) is weighing against him in his current ambitions.

[79] Robert Cecil is currently Treasurer, and perhaps this letter adds weight to the argument of those who say he has lost status at the court when the Great Contract fails. See p. 57.

Letter 18

13 November 1611: John Chamberlain to Dudley Carleton, from London[80]

[. . .] There is some speech that he shall go to Brussels. In the mean time he hath lessened his traine, having no more about him but his Dutch butler, Price, and his page. Master Morton is retired to his college at Cambridge, Master Parkhurst into Kent, and Bilford he hath preferred to the Prince, with asseveration and wagers of three of his choice pictures against three of the princes horses, that he shall draw or pourtray the Prince better than Isaach the French painter in the Blackfriars:[81] but the common opinion is that he must have many grains of allowance to hold waight with Isaake: the Prince in favour growes very like the Quene his mother: and Sig[or] Fabritio insinuats what he can with him, and the Scottishmen about him: I heare for certain he is in hand with the historie of all that passed twixt the Pope and State of Venice during the time of the interdict and that yt is to come foorth very shortly.

[After news of the arrest of Jesuits thought to have been connected to the Gunpowder Plot, and of the ubiquitously interesting selling of baronetcies, Chamberlain notes Thomas's return to court in passing near the end – the final element of a long list of recent events.]

Sir Thomas Overberie by much suit is restored to the court, and there is hope in time to the Quenes favor.

Letter 19

13 November 1611: John Thorys to William Trumbull, from London[82]

[. . .] Returning from the country I had yours of 23rd Oct. I cannot requite your news not being a courtier now. Sir Thomas Overbury is by the Queen's consent admitted to Court, though not to her side [. . .]

[80] The letter is printed in *The Letters of John Chamberlain*, ed. by Norman Egbert McClure, 2 vols. (Philadelphia: American Philosophical Society, 1939), Vol. I, pp. 311–15.
[81] Albertus Morton, son of Wotton's half-brother, had accompanied Wotton to Venice as secretary. William Parkhurst and Bilford were similarly Wotton's secretaries during this time.
[82] The letter is printed in *Downshire III*, p. 180. I have been unable to find out the details of John Thorys, though he seems to be a go-between for Trumbull and his correspondents

Letter 20

17 June 1612: John Chamberlain to Dudley Carleton, from London[83]

[He lets Carleton know that the former French ambassador, George Carew, has been appointed Master of the Rolls (over the heads of several others in the running for the position). This post, Chamberlain says, has either been given to Carew because his wife is close to the Queen, or because of the patronage of Robert Carr. There is then discussion of the candidates for the Lord Treasurership, and Chamberlain feels it will go to the Earl of Northampton.[84]]

Sir Walter Cope wishes you shold write now and then to Master Chancellor for he may stand you in great stead. I inquired of him both before my going out of towne and now since my coming backe whether there had ben any meaning to recall you and for what intent: he told me that my late Lord Treasurer saide not long before he died that some about my Lord of Rochester had gon about such a matter, belike to serve theyre owne turne, and put in some of theyre owne creatures: how likely this is you may judge, but yt doth not sound with me, and so I told him, for Sir Thomas Overburie for ought that ever I knew doth not wish you yll, and Sir Robert Killegree who is one of his next favorites is your fast frend: and I heard but yesterday that Master Packer your old frend is become his secretary:[85] but the surest card of all Sir Henry Nevill will never see you wronged where he may helpe. Yf he had not ben strongly oppugned every way he had ben setled before this in the secretaryship; but yt is saide too much solliciting hath hindered him, and the flocking of parlement-men about him, and theyre meetings and consultations with the earle of Southampton and the Lord Sheffield at Lord Rochesters chamber, (as is informed to the King but whether truly or no is a question) hath don him nor them no goode, for the King sayes he will not have a secretarie imposed upon him by parlement: and the erle of Southampton is gon home as he came without a counsaillorship, and the Lord Sheffield hath gotton a graunt of papists in Yorkshire. In

---

in 1611. Internal evidence in this letter suggests he is associated with Lord Roos (see *Downshire III*, p. 118).

[83] The letter is printed in *The Letters of John Chamberlain*, Vol. I, pp. 356–61.

[84] After the death of Robert Cecil in May, there was much competition to replace him in his various roles. This discussion of his replacement at Lord Treasurer is followed in the section quoted here by reference to some of the names in the running for Lord Secretary. Henry Neville's desire for this position, and Thomas's possible help in his ambition, is the subject of several of the letters included here from 1612.

[85] John Packer was Carr's secretary (see *ODNB* entry on Sir Robert Naunton). He went on to become Buckingham's secretary after Carr's removal.

the mean time the King himself supplies the secretaries place, and all the packetts are delivered to the Lord Chamberlain and so to the King and the aunswering of French affairs is referred to Sir George Carie, of Low Countries busines to Levinus, of Spanish to Master Calvert, as likewise those of Italie to him, or as other say to Master Edmonds clarke of the counsaile: and Sir Thomas Lakes is for matters at home as he was before: though they say he offer largely underhand for the higher place and his wife rather than fayle will furnish 5000 to make up 15000.[86] Kirkham is secretarie to the commissioners for the Treasurie, and Norton hath the reversion of Sir Richard Cookes places in Ireland both of secretarie and chauncellor of the exchecquer. But the likeliest now in the worlds eye for secretarie of state is Sir Henry Wotton and yt is a general opinion that the place is reserved for his comming home. He hath very great friends and the late Lord Treasurer recommended him to the King at his going away, and in his last letter wherein were many other remembrances and was redy written, but sealed after his death: and his living friends labor much for him. His brother is saide to have offered to resign his controllers staff on condition he may be receved secretarie, but I am not of that opinion, for I know he stoode lately upon 5000^{li} which I know I more than he wold spare for that purpose. For the King being geven to understand that he is yll served in parlement by reason of the paucitie of counsaillors and officers of household that were wont to beare great sway in that house, is minded to reduce yt to the forme yt had in the late Quenes days, and so caused the Lord Knollis and him to be dealt with about yt offering each of them 200^{li} a yeare during theyre lives to resigne theyre places. But the Lord Knolles stoode upon an earldome, and the Lord Wotton had rather have 5000li in hand, and so stands the case yet. But the Queen and the Prince are earnest in Sir H. Wottons behalfe, and the Lord of Rochester is not willing after his late reconciliation to oppose himself, or stand in the breach against such assaillants: specially having yrons in the fire now of his owne, and a patent (as I heare) beeing drawing to creat him earle of Devonshire, and great meanes made to the earle of Worcester to resign his mastership of the horse to him, and so to become Lord Privie Seale when the earl of Northampton removes to be treasurer, but these things are not yet don though much talked of.[87]

---

[86] Chamberlain sums up for Carleton how business is handled after Cecil's death. We see the involvement of diplomatic secretaries we've already heard from/about in earlier letters (e.g. Levinus Munck in Letter 17).

[87] This was a position of some importance, as James liked to hunt so much. Rochester was in some dispute with Pembroke about it, which may be the 'jarring' mentioned in Letter 23.

[The letter continues to discuss Wotton's success in his current place-ment in Savoy, from which he is recalled at the king's pleasure, and Chamberlain speaks in the following, slightly disapproving, tone about him.]

Touching all that I wrote to you before of Sigor Fabritio I should not nor could not beleve yt, but that many times unfitnes and unlikelines make a thing the more likely. [. . .]

Letter 21

12 July 1612: Sir Henry Neville to Ralph Winwood, Westminster[88]

[. . .] I sent yesternight to Sir Tho. Overbury to know what time I might come to him this morning; and he made me answer that he went out of town early, but would return about 6 of clock in the evening, and prayed me to come to him then. Hereof I thought fit to send you word, that you might not expect me according to my appointment yesternight. [. . .]

Letter 22

13 July 1612: Sir Henry Neville to Ralph Winwood[89]

[. . .] I feared that which happened: that Sir Tho. Overbury would not return yesterday till it was very late. Therefore I sent not to you, neither did I speak with him myself; but this afternoon, about two of clock, he will be with me, because I am not well, and cannot go to him. And he is desirous to meet you here, if you be returned from Court. [. . .]

---

[88] The letter is printed in *Buccleuch Whitehall I*, p. 109.
[89] The letter is printed in *Buccleuch Whitehall I*, p. 109. The date on the letter is 12 July, but due to the contents, referring to the events of the previous day in Letter 21, it is clearly written on 13 July.

Letter 23

1 August 1612: George Calvert to Sir Thomas Edmondes, Charing Cross[90]

[. . .] I doubt not but your lordship hath, by the industry of your agents and other friends here, heard that already which I must tell you for news, if I write anything at all. You know the *primum mobile* of our court, by whose motion all the other spheres must move, or else stand still; the bright sun of our firmament, at whose splendour or glooming all our marigolds of the court open or shut. In his conjunction all the other stars are prosperous, and in his opposition mal-ominous. There are in higher spheres as great as he, but none so glorious. All this is no news to you. To leave allegories, the king is in progress, and we are far from the court now to hear certainties, but it is told me yesterday that my Lord of Pembroke and my Lord of Rochester are so far out, as it is almost come to a quarrel. I know not how true this is, but Sir Thomas Overbury and my Lord of Pembroke have been long jarring; and therefore the other is likely. Our secretaries no man can tell who shall be; but the fairest is Neville, and some say Winwood also. He is returned back again into the Low Countries, not without great danger of shipwreck, so I hear. [. . .]

Letter 24

6 September 1612: Sir Henry Neville to Ralph Winwood, from Windsor[91]

[. . .] This tumultuary and uncertain attendance upon the King's sports affords me little time to write. But shortly I must pray you to understand that I have both received your letter to myself, and seen that which you wrote to Sir Thomas Overbury; upon both which I took occasion to press him in the point of the time of your revocation. I found him a little apprehensive, as if you mistrusted some neglect in him or other of the business that concerned you. And thereupon he renewed his protestations of all sincere meaning both on his part and his friends'. But for the time he prays you to have patience, and to refer it to the King's own humour, which must be followed, and against which there is no striving, without hazard of doing hurt. Yet he is in good hope of some speedy

---

[90] The letter is printed in Birch's *The Court and Times of James I*, Vol. I, pp. 190–2.
[91] The letter is printed in *Buccleuch Whitehall I*, pp. 111–12.

resolution, for upon the 21ˢᵗ of this month he [the King] hath appointed his Council to attend him, and put off their meeting till then which was purposed here as yesterday. For my part, I have had another conference with him of late, and find the matters well tasted which I proposed in the former. Much kicking there is both against you and me severally, but more against the coupling of us together. Yet I think it is done more out of animosity than hope; for Lake, in all men's opinions, is excluded, and Wootton hath rather lost than gotten by his late appointment. About a fortnight hence the King hath let me know that I shall hear from him some resolution about the matters whereof we have now twice conferred; whereupon I shall be able to make a more certain judgment of his purpose touching this whole business, and will speedily make you partaker of my conceit in it. In the mean time I do very much congratulate with you for the good amendment of my Lady, and wish you both health and happiness.

Letter 25

15 September 1612: Overbury to William Trumbull, from Theobalds[92]

[. . .] I have done my best offices for you toward my lord of Rochester, and my lord hath done such toward the king as I hope you shall find good effects of it in due time. In the mean time be vigilant and large in promises toward such as only offer their service and for such as perform the king will prove as bountiful, nor shall you want means to recompense merit, and you of all the rest it behoves to look about you, for your residence is in the shop of wickedness.[93] If upon the death of any great man in that country, you can help my lord of Rochester to any good bargain of excellent hangings at the second hand, or pictures or any household stuff which they have there better than ours, it would be a very acceptable service to my lord. [. . .]

---

[92] The letter is printed in *Downshire III*, p. 369.

[93] Thomas's instructions to Trumbull show his authority, but perhaps are not needed by the experienced diplomat. The writer suggests his power by making promises on behalf of the king. The 'shop of wickedness' suggests his view of (Catholic) Brussels.

Letter 26

25 September 1612: Sir Robert Naunton to Ralph Winwood[94]

Your letters of the 24th of August I received by Mr. Sa. Calvert about the 5th of this September. The same day, hearing that his Majesty was determined for Windesore, I went thither, and the next morning delivered your enclosed to Sir H. Nevill at Sir H. Savill's in Eaton, where I was by him resolved of a steady purpose in your honourable friends towards you and myself, but was at no hand to give suspicion of any such intention at all there, much less of any privity of his, in respect of their feeling sympathy with the Ambassador of Venice.[95] So I held it fitting not to trouble my Lord of [Ro]ch[este]r, lest an inexpe[cted?] visitation should seem a faint kind of importunity, but saluted Sir Thomas Overb[urie] *en passant*, which was sufficient to continue me in both their remembrance.

> *. . . volunt, valde velint . . .*

The day I came thither Sir H. [N]evill had speech [with his] Majesty as he hunted, for two hours, and received good approbation in the most of his advices, and by conference made good the rest, whereof his Majesty seemed to doubt at the first apprehension; but *de re tota quam tantopere avemus, verbum nullum*. His directions from his friends, you know, continue the same – not to obtrude himself into any petition or pursuit, but to leave it to them wholly, to cull out a time proper for the propounding it with success.[96] Hereupon some standers by are apt to conceive that the King mea[neth] to keep these places in suspense between himself and my Lords of Roch[este]r, as they we[re] after Sir Fr. Walsyngham's death; and that meanwhile Sir Tho. Overburie may fit himself with as good a probability to furnish the place in time, by the practice and experience he is now in, as Sir Tho. Lake and his Lady bare [bore] themselves strong upon. But we can admit no suspicion of any such underhand meaning in any of the 3, his Majesty's reservations having too many occasions in this undermining age of the world. I met with Mr. More at Windesore, who told me that in speech with my Lord of Roch[este]r he found him fixed in opinion that it would be very fit that your successor should be there en[coun]tered by you before

---

[94] The letter is printed in *Buccleuch Whitehall I*, p. 112–14. Robert Naunton is another who knows he must rely on the good offices of both Thomas and Carr, but he is considerably more needy than Neville.

[95] Dudley Carleton.

[96] The advice sounds like that of Thomas, making all of Neville's success dependent on him.

yourself should be called home; and that he heard, that when [his] Lordship was moved for him of Venice to succeed you, his answer was, that his fashion of carriage and countenance was somewhat with the loftiest to for [. . .] that people.

[. . .]

The King removed hence to Hampton yest[erday], whither the Lords are to follow him tomorrow, and to attend him there some four or five days, within w[hich time] the world expects his Majesty will declare his resolution further touc[hing] the Secretary[ship] [. . .] the Treasurership, and other offices that may receive alteration in c[onseq?]uence. Sir H. [Nevill] converseth now more professedly with my Lord of Rochester, and removed hence [with] the King, I mean *simu[l] tempore*. Myself hold on to my old course like a poor Chancery man that dreams of nothing but law and conscience, and resort only to Sir H. Nevill when he is in town, *et hoc parcius*. When you write to my Lord of Rochester, or to Sir Tho. Overbury, if it please you to use me for delivery of your letter, it may happily occasion me some further overture.

Letter 27

8 October 1612: William Trumbull to Overbury[97]

[gap] contentment, and no less thanck= [gap] your worthy letters dated the 15th of [gap] my carriage hereforward (by Gods assistance) [gap] shall rather have cause to [gap] nor my honourable Lord of Rochester to apoint him of any favour which his Lordship either hath already or shall please hereafter to extend towards a poor man of my rank. I will carefully observe those worthy and fatherly advice which are contayned in your said letter, and I protest unto you upon my faith, and the interest I have in your Lordship, & good affection, that I wilbe as carefull to husband his majestys moneys, (which are the publique treasure of my country) as if they were to be imployed for myne own particular benefitt. There shall not want in that care, paynes, or dilligence on

---

97 The letter is transcribed from NA SP 77/10/231. The top left corner of the MS is torn away, making the text difficult to read. It is clearly in response to Letter 25 and gives an indication of Trumbull's ongoing relationship with Thomas, who is now beginning to be influential. Trumbull shares his views on the recruitment of Englishmen to Catholicism on the continent in response to Thomas's comment on the 'shop of wickedness' in which Trumbull lives. The purchase of luxury goods for Carr is requested by Thomas.

my part to discover the dayly practises which are sent forward against his majesty, and his kingdoms. But what shall I say when, as without limitation, or restraint, there are such multitudes of his majestys evill afforded subsidy, suffered to repair unto these corrupted Provinces: and such daily confluence of Papists out of England to the Idoll of [illegible], under pretence of travell, and other fayned excess. If you will have the effect to cease, you must take away the cause, which is to hinder the liberallities of our countrymen from being transported hither, whereby there are so many seminaryes maintayned, and so many [illegible] monasteries builded; which serve for nurseries to p[illegible] the privacy of vypers; and with tyme to expose our country to the hazard of a dangerous rebellion. Consider such your self [gap] and discretions, whither [gap] distinction between a [gap] that as no practiser: [gap] for the advauncement of [gap] advise my Lord to fynde out [gap] of the less hurteful [gap] the more wicked. [gap] behold the numbers of your great issue, of noble and auncyent houses, which (as enfants perdues) are constantly sent over to Doway, and St Omers, to abjure their allegiaunce to his majesty, and render themselves the captayns of the Pope, and the Jesuitts, our capitall enemyes. Of this abuse both Sir Thomas Edmondes and myself have made many complaint; but could not yet ever fynde any redress. The evil is to be perceived here, but to be amended at home. For I dare boldly assure you that it is not the opinion of Spain, which alone doth maintayne these cloistered collidges; but the exhibitions of the bewitched English which if they could be rescued, or taken away, would soon make them bankrupt, and without inhabitant.

To the second point of your letter concerning the provision of some excellent hangings, pictures, or household stuff for my Lord of Rochester upon the death of any nobleman here. I will take such care and you shall see that your commission is not neglected. I understand that some such moveables of the late Duke of Anschot, who was exceedingly well fitted in that kynd, wilbe exposed to sale. Of excellent pictures he hath exceeding great abundance and I know some of them wilbe sold. But you must note that this people [gap] any other can be of that kynd of [gap] anie will not be had without much [gap] I will procure you a note of [gap] are to be had here; and request [gap] Antwerp, to lay wayte for such stuff [gap] to be rented there, as many [gap] that there are both good moveables, and [gap] be had in that town. Before I adventure to agree for any thing of this nature, I will both send you a description of it, and the lowest price. So I pray you to excuse this importunity, which my confidence in your love hath driven to a greater length than at the first I did resolve; and take my leave at this time, to remayne for ever,

Your assured loving friend to command
William Trumbull

Bruxelles this 8th of October 1612

Letter 28

9 October 1612: Overbury to Ralph Winwood, from Royston[98]

[. . .] My Lord [Rochester] will move for your coming over with the Count, and what answer he receives you shall presently hear. In the mean time, I pray you fasten the Count upon my Lord; and if you please, you may name me to him. [. . .]

Letter 29

24 October 1612: Ralph Winwood to Overbury[99]

Sir. Your letter of the 10 of thys month I receaved the 21st brought by a servant of Suastors(?) the postmaster who now twice in 20 days hath been sent hyther with letters from the Lord Haye to Monsieur Schooneberg. What the latter importuneth I know not: but the fyne was of little purpose; neyther did require as Schooneberg did openly declare to be sent by an express messenger, much less at the kings charge. Whilst the Elector Palatine was here, for that is his due title both in private to him and apart to his Counsel, and in public to them all together I have given this advyce in plain and direct terms entirely to repose themselves for the content and carriage of their business upon the counsel and directions of my Lord, who for the soundness of his judgement, his affection to their cause, his favour with his Majesty, was most willing, and best able to do them all real and powerful offices. Thys they severally and jointly promised. When of it they shall fayle, you shall do well, to make them somewhat sensible of their error: for my Lordship knows much

---

[98] The letter is printed in *Buccleuch Whitehall I*, p. 114.
[99] The letter is transcribed from NA SP 84/68/303. The letter is marked to 'My honorable friend, Sir Thomas Overbury, knight' and the tone is suggestive of that friendship.

contained in thys their negotiation whereof his servants cannot but be jealous. I have written to Schooneberg. Moore hath order to show you the letter and to follow your directions, eyther to delight at or suppress it. And now I cannot forebear to acquaynt you with a letter which yesterday I receaved from Sir Thomas Lake: wherein he writes that he hath commandment from hys Majesty, once in 14 days to advertyse all his Ministers abroad of all occurrences, eyther foreign or domesticall, the knowledge wherof he shall judge to be necessary for hys Majesty's service.[100] He ends hys letter with these words, that the vacant offices hang yet in suspense and so are like to do yet for some tyme yf thys order, that is for Thomas Lake to advertyse etc., be given with the privitie and approbation of my Lord. I am not so inconsiderate to except agaynst it. Otherwise you best wyll be able to judge, the prejudice hys Lordships honor will create thereby really and in very substance, not only in those nearly, of the whole world. For this feynt of advertising ys the principall charge and office of a principall secretary. To be able to do that, all dispatches must pass through his hands, and so come to hys hands, for the Ambassadors to whom he writes cannot but out of civility return him answer. Such will not be only ceremony, and compliment, and all Ministers abroad wyll stryve, all envy, who best shall advertyse him to receave from him the like measure. Neyther can I judge what the purpose ys to take from him the signets which are but the marks and *instrumenta inanimata* of the secretayrie, and to confer upon him the life and soul of the secretariship.[101] *Principiis obsta.*[102] There ys no medium in matters of thys nature between summa and principia and in the course you are in, *non progredi, est regredi.*[103] I for my particular, not[ing] with humility Sir Thomas hys letter, will continue the course I have followed since my return out of England, that is to make my addresses and [illegible]

[100] Winwood complains of Thomas Lake's request to receive all news from ambassadors. Clearly Winwood's anger at this is partly due to the importance of news exchange, and the perceived advantage to Lake in receiving it – as well as, of course, the assumption of position Lake has made here, taking upon himself one of the key roles of the Secretary. This is evidence of Winwood's political closeness to Thomas and he clearly feels Thomas can be useful in rectifying the problem here, but suggests his reliance on their common purpose. It is interesting, too, though, that this letter shows little of the 'socially binding' language we see in other letters, perhaps revealing something about the relationship between Winwood and Thomas.

[101] The phrase *instrumenta inanimata* appears to allude to Thomas Aquinas's *Summa Theologiae*, Part III, Qu. 78, in a discussion of transubstantiation. Winwood uses it humorously, with the accoutrements of the Lord Secretary as an analogy to bread and wine.

[102] *Principiis obsta* means 'resist beginnings': probably a quotation from Ovid's *Remedia Amoris*. Clearly he assumes a shared educational background with Thomas.

[103] *Non progredi est regredi*, meaning 'not to go forward is to go backwards', is a Latin idiom; perhaps Winwood is alluding to a specific usage of it, but it is not clear.

dispatches to my Lord untill from hym self I shall receave other directions. then I wyll strike safe and oblige him for that.

The best news I hear from abroad is thys: that the kyngs of Denmark and Suede are now entering with a treaty of peace. And so desyrous to hear from you to the purpose of your last, for my revocation I am

> yours ever to do you service,
> Raphe Winwood

Letter 30

6 November 1612: Sir Robert Naunton to Ralph Winwood, from Holeburne[104]

[. . .] If by my freedom with your Lordship you find me apt to distrust any, it is but my direct trust in the Psalm which directs us *Nolite confederer, &c.*, you know in whom; and so a diffidence not in either of you, but for you, and for our Church and State, which both promise themselves so much from you [. . . hears that] Sir Edward [Cecil] is a professed suitor, and that Sir Jo. Radclyf labours it for him here, in hope to succeed him at the Briel. [. . .]

Letter 31

17 November 1612: Sir Robert Naunton to Ralph Winwood, from Holeburne[105]

[. . .] Since by conference with Mr. More I find that Sir Tho. Overbury, out of an affection to introduce Sir Jo. Radcliffe into Sir E. C[ecil]'s employments there, is likely to endeavour for his cousin to become your successor;[106] and withal that my mediation to bring Sir F. Gr[eville] and him to meet, which I intended to advantage myself with Sir Thomas, was, I know not how, turquesed into a reprobate sense with Sir

---

104 The letter is printed in *Buccleuch Whitehall I*, p. 116. Thomas's plan to replace Edward Cecil at Brill with John Radcliffe is also mentioned in Letter 31, p. 92.

105 The letter is printed in *Buccleuch Whitehall I*, p. 118.

106 Thomas was backing Sir John Radcliffe (1582–1627) to succeed Edward Cecil to the governorship of Brill. It is unclear who exactly he has in mind to replace Winwood, or even for the secretaryship (since Naunton here seems to doubt his support of Neville), but it is a good example of the constant political plotting in which he seems to have engaged.

H. Nevill, as if I were too supiciously inward with Sir F. Gr., who holds
good quarter with my La[dy] of Suff[olk], &c.[107] Hereupon, finding Sir
H. Nevill somewhat drier (as methought) the last time I was with him
than in former times I had, I thought long to express myself unto him.
And this very morning having received letters from Sir Ed. Carre to my
Lord of Rochester in my behalf in general (who knows not of the place I
affect in particular) hard before the King's remove to Theobalds, I delivered them to his Lordship, who, reading them as he was going to the
King through the Gallery and calling me to him, told me they were to the
same effect he had before spoken to him, and bad me assure myself of
his best endeavour upon the first occasion, I went straight to Sir H. N. to
acquaint him what I had done, who told me my Lord, in his understanding, was resolved of m[e] for that place, but what Sir Tho. might write
for Sir Jo. Radclyf's sake, he co[uld] not tell, but to me he would impart
what he should discover [. . .] Touching our Palladium which we have
lost, I hold it neither fit for me to write what I conceive, and less fit to
be written to your Lordship.[108] It is given out by some of his confidants
that he had a design to have come over with the Palsgrave[109] and drawn
Count Maurice along with him, with some strengths, and done some
exploit upon the place that shot the Palsgrave's harbinger, and haply
[happily] have seen the Lantsgrave's daughter, or I know not what. That
this he meant to have done, whatsoever it was, *clam Patrem et Senatum
suum*; and hatching some such secret design, which was made subject
to misconstruction, it is now become abortive, like that of Henry the
4th in France. Sir H. Nevyll told me he had vowed that never Idolator
should come into his bed. And I was ascertained that in his sickness
he applied this chastisement for a deserved punishment upon him, for
having ever opened his ears to admit treaty of a Popish match. The best
news I can send you is, that by the noble and Christian intermise of Sir
H. Nevyll, there is a concentration made between my Lords of Penbroch
and Rochester, at which Sir H. N. himself was present; which was at
first put over by Sir Tho. Overbury, being with an intent to make the
cure the more sound. I hear the King hath done the like between the
Archb[ishop] and my Lord Northampton, but not from so good a party
as the other. There is hope the King will now declare himself, if he have
not done it already this afternoon, at his parting with the Lords. I am

---

[107] The *OED* lists the obsolete verb 'to turkish' or 'turkess', with examples from the late
sixteenth and early seventeenth centuries, meaning 'To transform, esp. for the worse; to
pervert; to turn into something different', of which 'turquese' is listed as a seventeenth-
century variant spelling.
[108] Referring to the death of Prince Henry.
[109] The Count Palatine.

in some haste, for fear Mr. More should send away before this come to him, which makes me write thus rhapsodically. The Palsgrave grows in grace every day with the King, who will have him down with him to Royston for some weeks. It is conceived he will hold him here till St. George's day be past, and after that investiture will consummate the marriage, and send them over together in May [. . .]

Letter 32

18 November 1612: Isaac Wake to Dudley Carleton[110]

Wake records that he gave Carleton's letters to Overbury, who said Rochester was gone with the King to Theobalds and Royston. He went to Theobalds, and found out 'Rochester's lodgings by the store of company that was about it'.

Letter 33

3 December 1612: Thomas Lake to Robert Cecil[111]

[A post-script comment after a business letter.]

The bill I wrot of to your lordship concerning Sir Thomas Overbury was sent from me as being to[o] cold in it, and I hear is procured to be signed after some contestation yet with importunity of Sir Robert Carre.[112]

---

[110] See *Calendar of State Papers, Domestic Series, of the Reign of James I, 1611–1618, preserved in the State Paper Department of Her Majesty's Public Record Office*, ed. by Mary Anne Everett Green (London: Longman, Brown, Green, Longmans, & Roberts, 1858), p. 156. This gives evidence of Thomas receiving packets of information from ambassadors, and Bacon accuses him of this at the trial. See Howell, *State Trials*, p. 973: 'packets were sent, sometimes opened by my lord, sometimes unbroken unto Overbury, who perused them, copied them, registered them, made table-talk of them, as they thought good. So I will undertake the time was, when Overbury knew more of the secrets of state, than the council-table did.'

[111] The letter is a transcription of NA SP 14/50/20.

[112] The letter shows the support Carr gives to Thomas in their court business in late 1612.

Chapter 3

The Fall of Icarus:
Overbury's Imprisonment

> one drop of bloud shed lawlesse,
> Will be the fountaine to a purple sea:
> The present lust, and shift made for Kings liues
> Against the pure forme, and iust power of Law,
> Will thriue like shifters purchases
> *Revenge of Bussy D'Ambois*, 5.4.52–6[1]

Thomas's presence in Royston in October and November 1612, where we left him at the end of Chapter 2, and then again the following April, indicates how often the court was there.[2] Sir George Calvert, whom we last met as a possible replacement for William Trumbull in Brussels, wrote to Edmondes, ambassador in Paris, in the middle of the 1612 dispute over the secretaryship.[3] His witty and articulate letter, in its outline of current news, characterises James's power, and makes reference to his hunting expeditions:

> You know the *primum mobile* of our court, by whose motion all the other spheres must move, or else stand still; the bright sun of our firmament, at whose splendour or glooming all our marigolds of the court open or shut. In his conjunction all the other stars are prosperous, and in his opposition mal-ominous. There are in higher spheres as great as he, but none so glorious. All this is no news to you. To leave allegories, the king is in progress, and we are far from the court now to hear certainties [. . .]

---

[1] George Chapman, *The Revenge of Bussy D'Ambois: A Tragedie*, ed. by Robert J. Lordi, in *The Plays of George Chapman: The Tragedies with Sir Gyles Goosecappe*, gen. ed. Allan Holaday (Cambridge: D. S. Brewer, 1987). All references in the text will be from this edition of the play.

[2] Cf. Letter 28, p. 90, sent from Thomas to Winwood from Royston on 9 October 1612. Isaac Wake, in Letter 32, p. 94, to Dudley Carleton on 18 November, records giving letters to Thomas to take to the king and Robert Carr in Royston. Letter 36, p. 126, Neville's letter to Winwood, refers to Thomas's letter from Royston; this must be written earlier than 21 April as it does not make any mention of Thomas's arrest.

[3] Letter 23, p. 85.

Calvert's 'allegory' presents a traditional image of the celestial power of the king, but with the mockery of those reliant on the king shown in the image of the 'marigold' courtiers, opening and shutting to the light of James's presence. Thomas is, of course, by 1612, one of these courtiers. In this chapter, I will continue to examine Thomas's power: this time looking at his arrest, his imprisonment and, ultimately, his death. The chapter therefore will see Thomas move from the centre of the homosocial court at Royston to a grave in St Peter ad Vincula, the church in the Tower of London.

The opening quotation establishes a perceived antithesis between 'the pure forme, and iust power of Law' and the 'shift made for Kings liues', with 'shift' in the sense of subterfuge or stratagem: more specifically a verbal stratagem, as legal judgements rely on the language of artificial proof presented, so 'shift' here has the verbal quality of sophistry.[4] In earlier chapters, I have shown how Thomas has risen in the presence of the king, initially as his server, and then by preferments associated with his being a close friend of the king's favourite. These chapters have focused on the social mobility accessible to educated men, and on the male friendship that enabled them to rise. This third chapter looks at the events of Thomas's final few months in the context of the legal debate in Jacobean England over the personal power of the monarch, and thus it looks too at the vulnerability of a courtier who has risen through the influence of that monarch. This chapter will begin with letters discussing the perceived change in Thomas's position as Carr builds ties with the Howards, and reflecting on whether to commit to paper their feelings about those in power. This leads into a section setting the legal context as many feared the growing risk of absolutism in England, especially in the changing political circumstances of 1612. I will then look at how Thomas's arrest was reported in April 1613, in the context of the king's power, and, finally, examine his letters to Carr from the Tower, where he was made a close prisoner and died in the September. The final letter from Thomas brings us back to all three areas this book establishes as key to successful courtiership.

A Courtly Fear of Absolutism

Thomas's career grew ever more successfully, as we have seen, through 1612 and into 1613, before the events of that spring were to bring it

---

[4] *OED*, 'shift' n., meaning 4a): 'A fraudulent or evasive device, a stratagem; a piece of sophistry, an evasion, subterfuge'.

to an abrupt end. Letter writers continue to tell their diplomatic correspondents about how 'Sir Thomas Overbury and my Lord of Pembroke
have been long jarring', and how this perhaps connects with a disagreement between the latter and Robert Carr; how rumours are spreading
that 'Sir Tho. Overburie may fit himself with as good a probability to
furnish the place in time', that is, Thomas may possibly become the new
Lord Secretary himself; or about how 'Sir Tho. Overbury, out of an
affection to introduce Sir Jo. Radcliffe into Sir E. C[ecil]'s employments
[at Brill], is likely to endeavour for his cousin to become [Winwood's]
successor' at The Hague.[5] The assumed political influence that lies
behind these comments, whether the rumours themselves are true or
not, makes it obvious that Thomas is thought to be a powerful and
influential player at court. For those writing at the time of his downfall,
Overbury was the courtier favourite who was able to make or break the
fortunes of his fellows, and attitudes towards him during the course of
his imprisonment and after his death showed distrust of the man that
people rarely voiced while he was in the ascendant.

By the beginning of 1613, Robert Carr had been working for some
months alongside the Howards: both Suffolk as Lord Chamberlain and
Northampton as leader of a team of commissioners at the Treasury.
The growing relationship between Carr and Frances Howard looked
likely to cement that connection still further, and there is little doubt
of Thomas's disapproval of such an outcome. His own letters from the
Tower show his disdain for 'that woman', and a great deal of evidence
is presented at her subsequent murder trial in 1615 of her dislike of
him. As the relationship between Carr and his lady develops, the influence of Thomas begins to wane, and the unease to build amongst his
political allies. The change in the relationship between the men who
have so far been working together against the Howard faction is seen
in a letter from Neville to Winwood; it is simply dated 'April', but must
have been written before Thomas's arrest on the twenty-first of that
month. The men continue to hope that his support will ensure their
preferment, but Neville is increasingly frustrated by the courtier's lack
of action:

> How it hath cleared up since the King's going to Roiston I know not other-
> wise than by Overburie's letters, who in this letter writes coldly as you see of
> you, and in a later concerning myself saith he is not in despair: which is a far
> different style from that he was wont to use.[6]

---

[5] Letter 23, p. 85; Letter 26, p. 87; Letter 31, p. 92.
[6] Letter 36, p. 126.

Accused of coldness and changeability by his allies, Thomas could be distancing himself from Neville and Winwood.[7] When writing to Winwood, Sir Henry Neville seems willing to identify the courtier's faults which he now believes may have caused them to lose their chances of preferment. Implicit in these comments are Thomas's self-assurance, his unwillingness to pander to the *amour propre* of great men, and his contrary, argumentative nature.

Neville's apparent distrust of his former ally at this point suggests his impatience and he is moved to express his frustration. As letters were rarely read simply by the intended recipient, most men were wary of committing their more extreme views to paper; Henry Wotton, for instance, writing rather obliquely to his close friend Edmund Bacon about Thomas a few days after his imprisonment, dare say nothing precise about the formerly influential courtier and instead reassures his correspondent, 'we shall discourse more particularly when we meet; which I now long for, besides other respects, that we may lay aside these metaphors'.[8] As if to strengthen the point, and show his real fear of epistolary indiscretion, he continues with an anecdote about one Sir Peter Buck, whose rather innocuous letter to a friend about activity at court led to his imprisonment and to his trial at the Star Chamber. Wotton quips, 'I set down these accidents barely, as you see, without their causes [...] but my lodging is so near the Star Chamber that my pens shake in my hand.'[9]

The reference to the Star Chamber leads us to the complex legal infrastructure of early seventeenth-century England, and opens a key issue for this chapter: the relative powers of the common law, courts with royal jurisdictions and the king's own prerogative. The Star Chamber was a royal court, originally indistinguishable from the king's Privy Council. Unlike the court of Chancery that also originated in the fourteenth century, it was not an equity court that amended miscarriages of justice between the letter and the intention of the common law. Rather, the Star Chamber, and other conciliar courts, with the power of the monarch

---

[7] Perhaps Carr's growing closeness to the Howard faction has led his favourite to consider that he should not be so clearly on the opposing side. The relationships are clearly more fluid than the concept of opposing factions would suggest, as we have seen in George Calvert's reference to Thomas and the Protestant Pembroke 'long jarring' (Letter 23, p. 85), though Thomas's final letter (Letter 78, p. 168) from the Tower blames that conflict on Carr.

[8] Letter 45, p. 136. Edmund Bacon, cousin of Robert Cecil, grandson and heir to the former Lord Keeper, Sir Nicholas Bacon, and married to Wotton's favourite niece, was one of his closest friends and regular correspondents.

[9] I have written further on this letter, and on the fear of letter writing; see Watson, '"My lodging is so near the Star Chamber that my pens shake in my hand": Letters, Truth and Lawyers' Fears', pp. 46–59.

behind their extraordinary powers, existed as a means of redress against possible corruption of judges and juries; it used, and contributed to the development of, common law, with chief justices sitting alongside privy councillors, but '[t]he advantage to the Crown was that proceedings were begun by information and tried summarily, with no need to satisfy a grand jury and a trial jury'.[10] The Star Chamber could, and sometimes did, prosecute those who were nobly born, who might not receive due justice from an overly reverential judge and jury. However, by the early seventeenth century, it was also known for a different kind of political role: 'The Star Chamber [. . .] offered a convenient forum for prosecuting offenders who opposed unpopular policies, cases in which juries might be too sympathetic to defendants.'[11] In other words, it could be used as a tool of absolute power, whether for the good or ill of the commonwealth or individual citizens. The fear that the Star Chamber provoked in those who commented on political matters in their letters is illustrated in Wotton's letter of April 1613.

Alan Cromartie assesses the power of royal prerogative in his work on constitutionality in early modern law, illustrating the debate in the attitudes of two medieval treatises that retained their influence into the sixteenth and seventeenth centuries. Where the Chief Justiciar of Henry II and writer of the *Tractatus de legibus et consuetudinibus regni Angliae*, Ranulf de Glanvill, argues that 'what pleases the prince has the force of law', shortly afterwards Henry de Bracton, in his *De Legibus et Consuetudinibus Angliae*, responds that the king puts himself under the law, as Christ did.[12] While their support of monarchy is clear, these two early legal writers form the basis for an ongoing debate on the relationship between the king and the law. Though his book argues that the sixteenth century showed 'the steadily growing imaginative purchase of the idea of English monarchy', Cromartie explains that it was 'only in the period's "Protestant" phases, under the two Edwardian dukes and Queen Elizabeth, that there emerged a bias towards law-bound government'.[13] All the Tudor monarchs, at some time or other, relied on the extra-legal powers of their prerogative, though Elizabeth, particularly, showed 'a willingness to respect judicial independence'.[14]

---

[10] John H. Baker, *An Introduction to English Legal History*, 5th edition (Oxford: Oxford University Press, 2019), p. 128.

[11] Baker, *English Legal History*, p. 128.

[12] Cromartie, *The Constitutionalist Revolution*, pp. 14 and 16. The treatises of these two lawyers, though written several hundred years before our period, were not replaced by later equivalents.

[13] Cromartie, *The Constitutionalist Revolution*, p. 89, p. 80.

[14] Cromartie, *The Constitutionalist Revolution*, p. 94.

However, by the end of the sixteenth century, legal heavyweights such as Edmund Plowden were writing that 'the political powers enjoyed by English monarchs were properly rights granted by the English common law'.[15]

By the time of James's accession, therefore, influential lawyers were usually not opposing prerogative powers, but trying to position these powers within the framework of common law, inevitably limiting them to some degree, and helping ward off fears of royal absolutism. As Cromartie comments, 'All that was actually required to justify an absolutist state was an "extraordinary" prerogative, that is, a right to involve *epieikeia*, whenever, in the king's sincere opinion, the good of the whole realm demanded it.'[16] The issue of *epieikeia*, or equity, is important to consider in this context. Plowden's *Commentaries* show the preoccupation with this Aristotelian concept permeating Elizabethan legal writings on common law, and it concerns the tension between the letter and the intention of a legal statute. As printing grew more common in the sixteenth century and common law rulings were increasingly written down, works such as those of Plowden discussed the issues arising out of them. There were inevitably situations when the letter of the law led towards a particular legal judgement, where the law's spirit would not have penalised a defendant in the same way; *epieikeia* is therefore 'the equity that "rectified" the law's unpalatable consequences', and it is this interpretation of written statute that is a key focus of Plowden's writings.[17] The Middle Templar explains that there are different possible ways of making a legal judgement based on statute, even though reason has led to that statute's construction:

> maxims are the foundations of the law and the conclusions of reason and therefore they ought not to be impugned, but always to be admitted; yet these maxims may by the help of reason be compared together and set one against another (though they do not vary) where it may be distinguished by reason

---

[15] Cromartie, *The Constitutionalist Revolution*, p. 109.

[16] Cromartie, *The Constitutionalist Revolution*, p. 149.

[17] Cromartie, *The Constitutionalist Revolution*, p. 8. Cromartie argues that this focus on equity is only one of two key ideas in Plowden's *Commentaries* – the other, after Ernst Kantorowicz, being the king's political body. But this is challenged by Lorna Hutson in 'Not the King's Two Bodies: Reading the "Body Politic" in Shakespeare's *Henry IV, Parts 1* and *2*', in *Rhetoric and Law in Early Modern Europe*, ed. by Victoria Khan and Lorna Hutson (New Haven: Yale University Press, 2001), pp. 166–98. Hutson argues that, when it is read correctly, there is little evidence of an interest in the theory of the king's two bodies in Plowden's writing; instead 'Plowden's record of the concerted and persistent attempts of the Tudor lawyers to apply an Aristotelian *epieikeia* to a burgeoning body of legislation' was key, and this 'was central to the emergence of the kind of political consciousness that later brought the issue of parliamentary sovereignty into sharp focus' (p. 172).

that a thing is nearer to one maxim than to another, or placed between two maxims.[18]

The importance of this is, as Cromartie argues, that the *Commentaries* are 'usually approached as an uncomplicated rendering of later sixteenth-century legal doctrines' but should 'be read as a form of political action', and such lawyers are at the centre of a debate on the relative power of the king and the law.[19] The concept of equity or *epieikeia* is important as if the king were capable of using it as a reason for rejecting a common law statute, and acting on his own prerogative instead – ultimately, he might argue, for the good of the commonweal – then it is a short step to seeing the king's decision making as being outside the control of the law.

This focus on *epieikeia* at the Inns towards the end of the sixteenth century led to Temple readings by Plowden's fellow Middle Templars James Morrice and Robert Snagg. Both also used the growing interest in legal history to argue that common law had its roots in the custom of the land. Snagg, in his reading on Magna Carta, for instance, argues for the different levels of power inherent in different kinds of legal jurisdiction:

> So as the Custom of the Realm revived by Parliament, is the Law of the Land, which is *Genus* to all; And the Parliament and the Acts thereof, and the Prerogative of the Prince, and the particular Customs of several Counties, Cities, Boroughs, & Manors, be all but *Species* of it: For that General Custom of the Realm, which is the Law of the Land, authorizeth the Parliament, limiteth the Prerogative [. . .][20]

Thus, by the end of Elizabeth's reign, there is much consensus amongst lawyers that the royal prerogative is within the compass of common law, and is subject to it. This is not, though, what James believed on his accession.

Francis Bacon, a professional lawyer and member of Gray's Inn, who was keen to succeed in royal service, wrote in support of the prerogative

---

[18] Edmund Plowden, *The Commentaries, or reports of Edmund Plowden, Of the Middle-Temple, Esq; An Apprentice of the Common Law, containing divers cases upon matters of Law, argued and adjudged in the several Reigns of King Edward VI, Queen Mary, King and Queen Philip and Mary, and Queen Elizabeth. Originally written in French, And now faithfully translated into English, and considerably improved by many marginal Notes and References to all the books of the Common Law, both ancient and modern* (London: In the Savoy, Printed by Catharine Lintot, and Samuel Richardson, Law Printers to the King's Most Excellent Majesty, for the Translator, and to Be Sold by the sellers in London and Westminster, 1761), p. 27.

[19] Cromartie, *The Constitutionalist Revolution*, p. 108.

[20] Robert Snagg, *The antiquity and original of the Court of Chancery and authority of the Lord Chancellor of England. Being a branch of Sergeant Snagg's Reading, upon the 28 Chapter of Magna Charta* (London, 1654) p. 17, discussed in Hutson, *Circumstantial Shakespeare*, p. 153.

powers of the Stuarts. As early as 1607, he had written a paper revealing his absolutist sympathies, where he declared that the king's prerogative came 'mediately from the law, but immediately from God'.[21] Ten years later, now Lord Keeper and member of the Privy Council, he confirmed his view that 'the king's prerogative and the law are not two things; but the king's prerogative is law, and a principal part of the law'.[22] Bacon's royalist ideology, though, Cromartie argues, attempts to counter an anxiety in Jacobean England over the royal prerogative; he notes 'growing English worries about extra-legal power' that 'reflected, amongst other things, a new understanding of the law'.[23] There was an understanding that absolutism was already possible, illustrated in Wotton's fear of the Star Chamber: a fear in those who, like him, were close to the court, of the king's use of his extraordinary power to control those who oppose royal policy.

Robert Cecil's death in 1612, and the death of Prince Henry, caused power to focus further on James himself. Not only did the alternative locus of power at the prince's court disappear, but so did the optimism that had existed there for a different kind of rule.[24] At the same time, the queen was simultaneously in mourning for her lost elder son and increasingly prone to ill health herself, and she undertook protracted travels away from London to seek cures in 1613 and 1615; thus, she grew to be less of a centre of power too, and the sole source of authority became the king himself. As Chapter 2 demonstrated, after Cecil's death, the king initially kept power from the competing factions in the court by delaying the appointment of a new Lord Secretary; but as 1612 moved into 1613, the king became ever more focused on his favourite, Robert Carr.

Thomas became increasingly important to Carr as, instead of appointing a new secretary, James devolved much of this work on his favourite, who used Thomas as *his* secretary and made the most of the courtier's education and political acumen. It was also during this period, in late

---

[21] *The Works of Francis Bacon*, ed. by James Spedding, Robert Leslie Ellis and Douglas Denon Heath, 14 vols. (London: Longmans, Green, Reader, and Dyer, 1857), Vol. X, p. 371.

[22] *The Works of Francis Bacon*, Vol. XIII, p. 203.

[23] Cromartie, *The Constitutionalist Revolution*, p. 153.

[24] As Sara Fraser puts it in *The Prince Who Would Be King: The Life and Death of Henry Stuart* (London: William Collins, 2018), p. 256: 'At St James's, Henry had created a dazzling and fully functioning court for the Prince of Wales [. . .] The new heir only had to step into Henry's shoes and fill a loss Charles's future people experienced as their own. James had arranged it so Henry's court developed a close-knit, collegiate character', but James was not to place Prince Charles amongst them and the despair was great at the loss of the hope Henry had represented.

1612 and early 1613, that things began to shift in their relationship as a result of Carr's involvement with Frances Howard. In the proceedings against Carr in his 1615 trial for Thomas's murder, Francis Bacon presents arguments to the court that give important evidence for events and motivations during this period. Bacon's overt antipathy to Thomas has to make us question his inferences: that the courtier 'had little that was solid for religion, or moral virtue, but was wholly possessed with ambition and vain-glory', that he was 'naught and corrupt', and that he was a man of 'unbounded and impudent spirit'.[25] His obvious dislike makes us read with scepticism his comments on Thomas's motivation and actions; but he is talking of events a mere two years beforehand, and his assessment of those and of the man himself must be a depiction that listeners, who knew the key players, would think credible.

Bacon uses Thomas's supposed involvement in the relationship between Carr and Frances Howard as a rhetorical circumstance to make his later opposition to the relationship more culpable. Thomas, he comments, 'made his brags, that he had won him the love of the lady [for Carr], by his letters and industry'.[26] This claim to have written the letters that wooed Howard gives some credence to the friends' initially jocular homosocial approach to her: a combined enterprise that disintegrates as Carr's affection for her grows. As long as she remains a joint project, and the real bond is between Thomas and his lord, she isn't a threat; but once Carr's allegiance is more to her than to his friend, the nature of their relationship shifts, and Thomas is seen as a danger to the couple. Bacon comments on the exclusivity of their friendship, noting in a way that implies an inappropriate personal, as well as professional, relationship that he is 'loth to have any partners in the favour of my lord of Somerset'.[27] It is worth remembering the political structure of the Jacobean court, at this point with a loosely attached group of Protestant nobles opposing the power base of the crypto-Catholic Howards, led by Henry Howard, Earl of Northampton, and Thomas Howard, Earl of Suffolk. As Chapter 2 showed, Thomas Overbury was often associated in terms of policy and sympathies with the former, despite his occasional 'jarring' with individuals. After his description of the argument with the queen in May 1611, Mr Taverner names the Earl of Pembroke as visiting Thomas in his lodgings to show support, but this is not to overstate the case. Taverner does more generally say 'almost all men' were there, and certainly pragmatism would have meant that even those

---

[25] Howell, *State Trials*, p. 974.
[26] Howell, *State Trials*, p. 973.
[27] Howell, *State Trials*, p. 974.

who disliked him would have felt the need to show sympathy with the favourite courtier's favourite secretary. Thomas would have had to maintain some sort of working relationship with the Howards. They were very powerful men and to achieve anything in the court, he would need their cooperation at times; but his support for Neville as secretary, a man opposing the Howards' favoured candidate, Thomas Lake, would have added to the evidence of his being opposed to the plans of the family. Indeed, that opposition seems to have been an accepted one as, referring to Thomas's relationship with Northampton, Bacon comments on his 'malice to himself and to his house'.[28]

The relationship between Carr and Frances Howard was of necessity illicit until she was in 1613 freed from her marriage to the third Earl of Essex in the infamous Nullity Trial. The pair were undoubtedly having a physical relationship, probably known to Thomas, for some time before this, and this would have given the latter the potential for exposure of the liaison, and thus power over his friend, should he wish to use that. Again, Bacon's evidence does perhaps show something of the relationship between the two men at this time, as he comments that Thomas, 'supposing that he had my lord's head under his girdle, in respect of communication of secrets of state, as he calls them himself secrets of nature; he therefore dealt violently with him, to make him desist with menaces of discovery and the like'.[29] Again, Bacon's image implies both Thomas's lack of respect for 'secrets of state', and his lack of political wisdom: the latter stemming, he implies, from his arrogance.[30] The changing political circumstances, in the legal context I have explored above, enable us to see more clearly the danger inherent in Thomas's position and what lay behind his arrest.

[28] Howell, *State Trials*, p. 974.

[29] Howell, *State Trials*, p. 974. For 'my lord's head under his girdle', see *OED* meaning 2c), phrases regarding girdles: '*(to have, hold) under one's girdle*: in subjection, under one's control'. Bacon's use of it may have this primary meaning, but it's also suggestive of the transgressive nature of their relationship – perhaps to provoke humour in the court-room at Carr's expense.

[30] Thomas himself asks Carr 'what secrets have past betwixt you & me', as, in his final letter from the Tower (Letter 78, p. 168), he berates his friend with his betrayal. The context of these secrets could be personal, and is not necessarily political, as Bacon argues at the later trial, though working together at court as the two men did, it is not an unreasonable assumption.

'[A] stroke of thunder': Thomas's Arrest

Overbury's arrest, on 21 April 1613, clearly surprised all observers, and the epistolary responses to it show that Bacon's dislike of Thomas was not unique. Two letters, for instance, were dispatched less than twenty-four hours after his arrest. John Packer, secretary to Carr and with some years of European intelligencing behind him, writes to Ralph Winwood in a deliberately objective and concise manner:

> there is fallen out an Accident whereof I thought fit to advertise your Lordship. Yesterday about Six of the Clock my Lord Chancellor and my Lord of Pembroke were imployed by the King to speak with Sir Thomas Overbury, and to make him an Offer of an Ambassage into the Low Countries or France [. . .][31]

He informs Winwood that Thomas declined the offer, citing as reasons his 'want of Language' and illness: his 'being so exceedingly troubled with the Spleen that if he had a long Letter to write he was feign to give over'. According to Packer, he goes on to tell his august visitors that

> he would not leave his Country for any Preferment in the World. Some say he added some other Speech which was very ill taken, but what it should be I cannot yet learn.[32]

He finishes with an account of Thomas's arrest and incarceration as a 'close prisoner' in the Tower. Packer's comment that '[s]ome say he added some other Speech which was very ill taken' is superficially objective, and it points out the lack of agreement amongst all observers. It could imply that Thomas might be expected to say things 'ill taken', and from earlier interpretations of his behaviour we can see that he is believed capable of thoughtless action and speech. A letter from Wotton – a man to his friend rather than an intelligencer to a diplomat – takes a rather subjective approach, and shows his pleasure in recounting the fall of a man he has never liked.

This second version of the events of the evening of 21 April is written by one man with a humanist education and an Inns of Court background to another. Trained in legal rhetoric and used to writing and speaking to

---

[31] Letter 37, p. 127. There is debate about where Thomas was asked to become ambassador. Packer here suggests places where Thomas's 'want of language' appears to be a ridiculous excuse; but the third place cited by others, Moscow, might be linguistically more challenging, as well as much further from the Jacobean court. The second letter written on the day of the arrest, Letter 45, p. 136, from Wotton to Edmund Bacon, which I go on to discuss here, also mentions France and the Low Countries.

[32] Letter 37, p. 127.

persuade his audience to adopt specific inferences, Wotton begins with the circumstances of time and place; in the council chamber which has been scene of Thomas's recent authority, and in the early evening, he is arrested. His reader feels the shock of the event as Wotton informs his friend that he happened to be an eyewitness when 'Sir Thomas Overbury was from the council chamber conveyed by a clerk of the Council and two of the guard to the Tower'. We have already discussed the power of eyewitness statement, and the expectation that it will establish credibility in the potentially slippery mode of epistolarity. Rather than the chronological account of John Packer, beginning with the events which he gave as reasons for the arrest, Wotton's choice is to open with juxtaposition of the centre of court business with the Tower, and this use of antithesis opens a more affecting narrative. His analeptic account continues with the origins of this arrest, as Wotton structures his letter to achieve maximum impact:

> both by the suddenness, like a stroke of thunder, and more by the quality and relation of the person, breeding in the beholders (whereof by chance I was one) very much amazement, and being likely in some proportion to breed the like in the hearers, I will adventure, for the satisfying of your thoughts about it, to set down the forerunning and leading causes of this accident, as far as in so short a time I have been able to wade in so deep a water.[33]

Having shocked his correspondent with the arrest of such a prestigious courtier in the 'first scene', he continues by expressing in metaphorical terms the impact it had on observers. He establishes the relationship between the drama he is recounting and its audiences (both the immediate 'beholders' and the later 'hearers' of the events, perhaps, like Edmund Bacon, through the reading aloud of letters). Again, unlike Packer, Wotton takes the opportunity to explore what caused the arrest more psychologically, and he gives an overview of Thomas's court position since the 'scandalous' incident with the queen:

> It is conceived that the King hath a good while been much distasted with the said gentleman, even in his own nature, for too stiff a carriage of his fortune; besides that scandalous offence of the Queen at Greenwich, which was never but a palliated cure. Upon which considerations, his Majesty resolving to sever him from my Lord of Rochester, and to do it not disgracefully or violently, but in some honourable fashion, he commanded not long since the Archbishop [. . .] to propound unto him the ambassage of France, or of the Archdukes' Court.

---

[33] Letter 45, p. 136. His use of the metaphor 'wade in so deep a water' conveys the difficulty of unpicking the motivation behind political events, as well as the danger in trying to interpret them. The depth he refers to is an image of the complexity of emotions and shifting alliances that this chapter explores.

In terms of rhetorical circumstances, Wotton is clearly interested in who and why – the person and motive behind the arrest. One of the motives is James's love for Carr; the king wants to 'sever him' from his friend and to do so in an honourable fashion, offering Thomas a diplomatic position to cover his disgrace. Yet disgrace it clearly is, as Thomas's refusal of first the Archbishop and subsequently the Chancellor and Earl of Pembroke demonstrates. In Wotton's metaphorical account, Thomas is a 'fish' that the hunter king is attempting to catch, and he refuses to take the bait:

> At this the fish did not bite; whereupon the King took a rounder way [. . .] Notwithstanding all which motives and impulsives, Sir Thomas Overbury refused to be sent abroad, with such terms as were by the Council interpreted pregnant of contempt in a case where the King had opened his will.

Having offered him a good diplomatic position, made it clear that it is the royal will, and tried to bribe him with the early assumption of the lucrative position of treasurer of the chamber, James had been refused. For such a king, there was no other option but to have Thomas arrested. Wotton's response is personal too: injured pride, that this insolent courtier should reject a position akin to that he had occupied in Venice and Savoy. Wotton thus draws a direct contrast between Thomas and those like himself who serve the king abroad; the difference is that the recalcitrant courtier resided in 'the bosom of a favourite'. The use of this intimate metonymic detail shows Thomas as a different kind of courtier, and encourages distrust in his reader:

> [the] refusal of his I should, for my part, esteem an eternal disgrace to our occupation, if withal I did not consider how hard it is to pull one from the bosom of a favourite. Thus you can see the point upon which one hath been committed, standing in the second degree of power in the Court, and conceiving (as himself told me but two hours before) never better than at that present of his own fortunes and ends.

Wotton refers to the Council and to Thomas's committal, showing the legal framework around the arrest, which, of course, supports the will of the king. Thomas's self-confidence and pride appear to have rankled personally with Wotton and there is an undoubted *Schadenfreude* in the latter's comments here.[34] It was, at the very least, thoughtless of Thomas to crow over a man whose diplomatic life was suspended and gives evidence of the man's propensity to '[s]peech which was very ill

---

[34] In 1613, Wotton is still suffering from the king's anger and is trying to redeem his position. See Chapter 2, footnote 18.

taken'.[35] Despite his growing influence and power in Carr's 'bosom', Thomas had not been able to recover fully from his altercation with the queen nearly two years previously: something a smoother courtier would have worked hard to reverse. The evidence seems to suggest that Thomas's overstated sense of his own worth led to problems submitting to others, even those who clearly outranked him – his behaviour thus forming another motive for James's actions against him. Thomas's political instincts seem to be guiding him towards behaviour which would offend such a king, whose writings on royal supremacy over his subjects are well known.[36] With the strongly Protestant beliefs Thomas had held since his days at university, and evidence in his *Observations* of his cynical attitude towards kingship in Europe, it is possible that he felt justified in 1613 in opposing the king's wishes.[37] Wotton realises that Thomas's behaviour is the death knell to his courtly ambition, and, again considering the circumstantial 'who' of the case, he mulls over whether the king's favourite is himself involved in the arrest:

> Now in this whole matter there is one main and principal doubt, which doth travail all understandings; that is, whether this were done without the participation of my Lord of Rochester? [. . .] in the meanwhile I dare pronounce of Sir Thomas Overbury, that he shall return no more to this stage.

Wotton's conviction that Thomas's life at court has firmly ended was one shared by others, even at this time of his arrest, and a week after this letter, the influential Thomas Erskine writes to the Earl of Mar giving his opinion, that Thomas 'shall never be more a courteoure'.[38]

So, at his arrest, Thomas's detractors begin to come out in force, using rhetorical circumstance to describe his imprisonment, showing surprise at it, but also implying their lack of sympathy. John Chamberlain, writing a week after Packer and Wotton, also examines person and motive and professes himself equally sure that the king, not Carr, was responsible:

---

[35] Letter 37, p. 127.

[36] The king had made clear his ideas on the divine right of kings through his publication of *The True Law of Free Monarchies: Or, The Reciprocal and Mutual Duty Between a Free King and His Natural Subjects* in Scotland in 1598, before he became king of Engand. In *Basilikon Doron*, written shortly after the birth of Prince Henry, he told his son that God 'maid you a littill godd to sitte on his throne & reule ouer other men' (*Basilikon Doron of King James VI*, ed. by J. Craigie (Edinburgh and London: Printed for the Scottish Text Society by W. Blackwood & Sons Ltd, 1944), 1.25).

[37] Thomas comments on the French 'Court of soueraigne Iustice; first the Presidents thereof are to be chosen by [the king], and to bee put out by him; and secondly, when they concurre not with the King, he passeth any thing without them': see *Sir Thomas Overbury His Observations*, p. 12.

[38] Letter 43, p. 135.

The King hath long had a desire to remove him from about the Lord of Rochester, as thincking yt a dishonor to him that the world shold have an opinion that Rochester ruled him and Overburie ruled Rochester wheras he wold make yt appeare that neither Overburie nor Rochester had such a stroke with him, but that he wold do what he thought fit and what he intended without acquainting either of them with his purposes.[39]

These letter writers are, in their examination of the king's responsibility and the motive for the arrest, concerned with what it has to tell them about the royal prerogative. Both Chamberlain and Wotton display a conviction that the motivator of the action was the king ('he wold do what he thought fit and what he intended') but they also show a fascination with how far the victim's friend should bear responsibility for what happened, or even have prior knowledge of it. Dependent as all are on the rise and fall of royal favourites, it is important whether this signals a falling from grace for Robert Carr, as all agree it has for Thomas. Chamberlain presents evidence of the favourite's continuing hold over James: 'The Lord of Rochesters ague continues with him still, so that he could not go yesterday with the King to Tiballs who tarried a day for him.' It is hinted here, of course, that Carr's ague was a response to his friend's arrest, and that he was pursuing the same course established when the queen engineered Thomas's banishment in 1611.

The friendship between Thomas and Carr is assumed, but there is a question mark for most courtiers over whether Carr's illness really does on this occasion reflect grief for his close friend. Wotton knows that he is still the reigning favourite, and alienating him through the revelation of a careless epistolary opinion would have been foolish:

My Lord of Rochester, partly by some relapse into his late infirmity, and partly (as it is interpreted) through the grief of his mind, is also this second time not gone with the King. Some argue upon it, that disassiduity in a favourite is a degree of declination; but of this there is no appearance, only I have set it down to show you the hasty logic of courtiers.[40]

Wotton's mention of the 'disassiduity in a favourite' may suggest his own belief, but it is countered immediately by a comment on 'the hasty logic of courtiers', which has the same reflective nature as the philosophical musings on the nature of preferment in his previous letter.[41] The passive 'it is interpreted' and distancing himself from the view with

---

[39] Letter 39, p. 131.
[40] Letter 40, p. 133.
[41] In Letter 45, p. 136, Wotton recognises this trait, commenting to Bacon, 'I take pleasure (speaking to a philosopher) to reduce (as near as I can) the irregularities of Court to constant principles.'

the objective 'some argue upon it' both demonstrate his refusal to ally himself to this opinion. As we saw earlier, obfuscation in letters often reveals the fear of advocating ideas contrary to the interests of men in power, but in mentioning them, of course, Wotton allows Bacon to draw his own conclusions.

Wotton, whose pens trembled in mere proximity to the royal power of the Star Chamber, writes in a similar manner to Edmund Bacon in May 1613, this time about the arrest of another courtier, Robert Killigrew. His correspondent's personal interest in the tale (Killigrew was related to Bacon) means that he wishes to talk of what has happened but Wotton did not feel he could discuss Thomas openly; instead, he uses ambiguous pronouns and the semantic field of medicine to give what must have been a rather confusing account of what had happened to the powerful courtier since his arrest just over a fortnight earlier:

> Of his case whose love drew him to it, I can yet make no judgement; the humour seemeth to be sharp, and there is wisdom enough in those that have the handling of the patient to manage the matter, so that at length his banishment from the Court may be granted as a point of grace. The nature of his alteration was (as you rightly judge it) in the first access somewhat apoplectical, but yet mingled in my opinion with divers properties of a lethargy; whereof we shall discourse more particularly when we meet [. . .][42]

Wotton's praise of 'those that have the handling of the patient' seems intended to protect him should the letter be opened and the subject matter deciphered. In his desire to meet Bacon and share ideas face to face, the honesty of spoken language is contrasted with the necessarily deceptive written word, as we have seen before. His epistolary metaphors are, in many ways, akin to the ciphers he and other diplomats use elsewhere, and to the pseudonyms we will see in Thomas's correspondence with Carr from the Tower.

These weekly letters to a friend show an intelligent but largely vicarious interest in court news. Viscount Fenton, however, was informing his Scottish cousin and ally of vital political intelligence and, as a member of the Privy Council, he was in a better position to know the persons and motivations of the principal actors. Fenton first assures the Earl of Mar, 'I will and maye assure your Lordshipe, that [Thomas's arrest] is fakt of his Majesties owin, and soe weill and judiciouslye caried that if it bein governed be onye uther I think it shuld never have done soe weill.'[43] In a further letter three weeks later, he is even firmer in his view that not only was James responsible for the arrest, but he is also sure that Carr

---

[42] Letter 45, p. 136.
[43] Letter 43, p. 135.

knew nothing about the king's plans. Having seen that James was determined to be rid of the courtier, though, the royal favourite has, quite
sensibly, decided nothing should prevent him from approving what the
king has done: 'althoe my Lord of Rotchester was noe thing aquented
vith his Majesties purpose in that [...] yet he is soe wyss and thinks
himselfe soe mutche oblished to his Majesties favore that there is noe
tye nor bownd shuld howld him quher his Majestie hes his interest.'[44]
Fenton's view that Thomas is doomed to stay in prison indefinitely is
clearly borne out by events. His comments on the conflict between court
factions, which rises closer to the surface after Thomas's removal, show
his inside knowledge and his perspicacity. He can see the self-seeking
duplicity of Carr, who will abandon any loyalty to his previous allies
to prove to the king that he is capable in his own right, and not entirely
dependent on Thomas:

> It maye be your Lordshipe will heir that there is lyke to be great factions, and
> that all theis that Overberrye drew to him and about my Lord of Rotchester
> are lyke to make a pairtye to the Howards, quitche I think theye wold doe if
> thaye culd sturr Rotchester to it, but he wilbe wiser.[45] Southehamptoun and
> Pembrouke are joined in that side, and thaye stand mutche to have Nevell
> Secreterrye. Thaye have vith them sume of the moste discontented nobill
> men of the younger sort, and all the Parlement mutineers; yet I think all will
> not worke to there end. I think his Majestie will let the world see that yet
> for a tyme Rotchester can make his Majesties dispatchis vithout the helpe of
> Overberrye.

Although his information is often less reliable than that of Fenton, John
Chamberlain, who has time on his hands to reflect on the events he witnesses, writes to a friend who is personally concerned in the outcome of
the affair. Still keen to secure a position in government, Winwood must
have been desperate for news from London. Chamberlain writes to him
that 'Sir Henry Neville is in a fair way, and his Friends look daily when
he shall be sworn Secretary', adding the flattering hope that 'he shall
tarry till a Colleague come to help to bear the burden; and I will not
believe otherwise but that we shall see you here shortly'.[46] Yet it is not
to be. The ascendancy of the Howards is secured, at least for the short
term, and Carr, still the king's favourite, is about to be secured too – as
more than their political ally.

Chamberlain adds, almost as an addendum, that 'There was speech
of a Divorce to be prosecuted this Term betwixt the Earl of Essex and

---

[44] Letter 53, p. 145.
[45] '[M]ake a pairtye to' = to oppose, become an enemy to, the Howards.
[46] Letter 45, p. 136.

his Lady', and he has already heard the rumour that she was 'aiming at another Mark', though he believes that there has been such scandal that it will not now proceed. However, the Nullity Trial to separate Frances Howard from the young Earl of Essex is to open a mere ten days later: the precursor of a general understanding that the fortunes of the Protestant faction at court, which included Essex, are declining. At the same time Carr's betrayal of Thomas begins to be more apparent, and Wotton notes at the end of May, 'Sir Thomas Overbury is still where he was, and as he was, without any alteration, the Viscount Rochester yet no way sinking in the point of favour; which are two strange consistents.'[47] He hints in his accustomed oblique way that, no longer ill and keeping his bed, Carr must have been complicit in the arrest, or, at the very least, have shifted his allegiance firmly away from Thomas afterwards. That is not apparent to the close prisoner in the Tower, who, fed poisoned food and poisoned information alike, does not realise for some time that he can no longer rely on his former 'bosom friend'.

The relationship between Thomas and Robert Carr is a key area of interest in the letters explored in this and previous chapters, which has demonstrated the homosocial environment of James's court as well as how affective rhetoric in letters between male correspondents was an epistolary expectation, even in political and diplomatic letters. Letters so far, between courtly observers and their correspondents, have looked at the relationship between the men as it appeared from the outside. The letters which follow, those between the men themselves, give alternative evidence.

A Growing Realisation: Thomas's Letters from the Tower

The letters between Thomas and Carr survive largely as a result of the 1615 trials. In the search for evidence of potential murder, the letters were seized and transcribed to be used in the prosecutions of the then Earl of Somerset, his wife and several others who played a role in events. The remainder of Chapter 3 will examine how these letters demonstrate Thomas's political style, and how this previously successful political approach fails him in these different circumstances: unknowingly opposed, as he is at this point, by the man he considers his friend. The first extant letter covers the mechanics of epistolary exchange: no easy process as he was a close prisoner and, therefore, forbidden to interact with anyone:

[47] Letter 54, p. 146.

Look well to your seals and mine, and mark them well. My letter yesterday was seald with soft wax ill favordly & seals; this is sealed with hard wax and my little seal.

Never write but upon some hope comming, then darkly and shortly. Call Neville hereafter Similis and because he is like Hen 8; call the king Julius. Remember those two changes; call Pembroke Niger.[48]

It is highly unlikely that Thomas would not wish to write to Carr almost as soon as he was arrested, so, though the prison letters largely exist in copy form and are not individually dated, we might estimate the date of this one to be in the latter half of April 1613. The tone is imperious; his quick thinking and the plotting of schemes to outwit his opponents are manifest in a stream of imperatives. He has apparently also found an unknown servant to deliver the letters to Carr: one with whom he is keen that his usual man, probably Lawrence Davies, shouldn't be seen.[49] The use of code names becomes a commonplace, though as he needs to explain the *dramatis personae* to Carr, it appears they have not used them before.[50] It perhaps shows Thomas's Middle Temple roots, with the satirical writing of contemporaries in those younger years often addressed to specific targets under alternative titles.[51] In a period where the king referred to his chief minister as 'my little beagle', and nicknames were regularly used as a form of affection, it is often playful.[52] Yet the use of such names also fits into the atmosphere of epistolary unease

[48] Letter 41, p. 133. Thomas's first letter is labelled 'Letter II' in the manuscript source and there is no extant Letter I, so there may be a short time lag after 21 April. It will only be a short lag, though, as Thomas alludes to what is probably Letter I in this letter and says it should have arrived with Carr 'yesterday att 3 a clock'. This is presumably the letter quoted by Bacon in Somerset's trial that I refer to in the Introduction (see pp. 1–2 above).

[49] In the 1615 trials, two men give evidence as Thomas's servants, Davies and Henry Payton. The former is said to have served him for eight or nine years, and is likely to have been the one he referred to as 'my man'. See Howell, *State Trials*, p. 919.

[50] Bacon comments, for instance, that 'they made a play of all the world besides themselves, so as they had ciphers and jargons for the king and queen, and great men of the realm' (Howell, *State Trials*, p. 973), and this is one of several references to the code names supposedly used between them. Men clearly did use code in letters (cf. for instance Thomas Bull in Letter 64, p. 157), but, if this is a regular habit between Thomas and Carr, it is odd that he explains in Letter 41 who all the code names refer to and gives instructions to Carr to use them.

[51] Examples lie in Benjamin Rudyerd's account of the 1597–8 Middle Temple revels, *Le Prince D'Amour* (London: William Leake, 1660). For further ideas on the roles played and names used in these revels, see Philip J. Finkelpearl, 'Sir John Davies and the Prince D'Amour', *Notes and Queries*, Vol. 10, No. 8 (1963), pp. 300–2.

[52] See NA SP 14/15/105, and the discussion of the nicknames applied to Cecil in Pauline Croft's 'Can a Bureaucrat Be a Favourite? Robert Cecil and the Strategies of Power', in *The World of the Favourite*, ed. by J. H. Elliott and L. W. B. Brockliss (New Haven: Yale University Press, 1999), pp. 81–95 (p. 88).

witnessed by Wotton's metaphors and ciphers, and, in the later trial, Francis Bacon implied a nefarious intent:

> they had ciphers and jargons for the King, the Queen, and all the great men; things seldom used, but either by princes and their ambassadors and ministers, or by such as work and practise against, or at least upon princes.[53]

Bacon manages to reduce Thomas's status here, suggesting he is below the rank of 'ambassadors and ministers', and his analogy hinting at treachery helps him to build his case against a man he is accusing of poison, a crime linked throughout this period with treason.[54] But Thomas's unease over the safety of writing also prompts him to ask Carr only to write 'darkly and shortly', with the code names adding to the 'dark' writing.

The letters go on to show that Thomas requested Carr procure a 'vomit' from their friend, Sir Robert Killigrew, to enable him to feign illness. The issue of Thomas's sickness is much discussed by all observing his incarceration, and there is no doubt that in the days leading to his death there was much evidence of it. He appears to have had some pre-existing conditions, and, over the time in the Tower, he ingested a great number of medicines given by court doctors, as well as poisons sent by Frances Howard in food and drink. Yet in these early letters it is also clear that he aims to use one such pre-existing leg condition deceptively, to engineer his release from the Tower. He muses, 'it shall be enough for me to shew my leggs wonderfull little, which I will impute since this though they were so afore', acknowledging his willing duplicity.[55] It is apparent that he is used to using deception to gain a desired outcome, and it is likely that he has regularly employed it professionally. This deception is not hidden from Carr, who becomes a co-conspirator. There appear to be several 'vomits' changing hands, though whether Killigrew supplied all of them is not certain.[56] Wotton's aforementioned account of Killigrew's arrest adds the intriguing detail that he was 'con-

---

[53] Howell, *State Trials*, p. 973.

[54] For a discussion of the regular linking of poison and treason, see Perry, *Literature and Favoritism*, pp. 95–103. He reminds us that Somerset was accused of poisoning Cecil too, and that in the trial of Thomas Monson for involvement in Thomas's murder, Coke hinted at Overbury's similar involvement in the death of Prince Henry (Howell, *State Trials*, p. 949).

[55] Letter 42, p. 134.

[56] Vomits are mentioned in the letters marked III, V and VI (Letters 42, 48 and 49, pp. 134, 139 and 139). In the *State Trials* record of Weston's trial (p. 917), the vomit is said to have been sent on 5 June, so this may help with dating one of these letters, though internal evidence conflicts; that marked Letter VIII (Letter 51, p. 140) is said to have been written when Thomas has been in prison a month, suggesting it would be dated 21 May or thereabouts.

ferring with a close prisoner in a strange language'.[57] Perhaps the contemporary desire for coded secrecy in letters was echoed in the friends' conversation by some kind of verbal cipher.

'Letter III' continues Thomas's plotting for his release and he asks Carr to send two royal physicians, John Craig and John Nasmyth, or possibly Allen, to attend him in the absence of the king's leading medicus, Sir Theodore Turquet de Mayerne. The power of medical specialists at this time was great; as Webster was to have Ferdinand comment in *The Duchess of Malfi*, 'Physicians are like kings. They'll brook no contradiction.'[58] Royal doctors would confer with the king, but he is not afraid of that; indeed, he plans to use this potentially threatening closeness. It doesn't really matter to him which of them are sent at this stage, he confides to Carr, as he does not plan to take their treatments; they will, instead, play their part in gaining his release. The physicians should be

> tow such as when they go back may go in to the king and relate how much my body is wasted with though[t] of the kings displeasure and this place. And that is all for I will take no phisicke of them, and uppon this reason, that till my mind be easd no phisicke can cure my body. And so having shewed them this I will desire them to com to you then you to carry then into the king, then for you to send them into the king by Pat. Mald. or so. Then presently after go you in your self.

The plot is full of alternatives and provisos. As he lists, slightly confusedly, who is to see whom, and who may see the king, Thomas gives the impression of much practice in this quasi-dramatic art, as well as being accustomed to instructing his lord. His next letter plans for the possibility of his leaving the Tower. The quick succession of apparently unconnected topics in this letter implies that communication between the extant 'Letter III' and 'Letter V' outlined plans upon which he is here commenting. The prisoner assumes he can rely on his correspondent implicitly, as he has done before.[59] However, 'the business' to which Thomas has referred does not seem to work and he asks his friend, 'I pray you answeare me directly to this: whether you will not use To. for a fortnight rather than leave me thus? I know that will carry it directly.' The phrase to 'use To.' has a particular meaning for the two men, and their use of in-group language such as this demonstrates the closeness of their friendship.[60] Thomas is asking Carr to take repeated doses of a

[57] Letter 45, p. 136.
[58] *The Duchess of Malfi*, 5.2.65.
[59] Letter 47, p. 138: 'Letter IIII' is a note from Killigrew to Rochester.
[60] In his discussion of Manningham's interest in Middle Temple coterie language, Chris

preparation which would make him ill, knowing that this will induce the king's affection for his favourite and manipulate him into giving in to Carr's request.[61] It appears he has done this before, perhaps in the aftermath of the queen's displeasure. After around a month of imprisonment, Thomas's imagination is still creating new ways to achieve his release, and he is still confiding everything openly to a man he has reason to trust.

This creativity reaches new heights in the very long 'Letter VIII': a masterpiece of plotting – both in the political and in the dramatic sense. Thomas here does the work of a playwright, deciding the action each of his characters should take and supplying them with lines. It shows his talent for *prosopopoeia*, and he gives words here first to the imagined 'Wolsey' (Suffolk), then to Carr himself, envisaging both in the presence of the king.[62] Firstly, Carr is to encourage 'Wolsey' to plead with the king to release the prisoner and there is clearly a sense here that, despite Suffolk's being part of the Howard faction, he may be prevailed upon to help.[63] There is a great deal of detail given: who is to engage Suffolk, what he is to be told to do, and even the words he is to deliver to the king:

> Hereuppon may Wolsee say, Sir, I hearing this, though[t] myself bound in honesty to tell to you, first for since if he dye in the night it might cost my Lord of Rochester his life to[o], who you see how passionattly he loves him [. . .] and lett my Lord of Rochester know nothing, but that you do it for his sake, never taking notice that I have sayd any thing [. . .][64]

Thomas proposes a structured speech predicated upon the king's love of Carr and Suffolk's high moral stance. The part he proposes for 'Wolsey'

D'Addario notes that 'groups under significant social pressure or which feel particularly uncertain of their place within a larger society tend to develop these obscurantist shared vocabularies in order to demarcate inclusion and exclusion clearly'. See 'The Texture of the Everyday in John Manningham's *Diary* (1602–1603)', *English Literary Renaissance*, Vol. 42, No. 2 (Spring 2012), pp. 203–22 (p. 209).

[61] See McElwee, *The Murder of Sir Thomas Overbury*, p. 85.

[62] See Chapter 2, footnote 28, on *prosopopoeia*. The skills that had so much use in the playhouse and in the giving of legal evidence were also, as we can see in the material in this book, useful in the writing of letters and in political plotting.

[63] Thomas's pragmatism has, I think, been underplayed by writers on this subject. Beatrice White is typical in her assertion that his opposition to Lake showed him 'taking the first open opportunity of running counter to the great family he so utterly detested' (White, *The Cast of Ravens*, p. 34). There is little evidence that he worked equally against all members of the family, or even that they formed an entirely unified faction. It appears just as likely that Thomas, like Carr, would have adapted his political behaviour to ensure the greatest chance of success at that point in time. His Protestantism may have led him to be a more likely ally of Southampton and Pembroke, but it did not prevent him from 'long jarring' with the latter (see Letter 23).

[64] Letter 51, p. 140.

contains the kind of persuasive case a legally trained mind might plot, with rhetorical circumstances clearly marking time and place (he 'must com to Julius on morning att Greenwich'), as well as the motives he should give for his action in coming to the king:

> for my own part I speak, for the world thinking me his enimye would lay his blood to my charge, which I would not have imputed to me for all the world [. . .][65]

Thomas's concluding comment on this triumph of imagination is a line that, on stage, would mark a Machiavellian courtier: 'here is a plot exquisitely laid'. His desire to manipulate and ventriloquise Suffolk appears matched by his desire to deceive the king. Only Carr is to know the truth.

Depending on the dating of letters, this plan to involve Suffolk may be 'the business' to which John Lidcote, Thomas's brother-in-law, refers when he writes in secret to the Tower at some point in May. He conveys a warning he has received about the potential involvement of Suffolk:

> One told me this day from Sir Humphrey Maye his mouth that my Lord Chamberlain is not so foolish to think that you will deny to yeald to anything for your Liberty but, when all is done, it will [be] pretended that that [sic] the Kings wrath will keep you there [. . .][66]

Not temperamentally suited to life at court, Lidcote is terrified of the subterfuge, pleading with his brother-in-law to recognise that he is 'cozened on all hands'. As we have just seen, Thomas's letters relish the intellectual challenge of securing his release, though filled with frustration at his imprisonment and anger at his treatment too. There is now little doubt that he blames the king entirely for his incarceration, and feels that his punishment, or at the very least the length of his punishment, is due to royal jealousy and is not equitable:

> sure the reason he keeps me close so long is to lay all wayes uppon you along, whether he can work your consent to a seperation, for after the dores are open, then he thinks we will mingle thoughts again [. . .][67]

---

[65] Presumably the choice of this place and time of day suggests Thomas's pragmatism – it is when and where James, perhaps, is most likely to be accessible; but, circumstantially, it also suggests openness, not in the dark of evening, in any kind of hidden venue. 'Wolsey's' explanation of his motive is also clever: that he doesn't wish to be thought complicit in Thomas's death in the Tower, which, as a Howard and the father of Frances, is entirely likely (and may, in reality, have been the case).

[66] Letter 52, p. 144. I am proposing a date in the last week of May, as his comment on Suffolk seems to respond to knowledge of the plot involving him proposed in 'Letter VIII'.

[67] Letter 51, p. 140.

Thomas gives, in the second person, reported speech showing how Carr can persuade James of his love for him, as a means of securing his real love's (Thomas's) freedom. The rivalry between Thomas and the king over Carr's affections is summed up neatly by Alastair Bellany: 'Overbury was James's main male rival for Carr's political and personal affections, and both men coveted the role of maker of the favourite's fortunes.'[68] 'Letter VIII' seems to give ample evidence of love between the two, though much of what is cited by popular writers as evidence of potential homosexual feeling is surely misread. The reminder, 'you are a naturall man; where your most love is, there your most company is', cited by Beatrice White as evidence of 'the "passionate" love between the two men', is actually a line Thomas supplies for Carr, to persuade the king that his love is for James just as his time has been always at the royal command.[69] Thomas's reasonable plan is to reduce the jealousy the king feels by supplying lines for Carr to assure the monarch of his loyal affections. Equally, what sounds like a slightly petulant reminder to a once-responsive lover, 'loving me better than him', is often taken out of context. The adverbial is the triumphant culmination of an imagined speech where Carr offers the king three options:

> [Either] I shall be reformd according to his instructions never to transgress, which he cannot but accept. If that will not, you will quit all business [. . .] or if both these fayle it will have a worse end [. . .] to shutt yourself up in a park and dye for this [. . .] & when he sees sure he will chuse the first, and presently tend toward it: for loving me better than him, what he touchd [on] you must never lett such a thing slid by unansweard

It is simply accepted in Thomas's view that Carr *does* love him more, and the complex plots he asks his friend to carry out are based upon this assumption.

The nature of that love is unclear from the epistolary evidence, though it does appear to go beyond the affective language typical of courtly and political letters. Roger Wilbraham, a contemporary writing after Thomas's death, notes in his journal that 'he [was] late before Somersett's bedfellow, mynion & inward councellor, for which he was much envyed in Courte'.[70] There are many accusations of betrayal and discussions of jealousy which, in another context, could be the words of a romantic lover, but it is not certain that the clearly strong bond

---

[68] Bellany, *The Politics of Court Scandal*, p. 50.
[69] White, *The Cast of Ravens*, p. 64.
[70] *The Journal of Sir Roger Wilbraham, Solicitor-General in Ireland and Master of Requests, For the Years 1593–1616*, in *The Camden Miscellany*, Vol. X (London: Royal Historical Society, 1902), pp. 115–16.

between the two young men was a physical one. More recent writers such as White continue to make this assumption: 'Both of them were strikingly handsome; of Carr especially it can be said that his face was his fortune – though Overbury, who never married, may have been more naturally homosexual.'[71] She attempts to contextualise the assumption by noting, 'It should not, however, be forgotten that in those days a friendship between two men often – and openly – involved emotional and sexual attachment', but this is less nuanced than recent scholarship on homosocial friendship suggests. Alan Bray's work, as we saw in Chapter 2, does suggest that attachment between men was a familiar feature of early modern life, but he makes it very clear that one cannot equate the passionate friendship of contemporary letters, and their evocation of literary models such as Virgil's second *Eclogue* and Cicero's *Amicitia*, with physical desire; such a letter 'was about [. . .] the "insensible" part of love, not sexuality but a Platonic meeting of minds'.[72] Due to the unusual motivation for their writing, Thomas and Carr's letters are perhaps not typical of these, but neither do they appear to reflect physical desire. In Thomas's letters, 'love' appears to be a type of contract which the two have entered into. He has given much to Carr, enabling the latter's smooth progress at court and, to support his friend, giving up opportunities he might otherwise have taken; now it is Carr's turn to repay that commitment and ensure his release. Though later writers were to assume a physical closeness between the two, it is by no means certain, and may even be evidence of an attempt to demonise Thomas, who was portrayed in the trials of 1615, and especially by Francis Bacon, as the very embodiment of corruption.

Whether their bond was emotional, sexual, pragmatic or a mixture of all three, it was clearly so strong that as 1613 progressed Thomas continued to trust and rely on his friend. He writes that the problem lies with how the king has been influenced by the talk of others:

> libells had told him you governed him, and I know not what, and Agrippina told him he durst do nothing to displease you. Now he to lett them see this tis not so but that he could discipline you when he pleased.[73]

The queen (Agrippina) and other enemies at court have spoken out in jealousy of Thomas's success and have successfully manipulated the king. In other words, they have outmanoeuvred the courtier in a way he might, in different circumstances, have chosen to use himself, and he

[71] White, *The Cast of Ravens*, p. 8.
[72] Bray, *Homosexuality in Renaissance England*, p. 61.
[73] Letter 61, p. 151.

recognises the effectiveness of their actions. He has clearly had informa-tion of the rumour to which Chamberlain referred just after the arrest.[74]

Despite his apparent realisation that Carr's actions are not assisting him in his release, as this letter progresses Thomas shows that he simply cannot believe in his friend's having betrayed him. He writes of court business and preferments for their friends: of deals in which he was engaged before his arrest. He continues to issue instructions to Carr, in the same manner he must have done throughout their time working together on the king's dispatches at court, and he continues to imagine scenarios for his release. At the end of 'Letter X', he considers again how he might parry the king's continuing attempt to send him abroad, using the excuse of his 'spleen' to avoid foreign air.[75] There are no conclud-ing calls here upon Carr's feelings; the calls are upon his sense of justice. They have worked closely together, and the Scottish lord owes his friend a debt for all he has given up on his behalf, and all he has done for him. Rather than calling upon legal process against this royal punishment, a course not open to him, Thomas can only call upon the contract implied in friendship.

As the summer progresses, Thomas's illness worsens, and 'Letter XII' opens with an account of his condition, the heat of his body and his water 'strangely high'.[76] The tenor of his communications is changing and he gives the impression, finally, of distrust. Closing by warning Carr that 'this is my last request to you, which if you deny me you will tempt me far', he seems to be moving from his previous mode of instruction to indistinct threat. In his growing illness and an unease 'that after so many promises' Carr might 'deal indirectly with me', Thomas also shows his fear, pleading that 'by God if you leave me here a week longer, I think I shall never see you more'. He was to die, unreleased, within three weeks.

The Final Communication

In the final few days before his death, Thomas wrote a last letter to Carr, and through the examination of this we return to all of the three key issues the first section of this book has raised: social mobility, homo-social friendship and the king's prerogative power. Wotton recorded in April Thomas's pride in his social status: that his position was 'in the

---

[74] Letter 39, p. 131.
[75] Letter 61, p. 151.
[76] Letter 63, p. 156.

second degree of power in the Court'.[77] But this position was clearly a precarious one. The role of secretary to a powerful man was in an uneasy balance with that of friend, and Thomas established both a notably close friendship and effective court power. The loss of both, ultimately, lay in the power held by James. The king's personal power allowed him to arrest a man at will; to imprison him through personal jealousy; and to keep him in the Tower without recourse to law. This led not only to Thomas's loss of status, and the end of his friendship with Carr, but also to his death.

Lidcote has clearly seen Carr, and sends Thomas advice that his 'unreverent style should make an alienation betwixt [himself and Carr] hereafter'.[78] Despite this, Thomas begins his last letter to Carr by declaring that he plans to change nothing in his usual tone: 'This paper comes under seals; & therefore shalbe bold to speak to you as I usde to do myself.' One might admire a man who, despite all the restraint he is now under, sticks to an open and honest declaration of his feelings. But it is clearly not politically effective, and he makes his survival a threat to his former friend, perhaps suggesting the truth of the accusations of insolence and political misjudgement levelled at him earlier. Carr's betrayal is, for him, a gross ingratitude to one who had other potential patrons at court and who, for the Scot's sake, abandoned those sources of preferment:

> With what face could you tell him that you would be less to me, to whom you owe more than to anie soul living, both for your fortune, understanding, & reputation? One who lost his fortune with Ignatius; entered into a quarrell with Niger; sufferd five month[s] banishment;[79] & now five years months [*sic*] miserable imprisonment [. . .]

Thomas argues that he secured power for Carr at his own expense and reminds him again of his tutelage and berates him for his ingratitude: 'what he speaks & writes howerly is mine, & yet can forget him that sowed that in him, & upon whose stock he spends'. To the prisoner, not only his relinquishing of Cecil's favour, but also his dispute with Pembroke and his altercation with the queen, which led to his banishment, lay at Carr's door.

However understandable his motive for berating Carr, the justness of his argument is clearly irrelevant at this final point; his reminding of the royal favourite of all he owed to his erstwhile secretary is not a

---

[77] Letter 38, p. 129.
[78] Letter 78, p. 168.
[79] It is unclear which banishment he refers to here; it could be five months from court in 1611 after the queen's displeasure (see Chapter 2).

politically effective strategy.[80] Thomas is not employing political skills to secure his release, but indulging in the human emotion he feels at his unjust treatment by a man he considered not only his ally but his friend. In this final letter, as he has not felt the need to do in those written earlier in the summer, Thomas calls directly upon the love between them. He challenges Carr bitterly that he 'forget[s] him, betwixt whom was nine years love, & such secreates of all kinds have past'. He characterises his friend damningly as 'the author of all'; by this stage he certainly blames 'the most odious man alive'.

Thomas's sense of betrayal is evident in his ongoing accusations. Friendship necessitated obligation, and in the placing of ambition above such obligations Thomas accuses Carr of having put aside common humanity: 'how litle (never name love) human affection: how litle compassion' he has shown in putting Frances Howard, 'that woman', above his friend of so long standing. His giving preference to the relationship with the woman Thomas has previously named 'the catopard' is merely the first in an excoriating list of accusations hurled at his correspondent in this final letter:[81]

> I heard how, notwithstanding my misery, you visited your woman; frizled your head, never more curiously; took care for hangings; & dayly were solicitous about your cloathes; officious in waighting; could prefer your cosen, and Gibb; held daily traffickes of letters with my enemies, without anie turning it to my good; sent mee 19 projects, & promises for my libertie; then, at the beginning of the next week, sent me some frivolous account of the miscarriage of them, & so slip out of town [. . .]

Carr's vanity, his craven ambition and his lack of honour are combined in Thomas's circumstantial vilification. It is highly unlikely that the man originally appointed to the position of server as 'a pretty yong fellow', and whose career at court had by this point lasted several years, ignored the requirement for appropriate appearance; the point here is not the fact of Carr's 'frizl[ing his] head' or being 'solicitous about [his]

---

[80] As Schneider comments in *The Culture of Epistolarity* (p. 77), 'The secretary had access to all sorts of sensitive and valuable information, hence the threat existed that he might betray such information; yet the secretary had to be trusted with information in order for the various organizational and administrative systems to function properly.' This has been Thomas's position in relation to Carr's state business, but his account, in his final letter to Carr, of writing all their secrets down, and sending it under seal to friends, with the plan 'to read it to them, & take copies of it', is political suicide.

[81] Letter 62, p. 155. Clearly a term of abuse, equating to something like 'wild cat'; cat was regularly used metaphorically to refer to a prostitute (*OED* usage 2b). 'Catopard' appears to be a unique usage in the period (there is no record in the *OED*) and it probably comes from Thomas's familiarity with languages; in Spanish or Italian 'gatopardo'/'gattopardo' is a leopard.

cloathes', but rather that he prioritised such things over the freeing of a friend to whom he owed obligation. As Thomas's letter exposes the daily preoccupations of courtiership, it also reveals the moral vacuum which he feels now lies beneath.

Thomas blames Carr directly for actions which have destroyed his career and happiness. His friend has

> stayde me here when I would have bin gone, & send for me twice that day that I was caught in the trappe, & long intending in your thought long ago, a marriage with that woman, denyde sending me to enquire of her, would speak ill of her yourself, & having bin now 2 months reconcilde to a league, not to have first, upon those hopes of theirs, made sure my libertie and return [. . .]

This is interesting evidence of Carr's involvement in 'the trap'. It appears Thomas was either about to accept the embassy or to leave the court when he was requested to stay by his friend. Peyton's testimony at the trial suggests that the argument between the two men at Whitehall, shortly before the arrest, ended with Thomas declaring his intention to part from the favourite, so it is possible that his plan to 'have been gone' was simply that. Dudley Digges, however, was to testify that he had a conversation with Thomas where the latter had said he would accept the proposed embassy.[82] Towards the end of this tirade Thomas's lament for their lost friendship acquires real pathos. He demonstrates the ability to produce *enargeia* with a style that, we have seen throughout these opening chapters, can be rhetorically highly effective:

> & now at last, when we may easily live the rest of our life in peace, & enjoy the remembrance of troubles, now you to leave me out, & take an occasion upon unrespective language, to say you will never be to me as you have bin.

In this final declaration of sorrow, he shows his genuine emotional involvement. He is not merely lamenting the loss of position and pecuniary reward, but his loss of their relationship. Contrary to the traditionally Petrarchan language of letters and to the terms Thomas used to other important correspondents, little about Thomas's style in the extant prison letters suggests love. Ironically, in this final letter, having been incensed that Carr has hinted he should change his writing style, and

---

[82] Digges' testimony went on to say that Carr had caused Thomas to agree to refuse the embassy, on the proviso that the Viscount would secure the king's agreement. Clearly, this suggests Carr's complicity in the setting of the 'trap'. See McElwee, *The Murder of Sir Thomas Overbury*, pp. 66–7, on Peyton's overhearing of the Whitehall conversation, and pp. 70–1, on Dudley Digges' evidence. The respective points in Howell's *State Trials* record are p. 919 (Peyton's testimony at Weston's trial), p. 920 (Digges' at Weston's trial) and p. 982 (Digges' at Carr's trial).

returning to this accusation cohesively again, showing how it rankled, he does just that; his sorrow at the loss of their previous relationship reveals the depth of feeling in this courtier that so many considered insolent.

At the height of his powers, Overbury ironically finds the limits of his social aspiration and his power at court in the face of the king's personal opposition. As Francis Bacon makes clear in the later murder trial where Thomas's closest friend is accused of the murder of the socially aspirant courtier, it is unusual for a man to be made a close prisoner in the Tower, for many months, 'on a contempt'.[83] Thomas's letters to Carr argue that his punishment has been longer than is usual for such an offence, and he instructs Carr to upbraid the king on the sentencing he has imposed with no legal trial: 'Say, Sir, twere well you thought of that having restrained a subjects liberty, of his quality, thus long and close, to which contempts never use to have above a week.'[84] The king's prerogative power, the implacable opposition of the Howard faction at court, and the personal betrayal of a man with whom he had worked and lived closely for nine years, all lay behind Thomas's death. It is the failure of this friendship and the opposition of a monarch that lead us to Thomas's final resting place at the end of this third chapter, as he is interred, with great hurry and little ceremony, in the church of St Peter ad Vincula in the Tower.

Appendix 3: Letters, 1613

Letter 34

24 February 1613: Overbury to Dudley Carleton[85]

Sir,

The business of this letter is to thanck you for yours. As for news, this place yiylds none because all things here hang in suspense but nothing is

[83] Bacon contradicts the views, for instance, of Fenton (Letter 53, p. 145), that Carr knew nothing about the arrest. He is keen to blame Carr too, and to make him appear more of a duplicitous and guilty man. But his comment about Thomas staying in the Tower for that long, 'but for a contempt' (p. 977), shows James's use of his prerogative powers. The king is at least complicit, even if he is driven by his love for Carr.
[84] See Letter 51, p. 140. A note in 1615 from Edward Coke, preparing the material for the trial of those accused of Thomas's murder, shows the continuing tension between the common law and the royal prerogative, as Coke decides 'on the advisability of proceeding in Sir Thos. Overbury's case by the ordinary course of justice, as was done in Queen Elizabeth's time, and not troubling His Majesty in it'. See *Calendar of State Papers, Domestic*, p. 307.
[85] The letter is transcribed from NA SP 14/72/67. (A version also exists in *Calendar of State Papers, Domestic*, p. 171.)

done [. . .] Your friends here present, Sir Henry Neville and Sir Robert Killigrew, salute and I command my love to you [. . .]

Your assured friend,
Thomas Overbury

Letter 35

16 April 1613: William Trumbull to Overbury[86]

Honourable Sir,

This bearer, servant to Mr. Quester, brought me your worships letter dated the 4th of this month upon the 9th of the same. And according to my Lordships commaundment, and your directions I would by the same means have returned you a pertinent answer at this present. But the party whom that business doth principally concern, being now absent at the Garrison, or some other place, whither he is gonne to discover the actions and practices of his countrymen, I must entreat you to make my humble excuses to his Lordship and to desire that I may have some 8 or 10 days respitt to make the dispatch of those papers which are required by his Lordship; which (by God's help) shalbe done with all [illegible] expedition.

Your advice concerning the nourishing of factions and divisions among the Irish, doth agree with my designement: and I will assure you that there is already such a fyre of diffidence, and disservice, kindled between the naturall Irish, and the transplanted English, as there wanteth but a small occasion to sett them together by the eares. If there be a little oyle of his majesty's liberalitie caste with that fyre, I suppose it shall hardly be quenched, although (as you shall find in my letters to his majesty) the fryers fearing a breach of this Regiment are in deliberation to exact an oath for the ending of their private quarrells; and counting of their affections to preserve the said Regiment. My next shall more amply upon this subject. In the mean while, I send you herewithall the publicacion of the Duke of Anschots (?) intended Porte-sale, which (as it is now resolved)

---

[86] The letter is transcribed from NA SP 77/10/286. The letter illustrates how involved Thomas had become with the receiving of the kind of intelligence and diplomatic news he had, in 1609, been writing to Cecil. Another letter from Trumbull (cf. Letters 25 and 27), this one shows Thomas's involvement in apparent plotting to 'nourish [. . .] factions and divisions among the Irish', as well as the usual discussion of potential continental acquisitions for Carr.

shall hold at Brussels the 15th of the next month new style. If you in your wisdom do find it convenient and fitt for my Lordship's view, I beseech you lett it be handed unto him, and in case his Lordship shall lyke of any thing mentioned therein, precure me order and instruction what to do, and it shall with all readyness be putt in practise with my best skill, and endeavour. I hope by this tyme that God Almighty for the good of our country shall restore my Lord to his former health, which I do wish and pray for as much as myne own. And so I take my leave from Brussels the 16 of April 1613.

Your assured poor friend to be commanded,
William Trumbull

Letter 36

April 1613: Sir Henry Neville to Ralph Winwood[87]

Before I give you account of anything else, I must not forget to thank you for the kindness it pleased you to do me of late, which together with many other shall be treasured up in a grateful memory. I made Sir Thomas Overbury acquainted with that which you wrote in your last letters to me concerning Sir Thomas Lake:[88] whose [Overbury's] answer from Roiston I send you herewith. But I have replied, that this is not enough, unless the King check him roundly and openly for it, and that my Lord [Rochester?] may signify anew his Majesty's pleasure unto his ministers abroad. For Lake's purpose is to engage the King as much as he may, and intrude himself as far as he can into the execution of the place, that his friends may pretend that he hath the more wrong done him, if he be excluded in the end; which language they begin to hold already.

For the point in the end of this letter concerning himself and me, this is the meaning of it. There hath been much poison cast out of late unto the King both against him and me, but more especially against him, and with more danger, because I doubt he hath given some advantage to take hold of; being, as you know, violent and open. And the tail of this

---

[87] The letter is printed in *Buccleuch Whitehall I*, p. 131. It must be dated before 21 April as there is no mention of Overbury's arrest; he is, implicitly, still in Royston with the court at the time of writing.

[88] Clearly Neville feels Thomas will help solve the problem of Lake's rising influence at this point. Is this linked to the problem Winwood first raised with Thomas directly the previous October, of Lake taking on activities of Secretary without having the position? See Letter 29, p. 90.

storm fell a little upon my Lord himself. How it hath cleared up since the King's going to Roiston I know not otherwise than by Overburie's letters, who in this letter writes coldly as you see of you, and in a later concerning myself saith he is not in despair: which is a far different style from that he was wont to use.[89]

Assuredly, if I miscarry, it is for his sake, and by his unadvised courses, having not only refused to take any help in the work, under pretence of not sharing obligations, but irritated and provoked almost all men of place and power by his extreme neglect of them, and needless contestation with them, upon every occasion.[90] Yet I have prevailed so much, as I have made a full reconciliation between my Lord and my Lord of Pembroke:[91] who hath showed himself a noble, wise, and worthy gentleman, not only in clearing himself from all the imputations our side had laid upon him without any just ground, but in remitting [the] injuries done him upon that false surmise, unto the public, [and] promising to join henceforth closely with my lord in all things he shall undertake for religion and the State.

I write you the rather of this, because I would wish you not to neglect him, out of any mistaking of his worth, but rather to bestow a letter upon him, which I will deliver with mine own hands. Within these two days both he and other of the Lords will be in town, by whom I shall understand somewhat more, how things are like to go, and then I will write again. In the mean time, with my best wishes unto yourself and my Lady and yours, I take my leave.

P.S. I send you a letter I received yesternight late from Roiston.

Letter 37

22 April 1613: Mr Packer to Ralph Winwood, from London[92]

Since I wrote to my Lady, there is fallen out an Accident whereof I thought fit to advertise your Lordship. Yesterday about Six of the

---

[89] This letter must be just before his imprisonment. Perhaps Thomas is in the midst of the conflict with the king over the foreign posting he is refusing to accept, and knows he is in difficulty?

[90] Neville's irritation with Thomas is voluble here. He selects his refusal to work with others, and his lack of tact with them, as key factors in their current difficulties.

[91] Cf. Letter 31 (p. 92) from Naunton above. This is another *rapprochement*, this time engineered by Neville. The earlier one Thomas brought about had apparently failed.

[92] The letter is printed in *Memorials of Affairs of State in the Reigns of Q. Elizabeth and*

Clock my Lord Chancellor and my Lord of Pembroke were imployed by the King to speak with Sir Thomas Overbury, and to make him an Offer of an Ambassage into the Low Countries or France, which he would. Whereunto he made Answer, that he was not capable of such Imployment for want of Language, nor able to undergoe it by reason of his Weakness, being so exceedingly troubled with the Spleen that if he had a long Letter to write he was feign to give over; therefore he should not be fit to attend any Busyness, as in accepting this Offer he must be forced to do:[93] And whereas it was alleadged that his Majesty intended this for his Good and Preferment, he would not leave his Country for any Preferment in the World. Some say he added some other Speech which was very ill taken, but what it should be I cannot yet learn. But not to trouble your Lordship with Length, this Report being made to the King, he sent my Lord of Pembroke for the Lords who were in Councill, (my Lord Chancellor staying with his Majesty,) to whom he declared when they were come, that he could not obtaine so much of a Gentleman and one of his Servants, as to accept an honorable Imployment from him. In Conclusion he gave them Order to send for him, and to send him to the Tower, where he is close Prisoner. I leave all Circumstances and Preambles to your Lordship. Now for my Lord of Rochester, who had but newly begun to leave his Chamber, he knew nothing till all was done and he gone, which your Lordship may imagine did much perplex him. But that Evening my Lord of Pembroke and Sir Henry Nevill were with him, and so were againe this Morning; who have given him so good Advice, that if he follows it, as I hope he will, all will be well with him, and no hurt to his Friend. Thus in haste I have but only given your Lordship a Taste of this Busyness, which your Lordship shall hear more particularly by Report of others [. . .]

K. James, Collected (chiefly) from the Original Papers of the Right Honourable Sir Ralph Winwood, Kt. (London: W.B. for T. Ward, 1725), pp. 447–8.

[93] Packer, who is secretary to Rochester by this time, is in a position to know what Thomas said, and his words, though a week before, are almost identical to those of Chamberlain to Carleton, 29 April (see Letter 39, p. 131).

Letter 38

22 April 1613: Henry Wotton to Edmund Bacon[94]

Sir,

The last week, by reason of my being in Kent, was a week of silence; and this I think will appear unto you a week of wonder.

The Court was full of discourse and expectation that the King, being now disencumbered of the care of his daughter, would towards this Feast of St. George fill up either all, or some at least of those places that had lain vacant so long, and had been in this time of their emptiness a subject of notorious opposition between our great Viscount and the house of Suffolk.[95] Thus, I say, ran the opinion; when yesterday, about six of the clock at evening, Sir Thomas Overbury was from the council chamber conveyed by a clerk of the Council and two of the guard to the Tower, and there by warrant consigned to the lieutenant as close prisoner; which both by the suddenness, like a stroke of thunder, and more by the quality and relation of the person, breeding in the beholders (whereof by chance I was one) very much amazement, and being likely in some proportion to breed the like in the hearers, I will adventure, for the satisfying of your thoughts about it, to set down the forerunning and leading causes of this accident, as far as in so short a time I have been able to wade in so deep a water. It is conceived that the King hath a good while been much distasted with the said gentleman, even in his own nature, for too stiff a carriage of his fortune;[96] besides that scandalous offence of the Queen at Greenwich, which was never but a palliated cure. Upon which considerations, his Majesty resolving to sever him from my Lord of Rochester, and to do it not disgracefully or violently, but in some honourable fashion, he commanded not long since the Archbishop, by way of familiar discourse, to propound unto him the ambassage of France, or of the Archdukes' Court; whereof the one was shortly to be changed, and the other at the present vacant. In which proposition it seemeth, though shadowed under the Archbishop's goodwill, that the King was also contented some little light should be given him or his Majesty's inclination unto it, grounded upon his merit. At this the fish did not bite; whereupon the King took a rounder way, commanding my Lord Chancellor and the Earl of Pembrock to

---

[94] The letter is printed in *The Life and Letters of Sir Henry Wotton*, Vol. II, pp. 19–21.
[95] Carr and the Howards are still seen by Wotton as opposing factions at this point.
[96] This comment on Thomas's 'nature' seems to show the 'insolence' mentioned repeatedly at the trial; perhaps it was something commonly agreed before his arrest, though Wotton clearly doesn't like him.

propound jointly the same unto him (which the Archbishop had before moved) as immediately from the King; and to sweeten it the more, he had (as I hear) an offer made him of assurance, before his going, of the place of Treasurer of the Chamber, which he expecteth after the death of the Lord Stanhop; whom belike the King would have drawn to some reasonable composition. Notwithstanding all which motives and impulsives, Sir Thomas Overbury refused to be sent abroad, with such terms as were by the Council interpreted pregnant of contempt in a case where the King had opened his will; which refusal of his I should, for my part, esteem an eternal disgrace to our occupation, if withal I did not consider how hard it is to pull one from the bosom of a favourite.[97] Thus you can see the point upon which one hath been committed, standing in the second degree of power in the Court, and conceiving (as himself told me but two hours before) never better than at that present of his own fortunes and ends. Now in this whole matter there is one main and principal doubt, which doth travail all understandings; that is, whether this were done without the participation of my Lord of Rochester? A point necessarily enfolding two different consequences; for if it were done without his knowledge, we must expect of himself either a decadence or a ruin; if not, we must then expect a reparation by some other great public satisfaction, whereof the world may take as much notice. These clouds a few days will clear; in the meanwhile I dare pronounce of Sir Thomas Overbury, that he shall return no more to this stage, unless Courts be governed every year by a new philosophy; for our old principles will not bear it.

I have showed my Lord and Lady sister your letter of the 18th of April, who return unto you their affectionate remembrances, and I many thanks for it. The King hath altered his journey to Thetford, and determineth to entertain himself till the progress nearer London. The Queen beginneth her journey upon Saturday [24 April] towards Bathe. Neither the Marquess di Villa (who cometh from Savoy) nor Don Pedro di Sarmiento (who shall reside here in the room of the present Spanish ambassador) are yet either arrived, or near our coast, though both on the way. So as I can yet but cast toward you a longing, and in truth an envious look, from this place of such servility in the getting, and such uncertainty in the holding of fortunes, where methinks we are all overclouded with that sleep of Jacob, when he saw some ascending, and

---

[97] Wotton draws a direct contrast between himself, and those like him who serve the king abroad, and Thomas. The difference is 'the bosom of a favourite', explicitly showing the sense of Thomas's courtiership as different, and disapproving of his refusal to conform. Wotton is, in 1613, still suffering from the king's punishment.

some descending, but that those were angels, and these are men; for in both, what is it but a dream? And so, Sir, wishing this paper in your hands, to whom I dare communicate the freest of my thoughts, I commit you to God's continual love and blessings,

Your faithful poor friend and servant,
HENRY WOTTON

I pray, Sir, let me in some corner of every letter tell my sweet niece that I love her extremely, as God judge me.

Letter 39

29 April 1613: John Chamberlain to Dudley Carleton[98]

[The letter mentions that both Arbella Stuart and her aunt remain close prisoners in the Tower too, and then he comes to the arrest of Overbury.]

I doubt not but you have heard of Sir Thomas Overburies committing to the Towre the last weeke. The King hath long had a desire to remove him from about the Lord of Rochester, as thincking yt a dishonor to him that the world shold have an opinion that Rochester ruled him and Overburie ruled Rochester wheras he wold make yt appeare that neither Overburie nor Rochester had such a stroke with him, but that he wold do what he thought fit and what he intended without acquainting either of them with his purposes and so caused the Lord Chauncellor and the earle of Pembroke to deale with Overberie and to tell him the Kings goode meaning towards him, wherby he had an intent to make use of his goode parts, and to traine him for his further service and therefore they offered him his choice to be employed either by the archduke, or into Fraunce or into Moscovie, (upon which place we have now new projects).[99] He excused himself as incapable of such places for divers wants and specially of language. They aunswered that he was young enough and with little labour might attain that in short-time, or otherwise he might be assisted and supplied by sufficient secretaries and other fit persons about him: he then alledged indisposition of body and want of health as beeing much subject to the spleen, wherto they replied that

[98] The letter is printed in *The Letters of John Chamberlain*, Vol. I, pp. 443–4.
[99] Chamberlain seems to be the first to mention Moscow. The other accounts simply talk of an embassy to France or the Low Countries.

chaunge of ayre might be a speciall remedy for such infirmities, but he stoode stiffly upon yt that he was not willing to forsake his countrie, and at last gave them a peremptorie aunswer that he could not yeeld to go, and that he hoped that the King neither in law nor justice could compell him to leave his countrie, with which aunswer the King was so incensed, that he willed the counsaile to consider what yt deserved who upon this contempt caused him to be sent to the Towre.[100] Some take this as a diminution of my Lord of Rochesters credit and favor, but the King told the counsaile the next day that he wold not have yt so construed, for that he had, and still did take more delight in his companie and conversation than in any mans living. The Lord of Rochesters ague continues with him still, so that he could not go yesterday with the King to Tiballs [Theobalds] who tarried a day for him. About Easter the Lord of Rochester shewed a noble part and example, for seeing the world at a dead lift and at theyre witts end for monie, he sent for some of the officers of the receyt, and geving them a key of a chest bid them take what they found there for the Kings use, which was 22000 in gold.

[. . .]

There was a divorce sued this terme twixt the earle of Essex and his Lady, and he was content (whether true or fained) to confesse insufficiencie in himself, but there happened an accident of late that hath altered the case: his Lady sought out and had many conferences with a wise woman, who (according to the course of such creatures) drew much monie from her and at last cousened her of a jewell of great value, for which beeing prosecuted and clapt in prison, she accuses the Lady of divers straunge questions and propositions, and in conclusion that she dealt with her to make away her Lord, (as ayming at another marke) upon which scandal and slaunder the Lord Chamberlain and other her frends thincke yt not fit to proceede in the divorce.[101]

[. . .]

Sir Henry Neville hath ben much employed in them and hath had much conference with the counsaile by the Kings commuandment, wherein they say he hath shewed himself a very redy and sufficient gentlemen. He is now in a fayre way and his frends looke dayly when he shalbe sworne Secretarie but I am still of opinion and have ben so ever since Christmas

---

[100] Thomas seems to have made a challenge here based in law: the king's prerogative has him imprisoned for contempt despite his call upon 'law' and 'justice'.

[101] Clearly Chamberlain doesn't make the link between Thomas's arrest and the divorce of Frances Howard, though he may or may not know the 'another marke' that he alludes to as being her aim is Robert Carr.

that he must tarie till the Lady Elizabeth be past the Low Countries and then our good frend there shall come to part stakes with him. I may be deceived, but yf that anchor fayle I will never make reckoning more of court holy bread nor court holy water but I am very confident yt will come so to passe, or els better and greater men then I are out of theyre account and besides theyre biais, and ye peradventure I know as much reason for yt as they that are neerer the helme. [. . .]

Letter 40

29 April 1613: Henry Wotton to Edmund Bacon, from London[102]

[. . .] Sir Thomas Overbury is still in the Tower, and the King hath since his imprisonment been twice here, and twice departed, without any alteration in that matter, or in other greater.

[. . .]

My Lord of Rochester, partly by some relapse into his late infirmity, and partly (as it is interpreted) through the grief of his mind, is also this second time not gone with the King. Some argue upon it, that dissiduity in a favourite is a degree of declination; but of this there is no appearance, only I have set it down to show you the hasty logic of courtiers.[103] [. . .]

Letter 41

Undated, but c. April 1613: Overbury to Rochester, from the Tower[104]

Letter II

Look well to your seals and mine, and mark them well. My letter yesterday was seald with soft wax ill favordly & seals; this is sealed with hard wax and my little seal.

---

[102] The letter is printed in *The Life and Letters of Sir Henry Wotton*, Vol. II, pp. 21–2.

[103] Again, we see Wotton's avoidance of writing anything culpable as he debates Carr's position in the letter.

[104] The letter is transcribed from BL MS Harley 7002, fol. 281. It is undated but it is clearly one of Thomas's first letters from the Tower, as it is full of instructions about sending letters, so I'm concluding it must have been sent at the end of April (or, at the latest, in very early May), but probably before the arrest of Robert Killigrew on 5 May.

Never write but upon some hope comming, then darkly and shortly. Call Neville hereafter Similis and because he is like Hen 8; call the king Julius. Remember those two changes; call Pembroke Niger.[105]

You must bid Giles warn my man not to be seen with this fellow, for that would make him suspected strayt.[106] Therefore call them next in some corner and not say a word, but write not till you have wonn some good point with passion. If you had the letter yesterday att 3 o'clock seald with soft wax, then sure all is safe. Lett my man bid him gett a wax candle that he may light as for his work and then give it me in a piece lighter to seal my letters, but let him not be seen with my man.

Letter 42

Undated, but c. end of April 1613: Overbury to Rochester, from the Tower[107]

Letter III

This after the receipt of your last. First for that of Robert Killegrew, send it as sonn as you can by this fellow, but very secretly for me to have in store.[108] But for to morrow, it shall be enough for me to shew my leggs wonderfull little, which I will impute since this though they were so afore. And then by my message by Pembroke and then will I use this vomitt tow days after, which will be a new occasion for you to be importunat to send me into the country to save my life, for tis not the close ayre but the apprehension of the place that hurts me, which you must stand uppon. I have now sent by the lieftennant to desire you (Mayerns being absent) to send young Crag hether and Nessmith; if Nessmith be away send I pray Crag and Allen, tow such as when they go back may

---

[105] The introduction here of the code names for key court players suggests this has not been a common factor of their previous communication.

[106] Giles Rawlins was Thomas's cousin as well as Carr's servant (see Howell, *State Trials*, p. 922).

[107] The letter is transcribed from BL MS Harley 7002, fol. 281. It is, like Letter II, undated, but there needs to have been a sufficient time between this and Letter II for Carr to reply and discuss Killigrew and his vomit. In Giles Rawlins' evidence to Coke (NA SP 14/81/32) he talks of taking the vomit from Killigrew to Thomas from Carr 'about x days after Sir Thomas Overbury was committed to the Tower', so this letter must be before that. Wotton's letter of 14 May (Letter 46, p. 137) discusses Nicholas Overbury's petitioning of the king for a physician on 13 May; though this letter instructs Carr to send doctors, it is likely that Carr doesn't do that immediately.

[108] The reference to 'that of Robert Killegrew' is to the vomit procured by him.

go in to the king and relate how much my body is wasted with though[t] of the kings displeasure and this place.[109] And that is all for I will take no phisicke of them, and uppon this reason, that till my mind be easd no phisicke can cure my body. And so having shewed them this I will desire them to com to you then you to carry them into the king, then for you to send them into the king by Pat. Mald: or so.[110] Then presently after go you in your self.

Letter 43

2 May 1613: Thomas, Viscount Fenton, to John, Earl of Mar[111]

I praye you to pardone me that I did not wret particularlye to your Lordshipe efter the commitment of Overberrye, but I desired my Lord Chanslaire to show your Lordshipe his letter. There is not onye thing more done in that matter since the first tyme. This I will and maye assure your Lordshipe, that it is fakt of his Majesties owin, and soe weill and judiciouslye caried that if it bein governed be onye uther I think it shuld never have done soe weill. I think he shall never be more a courteoure, and I think if the law will goe soe farr, never a man to staye in the cuntrye soe long as his Majestie leives. I have sume reasones that are not slycht ones to perswade me to this opinion.[112] [. . .] There is not appeirance of making onye Secreterrye in haiste, and I think there shalbe a Tresaurar first made; the steat heir hes great neid of bothe.

---

[109] The names are of several esteemed court doctors. Theodore Mayerne was the king's chief physician. John Craig, doctor, was nephew to old Crag (presumably!), who was Scottish and another of the king's physicians. John Nasmyth was another Scottish surgeon.

[110] It is unclear who 'Pat. Mald:' is, but I suggest it may be Patrick Maule, a Scottish courtier and close to the king.

[111] The letter is printed in *Report on the Manuscripts of the Earl of Mar and Kellie, preserved at Alloa House, N. B.* (London: His Majesty's Stationery Office, 1904), p. 50.

[112] Fenton does not, though, share those reasons in his letter. He seems very sure that Thomas's courtly career is over, and perhaps also his time in England. Interestingly, he notes that this possible expulsion is only possible 'if the law will goe soe farr'; he is not quite certain of James's prerogative power, it seems.

Letter 44

6 May 1613: John Chamberlain to Ralph Winwood[113]

[. . .] Neither can you choose but be perfect in the true cause of Sir Thomas Overberies committing to the Towre, which was a contemptuous aunswer and refusing of forrain employments offered him in the Kings name, and specially that he insisted that the King could not in law or justice force him to forsake his countrie. But some say he was most urged to that of Moscovie, which drave him to that peremptorie and unmannerly aunswer [. . .][114]

[He continues to speak disparagingly of the whole Muscovy project – which he calls 'discourses in the ayre' and does not feel will come to anything, despite Henry Neville's involvement.]

[. . .] Some say my Lord of Rochester tooke Sir Thomas Overberies committing to hart, others talke as though yt were a great diminution of his favor and credit, which the King doubting wold not have yt so construed, but the next day told the counsaile, that he meant him dayly more grace and favor as shold be seen in short time, and that he tooke more delight and contentment in his companie and conversation then in any man living.

[. . .] As I was now closing this letter I understand that Sir Robert Killigrew was yesterday committed to the Fleet from the counsaile table, for having some litle speach with Sir Thomas Overberie who called to him as he passed by his window, as he came from visiting Sir Walter Raleigh.

Letter 45

7 May 1613: Henry Wotton to Edmund Bacon[115]

Sir,

Your friend, Sir Robert Killegrew, hath been committed to the Fleet, for conferring with a close prisoner in a strange language; which were (as I hear) the two circumstances that did aggravate his error.

---

[113] The letter is printed in *The Letters of John Chamberlain*, Vol. I, p. 448 and p. 451.
[114] Chamberlain's comment on Moscow as the possible ambassadorship is unusual. Most name France and the Low Countries, and Thomas's claim to have little language for those seems unlikely; for Moscow, the excuse makes sense.
[115] The letter is printed in *The Life and Letters of Sir Henry Wotton*, Vol. II, p. 22.

Of his case whose love drew him to it, I can yet make no judgement;[116] the humour seemeth to be sharp, and there is wisdom enough in those that have the handling of the patient to manage the matter, so that at length his banishment from the Court may be granted as a point of grace. The nature of his alteration was (as you rightly judge it) in the first access somewhat apoplectical, but yet mingled in my opinion with divers properties of a lethargy; whereof we shall discourse more particularly when we meet; which I now long for, besides other respects, that we may lay aside these metaphors.[117] [. . .]

Letter 46

14 May 1613: Henry Wotton to Edmund Bacon[118]

Sir,

Your kinsman and friend, Sir Robert Killegrew, was in the Fleet from Wednesday of last week till the Sunday following, and no longer; which I reckon but an ephemeral fit, in respect of his infirmity who was the cause of it; which to my judgement doth every day appear more and more hectical.[119] Yesterday his father petitioned the King (as he came from the chapel) that his son might have a physician and a servant allowed him, as being much damaged in his health by close imprisonment; which for my part I believe, for the diseases of fortune have a kind of transfusion into the body, and strong working spirits, wanting their usual objects, revert upon themselves, because the nature of the mind being ever in motion must either do or suffer.

I take pleasure (speaking to a philosopher) to reduce (as near as I can) the irregularities of Court to constant principles. Now to return to the matter, the King hath granted the physician, but denied the servant;

---

[116] The close relationship between Thomas and Killigrew is clear here.

[117] Wotton here appears to suggest language, even in private letters, is open to infiltration and has to be coded. The letter continues with an anecdote about Sir Peter Buck, whose rather innocuous letter to a friend about activity at court led to his imprisonment and to his trial at the Star Chamber. Wotton quips that 'I set down these accidents barely, as you see, without their causes [. . .] but my lodging is so near the Star Chamber that my pens shake in my hand' (*The Life and Letters of Sir Henry Wotton*, Vol. II, p. 23). See my article on this letter and the deceptive nature of epistolarity: 'My lodging is so near the Star Chamber'.

[118] The letter is printed in *The Life and Letters of Sir Henry Wotton*, Vol. II, p. 23.

[119] That is, chronic. Wotton suggests, using medical metaphors, that Thomas's incarceration is likely to be a long one.

by which you may guess at the issue. For when graces are managed so narrowly by a King, otherwise of so gracious a nature, it doth in my opinion very clearly demonstrate the asperity of the offence. Sir Gervis Elvis (before one of the pensioners) is now sworn lieutenant of the Tower, by the mediation of the house of Suffolk, notwithstanding that my Lord of Rochester was the commender of Sir John Keyes to that charge; which the said Keyes had for a good while (and this maketh the case the more strange) always supplied even by patent, in the absence of Sir William Wade. Upon which circumstances (though they seem to bend another way) the logicians of the Court do make this conclusion, that his Majesty, satisfying the Suffolcians with petty things, intendeth to repair the Viscount Rochester in the main and gross. And therefore all men contemplate Sir Henry Nevil for the future secretary, some saying that it is but deferred till the return of the Queen, that she may be allowed a hand in his introduction, which likewise will quiet the voices on the other side; though surely that point be little necessary, for yet did I never in the country, and much less in the Court, see anything done of this kind that was not afterwards approved by those that had most opposed it [. . .]

Letter 47

Undated, but May 1613: Robert Killigrew to Rochester[120]

Letter IIII

My honorable lord, I have here sent you inclosed the vomitt you desired of me, but I would not concell your Lordship to take it unless the phisitians do aloe of it att this time, for though this be as good as any can be, then yet there is no such medicin good for all persons att all times, of which they are the best judges. But if your Lordship be resolved to take it, this bearer can give direction for the manner.

your honors devoted servant
Robert Killigrew

[120] The letter is transcribed from BL MS Harley 7002, fol. 281. Presumably it was written very soon after Letter III from Thomas, and before Killigrew's imprisonment on 5 May.

Letter 48

Undated, but May 1613: Overbury to Rochester, from the Tower[121]

Letter V

I seal this with my own seal; mark it well. I pray you seal with the stags head therafter, and send me my little seal again. By no means hear of my going out at all, beyond sea. Though for an hour but to Berry, not by commaund, but stolne thether by discretion.[122] Send me that vomitt inclosed, if I stay here four days longer. Lett this fellow be warnd to beware and gett to serve som body within [that] place, though but for a fortnight. For that letter under my own hand concerning you, putt all upon that; still stand uppon that. But urge nothing till that be done for this must be done, only by way of prayer and kindness. After justify when I am gone, though you have a grant, yet accept not delay for disputes. If this come safe writt me but word.

Letter 49

Undated, but May 1613: Overbury to Rochester, from the Tower[123]

Letter VI

I toke that vomitt to day but it worked only with me downwards. But one thing I am glad of, for so I have left it intire for you to use uppon occasion.

---

[121] The letter is transcribed from BL MS Harley 7002, fol. 281. It is undated, but is perhaps close in time to Letters III and IIII, as it also concerns a vomit. However, it could be a later one.

[122] It is unclear where Berry is; perhaps Bury St Edmunds. Cf. also Letter 61, p. 151, where it seems to have been a place Neville has been at with the king.

[123] The letter is transcribed from BL MS Harley 7002, fol. 281. Again, this is undated, but it must follow shortly on from Letter V as it concerns the outcome of vomit he has asked for.

Letter 50

Undated, but May 1613: Overbury to Rochester, from the Tower[124]

Letter VII

I sent to day a message to Dominick and had only a fayre answeare in generalities.[125] Look therefor you touch nothing but effects and urge dispaches, for my life lies upon it. And if this way fayle, I pray you answeare me directly to this: whether you will not use To. for a fortnight rather than leave me thus? I know that will carry it directly. If you deny me that, I am satisfied. Another request that you would convey that wonderfull tale to me under unknown names by Mayerne or the Apotecary now he is sick is a fitt time to urge a commiseration of my sickness, for I was never worse and if you leave me here, I shall never see you more. And that I fear my ennemies understand well enough, and hope so to com by my office. But do not you be accessory to my death, though you could not conceave my body should have overtired thus much; the tow lords should mitigate my fault, and say I was surprisd.

Letter 51

Undated, but May 1613: Overbury to Rochester, from the Tower[126]

Letter VIII

Now for Hansuffs new instructions;[127] first you must tell him, that you are so farr from speaking of this, as that you must make him swear, and so he Wolsee, that no man shall know this but only he and Wollsee, not Wollseys wife nor any child. Neither will you have any of your friends know it, but only me, but especially not Julius, because he must in apparance, after the offices be settled, be the author of this reconcilment, and must know nothing of this privatly done betwixt you three and me when

---

[124] The letter is transcribed from BL MS Harley 7002, fol. 282. Again, it is undated, but the numbering of the letters appears to be consecutive and as Letter VIII seems to be before 21 May, then this must also be written in May.

[125] Dominic(k) is the code name for Northampton.

[126] The letter is transcribed from BL MS Harley 7002, fols. 282–4. It is undated, but it refers to Thomas having been a close prisoner a month on Thursday, which implies it was written just before 21 May.

[127] It is unclear who, in their code, Hansuff is, but he is mentioned twice in this letter; the second time he is mentioned in conjunction with Pembroke's brother. This original mention suggests he has a connection with the Earl of Suffolk, code-named Wolsey in this letter.

I know it, and therefore Wolsey must take care, not to tell his wife, nor no soul living. Now for the first obligation betwixt you which is my delivery, say you have prepared it so that if Wolse[y] do but what you will propose, he and I together shall carry him out strayt, and that is that Wolse[y] must com to Julius on morning att Greenwich, and tell him that the Lieftennant *huius loci* is come to him and tell him Overbury is every night so sick as he is ready to dye, and that these tow or three nights, he hath sett one to wach him, in another rome, without his knowledge, who though[t] still he would not live an howre; and that he being of an haughty nature, and ashamed of this disgrace conceals it, and will not so much as confess a word of this to the phisitians.[128] Now for his part he is afrayd he will dye in his house except he be dismisd, and that uppon the suddaine ere any know, for to our knowlegde his keeper knows not of this. Hereuppon may Wolsee say, Sir, I hearing this, though[t] myself bound in honesty to tell to you, first for since if he dye in the night it might cost my Lord of Rochester his life to[o], who you see how passionattly he loves him; next Sir for my own part I speak, for the world thinking me his enimye would lay his blood to my charge, which I would not have imputed to me for all the world. Now Sir take no notice I pray you of what I inform, but what you do, do suddainly before it be too late, and lett my Lord of Rochester know nothing, but that you do it for his sake, never taking notice that I have sayd any thing; and, indeed, considering his offence being only a harsh answeare, a month of such close imprisonment is punishement enough. Hear is a plot exquisitely layd, Julius understanding no correspondence betwixt Wolsey and you. But now here is the caution of it; for, your enimies insulting, be sure they never hoped for such a day of publike glory, howsoever my friends conceal it from you.[129] You writt me nothing whether you have yet forbid Dominic, as he looks for any freindship from you, not to mingle his little business with these present, or else that he and you will be strangers, which I know he will not have a publick demonstration of and for him tis no matter; only traffick with Wolsey. You writt me nothing what security you have for the second with Similis, that is neglected; for if it be his man, except you have some foreknowlegde of it, they will count it no act of yours. Be ridd of these you keep and gett

[128] Thomas constructs a very detailed plot for Carr and Suffolk to enact here, giving them lines and talking of himself in the third person. See the discussion of the dramatic nature of this letter on pp. 116–20.

[129] In this rather confused passage, the transcriber makes an interpolation, 'Bullion Deputy of Ireland all Ambassadors hear of it'. It is unclear who 'Bullion' refers to. Thomas seems to have moved into direct address again, and the enemies are Carr's set up antithetically here against Thomas's friends.

me restored, and if ever you and I engage either for faction or publicke, never trust me! Lett everything go as it will, but if you now piddle with writting letters, and fitt these turns, wayt, go to church, be necessary about him till I be restord, then you betray me, for that is all he aims att.[130] But when he sees you make use of every opportunity to no other end, but to ridd me out of this place, and that for other business you will meddle with none, he will dispach me. Therefore look now to your fashion, for he observes well whether time work any thing, and you see how well he quiets you still with kind generalities; but in particular give you nothing in effect as the other day he told you to cure your sicknes, that if you would do but this, you should obtain you[r] ends sooner than you expect; uppon that presently you made an infamy recovered, gott abrod what done notwithstanding, so just a pretence for him as my sickness, he would not grant that of which never man for such an offence as mine, was restrained of, nay, such an offence as he himself sought; for he knew afore they came I would not go such a jorney.[131] Nay which is more, presently after would not beleve you about my sickness, nay in your last conference began to slyd back, and talk to you of showing his favor to you otherwise, so by that means, to call the poynt itself in question, which before you took for granted, and with speed by reason of his words, sooner than you lookd for. Do but mark this proceeding, and thereuppon leave of[f] your confidence, and suspect all but effects of that you have not had yet on, nay he hath not told you yett, that [if] I would reform I should retorne to court. Mark how you are handled. Today I hear nothing of having the liberty of this place, and the fellow is now to be put away and indeed I would be glad he were gone for our security, for now if you cannot gett present access for my frend, and uppon my sickness to[o], I never look for it.[132] [On] Thursday is a moneth close prisoner; sure the reason he keeps me close so long is to lay all wayes uppon you along, whether he can work your consent to a seperation, for after the dores are open, then he thinks we will mingle thoughts again, and after that he will not hope for it. Therefore now is the time he will try you all ways, uppon you alone, therefore leese [lose] no hours to declare your resolution, that God forsake you for sake me for any hope or fear, and lett it be an example to him that you can forsake him, and tell if ever you rest, eat or sleep quietly, till you have me restord, and this

---

[130] He appears to refer to James here.

[131] Here he refers to the embassy, proposed by Pembroke and Ellesmere after Overbury had already refused the Archbishop.

[132] Perhaps Thomas refers to access for Sir John Lidcote here, as he visits around this time. It is unclear why his brother-in-law manages to see him where Nicholas Overbury cannot.

boyish shame taken of you, and then show him your resolution for me. I shall be reformd according to his instructions never to transgress, which he cannot but accept. If that will not, you will quit all business, so take away the subject of this vexation, or if both these fayle it will have a worse end. You desire Hansuff or Nigers brothers liberty, or rather to shutt yourself up in a park and dye for this; you will never sure live thus, & when he sees sure he will chuse the first, and presently tend toward it: for loving me better than him, what he touchd [on] you must never lett such a thing slid by unansweard, for that you so you are a naturall man; where your most love is, there your most company is, and he can never say that any thing that this world had drew him one howre from you, nor ever was with me but when by reason of his business or other company you could not be with him;[133] and you fear the satiety of your company hath brought him to this little soundness of you. Indeed Niger, Southampton, Chandos, and Similis were company to[o] mean. Look upon their companions: More, Butler. And there was no gentleman, that applid himself to you but were of the best quallity and houses of England, as Jermin, Barkley, Radclife, Mansell, Killigrew, Udall, Lidcott: the best houses of England.[134] You are no old man, yet nor can delight in old company continually. That day Similis is made, be sure you never so much as take notice of it or look cheerfully; tell you can receave no honour till first you be freed from disgrace; tis the manner of benefitts pleaseth, not the matter, but you, for preferring a good servant, to lease [lose] a freind was an ill recompense. Beside for the thing itself, if it be well done now, it had been better done som ten months ago; the delay hath spoyled the world, and the ending of it worst, to take away on[e] that hath deserved as well as ever he can deserve. Even so, without any rejoicing, speak. There ingage Similis presently alone as the company is gone about me: perchance this man will send Unctius to deal about me.[135] If he do, never answear him, nor any else, but say you use not to

---

[133] This line is often misinterpreted as Thomas arguing that Carr loved him (see White, *The Cast of Ravens*, p. 64), but is actually another line for Carr to deliver to James; he is to persuade James that his love is for the king, and that he only went to Thomas when James wasn't available.

[134] The list of men associated with Thomas and Carr is discussed by Alastair Bellany in *The Politics of Court Scandal*, pp. 42–3. Sir Thomas Jermyn; Sir Robert Berkeley (who was bound to Thomas at Middle Temple in 1601) or one of the family from Berkeley Castle: perhaps Sir Henry Berkeley, as Bellany suggests); Sir John Radcliffe (whom Thomas was supporting as governor of Brill; see Letter 31, p. 92); Sir Robert Mansell; Sir Robert Killigrew; Sir William Uvedale (an alternative spelling for Udall), 'son of Elizabeth I's treasurer of the chamber, who eventually inherited his father's office at Carr's gift' (Aylmer, *The King's Servants*, p. 83); and Sir John Lidcote, Overbury's brother-in-law.

[135] Unctius is the name for Abbot, the Archbishop of Canterbury.

speak to your master by mediatours; you will speak with him himself. If you cannot do somthing presently, you must take that To: again and not recover till I am out, and be so dangerously sick that you much desire to speak with me before you dye. Tell him that is your last request to him, and so you must continuew till you have gott me out, and gott Patt. Mald. and Mont: to be there to be with him still.[136] This do rather than lett me live here a [in] this fashion, and my mind overthrow my body for ever. Do somwhat like an honest man and a freind, though you never do more. Gett me from hence, for the opinion of this deed. Alas, you bid me have a good hart; you must know that the best harts can ever worst bear shame, and victory; and for my part I wonder to hear that you [are] abroad, and are seen in the world, I liyng here. For God refuse me if I be not so ashamd of staying here so long that now I never dare open the windows to look out.[137] And for the offence he speaks, bid him beware, gravely beware; lest when all comes to all it prove my words imported no contempt.[138] Say, Sir, twere well you thought of that having restrained a subjects liberty, of his quality, thus long and close, to which contempts never use to have above a week.[139]

Letter 52

May 1613: Sir John Lidcote to Overbury[140]

Sir

For me to acquaint Sir Robert Killegrew with this busines were preposterous, for I know no man my Lord more mislikes, and that it should

[136] Perhaps Sir Patrick Maule and the Earl of Montgomery (for 'Patt. Mald.', cf. Letter 42, p. 134).
[137] This is mentioned in Giles Rawlins' testimony (NA SP 14/82/35) where he comments that, after 'a fortnight before his death', when Thomas had been hopeful of release (the time of Suffolk's letter (Letter 72, p. 164) and his optimistic letter to Lawrence Davies (Letter 73, p. 164)), 'he could never see him at the window, albeit he often attempted'. At this earlier stage, Thomas seems to be hiding from shame; but later it seems to have had a more sinister interpretation.
[138] The implicit threat in 'bid him beware' shows Thomas's continuing anger and resentment, and perhaps gives evidence of what others call his insolence.
[139] Thomas is conscious of the inequity of James's punishment; for a contempt such as his, a week would be more appropriate for imprisonment. This is the third mention in this letter of the inappropriate length of his incarceration. Thomas has already been in the Tower for a month, and will, by the time he dies there, have been a close prisoner for five months. See p. 124 for further discussion of the king's decision.
[140] This letter is transcribed from NA SP 14/72/257.

be concealed from him he desyres nothing more: wherefore for him to speak in it would but more enrage him, & do you no good, but harm. One told me this day from Sir Humphrey Maye his mouth that my Lord Chamberlain is not so foolish to think that you will deny to yeald to any-thing for your Liberty but, when all is done, it will [be] pretended that that [*sic*] the Kings wrath will keep you there; and in the mean tyme you are cosened on all hands. To avoyd that which I fear most of anything in the world, pray consent to me in this one thing: that Laurence may be sent out of the way.[141] For nothing cann hurt us but must be urged from him, which to prevent, he may send you up woord by Weston that he fynds your impatience soe great as all his pains cannot satisfy and that he is not able to endure the toyle you put him to, whereat you may seem so offended as you may put it to his choice and I will send him where he shall be safe (under another name) from all suspition. By this meanes shall we be free from theyre last trick, and whilst you are th[e]re Harry may do you any service you stand in need of.[142] I pray consider well of this for I think it very materiall. Study by all meanes your getting out speedily for by God never any man was so cosened as you are. But yett I would advise you not to see it, nor take notice of it, but to chaunge your stile if you write to my Lord of Rochester and cozzen him another while, for there is no honest quarter to be held with him. As you love me, burn this, and forbear wryting all you cann for it was never so dangerous.

Lett this cour[s]e for Laurence be soddanly resolved uppon which must proceed ~~from~~ out of some angry message from you.

Letter 53

20 May 1613: Thomas, Viscount Fenton, to John, Earl of Mar, 'at nycht'[143]

[. . .] I perceive be one word in your last letter that you are halfe a witche in the matter of Overberryes, for althoe my Lord of Rotchester was noe thing aquented with his Majesties purpos in that, but sume uthers quhom it did pleis his Majestie to make uss of there service, yet he is soe wyss and thinks himselfe soe mutche oblished to his Majesties favore that there is noe tye nor bownd shuld howld him quher his Majestie hes

---

[141] Referring to Lawrence Davies, who had been Thomas's servant for eight or nine years.
[142] Referring to Henry Peyton (or Payton), who was also Thomas's servant.
[143] The letter is printed in *Mar and Kellie*, p. 51.

his interest; and this matter is meerlye from his Majestie himselfe and upone soe good groonds that I think I maye assure you that he wilbe noe more a curteoure in haist, and for onye thing that I can heir not out of prisone, soe that we let him stike their and it maters not how long. It maye be your Lordshipe will heir that there is lyke to be great factions, and that all theis that Overberrye drew to him and about my Lord of Rotchester are lyke to make a pairtye to the Howards, quitche I think theye wold doe if thaye culd sturr Rotchester to it, but he wilbe wiser. Southehamptoun and Pembrouke are joined in that side, and thaye stand mutche to have Nevell Secreterrye. Thaye have vith them sume of the moste discontented nobill men of the younger sort, and all the Parlement mutineers; yet I think all will not worke to there end. I think his Majestie will let the world see that yet for a tyme Rotchester can make his Majesties dispatchis vithout the helpe of Overberrye. For the uther office, I think it shall lycht quher you will not be sorye; he best deserves it, and soe thinks his Majestie. This same daye was there in the Commissione Court, before the Artchebeshope, a nulletye of the mariage betuyxt my Lord of Essex and his ladye, for he did confes in presence of the Chamberlaine, Worsister, and Knowles, that he culd doe noe thing to hir; but since the matter hes bein intendit it is thocht that Southehamptoun and Pembrooke hes made him goe bake againe, but the matter is in prorsus quhat is done this daye. Quhitche is the first I doe not yet know, but it is thocht for certaine that it wilbe a nulletye. [. . .] The lieutennent is chainged, and Sir Gervas Elves hes the plaice that was squyer to the bodye.[144] [. . .]

Letter 54

27 May 1613: Henry Wotton to Edmund Bacon, from St. Martin by the Fields[145]

[. . .] Sir Thomas Overbury is still where he was, and as he was, without any alteration, the Viscount Rochester yet no way sinking in the point of favour; which are two strange consistents[146] [. . .]

---

[144] Made Lieutenant of the Tower in May 1613 by the interference of Northampton and Rochester, Gervase Elwes was, in the ensuing trials, one of the men accused of enabling Thomas's murder.

[145] The letter is printed in *The Life and Letters of Sir Henry Wotton*, Vol. II, p. 28.

[146] This seems to be a hint to Edmund Bacon that, although Wotton can't write it openly, there's more to this situation. It perhaps suggests his understanding of Carr's complicity in what has happened to Thomas.

Sir R. Drury runneth at the ring, corbeteth his horse before the King's window, haunteth my Lord of Rochester's chamber, even when he is not there, and in secret divideth his observances between him and the house of Suffolk: and all this (they say) to be ambassador at Bruxels. So, as *super tota material*, I see appetites are not all of a kind; some go to the Tower for the avoiding of that which another doth languish to obtain[147] [...]

Letter 55

Undated, but c. June/July 1613: Overbury to Rochester, from the Tower[148]

Letter IX

You must give order presently and send back for wine, gelly and a tart to be brought to me to morrow by James; and then for the jelly and the wine will I never have it up to my chamber att all, but have it convayed from James to the lieftennants wife, which is the best way. So too for a cold pasty of venison, I will send it to the lieftennants, but that cannot be done to morrow. He that brings me this letter brings no tart, which is ill lost, for to morrow I would have the wine and gelly delivered. Therfore you must send a footman away all night; the conveyance in is better by my man than Giles, for Giles is more suspected.[149] Instruct Similis if he can to fall in talk about me at Windsour, both for never speaking an undertaking word but modestly and discretly, and so for not sending messages to him from hence, leese [lose] not to morrow for sending.

I pray you lett me know to morrow afore dinner whether that in the scurvey greasy bottle were legible and whether I shall send an unctious

---

[147] That is, the embassy to the Low Countries, which he suggests here was offered to Thomas.
[148] The letter is transcribed from BL MS Harley 7002, fol. 284. It is undated, but suggests that the king is in Windsor at this point. Nichols's *The Progresses, Processions, and Magnificent Festivities, of King James the First*, Vol. II, p. 670 suggests that the king's journey was to begin on 16 July, but, as he was ill at Theobalds (p. 671), he didn't actually set off from there until the end of July. It is unlikely, though, that this letter dates from July if the numbering sequence is chronological. Letters coming after that marked Letter IX are clearly in June. Nichols has no mention of the king being out of London in June.
[149] Giles Rawlins.

message to th[e] Dominic by the lieftennant, which I think would do well.

Letter 56

3? June 1613: Henry Wotton to Edmund Bacon, from London[150]

[. . .] Sir Robert Mansfeld is still in restraint. Sir Thomas Overbury not only out of liberty (as he was) but almost now out of discourse [. . .]

Letter 57

Undated, but c. June 1613: Robert Carr to Overbury[151]

I have considered that my answer to you, and what I have otherwise to say, will exceed the bounds of a letter, & so having not much time to use betwixt my waiting on the King & the removes we do make in this our little progress, I thought fit to use the same man to you, whom I have heretofore many times employed in the same business. He has besides an account of a better description of me to give you to make a repetition of the former carriages of all this business, that you may distinguish that which he did by knowledge of mine & direction, & betwixt that he did out of his own Discretion without my warrant.[152] With all this he has to renew to you a former desire of mine, which was the ground-work of this, & the chief errand of his coming to you, wherein I desire your answer by him. I would not employ this gentleman to you, if he were, as you conceit of him, your unfriend, or an ill instrument betwixt us. I owe him the testimony of one, that has spoken so honestly, & given more praises of you than any man, that has spoken to me.

---

[150] The letter is printed in *The Life and Letters of Sir Henry Wotton*, Vol. II, p. 29.
[151] The letter is transcribed from BL Add. MS 4106, fol. 91. It is undated but marked 'about June'.
[152] There has, it seems, been some communication between them, via this servant, which has upset Overbury and needs explanation. The servant clearly has a separate verbal message to deliver alongside this written one, and must 'renew to you a former desire of mine' (unspecified presumably due to Carr's distrust of epistolary form). Cf. Schneider, *The Culture of Epistolarity*, p. 65: 'orality and writing worked as mutually verifying constructs: the sanction of the handwritten lines identified and authorized the bearer to speak, while the bearer's oral report lent confidentiality and immediacy to the letter.'

My life at this time makes me to and fro more than I expected: but the subject of my next sending shall be to answer that part you give me in your Love with a return of the same from

Your assured loving Friend,
R. Somerset

Endorsed
Lord Somerset's first
Letter[153]

Letter 58

Undated, but c. June 1613: Thomas, Viscount Fenton, to John, Earl of Mar[154]

I culd not omitted this occasione to let your Lordshipe know of the receate of your letters of the 9 of June from Allowye. To satisfie a lytill that point of your letter quherin your Lordshipe desires and wishes that we maye leive in paice and quyetnes heir for that will make you the quieter their, our present steat is at this tyme in tuo factions, the Howards one to quhom his Majestie inclines the moste, the uther Southe[hamptoun] and Pem[brooke] with sume of the Lower Houss men that heirtofore hes bein drawin to follow my Lord of Ro[tchester] by the maines of Overberrye. But you must understand that in my opinione Rotchester is soe wysse that quhotsumever show he makes he wilbe noe wayes but quher the King hes his interst, nather doe I see but that he is abill to forget Overberrye before he offend the King. Yet let me saye soe mutche to your Lordshipe, that it is thocht be the wisest that he hes bein soe long in sattilling him selfe to one of the pairteis that now he can not doe it without sume perrell to him selfe, quhitche I protest to God I shuld think muselfe if thaye had a lytill of our Scots humore, but you know heir thaye doe not mell but under boord all their playe is.[155] Essexx is

---

[153] This implies there were more letters from Carr to Thomas in Bacon's evidence. It is clearly not Carr's first letter to the Tower, but must have been the first Bacon found extant.

[154] The letter is printed in *Mar and Kellie*, p. 52.

[155] 'Mell' in *OED* means either (v.1) to discuss or talk or (v.2) to mix or have dealings (i.e. work together?). The former, in the sense of speaking out publicly? Or Fenton seems to be accusing English lords of working secretly and independently, unlike typical Scottish collaboration. 'Under boord' is the opposite to 'above board', hence secretly, deceptively; *OED* gives a 1603 example: Sir Christopher Heydon, *A defence of judiciall*

lyke to prove himselfe not woorthye of sutche a bedfellow as he hes had this tyme past imagend. To be short, that mariage wilbe made null, and the nyxt nevelles that your Lordshipe shall heir she wilbe married to our [*indecipherable*] and great courteoure.[156] There is mutche dealling from Spaine, France and Savoie for to have the Prince in mariage, but I think he shall licht in France, if my intelligence be trew.

Letter 59

10 June 1613: John Chamberlain to Ralph Winwood[157]

[. . .] At my return I found litle alteration here, saving that our frends affayres go rather backward then forward, one reason wherof (among many others) is that those businesses beeing parted among divers that were wont to have recourse only to one, every body is loth to leave his hold, or the advantage of valuing himself in the Kings favor, and having accesse to his eare.[158] Sir Thomas Overberie lies still by yt and for ought I heare is like to do [. . .] The divorce twixt the Earle and his Lady is on foote, and hath ben argued twise or thrise at Lambeth before certain commissioners, but *a huis clos*. The greatest difficultie is that though he be willing to confesse his insufficiencie towards her, yet he wold have libertie to marrie with any other, as beeing *maleficatus* only *ad illam*. Yet some lawiers are of the opinion that yf she will take her oath that he is impotent towards her, yt will serve the turne, wherof yt is thought she will make no bones, as presuming that she is provided of a second, which I shold never have suspected, but that I know he was with her three howres together within these two dayes, which makes me somwhat to stagger and to thincke that great folkes to compasse theyre owne ends have neither respect to frends nor followers[159] [. . .]

astrologie, ii. 67 – 'After the fashion of iugglers, to occupie the minde of the spectatour, while in the meane time he plaies vnder board'.

[156] Clearly Fenton knows about Frances Howard's relationship with Robert Carr. This is later in date than Chamberlain's comment to Carleton on 29 April about 'another mark' (Letter 39, p. 131), which uses a metaphor not a name. Fenton does not name Carr either, but he needs to be less circumspect.

[157] This is printed in *The Letters of John Chamberlain*, Vol. I, p. 458.

[158] This is undoubtedly a reference to the secretaryship, with which Winwood is closely involved; everyone who had some role to play in the current system was reluctant to see a Lord Secretary appointed, lest he lose his own little part of power. They were 'wont to have recourse only to one', i.e. Robert Cecil, before his death.

[159] This echoes his letter of 29 April (Letter 39, p. 131) about 'another mark'. He is still

Letter 60

24 June 1613: Thomas Lorkin to Thomas Puckering, from London[160]

[. . .] For the treasurership, the general voice confers it upon Northampton, as it did that of the secretaryship upon Sir Harry Neville; though, for this latter, I suppose his hopes quite dashed; for merely depending upon my Lord Rochester, he wants not opposition; and then, besides, Overbury being fallen into disgrace, he is thereby deprived of his best instrument. [. . .]

Letter 61

Undated, but c. late June 1613: Overbury to Rochester, from the Tower[161]

Letter X

Take heed you bee not cosend in the relation of this busines, for he that Julius hath appointed to warn the lieftennant and relate to him what is found, may say the lieftennant sayth this and that which he never spake; therfore the day Julius coms to this town, lett one be sent afore to the lieftennant to warn him to come to Julius as to speak about my Lady Arbella, and and [*sic*] there lett him ask of himself directly, whether there were any such paper afore, whether any since; so you go to the root, else the instrument of conveyance, may overthrow all your design, but this way you deceave him quite. I tell you what makes me think the lieftennant never said any such thing but they faine it uppon him; yesterday he and I talking of news, I told him how ignorant of all things I was since I cam in, he sayd nay you have receaved wine and tarts. I took it presently uppon the lift, and a testament lying on the table, I swore uppon it that none of all those things ever conveyed an[y] thing to me but themselves and he took up the book strayt again, and swore he never suspected that they did, and the same he swore to me

not mentioning Carr by name, but he clearly knows his identity and there is gossip about the affair. His first mention of a name is in a letter to Carleton on 23 June: 'The world speaks liberally that my Lord of Rochester and she be in love one with another' (*The Letters of John Chamberlain*, Vol. I, p. 461).
[160] The letter is printed in Birch, *The Court and Times of James I*, Vol. I, p. 248.
[161] The letter is transcribed from BL MS Harley 7002, fols. 284–6. It is undated but Thomas refers to Mansell's release and suggests he's been imprisoned now two months, both of which put the letter at the end of June.

again this morning, taking it unkindly that I would suspect his suspition. Therefore the man is belide, and Julius abusd by the instrument.
Now therefore look to it. This was on Tewsday night for the fellow
here [gap in text] being so far ingaged [gap in text] greedy villen, as
your [gap in text] he now and then seems dainty, is [gap in text] or a
promise from you [gap in text] under you. About what [gap in text]
and I will entertayne his [gap in text] him faithfull enough, but I [gap
in text] have spoken that they should [gap in text] but for that there is
but tow [gap in text] sure my landlord is sett on to be jealous, which
is no hard work att this time, for yester night again he wonderd at my
being here thus long: Mansell out and returnd again to court, whose
cause and manner and time of imprisonment, was much different from
mine, and he had the same enimies I have, and no such frend.[162] Then
he told me how much cause you had to venture, not only your fortune
but even your life for me, for 'twas well known all this malice came
uppon me, not for any fortune, or titles that I had, but for making a
stranger so great an actor in this state. Besides he knew that out of my
truth to you I had refusd tow thousan[d] pounds from Ignatius, and
entred into a quarrell against Niger.[163] I told him I wondred too, and I
knew twas without example such an imprisonment uppon a contempt;
and for a man to show first an utter inabillitye, and after that, and in
that respect to profess an unwillingnes, I thought it was a contempt
without example. Now I perceave by that you sayd of the lawspeakers
that you been made beleve that mine was a fault, and, if it were not
for you, much would be done. Sir, be not deceved, as my accusations
were all false afore, so is my fault no fault (what sayd the Duke about
going over?) nor had it been the uttermost contempt, is this kind of
imprisonment due to it? I sayd I would not [gap in text] that I must
maintayne [gap in text] for to gain that word [gap in text] them first of
thought, [gap in text] then the lawyer sayd [gap in text] not leave my
country which [gap in text] to be granted and Niger [gap in text] I be
not deceaved they [gap in text] Mansell out so to my [gap in text] compassion on both to the world [gap in text] what will you say if Julius,
as he told you att first, that you would not have me send him post to
Berry or Oxford strayt, so now he say, that you would not have me take

---

[162] Sir Robert Mansell was a naval officer and by 1613 was a courtier working for Carr.
He was arraigned on 12 June, so this letter comes after his release two weeks later.
Thomas's comparison of his case with Mansell's is part of his ongoing argument that his
incarceration has been too long.
[163] Ignatius is the code name for Robert Cecil. This comment on refusing money from
Cecil is repeated in his final letter to Carr (Letter 78, p. 168).

him out any degree; and so with form putt you of[f] again.[164] Am not I
then in a good state, the progress comming on, by trusting uppon you?
Or have not you done well, the people dissolving within four days, to
have those in your hands, that if this trick hit not, you are undone, for I
warrant few in England but think tis your plot and vanity to keep them
in your hands, though the state be ruind by it? O have you not hus-
banded this tow months well, both for mee and Similis? In what degree
we were both the first hour there we are still, and I fear that course
of quick dispach which I praescribed must be your refuge now when
all is done; for I hope you will neither suffer me here longer nor keep
those longer in your hands, whatever course you take: you so cosend
as to think Julius keeps me here in respect of my fault, or in respect of
Similis' business, for he knew att Berry I was as farr from that, as here
thus close; but the matter was libells had told him you governed him,
and I know not what, and Agrippina told him he durst do nothing
to displease you.[165] Now he to lett them see this tis not so but that
he could discipline you when he pleased, he hath continued this with
making objections and telling of informations, and so won time uppon
you by hearing answears and the like. I should be glad to hear Will
Udalls business of hydes went on, for his sake no less than mine own.[166]
For the reversion after Fulk[e] Greville for Jack Lyttcotts boy, you may
keep any other from having it, till a fitt time to passe it for him. For
Badgers stewardship, I would he had it. For Shirlies do somwhat; 'tis a
fine suit. This year hath been lost both for office and park. Make that
sure at the end of it. Upon you now my fortunes depend too; if I had
brought it to Nigers brother, or Hansuff, they had pas[se]d it sooner,
and I would have made my part £5000 for in all tis twelve. Niger can
cause Agrippina make Unctius cease, from being any more of the plot
with them, and shame him for what is past. Her nature is, if it be well
followed, now others would oppress me, to be as much for me, as afore
she was against me.[167] Do you and Similis set Niger uppon this, so there

---

[164] As in Letter 48 (p. 139), Berry may be Bury St Edmunds. It is referred to again later
in this letter, and it is clearly a place visited by the king and Neville too. Bury is not far
from Royston and Newmarket, so likely to be connected to the king's hunting visits.

[165] Thomas knows well that the king has been affected by the gossip Chamberlain relays
in Letter 39 (p. 131), and that the queen (Agrippina) has stirred him to take his revenge
on the rival for Carr's affections. See pp. 63–4.

[166] Thomas is keen to maintain his influence on patronage. Probably the William Uvedale
mentioned here is the man bound to him at Middle Temple in 1601 (cf. mention of
Udall in Letter 51, p. 140). The reversion of Treasurership of the Chamber, bought for
Overbury in 1613, passed to Uvedale on Thomas's death, so clearly he was part of his
and Carr's group of close associates.

[167] Despite her earlier opposition, Thomas feels the queen will support him now that he
is opposed by others.

is tow taken of[f], Unctius and Dominic, and then on[e] push will rid
me hence. If he have a design, or rather a wish, I think, then a hope to
have me go over, for 2 or 3 moneths, which I think he will not have,
the answeare to that is, that nothing helps the spleen so much as our
native ayre, and forraine, though better, hurts it.[168] Therefore of late
Mr. Burgess, the famous preecher, having the spleen though otherwise
of a strong body, was fayne to leave his charge att the Hag[u]e, only
to come to London, his native ayre, for the ease of his sickness; and I,
whiles I was abroad, was never well an hour, how[ev]er, as Mayerne
knows, which made mee return so soon.[169] This late example of Mr.
Burgess generally known, will prevent that motion, and best if it be
us[e]d by way of discourse before hand. Mr. Burges[s], the silenced
preacher, had att the Hag[u]e a great stipend and was fain for the
spleen to come to his native ayre, and leese [lose] all, being forbidded
to preach here. Mark that, will Julius mark by this particular? If all
the tricks and tales they put upon me were for my sake or to reflect his
anger toward me upon Similis business, which is a good observation,
for they made as if they were only angry at me, without any meaning to
hinder the k[ing's] intent. I am of opinion that villen Andrew gave them
notice of your sending tarts, and for your cosen (if you did not send for
him up for knowing my absence) 'twere well you sent him home, for
either his charg is to no purpose, or else he very negligent of it, to live
here so long, and you know in the progress, if he have not stable bed
as he please, then his murmering goes by your notion to Julius, and so
lights on mee, before God, and he have their offices in possession.[170]

---

[168] According to *OED* (meaning 1b), the spleen is the seat of melancholy or morose
feelings.
[169] This could be a reference to his travels in 1609, though it is unclear if he has been out
of England since. This has been suggested as the outcome of one of his arguments with
the queen, but there is no evidence of a later visit. His unwillingness to travel is perhaps
medical, as he suggested to the king's representatives when offered the embassy in April
1613; he certainly objects vehemently to going to France (see Letter 62, p. 155).
[170] An Andrew Hargason (?), groom of Carr's chamber, is mentioned in Giles Rawlins'
testimony to Coke (see NA SP 14/82/33).

Letter 62

Undated, but c. early July 1613: Overbury to Rochester, from the Tower[171]

Letter XI

You might do well to writt to the Catopard to night to will her make her father sure, which, except he think it will be a beginning of a perpetuall friendship with you, twill not be. You might do well to writt to Northampton tonight, as sorrowing both for his sickness and allso for his absence on Sunday; but desire him to show his love in making others sure though himself be away. Twere well, either tonight or to morrow, to make Julius not only passive, but to tell you what he will do aforhand. Be sure to be present yourself; that will do much. And for the Archbishop and Wolsey, not to trust to any mediation, but to speak to them your self. For my sicknes of consumption and *flatus hypocondriacus*, Mayerne may be cald upon his oath; if they doubt, your presence, when 'tis moved, will do much both with Julius himself, and the rest will not break promise afore you. Urge to the king, Ramsey and Mansell, that somthing may be done for your sake, to me as to others.[172] I pray you let the king know the intent of my letter, both before and now, which was to desire his pardon; that my hart was farr from offending him; for my words, they were spoken as being surprisd on the sudden, and spoken in regard of my sicknes, not of his command. So, by foretelling the effect of my letter, prevent that objection, that I sought not the king's favour, when you know I desird to writt ten weeke ago. So for suing to the Lords, that cannot be objected; for when the Lords were here last, I being then in a fitt of my fever, I gott the lieftennant to desire my lord Northampton to move the Lords, in my behalf, for their favor and mediation to the king. But my Lord Northampton returned that he would first speak with you about [it]. I pray you remember this offer of mine, for that prevents to that objection, that I sent not to them. If you would by your Catopard, by Dominic, or any way, make sure [of] Wolsey; all were gained in him only. A message from me to Wollsey would have done good, for otherwise he will fear that when I come abroad, however you stand now, I will divert you; but for that you must give him assurance for me to be his.[173]

---

[171] The letter is transcribed from BL MS Harley 7002, fol. 286. It is undated, but he notes that he would have liked to have written to the king to explain everything ten weeks ago, which may be when he was imprisoned; if so this letter dates from just into July.

[172] David Ramsay, or just possibly his brother, James, if the latter wasn't out of the country working for the Danes at this point.

[173] Thomas's letter to Suffolk is Letter 71 (p. 162). It is undated and it is possible that he

The Dominic being sick, if he deal betwixt you, will hurt it much, but when you see him speak with Wolse[y] yourself, and that is best of all. From France keep me, I pray you, though I take phisicke all the progress att my chamber.

Letter 63

Undated, but c. July 1613: Overbury to Rochester, from the Tower[174]

Letter XII

This morning (notwithstanding my fasting all yesterday) I find a great heat continue in all my body and the sam desire of drink and loathing of meat, and my water is strangly high, which I keep till Mayerns com. This distemper of heat contrary to my constitution makes me fear some fever at the last, and such an one, meeting with so weak a body, will quickly, I doubt, end it; and in troth I never liked myself worse, for I can indure no cloaths on, and do nothing but drink. This is the story. Now my request to you is, and it may be my last, is that you would gett me leave to go to my own chamber to night, and after nine o'clock. I may go thether in the lieftennants coach unseen and unknown. Not possible to gett me hence to night because of that business to morrow, then pressing tonight vehemently will make him condesend for to morrow night, and besides will keep the other from fayling to morrow; and to morrow night, however I am thought I dye for it, I will if I may go out of this place, if I cannot tonight. But if he deny you tonight, and to morrow night to[o], then this is my last request to you, which if you deny me you will tempt me far; that after mousing it to morrow and failing, to go to bed and to take To and not stir, though he remove, till I be out; you know the other busines being done you can have no politicke pretence to put me off. My hand is weak and I writt this much in payne. If you succeed nott in the neither of the former, if you deny me the third.

writes to him before the 20 August date Alastair Bellany proposes and which determines its position here (see *The Politics of Court Scandal*, p. 55).

[174] The letter is transcribed from BL MS Harley 7002, fol. 287. It is undated, but the growing sickness he comments on here might be that which Bull reports to Winwood on 20 July.

Letter 64

20 July 1613: Thomas Bull to Ralph Winwood[175]

[. . .]

Sir Tho. Ouverbury is still here in prison, shut up close, and very sick. For other occurrences I doubt not but your freer friends may more fully advertise you; only I have good cause to imagine your friend will not be Secretary.[176] Be reserved, therefore, in your proceedings, and attend upon such a guard as may with advantage offer however things settle, for it is thought Venus hath overthrown Mercury,[177] and will knit the two sides into one. Farewell, my dear Sigr. Ridolfo,[178] and believe my dearest love shall ever be with you, and return you the truest effects and services that can proceed from, &c

Letter 65

Undated, but c. late July 1613: Overbury to Rochester, from the Tower[179]

Letter XIII

My fever is relapsed, my water as high as ever; therfore this is the time to strike. What if you should take notice of the tale to Julius, and so cut it up by the root? Tis wonderfull to me, that after 3 moneths capitulation, he should offer to deal so with you at last; you wrot to me, that he sayd he would grant you all your suits.

---

[175] The letter is printed in *Buccleuch Whitehall I*, pp. 139–40.

[176] This is Sir Henry Neville, who appears to have been a casualty of Thomas's downfall.

[177] Venus seems to be Frances Howard, which makes Mercury Thomas. This is an interesting choice of god; see Janette Dillon, *Theatre, Court and City, 1595–1610: Drama and Social Space in London* (Cambridge: Cambridge University Press, 2000), p. 114, where she comments on the connotations of Mercury as the 'god of craft and cunning'.

[178] The use of code names seems to be common amongst those writing professional diplomatic letters, Bull even addressing Winwood as Sigr. Ridolfo (as Wotton was Sigr. Fabritio for Chamberlain; see Letter 18, p. 81).

[179] The letter is transcribed from BL MS Harley 7002, fol. 287. It is undated, but refers here to '3 months capitulation', so probably it dates from the end of July.

Letter 66

Undated, but c. late July 1613: Overbury to Rochester, from the Tower[180]

Letter XIIII

I was lett blood Wensday x [ten] a clock. To this Fryday morning my heat slackens nott, my water remains as high, my thirstines the same, the same loathing of meat, having eat not a bitt since Thursday was senight to this howre; the sam scouring and vomiting, for yesternight about eight o'clock, after Mr Mayerne was gone, I fainted and vomited: the very same dryness.

Letter 67

Undated, but c. late July 1613: Overbury to Rochester, from the Tower[181]

Letter XV

Though you may not take notice directly, yet you may say, Sir, after so many promises you will not deal indirectly with me. I should be sory to see that in your disposition. Then say, sure you will find your self pitifully abusd. So, a farr of[f], you may shame him out. What censure had Ramsey here? What censure had Parpoynt for the key?[182] O, this is strang[e]; you must arm the tow lords with thes particulars, especially those publicke partialitye[s] of Du: Mar: Ramsey:[183] if this fayle there is no way left, but immediately, upon the refusal and breach of promise, To: for a week. That is the last refuge, and your reason is honest, for my fever grows so uppon me a new that, by God, if you leave me here a week longer, I think I shall never see you more, for the fever will never leave me while I am here.

[180] The letter is transcribed from BL MS Harley 7002, fol. 288. It is undated, but talk of Thomas's worsening illness may lead to Lidcote's discussion of his will in the letter to Rochester on 26 July.

[181] The letter is transcribed from BL MS Harley 7002, fol. 288. It is undated, but the reference to Mrs Parpoint suggests a date after her release in July.

[182] This is a reference to Mrs Parpoint, and the key taken by Arbella Stuart, which is mentioned by Bull elsewhere in Letter 64. There he talks of her having twelve weeks' imprisonment, and presumably at that point she has just been released.

[183] Perhaps here he refers to the Duke of Lennox, and certainly Ramsey is the same man mentioned in Letter 62 (p. 155), but it is unclear who Mar: is.

Letter 68

26 July 1613: Sir John Lidcote to Rochester[184]

Right honorable

and my very good lord. According to your Lordships commaund I have
conveyed the notes which I receved from your Lordship. Dowbt not of
the good use will be made thereof: my brother utterly disclamed that he
ever had any mistrust in Mayerns phisick: there fore humbly prayeth
your Lordship if it be possible to remue [remove] that apprehension of
the king. That which I spake to Sir Robert Killigrew my self was rather
to shew the distemper that the violent working of the phisicke had
brought him to it than any distrust he had of it. I know your Lordship
hath h[e]ard that the worant for our going to him was presently recalled,
so that I have no more admittance to him, but this mor[n]ing it pleased
my Lord of Northampton to send for me, to let me know that he would
grant a warrant to Mr Lieftennant of the Tower to carrie in his will to
him: to see it published. The Lieftennant but yeasterday told my brothers man, Lawrence, that he wondred that his masters friends weare so
slack in finishing his will, for he said he doutted him now more than
ever he did. Yet he makes shewe to us to be more comfortabel in him
self than he was. He hath taken all your Lordships *Aurum potabele*, is
entered into an other glass & surely findeth much good of it, and eateth
broth every day. There fore we hope well of him. The greatest comfort I
can give him is the asuarance of your Lordships favor of which he hath
had so long; & so nobell triall as now he cannot doubt the continuance
there of, for which how much both himself and all his fri[e]nds stand
charged in duties to your Lordship, I cannot express; only for myne
owned particular, I humbly beseach your Lordship to stand assured:
that I will ne[i]ther have life nor any other ability that shall not really be
at your Lordships commaund.

I have receved since your Lordship went to Fernham 3 severall letters.

Your Lordships humble servant, John Lidcote

<hr />

184 The letter is transcribed from BL MS Harley 7002, fol. 288. He mentions the writing
of Thomas's will, but no record of this remains, if it were ever completed.

Letter 69

6 August 1613: Southampton to Ralph Winwood[185]

Sir,

I perceive by your last Letter that you have been of late particularly advertised of the Proceedings in England, and how the Busyness of which we desire so much to hear the Conclusion, is still in Suspence.[186] The Difficulty alledged, is the not having as then accommodated the Matter of Sir Thomas Overbury, which many times bred Disturbance, and hindred the Performance of the Resolution taken; and it is in vaine to hope for any good Issue of the other until that be settled, which I thinke to be done long ere this after this Manner; that upon his Submission he shall have leave to travail, with a private Intimation not to return until his Majestie's Pleasure be further known:[187] And much adoe there hath been to keepe him from a publique Censure of Banishment and loss of Office, such a rooted Hatred lyeth in the King's Heart towards him; and that Blocke being now removed, I find the same Confidence that I left touching Sir Henry Neville; which I shall be as glad of as any, but (as I wrote before) this often deferring hath made me doubtfull.

Of the Nullity I see you have heard as much as I can write; by which you may discern the Power of a King with Judges, for of those which are now for it, I knew some of them when I was in England were vehemently against it, as the Bishops of Ely [Lancelot Andrews] and Coventry [Richard Neyle, soon translated to Lincoln]. For the Buisness it self, I protest I shall be glad, if it may be lawfully, that it may go forward; though of late I have been fearful of the Consequence, and have had my Fears encreased by the last Letters which came to me; but howsoever, the manner of interposing gives me no cause of Contentment.

[. . .]

---

185 The letter is printed in *Winwood Memorials*, p. 475.
186 Presumably he refers to the secretaryship here.
187 It is interesting that Southampton feels Thomas will be released, with instructions to go abroad for some time. Perhaps this was the king's plan.

Letter 70

Undated, but c. August 1613: Overbury to Northampton[188]

To say I could have related any thing from your Lordship but the effects of your utmost displeseur I cannot yet, not with standing such hath been your Lordships nobleness as upon my Lord of Rochester's request to forget things past.

Your Lordship hath pleased to [have] been an earnest mediator to his Majesty for my liberty, by which intercession I understand [the] state of my liberty is much bettered, which favor received from your Lordship, considering things past, make a greater impression of gratitud in me than if I had proved it from one from whom I could [have] hoped for it.

But now, if it would please your Lordship to ad[d] again your Lordships hand to perfict this work so successfully begunn, and to be a means first for my presant liberty, and after for the recovere of his Majestys favour, I protest before the living god I will ever heare after be as faithful to you as your Lordships own hart, and when I digress from this protestation let this letter be testimonie to convince of dishonisty to all the world.

I am yet but weak, which will make the benefit of my liberty more pretious, and am not abell to writ[e] much, but so god dealle with me both for my libertie and helth as I do not this only out of necesitie of my presant state, but that I am with all desirous to receve favor from your Lordship in this business as the person of so much honour and directness as that next my Lord of Rochester I shall cast myself upon your Lordship, if your Lordship will be pleased but to accept me, and be to me as I shall deserve. So humbly taking my leave, I rest –

---

188 The letter is transcribed from BL MS Harley 7002, fol. 289.

Letter 71

Undated, but c. August 1613: Overbury (and Gervase Elwes) to Suffolk, from the Tower[189]

Right Honorable

That which your Lordship vouchsafed to do in my behalf, both on for the progress and at Salisbury, gives me this hope, though it were at the request of my Lord of Rochester: that your Lordship['s] heart is not irreconcilable towards me. But my desire [is] not to rest heare only to have your Lordship my enemy, but if all the service which I cann perform may winne your Lordships good opinnion and trust, and make me to be received as one of yours, much honor and directions have I ever seen in your Lordship; both towards freind and enemy, as I shall think it happily imploied – and with as much zeal I shall perform it as being creature of your Lordships living. And since it hath pleased your Lordship to concur so readily with my Lord of Rochester to his Majesty in my behalf, I profess, upon my faith and salutation, that it shalbe my endeavour to the uttermost of my credit to continue that freindshippe between your two Lordships firm and inviolable, that without respect to any either that is or to be, and this is the uttermost assurance that a Christian and an honest man can give. And so, humbly taking my leave, I rest.

Good my Lordship, excuse my blotting by reason of my weakness at this time.

Your Lordships to be commanded,

Thomas Overbury

The copy of Mr Lieutenants letter to me:

I humbly beseech your Lordship that my Lord Chamberlain, receaveing my letter, sent to gether with that of Sir Thomas Overbury, may understand that I write another man's wares, not my own, and that, wheare the cross is, he made me alter, as myne and not his own, least my Lord might again think his liberall profession was with reservation, for he is feared least my Lord should not be satisfied. His own direction I have allsoe sent for part his own hand to be a deed to the letter. In that which

---

[189] The letter is transcribed from BL MS Harley 7002, fol. 290. It is undated, but Bellany, *The Politics of Court Scandal*, p. 55, gives 20 August. It could follow immediately after Letter 62 (p. 155) when Thomas laments not having sent Suffolk a note. It appears in the MS copy just after Thomas's letter to Northampton dated 24 August, so looks likely to be around that date.

I delivered to your Lordship to be sent to Sir Thomas Monson his phrase falles short of that which he is now brought unto; [it] must be considered according to the difference of tyme between his resolutions.

Your Lordships etc
G: Helwise

I sealed my letter to my Lord in
his sight after he had writte[n] it
and if needbee will justify as his
act, whatsoever is therein.

Mr Lieutenant to my Lord Chamberlaine by
Overburys direction

Right honorable

I retourned to Sir Thomas Overbury the answer, which, because it was not so ample, he suspected his own straightnes. Therefore he hath thought good to enlarge himself, hoping, according to his plain and trewe heart, to receave a free and noble answer. The first effect of your Lordships favour, I hope, wilbe shewed in endeavouring his present liberty, and that as one party is dispatched for answer of your Lordships acceptance, so an other may be dispatched to sollicit his enlargement, else might the services which he intendeth must not become so profitable as he hart[i]ly wisheth; and so soon as he is free, [he] doth desire he might make this first address in some secret place, wheare your Lordship shall appoint, that he might shewe some further assurance of that which he hath hartily professed.

In [the] mean tyme [he] protesteth that these things past, which gave which gave [*sic*] your Lordship offence toward him, never proceded of any ill affection towards your Lordship, or yours, or any personal dislike, but upon ma[n]y provocations and injuries which his Lordship never knew, and such as no man but noted to be sensible. Thus remaining, etc.

Letter 72

Undated, but c. August 1613: Suffolk to Overbury[190]

My Lord Chamberlaine to Sir Thomas Overbury

Sir Thomas Overbury,

The free protestacion of your desier to give me satisfacion for former wro[n]gs hath taken so good impression in me as I shall be willing to give testimony therof, by my best assistance, for your liberty, wherin, notwithstanding, not to be mistaken, I must let you know that I dare not be a peremptory undertaker when I consider in how a degree his Majesty was offended with your contempt; so as I conceave your freedom, your freedom must be a work of some tyme.

But because you so freely offer your self to me specially, in employing your uttermost endeavours to mediate a fast freindshipp between my Lord of Rochester and myself, without respect of any [of] your new friends, so much am I affected I may call again for this your Letter written to mee with this assurance and which I now return to you as pledge and assurance of your promised good offices between my Lord of Rochester and me. By it you are engaged to do this, and for this I will be

your loving good friend,
T. Suffolk

Letter 73

Undated, but c. end of August 1613: Overbury to Lawrence Davies[191]

That letter I sent you, first shewe to my sister to comfort and to lett her see the tyme will not now be long godwilling ere we go down, for the knott is knit. But lett her only speak to her husband of it, for my Lord would not have his letter knowen.[192] Then wright out two copyss of it straite; one I will send to my Lord of Rochester; the other to my Father, to lett him see my busines is now come to certaynty and will have a short

---

[190] The letter is transcribed from BL MS Harley 7002, fol. 290. It is undated, but must follow closely after Thomas's letter to Suffolk (Letter 71, p. 162). A copy of the letter, in Lawrence Davies' hand, is NA SP 14/82/31; this is one of the copies requested by Thomas in his letter to Davies (Letter 73, p. 164).

[191] The letter is transcribed from NA SP 14/82/29, a copy of the letter made for Edward Coke during his examination of witnesses in October 1615.

[192] This must be the letter from Suffolk: Letter 72 (p. 164) here.

end. And wish him to not to speak of that letter, but desyre him to make haste back out of his circuit, for I hope to be at Borton afore him & lett my uncle William wright to my uncle that I hope to meet him without fayle at Borton at Michaelmas or sooner if he will come.[193] Lett Payton remember my duty to my mother and tell her I never longd more to see her & I hope I shall do shortly.

For my health I thank God I grow better again. That word in the letter (some tyme) is no long tyme: a week or tenne days. Tomorrow morning return me the letter again.

Letter 74

24 August 1613: Overbury to Northampton[194]

Right honnorable and my very good Lord:

I receaved an advertisement yesterday from your Lordship by Mr Lieftenant that my Lady of Essex hath been informed of some speeches of myne wherin I should wrong her in her honor. 'Tis trewe, my very good Lord, that I have heard from many, yea, and from my Lord Rochester himself, with what bitternes her Ladyshipp would often speak of me, and out of the sound of that 'tis possible I may have spoken with less respect of her than was fitt; but that ever I touched her in point of her honor, farr be from me, for I protest twas never in my words nor in my belief; and this I will professe to all the world, and if either my Lady of Suffolk or the Lady herself shall rest unsatisfied, I will be ready to tender as much to their Ladyshipps and to say the same which now I wrighte to your Lordship. And for my Lady of Essex, if I might be only freed from her ill will for [the] tyme to come, there shall be no man readier to respect and honor her than myself. And so with inexpressible thanckes to your worthy Lordship for the favour I have receaved from you, I rest

from the Tower the 24th of August 1613

your Lordships most obliged servant to com[m]and

Thomas Overbury

---

[193] Bourton-on-the-Hill, where Nicholas Overbury originates from.
[194] The letter is transcribed from BL MS Harley 7002, fol. 290.

Letter 75

25 August 1613: Overbury to Suffolk, and Gervase Elwes' accompanying letter[195]

The coppy of Sir Thomas Overburys second letter to my Lord Chamberlain

Right noble and my very good Lord,

Your Lordships so clear and hearty acceptac[i]on of my service, so that now I am bould to account myself as one of yours, hath [gap in text] and setteled my thoughts as I am confident they shall never again be removed; only my grief is that unhappily I have been a stranger thus long unto your Lordship.

I have returned heare my letter again aforehand and for the contents which engage me. Let me perish if I be not as faithfull servant between your two Lordships as to my own soul, and do conceave to foresee that knot so near tying which I am confident it will not [be] in the power of man to dissolve, and for my endeavour thearin, that it shall not be in the power of any to divert me, my Christianity lives on it.

Now good my Lord give me leave as your servant to make this onelie request, that whereas your Lordship says it will be a work of some tyme, that your Lordship will be pleased as much as in you lyes to shorten that tyme, which I crave of your Lordship, not onelie for my liberty itself, but principally for my health sake. For though my disease begone, yet the peircing air and solitariness of the place will not suffer my strength to grow, but slowly, which change of air will quicklie recover; and as soon as I am out & may be so happie as to speak with your Lordship in any private place that your Lordship shall appoint, I am confident I shall give your Lordship a testimonie that I intend to do your Lordship faithfull service.

The request I was bold to impart your Lordship, knowing that your noble nature could have some care of a weak man, were to that of a prisoner. So, with all taking leave, I rest

From the Tower 25th: of   yours faithfully till death
        August 1613   Thomas Overbury

        Mr Lieutenant's letter, August 25th,
        to my Lord Chamberlain.   (In my lord of Northampton hand)

Your Lordships letter was so welcome as he could not conteine himself for joy, and now no remedy but he will send the first wheerein he gave

---

[195] The letter is transcribed from BL MS Harley 7002, fol. 291.

that assurance, which he would have you to keep. He hopeth your Lordship wilbe so active in this business as his desires shall have a speedy end, which the rather he desireth that he may that of his part which above anything in the world, and doubteth not but presentlie to give such a beneficiall testimonie of his affection as your Lordship shall not thincke you have bestowed your favour on one unworthy. So, I humbly take my leave.

Letter 76

27 August 1613: Sir John Lidcote to Rochester[196]

Right honorable and my very good Lord,

I receaved a letter sent me from your Lordship, sent me by my Lord of Northampton. According to your Lordships directions therin, do I ime-diatelie send to my brother, who I find to be very well satisfied therwith. The other letter which you sent by his man was presently, although with very great difficulty, delivered to him before the comminge of your Lordships last letter. We cannot as yet persuade the keep[er] to bring an aunswere from him by reason of some late falling out between them, whereupon Weston hath vowed to convey no more letters for him; and besides the Lieftenante hath within these 4 days had him in very strict examinacion about his delivery of letters, which jealousie of the Lieftenante the keeper thinecketh hath growen out of something that my brother hath touched uppon in discourse with him which perhaps savoreth of some intelligence; but I doubt but within few days this vow of the keeper will be passed over, as many before have been. My brother hath been latelie very ill but is now well again. I am very sorry to hear your Lordship hath been sick, but I hope the worst is past and that your sicknes wilbe the cause of better health, for which I shall ever heartily pray, and wilbe allwaies ready at your Lordships comande as

Your Lordships humble and most affectionate

Westminster xxviith August   servant,

John Lidcote

196 The letter is transcribed from BL MS Harley 7002, fol. 291.

Letter 77

29 August 1613: Thomas Lorkin to Thomas Puckering, at Padua[197]

[Right-hand side of letter damaged, so some gaps. The opening of the letter concerns the Earl of Essex's plea against the Nullity.]

At the last hearing, my Lord of Rochester stayed heer in town (as is supposed) to hear the success; & rode presently post unto the King his Majesty therof, who shewes himself so passionate in this buisnes onely in favour with whom a new match would be presently concluded, if this ould were once absent. Sir Thomas Overbury is like to runne a short course, being sick unto death.[198] The L[ieutenant] of the Tower, together with the Phisitians that were there about him, have subscribed their hands that they hold him a man past all recovery.

Letter 78

Undated, but September 1613: Overbury to Rochester, from the Tower[199]

This paper comes under seals; & therefore shalbe bold to speak to you as I usde to do myself. I understand you told my brother, that my unreverent style should make an alienation betwixt you & me hereafter: at least such a one, as we should never be as we had bin. With what face could you tell him that you would be less to me, to whom you owe more than to anie soul living, both for your fortune, understanding, & reputation? One who lost his fortune with Ignatius; entered into a quarrell with Niger; sufferd five month[s] banishment;[200] & now five years months [*sic*] miserable imprisonment. And now to make so poor a pretence, to say you will alter towards me for the style in my letters? Alas, this shift will not serve to cover your vow. Your sacrificing me to your woman; your holding a firm friendship with those that brought me hither & keep me here; & not make it the first Act of anie good tearms with them, to set me free & restore mee to yourself again? And you bid

---

[197] The letter is transcribed from BL MS Harley 7002, fol. 280.

[198] The juxtaposition of the discussion of a new marriage occurring if the old one is put off, with the death of Thomas, implies Lorkin's possible understanding of a connection.

[199] The letter is transcribed from BL MS Cotton Titus B, vii, fol. 483. It is Thomas's last letter to Carr before his death. See the discussion of this letter on pp. 120–4 above.

[200] It is unclear which banishment he refers to here; it could be five months from court in 1611 after the queen's displeasure (see Chapter 2).

my brother keep your intent secreat: that you might steal away with
your wickednes. But that shall not be. You & I will come to a publicke
triall before all the freindes I have. They shall know what words have
past betwixt us heretofore, of another nature than theise. And I pray you
keep you my letters, that they may see how much I forget your Lordship
in my style. I shalbe upon the rack; you at your ease, negligent of mee; &
I must speak calmly. If Hector of the Harlow be so infamous for betray-
ing a stranger, your storie shall put down, to betray, & so quit a freind.
But now I will confess to you: so soon as I perceived how litle (never
name love) human affection: how litle compassion (no not so much as to
the colt in Enfield chace) when I heard how, notwithstanding my misery,
you visited your woman; frizled your head, never more curiously; took
care for hangings; & dayly were solicitous about your cloathes; officious
in waighting; could prefer your cosen, and Gibb; held daily traffickes of
letters with my enemies, without anie turning it to my good; sent mee
19 projects, & promises for my libertie; then, at the beginning of the
next week, sent me some frivolous account of the miscarriage of them,
& so slip out of town; & all this ill nature shewed by the man, whose
conscience tells him, that trusting to him brought me hither, & by him
that conveighed all my service to Julius, & made himself valued by his
maister for it; & my share to be a prison, upon such tearms; yet that
never man suffered to my knowledge that what he speaks & writes
howerly is mine, & yet can forget him that sowed that in him, & upon
whose stock he spends: nay forget him, betwixt whom was nine years
love, & such secreates of all kinds have past, & in the noyance my father
& my mother languishing for me, my mistress wisheth she might but lie
upon the boards by me, to bear me companie, my brother Lidcote overthrown by it, his aunt discharging him from her house, which saved 300
li. a year;[201] & he that is the author of all, & that hath more cause to
love me, yea perish for mee, rather than see me perish, to stand stupid,
& leese [lose] a jot of aniething that concerns himself, go on make much
of, nay let my enemies play upon me, send for tickets under my hand,
so [that], by God, since I came in, I have not found the advantage of a
straw, by no not so much as a servant in my extreame sicknes[s], nor my
freinds free to speak my last words to. When I had observed this the bitternes of my soul cannot conceal it self in letters. And that this wickedness may never die, I have all this vacation wrote the storie betwixt you
& me, from the first hower to this day: what I found you at first; what I
found you when I came; how I lost all the great ones of my countrie, for

---

[201] It is unclear who the mistress he refers to here is. The *Winwood Memorials* transcription has 'soul' here, instead of mistress.

studying your fortune, reputation, & understanding; how manie haz-
zards I have runne for you; how manie gentlemen, for giving themselves
to you a stranger, are now left to the oppression of your enimies; what
secreates have past betwixt you & me; & then, for the last part, how
when you fell in love with that woman, as soon as you had wonne her by
my letters, & after all the difficultie being past, then used your own for
common passages (then you used your own, and never after but denied,
concealde, & jug[g]led betwixt your man and yourself) & upon that
cause there came manie breaches, as Huntingdon, Newmarket, after at
Whitehall; thereupon you made your vow, that I should neither come in
the court nor with my friends and many years which are now fulfilled,
stayde me here when I would have bin gone, & send for me twice that
day that I was caught in the trappe, & long intending in your thought
long ago, a marriage with that woman, denyde sending me to enquire
of her, would speak ill of her yourself, & having bin now 2 months rec-
oncilde to a league, not to have first, upon those hopes of theirs, made
sure my libertie and return, & now at last, when we may easily live the
rest of our life in peace, & enjoy the remembrance of troubles, now you
to leave me out, & take an occasion upon unrespective language, to say
you will never be to me as you have bin. All theise particulars I have set
down in a large discourse, & on Tuesday I made an end of writing it
fayre, & on Friday I have sealde it up under eight seals, & sent it by a
freind of mine, whom I dare trust, (taking his oath not to open it) I send
[it] to him that is truer I fear than lett & then to call all my freinds, noble
and gentlemen, & women, & then to read it to them, & take copies of it,
& I have vowed to have wrote the truth. This I think you will not denie
a word. So thus yf you will deal thus wickedly with me, I have provided
that whether I die or live, your nature shall never die, nor leave to be the
most odious man alive.

Letter 79

Undated, but September 1613: Northampton to Gervase Elwes[202]

Worthy Mr. Lieutenant,

My Lord of Rochester desiring to do the last honour to his deceased
Friend, requires me to desire you to deliver the Body of Sir Thomas

[202] The letter is printed in *Winwood Memorials*, p. 481. It must have been written on the
day Thomas died, 15 September 1613.

Overbury to any Friend of his that desires it, to do him Honour at his Funeral. Herein my Lord declares that the Constancy of his Affection to the Dead, and the Meaning that he had in my Knowledge, to have given his strongest Strain at this time of the King's being at Tibballes [Theobalds], for his Delivery. I fear no Impediment to this honourable Desire of my Lords, but the Unsweetness of the Body, because it was reported that he had some Issues, and in that case the keeping of him above must needs give more Offence than it can do Honour. My Fear is also, that the Body is already buried upon that Cause whereof I write; which being so, it is too late to set our Solemnity.

Thus with my kindest Commendations I end, and rest
          Your affectionate and assured Friend,
                    H. Northampton

Postscript.

You see my Lord's earnest Desire with my concurring Care, that all Respect be had to him that may be for the Credit of his Memory; but yet I wish withal that you do very discreetly inform yourself whether this Grace hath been afforded formerly to close Prisoners, or whether you may grant my Request in this Case, who speak out of the Sense of my Lord's Affection, though I be a Counsellor, without Offence or Prejudice.[203] For I would be loath to draw either you or myself into Censure, now I have well thought of the matter, tho' it be a Work of Charity.

Upon the Back of this Letter are the following words in Sir Gervaise Helwis's own Hand.

So soon as Sir Thomas Overbury was departed I writ unto my Lord of Northampton; and because my Experience could not direct me, I desired to know what I should do with the Body, acquainting his Lordship with his Issues, as Weston had informed me, and other Foulness of his Body, which then was accounted the Pox.[204] My Lord writ unto me that I should first have his Body viewed by a Jury, and I well remember his Lordship advised me to send for Sir John Lidcote to see the Body, and to suffer as many else of his Friends to see it as would, and

---

[203] Either Northampton reflects Rochester's real distress here, or he colludes with Rochester to make the latter appear distressed: probably the latter if we assume the second letter (Letter 80), written 'at 12', and perhaps after Rochester has left, is sent without Rochester seeing it.

[204] This rumour is echoed by Chamberlain in his letter to Carleton on 14 October (Letter 82, p. 173).

presently to bury it in the Body of the Quire, for the Body could not keep.[205] Notwithstanding Sir Thomas Overbury dying about five in the Morning, I kept his Body unburied until three or four of the Clock in the Afternoon. The next Day Sir John Lidcote came thither; I could not get him to bestow a Coffin nor a Winding-Sheet upon him. The Coffin I bestowed; but who did wind him, I know not. For indeed the Body was very noisome; so that notwithstanding my Lord's Direction, by reason of the Danger of keeping the Body, I kept it over long, as we all felt.

Ger. Helwysse.

Letter 80

15 September 1613: Northampton to Gervase Elwes (as Letter 79)[206]

Worthy Mr. Lieutenant,

Let me intreat you to call Lidcote and three or four of his Friends, if so many come, to view the Body, if they have not already done it; and so soon as it is view'd, without staying the coming of a Messenger from the Court, in any case see it interred in the Body of the Chapel within the Tower instantly.

If they have viewed, then bury it by and by; for it is time, considering the Humours of that damn'd Crew, that only desire means to move Pity and raise Scandals.[207] Let no Man's Instance move you to make Stay in any case, and bring me these Letters when I next see you.

Fail not a jot herein as you love your Friends; nor after Lidcote and his Friends have viewed, stay one Minute, but let the Priest be ready; and if Lidcote be not there, send for him speedily, pretending that the Body will not tarry.

Yours ever.

In Post-haste at 12.

---

205 The choir of St Peter ad Vincula, the Tower's chapel.
206 The letter is printed in *Winwood Memorials*, p. 482.
207 Northampton is scathing about Thomas's family and the threat they pose.

Letter 81

20 September 1613: Rochester to Giles Overbury[208]

My Lord of Rochester to Mr. Overbury upon the death of his brother Sir Thomas Overbury.

Sir,

      I am sorry that the first tyme of my writing to you should be upon the worst occasion that could happen to either of us: being to you the loss of a brother, & to me of my dearest friend, which makes a first conjunction betwixt us in sorrow & in heavie regrayt for the loss, which I wish I could redress with the loss of any thing in this world I can call myne. But it shall not be fitt I contynue what I have a will to say upon this ground, for it should be to neither of our bests, for the discharge of my springs should but keep free your vessells with greife & heap sorrow too much aloft, whom our care should be to depress. But my part of care now shall now be to express a dearness to [the] memorie of him whom living I could not be suffered to enjoy.[209] And witness by the goodnes I shall be author of, I hope to these belonged him; how high a valeur [value] I set on himself, as you are the first in order and nixt to him so shall you be the same esteem. And that although my affection to all men in comparison with him is lost & neyer to appear again. That ne[ver] theles my indeavoyrs shall be quick & active to the good of thos that he loves, but to yourself principally. And of this I will devise with you farther both for your present & future coarse, which shall sho[w] that as I beginne, really so I will poursue it constantly. And will give testimony that I am

Extraordinarilie your friend
Lord Rochester

Letter 82

14 October 1613: John Chamberlain to Dudley Carleton[210]

[. . .] I am newly come to towne and know not what is newes to you but at all adventures you shall have all I can call to remembrance. Sir

---

208 Transcribed from BL Add. MS 31922, fol. 14.
209 Carr implies to Thomas's brother that he was powerless in the events of 1613. His affective style here shows that he, like Thomas, could write an effectively emotional letter.
210 The letter is printed in *The Letters of John Chamberlain*, Vol. I, p. 478 and p. 480.

Thomas Overburie died and is buried in the Towre. The manner of his death is not knowne for that there was no body with him not so much as his keeper, but the fowlenes of his corps gave suspicion and leaves aspersion that he shold die of the poxe or somwhat worse: he was a very unfortunat man, for nobody almost pities him, and his very frends speake but indifferently of him.[211]

[. . .] and for Sir Henry Nevill I thincke he is now *chiarito* that there is no truth in promises, and I marvayle that he wold be caried away so long with vaine hopes, for since the conjunction (as they call yt) of the cheife favorites of both factions he might easily see how the world went. Sir Thomas Lake begins to come again in request and much busines passes through his handes, and I am fully of opinion that he shalbe wholly employed under my Lord of Rochester, who to geve some contentment to Sir H. N. presently upon the death of Overberie (who had the reversion of the treasureship of the chamber) bought the place of the Lord Stanhop for 2000[li] and wold have bestowed yt on him, but he refused to take monie or anything bought with monie at a subjects hand, and withal thought himself undervalued to be rancked with Overberie, and after he had ben so long upon the stage for a secretarie to accept a meaner place.

Letter 83

23 December 1613: John Chamberlain to Dudley Carleton[212]

[Chamberlain informs Carleton that little is moving politically since his last letter, and that Winwood ('our goode frend of St. Bartlemewes') feels the same.]

[. . .] for though he be by common voyce and opinion already as yt were in possession of the place so much spoken of, and in great favor with the great man [Rochester], and injoyned to attend him (as he doth duly) every day: and further hath more assured and direct promises then ever your Berkshire frend [Neville] had; yet he is not caried away to build upon these foundations, but yf nothing be don between this and Twelftide, is resolved to demaund his dispatch and to return whence

---

[211] This is perhaps the most damning line on the death of Thomas before anyone suspects murder. There is a sense of the extent of the dislike at least some others at court felt for him.

[212] The letter is printed in *The Letters of John Chamberlain*, Vol. I, pp. 492–3.

he came [The Hague]: he is told by him whom he may beleve, that but for Sir Thomas Overburie he had ben in the place longe since, when he was sent for sommer was twelvemoneth:[213] so that in reason there shold be no let now, but that he seekes not to by-saints, or that he is reputed somwhat harsh, and too plain a speaker for the tender eares of this age: indeed he is somwhat too quicke and nible to kepe tune with the slownes and *faineantise* of this time.

---

[213] After his death, the rumours circulate about his Machiavellian undermining of Winwood. They may or may not be true (and are certainly not beyond him), but he must have been open to blame for many things at this point.

Chapter 4

Royal Prerogative and the Role of Counsel in *The Winter's Tale*

> Our prerogative
> Calls not your counsels [. . .]
>   [. . .] if you, or stupefied,
> Or seeming so in skill, cannot or will not
> Relish a truth like us, inform yourselves
> We need no more of your advice.
>
> *The Winter's Tale*, 2.1.163–8[1]

As this section of the book moves on to look at staged representations of courtiership, I begin with a play written and first performed when Thomas was rising in his court career. The questions generated by *The Winter's Tale* are profoundly important to anyone thinking about royal power and courtiership in this period, as the play explores the relationship between counsel and the king's power. To see the impact of this on the mechanisms for success in Jacobean courtiership discussed in the first three chapters, I shall first look to understand how the play asks its audience to consider the relative status of common law and the king's prerogative in the staged Sicilia, a political state with much in common with early modern England. Having established the legal context, I shall then look at the relationship between Leontes and his chief courtier, and how, rather counter-intuitively for a ruler with much of the autocrat about him, the king works hard to persuade Camillo to believe his proofs of Hermione's guilt. Finally, I shall move from issues of Camillo's personal virtue to examine what we might infer from the play about the art of courtiership more generally and whether a man who would be a courtier can possibly be honest. Thus, I shall develop further my argument on the moral flexibility needed to secure success at the Jacobean court.

---

[1] All references to *The Winter's Tale* are taken from the Arden 3 edition of the play, edited by John Pitcher (London: Methuen, 2010).

As Chapter 3 outlined, the late sixteenth and early seventeenth centuries were a time of tension in legal thinking. The developing centrality of the common law, largely accepted in the Elizabethan period, was beginning to be challenged as a new king came to the throne wanting to assert his rights to use extraordinary, or prerogative, power. Though the relationship between the statutes of common law and *Prerogativa Regis* had been considered for some time before the rise of the Tudors, as Chapter 3 showed, and later Tudor monarchs had certainly used extraordinary powers, there was a growing anxiety over its status under a king with more obviously autocratic instincts. Many trained at the Inns of Court, some professional lawyers, and others working in parliament or at court, preferring to consolidate the power of common law, were unwilling to acknowledge the equivalent status of prerogative law, and many disagreed with Francis Bacon that 'the king's prerogative is law, and a principal part of the law'.[2] Bacon, of course, although a lawyer, was keen to secure preferment at court, and his legal argument cannot be said to be impartial, but it illustrates the centrality of the issue of legal decision making in this period. If the king is to judge, and use extraordinary powers more frequently to argue cases of equity, there was a concern about his motivation and those who advised him.

Shakespeare writes *The Winter's Tale* in a period which is, therefore, very interested in the question of the relationship between the monarch and the law, and the consequence of increasing autocracy on honest counsel. It is a period very interested in establishing what is true, and in how one goes on to prove that, and much of the forthcoming analysis relies on how artificial proof is used in a court of law. As Lorna Hutson has argued persuasively, the fascination with legal proof at this period is a consequence of the post-Reformation importance of the jury trial in English law and the need to present verbally testimony that can lead to a verdict.[3] Linking the production of argument in an early modern court of law to the learning of the classically inspired rhetoric which was a key part of humanist education, Hutson demonstrates how the generation of circumstantial proofs is the product of an education based on the ideas of Cicero and Quintilian, often by way of Erasmus' *De Copia* in

---

[2] *The Works of Francis Bacon*, Vol. XIII, p. 203.
[3] Hutson, *The Invention of Suspicion, passim*. See for instance the initial claim of the book, that 'what changed in popular vernacular dramaturgy' at this period 'involved dramatists' awareness of affinities between the judicial or forensic rhetoric that drives the action of the Latin comedies of Plautus and Terence [. . .] and the rapidly developing sophistication of evidential concepts in English common law' (p. 3). Her subsequent book, *Circumstantial Shakespeare*, develops this argument looking at the use of circumstances to show the 'unscene', or 'extramimetic, *imagined or conjectured* locations and temporalities' (p. 7).

the schoolroom. I have argued that familiarity with these texts enables writers of courtly and diplomatic letters (who, like lawyers, often also benefited from classical learning) to engage their reader, but this is particularly clear when looking at the writing of drama. As we saw in the letters of Mr Taverner, or Henry Wotton, the creation of circumstances allows readers and audience members to infer what cannot be seen: motivation, for example, or emotion. This combination of defining what is true, and who should make a judgement of what is true in a matter of immorality or legal misdemeanour, lies behind the matter of *The Winter's Tale*.

Leontes' Legal Anxiety

Like Jacobean England, Sicilia appears to embody the tension between common law and open legal practice on the one hand, and more autocratic decision making, by a king keen to establish his own prerogative, on the other. Leontes makes decisions in Sicilia that, despite the initial opposition of the court, he is able to insist upon. The accusation of adultery he makes against Hermione is, for the on-stage and off-stage audience, obviously unjust, but Leontes' belief in her guilt is absolute. He is opposed first by Camillo (I shall return to the end of Act 1, Scene 2 in the next section of this chapter), then his judgement is challenged in the following scene by the assembled lords of the court. Demonstrating that he is not an entirely autocratic ruler, and implying that he has not behaved in this way before this point, the lords expect to question Leontes and he hears the lords' opposition, though with increasing frustration. He seizes Antigonus physically, but the courtier continues to argue that the king's judgement is wrong and the queen honest: 'If it [your belief] be so, / We need no grave to bury honesty' (2.1.154–5). Leontes is angry about having no 'credit' (l. 157), and demands of the court whether they believe him or not. An autocratic monarch who was feared by his subjects might expect opposition to stop at that point, but the lords continue to argue against him; it is weirdly comic that a man with the power to condemn others to death can be challenged as he is, with even his own wording turned back upon him in clever ripostes. Leontes is forced to explain to them (and to the theatre audience, of course) the legal context of Sicilia, similar to that James believes exists in England under his rule. He reminds them of his 'prerogative' (l. 163) and that he does not need to ask their 'counsels' (l. 164); instead '[t]he matter, / The loss, the gain, the ordering on't, is all / Properly ours' (ll. 168–70). If he wishes to condemn the queen for adultery, he can do that, without engaging in a debate with his courtiers. Yet, Leontes cannot, it seems, resist continuing the argument. As the next section of this chapter will show, the king wishes to convince his courtiers, not simply to override them. He explains that he has seen the 'circumstances' (l. 178) that prove her guilt and apart from ocular proof he has all he needs to convict. But he wishes for their approval, and after he tells them that they'll soon have the further evidence from Apollo's oracle, he asks them rather childishly, 'Have I done well?' (l. 187). He wishes, he declares, to '[g]ive rest to th'minds of others' (l. 191) who don't have his ability to see the truth, suggesting that he is more rational and conforms to the political and legal framework in which he is monarch. This scene, and Act 2, Scene 3 to come, seem to ameliorate the danger we imagined at the end of Act 1 and show, of course, the tragicomic nature of the play; Leontes is not a tyrant such as Ferdinand or the cardinal in *The Duchess of Malfi*, a play I shall discuss in the next chapter. Camillo may have feared that he was in danger of his life and Leontes may have demanded Polixenes' murder, as if we were in the midst of a tragedy, but this later scene set in the wider court suggests instead that this is a newly autocratic king, who has lost his wits and is showing poor judgement: a king who asks for the approval of his courtiers and who can even be mocked by one of them, Antigonus, in an aside as he leaves the stage.

As it was by the lords, Leontes' judgement of Hermione is also challenged by Paulina, and the grounds on which she makes that challenge lie in his lack of legal procedure. Surrounded by the gentlemen of the court, whom she has not seen challenging the king, we wonder if she exaggerates when she tells him:

> I'll not call you tyrant
> But this most cruel usage of your queen,
> Not able to produce more accusation
> Than your own weak-hinged fancy, something savours
> Of tyranny, and will ignoble make you,
> Yea, scandalous to the world.   (2.3.114–19)

Though declaring that she is not calling him a tyrant, her accusation is that he has made judgement of Hermione without any evidence beyond his own surmise, and that 'savours of tyranny'. Instead of hearing witnesses, and listening to the advice of his counsellors, he has simply relied on his 'weak-hinged fancy', and thus the decision is not rooted in objective proof. He is correct in retaliating that, if he were actually a tyrant, she would be in danger of her life; we have seen in the previous court scene that lords do challenge him and neither they nor Paulina die at his command. Indirectly, her husband Antigonus, of course, will do just that, but the question that hovers over this scene, of whether Leontes is a tyrant, is a more complex one. A tyrant would not need proof. She is correct that his 'weak-hinged fancy' is all he appears to be relying on in his arrest of the queen, and his belief that he is 'blest [. . . i]n [his] just censure, in [his] true opinion' (2.1.36–7) shows his conviction. Yet, a tyrant would act on that conviction alone: not just arrest the queen, but have her executed for treason, and Leontes does not do this. He appears to believe that his judgement is a revelation from a divine power; he is 'blest', and his recourse to the oracle is as much a desire for the public confirmation of that blessing than to find out anything. We can see this when he refuses to accept Apollo's judgement in the trial scene, but when he sends Cleomenes and Dion to the oracle he acclaims the transparency of the process of which this journey is a part: 'as she hath / Been publicly accused, so shall she have / A just and open trial' (2.3.201–3). Paulina was perhaps correct in assuming that Leontes would not want to be seen as 'scandalous to the world'; he seems at this stage sensitive to the opinion of his court and keen to prove himself correct in his judgement.

The Winter's Tale thus explores Jacobean ideas of law and kingship, and the tension between two kinds of rule: a monarchy that defers to the centrality of the law, as advocated by many at the Inns of Court, and the kind of autocracy verging on tyranny, where the king sees his prerogative as superior to the decisions of common law. As the trial of Hermione proceeds, and Leontes' pre-judgements are challenged by the queen's articulate and affective testimony, it becomes clear that the appearance of legally determined rule is simply that: an appearance. Leontes declares she should 'look for no less than death' (3.2.89), and were it not for the intervention of the divine, through the agency of the oracle, a conviction and execution would clearly have been the outcome. Hermione is correct in her conclusion that she will 'be condemned / Upon surmises, all proofs sleeping else / But what [Leontes'] jealousies awake' (ll. 109–11). There is an oscillation between tragedy and comedy in this opening half of the play, but the trial, like the earlier scene showing Leontes' conflict with his chief counsellor, has its roots in a darker kind of drama where tyranny and absolutism deny law the power to bring truth to light.

Persuasion and the Pursuit of Knowledge

In Hermione's trial scene, as she realises that, despite all the persuasive testimony she has to offer and her knowledge of her own innocence, she is to be found guilty, she says to her husband, 'You speak a language that I understand not' (3.2.78). This question of how far the truth can be determined through language, and how powerful words are in legal testimony, is equally important in the earlier scene between Leontes and Camillo. In the disagreement it stages between king and courtier, this scene enables us to see Leontes' desire to persuade his chief counsellor of Hermione's guilt and to use language to convince. His need to do this, rather than to use the executive powers we have just seen that he has at his disposal, suggests something about his relationship with Camillo.

Leontes has judged Hermione to be guilty before this dialogue begins towards the end of the second scene of the play. He believes he has done this by interpreting the behaviour of his wife and Polixenes, and the audience has heard him begin to rehearse circumstances and infer from them the motivation of the pair.[4] They were, he tells us aside, 'paddling palms and pinching fingers, / [. . .] making practised smiles / As in a looking-glass; and then [. . .] sigh[ing], as 'twere / The mort o'th'deer' (1.2.115–18). The use of familiar courtly analogy, with references to looking glasses and the hunting of which James was so fond, as well as the angry plosives describing their hands, build evidence against them. He continues, observing them walk away shortly after this, 'How she holds up the neb, the bill to him, / And arms her with the boldness of a wife / To her allowing husband' (ll. 182–4), seeing the gestures she makes and interpreting them to prove her unfaithful. As soon as he is in private conference with his trusted counsellor, Camillo, he presents the case for the prosecution in what prefigures a trial scene. Camillo, preferred and raised to his position in Sicilia by Leontes, is clearly expected to understand, to 'relish', the situations the king describes in the same way that the speaker does.

The scene shows Leontes, King of Sicilia, asking his chief minister, Camillo, to carry out his commands. Although we have witnessed the king's jealousy erupt earlier in the scene, and we have heard him present the circumstances behind his belief, nonetheless his demand that Camillo kill Polixenes for him is shocking to both courtier and audience. The staged conflict between the courtier and his lord after he has given this command presents a disagreement over the interpretation of what is true from what is witnessed. Leontes simply cannot believe that a man he is close to could interpret evidence so differently to him, and the play leads the audience to question whether a courtier should deny

---

[4] The relationship between gesture and behaviour, and persuasive speech, is discussed at length by Julie Stone Peters in *Law as Performance* (*passim*, but see p. 71 for a discussion of the use of both *actio* and *pronunciatio* to achieve pathos in Roman explorations of rhetoric). Leontes' inference of Hermione's guilt from both her words and her actions relies upon the assumption of this connection.

the evidence of his own senses to adopt his lord's perspective.[5] It is a question of epistemology and the audience is engaged in the quasi-legal debate about proof and belief, while simultaneously aware of the illegality and immorality of what the king asks Camillo to do.

One of the key issues for an audience considering this scene is the kind of relationship between the two men. Has Leontes preferred an unworthy man simply because he will support him? Is Camillo presented as a flatterer, deferring to the king's authority despite his own judgement? As we have seen through the opening section of this book, the success of men at the Jacobean court was rooted in homosocial bonds. The bond between Camillo and his lord is initially shown to be a strong one but, though it appears to be rooted in a kind of Roman *amicitia*, there is an asymmetry to a relationship with a king that prevents it from being defined as friendship. I shall suggest later that this power imbalance may not be quite as it appears, but as the dialogue between Leontes and Camillo moves to its crisis point, the king stresses Camillo's dependency on him; he reminds the courtier how he was preferred by the king to this position of trust and how he plays an important role in the current royal visit:

> thou
> His cupbearer – whom I from meaner form
> Have benched, and reared to worship, [. . .] mayst see
> Plainly [. . .]   (1.2.310–13)

The king has, 'from meaner form', 'benched' him and Leontes' use of the synonymous terms here shows the instinctive rhetorical wordplay that so often shows his emotion. Even earlier in the scene, where his language on Polixenes and Hermione's exit seemed to grow disjointed and less controlled, he relied on wordplay to convey an ironic sense of his betrayal. By the time he talks to Camillo, his language plays on forms and benches in a legal context, with an allusion, perhaps, to the King's Bench or the benchers who had seniority at the Inns. The reference to the courtier's rise therefore alludes to the audience's awareness of legal process, but also brings a legal context to his ensuing prosecution: a prosecution of Hermione initially, but increasingly a prosecution of Camillo himself.[6] The often rapid courtly success consequent upon

---

[5] Quintilian emphasises the importance of the senses in the effective working of rhetoric. Seeing and hearing are both important as 'these are the two senses by which all emotion penetrates to the mind' (*Institutio oratoria*, 11.3.14).

[6] Though the *OED* does not suggest the verb 'to bench' as connotative of legal benches (usage 3b cites this quotation), a search of Literature Online shows that, overwhelmingly, uses of the noun 'bench' in drama of this period have connotations of the law, though

such a bond between king and courtier is matched by the swiftness with which the king can demolish it. Leontes' subsequent assessment of Camillo as 'a gross lout, a mindless slave' (l. 299) as he will not accept what the king tells him about the queen challenges both the social status and intelligence important in the self-fashioning of an early modern courtier, and emasculates an advisor opposing his royal prerogative.

A key area of vulnerability for a courtier was how others viewed his origins, though the 'upstart' courtier – often the target of those jealous of his rising – was not usually the object of his own master's attack as Camillo is here.[7] He shows the expected appearance of courtliness throughout the opening two scenes and an audience member would not be conscious of his social mobility were it not for Leontes' challenge. In the opening scene of *The Winter's Tale*, the dialogue with Archidamus establishes Camillo's smooth rhetorical skill, as the two lords model the flattering language of the successful courtier in a formal setting. This language is part of what Pierre Bourdieu called *habitus*: 'durable, transposable dispositions' that enable interaction between people in a particular context.[8] As Penelope Geng notes, looking at the *habitus* of common lawyers, it 'might be manifested in one's speech, mannerism, dress, aesthetic taste, or other outward signifiers'.[9] Camillo reflects to his visiting counterpart a sophisticated urbanity, and consolidates his own status;

---

sometimes it can refer to a church bench (perhaps with echoes of the consistory court). It is used of ordinary household or inn furniture very much less often. The only three dramatic uses of 'bench' as a verb in this period appear in Shakespeare. In *Coriolanus* Brutus comments that he hopes his 'words disbenched you not' as Coriolanus rises to exit the Senate (2.2.69). In *King Lear*, it is evocative of the legal court, as I argue is this example from *The Winter's Tale*. On the Heath, Lear conducts his mock trial of Goneril and Regan, telling Edgar, in his guise of Poor Tom, 'Thou robed man of justice, take thy place'. A similar command is issued to the Fool: 'And thou, his yoke-fellow of equity, / Bench by his side' (3.6.36–8). The use of the noun 'form' here is the *OED* usage 17; its being used in a legal context is supported in the description of a 1620s wooden form, in the V&A collection; see https://collections.vam.ac.uk/item/O78980/form-unknown/ (accessed 2 August 2021), where the website entry comments that '[b]enches, or forms, were a simple and functional form of seating for dining halls, school rooms, law courts and so forth'.

[7] This was part of the conflict between the aristocratic faction at Elizabeth's court, led by the Earl of Essex, and others promoted by the queen from less exalted backgrounds. William Cecil, for instance, was the son of Henry VII's yeoman of the chamber and sergeant-at-arms, and only two generations away from the family's roots in the minor gentry on the Welsh border. Curtis Perry comments on the Elizabethan 'paranoia about the political domination of a corrupt court focused predominantly [. . .] on the idea of the *regnum Cecilianum* and on the image of Lord Burghley and his son Robert Cecil as upstart traitors hostile to tradition and degree' (*Literature and Favoritism*, p. 188).

[8] Pierre Bourdieu, *The Field of Cultural Production: Essays on Art and Literature*, ed. by Randal Johnson (New York: Columbia University Press, 1993), p. 5.

[9] Geng, *Communal Justice*, p. 3.

he is familiar with the detail of royal life, and his position is sufficiently long-standing for him to have been privy to Leontes and Polixenes' friendship as children. The 'affection' (1.1.24) they discuss between the two kings, who were 'trained together in their childhoods' (ll. 22–3), sets the homosocial tone to the play as a whole. In a sequence of past events, using rhetorical *incrementum* to show increasing intimacy, Camillo tells Archidamus that they have, though absent from each other, 'seemed to be together', 'shook hands' and 'embraced' (ll. 29–30). As we have seen in the letters of courtiers in earlier chapters, practical relationships between men at court are established and sustained through the language of love. Camillo echoes this here with the listing of love tokens between the two kings, 'gifts, letters, loving embassies' (l. 28), and in the hyperbole of love poetry to describe their affections for one another; they have, for instance, 'embraced as it were from the ends of opposed winds' (ll. 31–2).[10] This opening scene positions Camillo at the centre of the Sicilian court, and the audience notice his presence alongside Leontes as the ruler enters in Scene 2, with, otherwise, only his wife, his son and his brother king. The audience seem encouraged to infer that he is a favoured courtier, and his projection of appropriate courtly behaviour continues; Camillo is quietly present throughout Leontes' growing unease and he is the first to whom the king turns. He is relied upon for advice, and initially the relationship with the king appears to be a very close and trusting one. Indeed, Camillo's success appears so marked that, as the play opens, he models behaviour for aspirant courtiers in the theatre audience. Janette Dillon has proposed that the theatre could act as a shop window for such men, and here the actions of Camillo display a 'mode[] of being' for them to peruse and judge.[11] The process of becoming a courtier necessitated the adoption of acceptable language and behaviour and, showing these outward signs of successful courtiership, Camillo has been 'bench'd' by his king as reward. However, the essential emptiness of these signifiers of success, and the vulnerability of even the most apparently successful courtier, is made clear by the king's withdrawal of his favour in the face of his counsellor's refusal to interpret events as Leontes presents them in his evidence.

Important to an assessment of Camillo's courtly virtue are the competing justifications presented in the dialogue between king and courtier:

---

[10] See, for instance, p. 31, for a discussion of what Gary Schneider calls the 'emotion-laden rhetoric that regularly mediated political negotiation'. The example from Camillo's language here, of course, reminds us of the parity between Leontes and Polixenes that enables true *amicitia*; they are each an *alter idem* for the other, as Camillo, a courtier, cannot be.

[11] Dillon, *Theatre, Court and City*, p. 41.

that of the command, and that of the opposition to that command. The audience, of course, witnesses the development of Leontes' irrational jealousy, and approves of Camillo's refusal to kill Polixenes as his king demands. His challenge to this overweening royal authority cannot do anything but increase his virtue in the eyes of audience members. Typically, courtiers on stage who oppose the wishes of their king face death, as Leontes suggests in his later confrontation with Paulina, and as it could be argued that, in a less direct way, Thomas Overbury did. Camillo certainly feels he risks this, and his decision to refuse the command he is given is made in this context. It would be a counter-reading of the play for anyone to approve of the king choosing to exercise his royal power in this way: counter to all legality, not to mention conventions of hospitality and even expectations of family, as the two men are often described as brothers. The murder of Polixenes would verge on fratricide. It is possible to argue, as we saw Francis Bacon do earlier, that the king's prerogative power was not counter to English law and, instead, a part of it; but it would be difficult to develop that argument to justify the wishes of Leontes, whose irrationality is shown in the suddenness of his jealousy. Yet, of course, Leontes does try to justify his command, and his means of doing this is rhetorical; he attempts to persuade Camillo using elements of a legal case and creating a kind of artificial proof. Underlying the king's dialogue with his minister is the classical *status* system and the point of contention in the controversy: what he thinks Hermione has done, how we should define that act, and how we should judge the guilt of her actions. All of this would be proof for his chief minister of her adulterous behaviour.[12] Yet Leontes' case is not set out in such a structured way, as the king assumes that the conjectural, definitive and qualitative questions underlying his prosecution must be already understood by a man of such intelligence as Camillo.

But before we look closely at the prosecution that he offers in order to persuade his chief courtier to act, we might ask why an apparently autocratic monarch such as Leontes bothers to 'persuade' Camillo at all. He is angry at his advisor's refusal to see what appears obvious to him – Hermione's guilt. It seems more natural in such a ruler simply to threaten with violence the courtier who opposes him or even to carry out such a threat. In fact, I suggest, what lies behind Leontes' behaviour

---

[12] For a discussion of the importance of the *status* system in classical, and then in early modern, legal and literary writing, see Eden, *Rhetorical Renaissance*, chapter 1. She discusses how Renaissance writing was influenced by rhetorical texts such as Cicero's *De Oratore*, which outlined this core set of questions to establish a case: 'The first asks "did it happen?" (Lat: *sitne?*), the second "what happened?" (*quid sit?*), and the third "what kind of act was it?" (*quale sit?*)' (p. 16).

has its origins in the relationship between the two men. As I suggested before, rather than echoing the balance implicit in the *alter idem* of *amicitia*, there is a structure at play here that forces an asymmetrical power relationship. At a court led by a monarch who is conscious of his prerogative and who has autocratic tendencies, as Leontes appears to have, the expected asymmetry of king and courtier would see the power lie entirely with the king. But it is possible to see a different perspective, not quite as one might expect, leading to Leontes' need to prove himself right to Camillo. To explore the complexity of the power structure we see on stage here, we need to return to the opening of the conflict between them.

Looking closely at the dialogue following Mamillius' exit reveals how this previously successful courtly relationship begins to shift under the pressure of different perspectives:

> Leontes: Camillo, this great sir will yet stay longer.
> Camillo: You had much ado to make his anchor hold;
> When you cast out, it still came home.
> Leontes: Didst note it?
> Camillo: He would not stay at your petitions, made
> His business more material.
> Leontes: Didst perceive it?
> [*aside*] They're here with me already, whispering, rounding,
> 'Sicilia is a so-forth.' 'Tis far gone
> When I shall gust it last. – How came't, Camillo,
> That he did stay?
> Camillo: At the good queen's entreaty.
> Leontes: 'At the queen's' be't: 'good' should be pertinent,
> But so it is, it is not. Was this taken
> By any understanding pate but thine?
> For thy conceit is soaking, will draw in
> More than the common blocks. Not noted, is't,
> But of the finer natures? By some severals
> Of head-piece extraordinary? Lower messes
> Perchance are to this business purblind? Say.
> Camillo: Business, my lord? I think most understand
> Bohemia stays here longer.
> Leontes: Ha?
> Camillo: Stays here longer.
> Leontes: Ay, but why?
> Camillo: To satisfy your highness and the entreaties
> Of our most gracious mistress.
> Leontes: Satisfy?
> The entreaties of your mistress? Satisfy?
> Let that suffice. I have trusted thee, Camillo,
> With all the nearest things to my heart, as well
> My chamber-councils, wherein, priest-like, thou

Hast cleansed my bosom; I from thee departed
Thy penitent reformed. But we have been
Deceived in thy integrity, deceived
In that which seems so.

Camillo: Be it forbid, my lord.   (1.2.212–41)

The second person pronouns appear to show the expected power differential. To Camillo's polished and reverential 'you', Leontes responds with 'thou', with all the connotations of superiority in this courtly context. But this would suggest the king's confident power over his courtier and this is not quite as it appears. As evidence of Camillo's success as chief counsel to the king, it is apparent that Leontes relies on his advice. He stresses the courtier's quasi-religious role, where he has been accustomed to an almost confessional relationship with his 'priest-like' counsellor and the latter has 'cleansed' him. The king's esteem is implied as he asks Camillo whether the putative cuckoldry is apparent to 'any understanding pate but thine'. He clearly relies upon Camillo's intellect and perceptiveness, and perhaps he is not used to acting without the courtier's approval. This makes sense if one considers the obvious difference in age between the two. The father of a new baby and a ten-year-old, Leontes is presented by the internal evidence to be thirty-three at the time of the play.[13] The talk of the courtier's advice for the monarch, of his 'priest-like' cleansing of the king's soul, suggests the likelihood of Camillo being older than this. As he has told Archidamus, he knew the kings as children, and this is reinforced when, later in the scene, Polixenes – a similar age to Leontes – tells Camillo, 'I will respect thee as a father if / Thou bear'st my life off' (1.2.457–8). The power inherent in the courtier's seniority and in his habit of advising the younger man thus means that the asymmetry isn't quite as it first appears.

In a play concerned with the passing of time, the age of the characters, which shifts sixteen years through the course of the action, is important. The more mature 'integrity' of Camillo, in which Leontes has not been deceived at all, is accentuated by his older years and the Sicilian king's quasi-filial reliance on him. The shift from his opening compliments in this speech to 'we have been / Deceived in thy integrity, deceived / In that which seems so' echoes the sudden shift in his assessment of Hermione earlier in the scene, and in both cases Leontes rejects someone emotionally close to him, counter to his past experience. As the dialogue above begins there is no challenge to Camillo's social status. Indeed, he is someone who has shared Leontes' thoughts, discussed them with him,

---

[13] See 1.2.154–5, where Leontes tells Polixenes and Hermione that he imagined he was Mamilius' age, ten years old, and that it required him to 'recoil / Twenty-three years'.

and been an intellectual equal with his 'understanding pate'. Yet Leontes' use of the verb 'seems' suggests a question mark over all of this. The king's distrust of what courtiers project – of what appears to be so but is not necessarily as it appears – is a comprehensible response to the self-fashioning necessary for courtly success. The equation is made between virtue and transparency, calling into question the possibility of virtue in one whose public role demands the assumption of an appearance: a deception. The dialogue between Leontes and Camillo is a challenge to the assumption of a natural link between events and their representation – visually, or, as here, in speech; in other words, it is a challenge to the very existence of honest perception, and honest language.

The different perception of the events they have both just witnessed leads to each challenging the words the other chooses. Camillo's courtly epithet, 'the good queen', is questioned by Leontes, who casts doubt upon the qualitative judgement here. Leontes' deictic reference to 'this business' – the action he conjectures happened, and which he believes is defined by being apparent to all – is challenged by Camillo, who queries, 'Business, my lord?'. In what increasingly savours of cross-examination in a courtroom, Leontes challenges Camillo's choice of lexis again, with 'Satisfy? / Th'entreaties of your mistress? Satisfy?'. The danger Camillo is faced with is shown in the half-line and the consequent pause: 'Ay, but why?'. The courtier's usual linguistic smoothness almost covers his realisation of the danger, but his 'understanding pate' is betrayed by the pause. As Camillo increasingly understands, the danger lies in the limitations of his language to represent Leontes' truth. Legally trained audience members can see that, having not established the key questions of his case, Leontes is asking Camillo to make the same assumptions as he has, without guidance towards that qualitative judgement. More than this, the audience are being asked to judge whether language can indeed convey an objective reality, or whether, presenting as it must a subjective and mediated version of events, it is always unreliable or untrustworthy.

In self-fashioning, a courtier's adoption of a particular linguistic mode – like his assumption of a visual appearance – is only worth the years of preparation because of the general acceptance that what one could see or hear of a man (his *habitus*, as Bourdieu might have labelled it) *did* reflect reality. Only this belief explains Quintilian's comment on the power of the eyes and ears in a law court, or the industry of courtier manuals and the training of those with courtly aspirations at places such as the Inns of Court.[14] Ben Jonson asserts the supremacy of language: that '*Language* most shewes a man [. . .] the image of the Parent

---

[14] For Quintilian's comment, see n. 5 above.

of it, the mind. No glasse renders a mans forme, or likenesse, so true as his speech.'[15] Yet increasingly the knowingness of Jacobean theatre challenges these assumptions. Plays such as *The Winter's Tale* question whether appearance or speech are reliable signifiers or have fixed meanings, and a courtier's potential for virtue is thereby challenged. The presentation of this leading courtier, how he reacts to the questions and assertions of his monarch, enables the audience to make an assessment of the honesty possible in a courtly position.

Honesty and the Art of the Courtier

The question of honest counsel was clearly a matter of interest to literary writers before the accession of James, and good counsellors, who give advice for the good of the kingdom, were set up antithetically to those who give bad advice for personal gain throughout Elizabethan literature. For an earlier example, one might look at Sidney's *Arcadia* and the contrast set up between Philanax, a loyal courtier, and Dametas, his self-seeking servant. As Curtis Perry argues, the counsellor who flatters rather than advising on behalf of the kingdom 'reinforce[s] and magnif[ies] the errors of the prince's judgment. The result is a preposterous disruption of natural social order.'[16] It is Perry's aim to demonstrate that this interest in counsel, as James accedes to the throne, develops into a shifting debate over court favouritism. The process of what was pejoratively labelled favouritism had been argued under Elizabeth to be a way to promote meritocratic men, typically those with a humanist education and talent, but from backgrounds outside the entrenched privilege of a small number of families with long-standing court connections. Men such as William Cecil and Francis Walsingham had been promoted in that way by Elizabeth, and even in this earlier period they had faced opposition at court from aristocratic heavyweights such as

---

[15] From *Discoveries*, ed. by Lorna Hutson, in *The Cambridge Edition of the Works of Ben Jonson*, ed. by David M. Bevington, Martin Butler and Ian Donaldson, 7 vols. (Cambridge: Cambridge University Press, 2012), Vol. VII, p. 567. Jonson hints at the common similitude, comparing speech and appearance, which had formed part of the discussion of rhetorical style since the ancients. Cf. Kathy Eden on 'the garment of style' in *Rhetorical Renaissance*, p. 152: 'Like fashion differences, in other words, differences in literary style point resolutely [. . .] to personal differences between stylists.' Adam Fox argues that a key purpose of language in this period is seen to be to 'underpin social hierarchies, to provide a litmus of rank and degree and a vehicle for status differentiation', in *Oral and Literate Culture in England, 1500–1700* (Oxford: Oxford University Press, 2000), p. 53.
[16] Perry, *Literature and Favoritism*, p. 60.

the second Earl of Essex.[17] But after James's arrival in London, surrounded by Scots that he trusted and promoted over Englishmen keen for court position, favouritism was perceived to be endemic. The issue was whether men preferred by the monarch, that is those who were not at court because of their noble English birthright, could be more than flatterers; the possibility of honest counsel thus became even more hotly debated in Jacobean London.

In his discussion of Sir John Fortescue's influence on the development of common law, Alan Cromartie shows that this early and influential lawyer urged the issue of good counsel to prevent autocracy and to make sure that the king ruled for the good of the commonwealth. Fortescue was adamant, as many of the Elizabethan and Jacobean Innsmen were to be, that the king had no right to ask his subjects to commit an action that broke common law and that subjects should refuse to do so: 'Nay, even the judges of that kingdom are all bound by their oaths not to render judgement against the laws of the land, although they should receive the commands of the sovereign to the contrary.' He continued to stress the importance of courtiers speaking truth to power: 'the opinion of a king, whoever he may be, is not sufficient to rule a kingdom without the support of counsellors, even though that king were son of Solomon.'[18] Suggesting the difficulty of doing this, Thomas More, Cromartie goes on to show, believed that good counsel to monarchs was not always possible, and, in the first chapter of *Utopia*, More 'addresses the problems of counsellors to *princes*, that is, of those who [. . .] are obliged, in consequence, to make compromises'.[19] These 'compromises' recognise the tension between a courtier's conscience and the commands the king can make of him. The courtier's position relies on the preferment of a monarch who expects loyalty and obedience to his wishes, and this may not sit easily with being an honest counsellor. It is this tension that we see played out in the second scene of *The Winter's Tale*.

---

[17] Characterising a cultural shift in attitudes to counsel during the Tudor period, John Guy suggests a dichotomy growing between a '"humanist-classical" idea of counsel and an alternative "feudal-baronial" tradition'; the rise of influential men such as William Cecil and Frances Walsingham under Elizabeth consolidated the importance of humanist ideals amongst men of influence and power at court, at the same time embedding the idea of social mobility. The discussion of the relationship between counsellors and the monarch in Jacobean England thus comes out of the disputes of the previous reign. See John Guy, 'The Rhetoric of Counsel in Early Modern England', in *Tudor Political Culture*, ed. by Dale Hoak (Cambridge: Cambridge University Press, 1995), pp. 292–310 (p. 304).

[18] Sir John Fortescue, *De laudibus legum Angliae*, ed. by S. B. Chrimes (Cambridge: Cambridge University Press, 1942), p. 85, cited in Cromartie, *The Constitutional Revolution*, p. 27.

[19] Cromartie, *The Constitutional Revolution*, p. 88.

Ironically Leontes sees Camillo's honest counsel in this scene, defending the woman we know is innocent, as showing a lack of honesty; we realise that honesty here is a contingent term as the king insists '[T]hou art not honest' (l. 240), and accuses the courtier of being negligent, cowardly or foolish. Camillo's response is to assert his integrity, demonstrating his training. Despite his evident surprise, he shows instinctively his rhetorical dexterity; unlike the confusion of the king's verbal structure, he deals with each accusation logically and methodically, with the syntactical patterning of someone for whom rhetorical style is second nature:

> My gracious lord,
> I may be negligent, foolish and fearful;
> In every one of these no man is free,
> But that his negligence, his folly, fear,
> Among the infinite doings of the world
> Sometimes puts forth.   (ll. 247–52)

As Leontes' anger grows at Camillo's apparent refusal to say what he has witnessed – as the king sees it, to put reality into words – he finally bursts into an accusation, not quite so linguistically disjointed as his earlier exclamations in this scene, but the staccato rhythm contrasting with the smooth rhetorical skill of his advisor:

> Ha' not you seen, Camillo –
> But that's past doubt; you have, or your eye-glass
> Is thicker than a cuckold's horn – or heard –
> For, to vision so apparent, rumour
> Cannot be mute – or thought – for cogitation
> Resides not in that man that does not think –
> My wife is slippery?   (ll. 267–73)

As he embellishes his list of sensory evidence by which he considers Camillo must have perceived Hermione's guilt, the twisting of his syntax reveals his rambling thoughts until the clarity of his final statement – the only thing he is certain of – 'My wife is slippery'. The *status* questions by which Hermione's guilt should be established are not addressed directly by Leontes. He doesn't say what she has done, or define what he argues has happened, in any clear way at all, until he makes the qualitative judgement that she is 'slippery'. In doubting the case the king thus believes to be proven, Camillo must be at fault:

> If thou wilt confess,
> Or else be impudently negative,
> To have nor eyes, nor ears, nor thought, then say
> My wife's a hobby-horse, deserves a name

> As rank as any flex-wench that puts to
> Before her troth-plight: say't and justify't!   (ll. 273–8)

Leontes wishes Camillo to use language to support the king's own view of events, one he sees as self-evident, and he twists a variety of words concerning speech out of their true meanings to challenge his counsellor to argue his definition of truth. 'Confess' not to the truth but to falsehood; 'say' and 'justify' error; give 'a name' to something when the signifier does not signify the signified (that is, the term 'hobby horse' does *not* equate to Hermione, but Camillo is being asked to assign the label as though it does). A virtuous courtier would speak the truth, and 'seem' to be what he was; language would equate to reality. He would also challenge a ruler whose actions were against the good of the state. Leontes' demand is, on the surface, for Camillo to speak truthfully, but, as the courtier and the audience realise, if the truth is that Hermione is innocent, then the king's demand is for him to lie. Yet, after Leontes challenges him with more detail of his suspicion, Camillo continues to present himself as an honest counsellor, defying the king when he believes him to be in error: 'You never spoke', he says, 'what did become you less / Than this' (ll. 280–1).

The scene reveals the difficulty of establishing linguistic truth in an absolutist court where the power to define truth lies with the monarch. It forces the play's audiences to question the proper action of a counsellor and the possibility that truth can exist at all in such an environment. The debate, of course, was an especially interesting issue to those men of the Inns of Court, trained as Thomas Overbury, used to debating political and legal points, establishing the *status* of a case, and who would undoubtedly see the weakness of what Leontes puts forward, where so much is implied and assumed, and not proven. The careers of such men were to rise or fall by their understanding of the tension staged here. After a crisis point in the scene where the king demands he '[s]ay it be, 'tis true' (l. 296), the courtier refuses. Their evident closeness underlies the conflict, even as it reaches its climax, and any vestige of legal argument in Leontes' speech is replaced entirely by emotion:

> It is – you lie, you lie!
> I say thou liest, Camillo, and I hate thee,
> Pronounce thee a gross lout, a mindless slave [. . .]   (ll. 297–9)

The pronouns wobbling between formal and informal, and the child-like exclamation 'I hate thee', reveal his sense of betrayal, and he hits out by reversing all the status he has conferred upon Camillo, and his esteem for his 'understanding pate'. Despite his desire for Camillo's support, shown to be the driving force behind this argument and proving the asymmetry of the power balance to be more complex than we might have thought, the king can, in a state like Sicilia, assert his own judgement as truth. A courtier has no choice but to agree.

Confronted with the power of a monarch who could order his death, Camillo is forced to submit and to use the language acceptable to the king: 'I must believe you, sir' (l. 331). However, unhappy with the moral position this puts him in, he finds an answer which again involves a manipulation of semantics and betrays the moral ambiguity of the dependent courtier's position. His response to Leontes' demand that he poison Polixenes deepens the moral complexity of his portrayal. Initially, he appears to submit to the command of Leontes to kill the visiting king, agrees to 'do't', and projects an image of obedience. To justify what would, in fact, be murder, he claims innocence of immoral action, as he would kill on his lord's behalf and in response to his lord's wishes. The complexity of courtly morality consists here in the paradoxical need for courtiers to be deceptive in the honest service of their lord, and it poses a debate for the audience. The positions taken in this altercation between Leontes and Camillo can be seen as analogous to those adopted in Inns of Court mooting. What kind of defence is possible for a man in a position of service committing such a crime at the behest of his lord? We are driven to ask whether honest courtiership is, in itself, paradoxical: whether to be a successful courtier implies at the very least an ability to manipulate truth.

Courtiership and its 'art' is thus deceptive, and analogous to the assumption of a role on stage; this is clear from examination of the advice given to rising young men in courtier codes of conduct. Those writing these manuals make explicit what plays such as *The Winter's Tale* suggest: that courtly morality relied greatly on which deeds were perceptible and which could remain hidden. One example of this can be seen in such a text, *The Civile Conversation of M. Steeven Guazzo*, translated by Innsmen in 1581. The advice of an Italian courtier, servant and ambassador of the Gonzago family, Guazzo reveals his views in the text through the words of two speakers, his brother, William, and Annibale. The latter discusses this issue of reality and perception, noting that

> It is a common saying, That he which is evill and taken to bee good, may doe muche mischiefe, and no man thinke him to bee the worker of it. Notwithstanding, I put these same in the number of the tollerable: for though it trouble your conscience to come in their companie, yet you give no occasion of mislike to the worlde, for that they are not reputed evill, and in this point wee ought to satisfie rather others than our selves, and to give place to the common custome.[20]

---

[20] *The Civile Conversation of M. Steeven Guazzo.* Books 1 to 3 were translated

What is the importance of virtue if its appearance is, as Annibale argues here, the vital factor? Guazzo's text suggests that what many dreaded about court life is true: that not only is lowly background concealed beneath an appearance of courtly manners, clothing or speech, but immorality is also hidden under the guise of virtue: *habitus* conceals much.

Francis Bacon, as an illustration of the art of courtiership, argued that 'if you dissemble sometimes your knowledge of that you are thought to know, you shall be thought another time to know that you know not'.[21] In this, of course, lay the less positive 'arts', and it was a small step from adopting the appearance of more knowledge than you really have to pretence, cunning and deception. If actions and language form an apparent social identity, and, like a dramatic role, these can be adopted, then identity itself acquires fluidity. Martine Van Elk, developing Frank Whigham's work on courtier literature to evaluate female courtliness in *The Winter's Tale*, notes that 'the court [is] a place where social identity is constructed through public, rhetorical performance'.[22] She explains that she uses 'the term "performance" [. . .] to denote an early modern awareness of self-presentation as not necessarily directly reflective of inner identity but determined by social constraints and strategic con-siderations'. The term 'performance' encompasses both the visual and the auditory, and *The Winter's Tale* demands that its audience judge the morality of Camillo's performance of courtiership in Sicilia. If the essence of the courtier is constructed – that is, a carefully formed series of skills and projected appearances which does not actually convey real substance – then the possibility of virtue in a courtier is called into question. If effectively done, this 'art' leads a man to success in his role and, ironically, over time, he becomes the thing he pretends to be; that is, his appearance gradually becomes his inner identity. Yet it is unclear whether this process can allow such a polished courtier to be counted as virtuous, though he may be accomplished and practised; it is this judge-ment that an audience must make of Camillo.

Camillo faces immoral commands and is reliant for his position on the power of monarchy. Yet, as Stuart Kurland has shown, '[t]he play

by George Pettie in 1581, reproduced in *The Tudor Translations*, 2 vols. (London: Constable, 1925), Vol. I, p. 62.

[21] Francis Bacon, 'Of Discourse', in *The essayes or counsels, ciuill and morall, of Francis Lo. Verulam, Viscount St. Alban* (London: John Haviland, 1625), p. 196.

[22] Martine Van Elk, '"Our praises are our wages": Courtly Exchange, Social Mobility, and Female Speech in *The Winter's Tale*', *Philological Quarterly*, Vol. 79, No. 4 (Fall 2000), pp. 429–57 (p. 431). Cf. also the relationship between rhetoric, performance and the law proposed in Julie Stone Peters' recent work in *Law as Performance*.

depicts royal counselors who are willing to frustrate the wishes of their royal masters and act according to their own conceptions of justice or the common good – or their own self interest'.[23] As Camillo, of course, does not plan to *commit* the sinful act his king demands, his projected image of obedient submission is a performance. Rather than Camillo's eyes being unable to see the truth, it is Leontes whose vision is unreliable. Unable to see the honesty in Camillo's defence of Hermione to begin with, now the king cannot see the courtier's deception. Through the permutations of the scene, the audience segment accustomed to such debate and the analysis of criminal action, and familiar with the workings of the royal court, would be able to draw conclusions from this modelling of a courtier's response and learn possible ways of dealing with the immoral demands of a king whose belief is in the supremacy of his own prerogative.[24]

Thus, in subsequently promising to poison Polixenes at Leontes' request, the courtier ironically reclaims his honesty by lying and the satisfaction of this paradox would not have been lost on this audience segment. Camillo has no intention of poisoning a king, and instead tells Polixenes of the danger he is in, fleeing Sicilia to escape the linguistic demands of a king whose inability to see the difference between truth and falsehood threatens mortal danger. The scene as a whole shows the danger that linguistic truth could lose its existential reality in a court where a monarch controls semantics and the use of language to define events in the way he perceives them. Within this play more widely concerned with the value of truth, Act 1, Scene 2 illustrates through the decisions made by Camillo the dangers that come from the need to fashion a courtly image, with all the consequent doubts about what lies beneath such an image. Equally, it shows the danger when speaking to one in authority, and the necessity of slippery, morally ambivalent language to avoid that danger. Shakespeare's play challenges the possibility of transparent virtue in courtiership. Even a character such as Camillo

---

[23] Stuart Kurland, '"We Need No More of Your Advice": Political Realism in *The Winter's Tale*', *Studies in English Literature 1500–1900*, Vol. 31, No. 2 (Spring 1991), pp. 365–86 (p. 376).

[24] For discussion of the response of groups within an audience, as opposed to reading a more homogeneous audience response, see Andrew Gurr, *Playgoing in Shakespeare's London* (Cambridge: Cambridge University Press, 1987; 3rd edition, 2004), and Charles Whitney, *Early Responses to Renaissance Drama* (Cambridge: Cambridge University Press, 2006). The term 'segments' is coined by Whitney, who notes that playwrights 'and their plays perform complex and varied services for different audience members who act as free agents in the dramatic transaction' (p. 147). It is interesting that he sees the importance at this period, in particular, of Innsmen such as Thomas: 'The sensibility of the most important audience segment, the Inns of Court, is profoundly performative' (p. 115).

cannot avoid the need for the deception and moral confusion implicit in the role of courtier.

This ambiguity is even more interesting when one realises that Shakespeare chooses to add virtue to his drawing of Camillo in the adaptations he makes to the source text for the play, Greene's *Pandosto*. These changes make the courtier more complex and his virtue more difficult to judge. He diminishes the obvious, self-seeking immorality of Franion, Greene's courtier, who presents several persuasive reasons to commit the murder, leading to the interim conclusion: 'Care not then though most count thee a traitor, so all call thee rich.'[25] As Lorna Hutson notes of this speech in Greene:

> Anyone who has read any prose fiction of the sixteenth century will be aware of how frequently scenes of what seem at first to be private cogitation turn out to be scenes of the solitary and sometimes vocal rehearsal of *pro et contra* arguments. So, for example, in Robert Greene's *Pandosto*, Franion, the King's cupbearer, is asked by his master to commit treason. He withdraws to be 'secret in his chamber' where he 'began to meditate with himself'. His 'meditations' take the form of *sententiae*, offered as *pro et contra* arguments ('treason is loved of many, but the traitor hated of all') and we are told that he 'muttered out these or suchlike words'.[26]

In the soliloquy Shakespeare gives Camillo, we see the courtier with a humanist education rehearsing arguments in an apparently similar way but a key thing is that in his rewriting of Greene, Shakespeare reduces the 'pro' argument to one line: 'To do this deed, / Promotion follows' (1.2.353–4). Camillo dismisses the immoral deed, and the promotion that would instantly hang on it. But despite this apparently greater virtue than that of Franion, it is important to recognise the remaining ambivalence of Shakespeare's character. His 'contra' argument initially is not one of morality; he does not instantly argue that murder is wrong in itself, or that killing an anointed king is in particular against God's law; instead, he tries to think of *exempla* – men who have done what they were asked in this way and 'flourished after' (l. 356) – and he cannot. It is thus that he concludes, 'I must / Forsake the court' (ll. 358–9).

Shakespeare retains further elements suggesting Camillo's moral ambiguity. In response to Leontes' request that he 'bespice a cup', Camillo answers, with instinctive rhetorical smoothness, that he 'could do this, and that with no rash potion, / But with a lingering dram that should not work / Maliciously, like poison' (1.2.317–19). There remain hints

---

[25] Robert Greene, *Pandosto. The Triumph of Time* (1588), in *The Winter's Tale*, ed. by Stephen Orgel (Oxford: Oxford University Press, 1996), p. 238.

[26] Hustson, *Circumstantial Shakespeare*, p. 53, quoting Greene's *Pandosto*, pp. 238–9.

that this is, perhaps, a man not unfamiliar with the hidden instruments of death. The mere fact of his tricking Leontes and escaping the court shows that, despite his honourable defence of Hermione and his refusal to kill Polixenes, Camillo possesses the arts of a skilled courtier-deceiver.

Corruption and Courtiership

Thus, I close this discussion of Shakespeare's tragicomedy with an issue that hints towards tragedy, and prepares the ground for the next chapter's exploration of *The Duchess of Malfi*. In *The Winter's Tale* we have seen that the existential nature of honest courtiership is challenged. Under the rule of an autocrat, a courtier has to be flexible in his virtue or, at the very least, in expression of that virtue, if he is to survive. The argument running through this book, that virtue has to be a flexible concept if a man is to achieve courtly success, is supported by evidence in this text. The king's prerogative powers are presented too as antithetical to the process of common law, and as having the potential to disrupt it, though the power of the idea of common law is shown in Leontes' determination to 'prove' Hermione guilty, using a variety of quasi-legal means, rather than simply condemning her through his own extraordinary judgement. He needs to be seen to be adhering to legal process, and not just asserting his own decision, though that, in fact, is what he does at the crisis point in Hermione's trial. As we move on now to look at Webster's representation of law, courtiership and the potential for truth in his revenge tragedy, we can see the continuing fascination with the corrupting nature of court life. As the Jacobean period builds on increasingly fashionable late Elizabethan ideas, I shall discuss how lessons from Roman history were used to interpret what was happening at James's English court.

Chapter 5

Defining Successful Courtiership in *The Duchess of Malfi*

> though I loathed the evil yet I loved
> You, that did counsel it [. . .]
>
> *The Duchess of Malfi*, 4.2.321–2

Bosola cries out his love for Duke Ferdinand in Act 4 of *The Duchess of Malfi*, in a dialogue created by John Webster in 1612–13, years that saw Thomas at the height of his career and then, suddenly, in the Tower. The intelligencer and courtier uses the language of *amicitia* to justify his indefensible actions, in a power relationship similarly asymmetrical to that we saw between Camillo and Leontes in *The Winter's Tale*, but not in this case with the ambivalence of the king and the quasi-paternal courtier. Bosola is simply under the duke's control. The relationship is firmly outside Webster's source material in William Painter's earlier *Palace of Pleasure*, though both the story he adapts and his dramatic version of these events are warnings against overreaching. Both the play and the prose romance punish men whose desire for social mobility forces them to act in different ways beyond contemporary limits and acceptability. Webster, of course, is not merely writing at the time Thomas is at the height of his court influence, is imprisoned and dies; he probably knew him well. Both men arrived at Middle Temple in 1598, and when called upon to create a successful courtier in his play, one of the models he had at his disposal was a man he was likely to have known for fifteen years, and who was by 1612 a leading figure at James's court. Later evidence consolidates this connection between the men. Webster perhaps wrote the preface to the second edition of Thomas's posthumously published poem *A Wife*, and one critic has suggested he, 'in effect, became Overbury's literary executor'; his poems are printed alongside later publications of *A Wife*.[1] As well as Webster's reading of Painter's tale, his

---

[1] See Charles R. Forker, *Skull Beneath the Skin: The Achievement of John Webster*

interest in one of his famous contemporaries is likely to lie behind a play that is centrally concerned with the nature of courtiership.

In that context, this chapter focuses on two characters from Webster's play, Antonio Bologna and his murderer, Daniel de Bosola, who illustrate this chapter's claim that effective social rising and successful courtiership relied upon the joining of humanist education and homosocial connection to a willingness to accept royal command, whatever is demanded: as Bosola says, to 'loath[] the evil yet [. . .] love[]' the monarch. Antonio is a character at the heart of Painter's version (and, before that, of Belleforest's and Bandello's). In all the sources his marriage to a woman who is his social superior is punished, though the texts create differing degrees of sympathy for him. Bosola, though not an invention of Webster, is very much developed by him. A character mentioned in the final page of Painter's tale as the man hired by the cardinal to kill Antonio is developed by Webster into a central focus of his dramatic adaptation. In order that they should understand why he acts as he does, to be able to infer a *fabula* from the *sjuzhet* presented, the audience is given detail on his upbringing and his earlier history.[2] A seventeenth-century audience member would have seen him in the tradition of staged malcontents. I will argue here that both of Webster's courtier characters echo elements of the life of Thomas Overbury and that both characters owe their lamentable end to the lack of one of those three key constituent elements.

Court scenes in plays such as *The Duchess of Malfi* are vital, yet so often they are cut from modern performance. The opening scene of Webster's tragedy is often reduced considerably, though it usually retains the famous comparison of the French court to a fountain that should flow throughout the commonwealth with 'pure silver drops'

(Carbondale, IL: Southern Illinois University Press, 1986), p. 122. Several critics have found it useful, despite the earlier date of *The White Devil*, to explore parallels between Frances Howard and Vittoria Corombona; see David Lindley, *The Trials of Frances Howard: Fact and Fiction at the Court of King James* (London: Routledge, 1993), for instance pp. 184–5, and, more recently, Stevie Simkin, *Cultural Constructions of the Femme Fatale: From Pandora's Box to Amanda Knox* (New York: Palgrave Macmillan, 2014), pp. 74–7.

[2] It is useful to consider the presentation of Bosola in terms of structuralist narratology, since an audience's response to the courtier develops as Webster's characterisation progresses. We begin with lack of sympathy for a self-seeking courtier, and learn to understand his motivation in a more nuanced way as we are able to infer more from the detail of the backstory provided. See Keir Elam's *Semiotics of Theatre and Drama* (New York: Methuen, 2002), where he explores how in this approach 'actions and events supposedly occurring in W_D [the imaginative world] have to be inferred from a representation which is non-linear, heterogeneous [. . .] discontinuous [. . .] and incomplete' (p. 106). Thus, the analeptic account, of Bosola's time in the galleys or his education, influences the inferences the audience make from his subsequent on-stage action.

but is often poisoned 'near the head' and thus 'Death and diseases through the whole land spread' (1.1.13–15). Evocative of something being 'rotten in the state of Denmark', the image is used as a metaphor for the representation of rule and presents Webster's play as a challenge to absolutism. This chapter will go on to show how Webster's representations of Italian courtiers Antonio and Bosola tell audiences much about the complexity of gaining and sustaining a position in the complex Jacobean political landscape. Firstly, I examine Antonio, clearly educated and able to thrive in a homosocial court, but incapable of the moral flexibility needed in a corrupt, absolutist regime. Then I explore further how contemporary ideas of court corruption relied on earlier writing about imperial Roman court life. Contrasting the Roman Empire with its earlier Republic, historians such as Tacitus illustrated a moral decline, and writings such as his, newly translated in the late sixteenth century, were appealing to those opposing a rise in what they saw as autocratic and corrupting tendencies at the English court. Finally, the chapter explores how this context informs our understanding of Bosola, a character with all the moral flexibility that Antonio so conspicuously lacks.

Antonio's Social Mobility and Friendship

In his adaptation of Antonio Bologna, Webster makes strategic changes to a figure that, in Painter, has built a great reputation as Master of the Household of Frederick of Aragon, King of Naples, before he flees to France on the expulsion of the king, and is thence invited to Malfi by the duchess. Webster's Antonio appears to be a native of Malfi, though, keeping elements of the original, he has just returned from travels in France. In choosing to make the courtier an apparent native, the playwright contrasts more powerfully the sense of home and safety in the first part of the play with the roaming banishment of the latter part, and is able to make the wanderings of the duchess and her family feel more desperate. Thus, as the play opens, Antonio is the returning traveller who knows everyone at the Malfi court and informs his friend, Delio, about them. His time in France allows him to compare political systems there and at home, and in response to Delio's questions about the court he has just left, he declares, 'I admire it' (1.1.4). Antonio, in his opening remarks, reflects one of the key facets of a successful courtier; he is educated and articulate, shown in his ability to discuss what he has learnt politically from those travels. His humanist education has enabled his social mobility.

In the key court post of Master of the Household, as we saw with Camillo in the previous chapter, Antonio shows that he is of high status and well connected, although he is not of the royal blood. He is required to act as the duchess's secretary, invited in to her private quarters later in the opening scene apparently to take a letter. The education required for such a position was well known to the audience at the original performances of *The Duchess of Malfi* by the King's Men in the Blackfriars in 1614. At this smaller, indoor playhouse, a substantial segment of those paying the higher entry fees were from the nearby Inns of Court, and had themselves the legal training and the classical education that would have enabled Antonio to do his job at the court of Malfi. William Painter's source says 'he had by Arte gotten that: which is most worthy of prayse, which was, the knowledge of good letters, wherein he was so well trayned, as by talke and dispute thereof he made those to blush that were of that state and profession'.[3] Webster makes his audience infer that part of the *fabula* as the first scene reveals the verbal articulacy that Painter describes. Antonio's dialogue with Delio allows the two a quasi-choric role as the rest of the cast come on and off stage observed by them. As Jonson had done in comic form with Cordatus and Mitis – the Grex in *Every Man in his Humour* – Antonio and Delio begin the play as intermediaries between the audience and staged characters, guiding the opinion of the latter held by the former.

The duchess is attracted, though, not simply to a low-born and bookish secretary with a humanist education. Instead, Antonio is shown to be a man at the centre of Amalfi's homosocial court. His masculine appeal is often overlooked in productions that miss out much of the first scene, but he is reported as the winner of the tilt that has taken place just before the action begins; he 'took the ring oft'nest' (1.1.86) and is given 'the jewel', his prize, by Duke Ferdinand. In the source story, he is described as 'valiant of his person, a good man of Warre' (S2ᵛ), and this is translated by Webster into the otherwise irrelevant court games. Many courtiers of Thomas Overbury's generation illustrate the court context in which Antonio might be seen to thrive; they valorised martial action and this was a key part of the homosocial milieu.[4] It is worth

---

[3] William Painter, *The second tome of the Palace of pleasure contayning store of goodlye histories, tragical matters, & other morall argumentes, very requisite for delight and profyte. Chose and selected out of diuers good and commendable authors, and now once agayn corrected and encreased. By VVilliam Painter, clerke of the ordinance and armarie* (London: Thomas Marshe, 1580), fol. S2ᵛ. All other references are in the text.

[4] The 1607 tilt was the making of Robert Carr. In his *ODNB* article on Carr, Alastair Bellany notes: 'At the accession day tilt in March 1607 Kerr (or, as the English spelt it, Carr) fell from his horse and broke his leg. The accident proved a turning point in his fortunes. The king decided to help nurse the injured groom and was soon captivated.'

remembering that, in a protracted Elizabethan peace in the 1590s, many of these as young men had followed the Earl of Essex in his sea-going expeditions or fought with him in Ireland shortly before his ill-fated rebellion. One such was a man we have seen often through the first three chapters of this book, and who was well known to Thomas: Henry Wotton, who had an Oxford degree and was fluent in several European languages. Wotton's verbal dexterity was a great asset to him as the Earl of Essex's secretary in the last years of the 1590s, and he was part of Essex's circle.[5] He took part in the Cadiz and Azores expeditions, travelled with the earl to Ireland and remained in his employ until the end of 1600, when, seeing the increasing displeasure of the queen, he prudently chose to leave it and travel abroad. Nonetheless, his passion for Essex's leadership was clear. In a letter to John Donne from Ireland he comments that 'we have a good cause and the worthiest gentleman of the world to lead it'.[6] Gaining the by then rather empty title of Earl Marshal in 1597, Essex grew to be the champion of young men frustrated in their pursuit of a court position, who yearned for an active and military opposition to Catholic enemies in Spain and Ireland. Donne himself was another of these men, craving court preferment for many years before he replaced Thomas as Robert Carr's secretary in 1613. Yet another was William Cornwallis, whom we last saw in Chapter 1 travelling to Edinburgh with Thomas. Before success in James's Privy Council, Cornwallis showed frustrated ambition under Elizabeth. Knighted by the Earl of Essex in Ireland in 1599, he was as inspired by the martial aristocrat as Wotton or Donne. Cornwallis's essays, influenced by Montaigne, were published immediately after his time with Essex, but before the ill-fated rebellion. One essay, on ambition, extols the valour of his ideal courtier over those who hope to succeed by less physical means. Attacking those who do not sufficiently value men like the earl, Cornwallis argues:

> It is worthinesse to plucke Honour from daungers, and hazards, to aduenture something in a siege, to be the first at a breache, to lay hold at the grappeling of shippes, vntil the losse of both hands, and then to hold by the Teethe: this is the way to Honor directly; for which if there be not recompence, vpon their heades let it lye.[7]

---

[5] We saw his facility with languages illustrated in Chapter 1 on his disguised visit to James's court in Edinburgh.

[6] *The Life and Letters of Sir Henry Wotton*, Vol. I, p. 309. The letter is cited in Luke MacMahon's *ODNB* entry on Sir Henry Wotton, which provides fuller details of both Wotton's activities for the Earl of Essex and his friendship with Donne.

[7] *Essayes, by Sir William Corne-walys, the younger, knight* (London, 1600), chapter 10, 'On Ambition'.

Warm now to his task, he demands rhetorically, 'Are not these vertues better then to wooe preferment as if shee were a wench, to send presents, to praise all, because we like some?' Going to Scotland with Thomas as these essays were fresh in Cornwallis's mind, and leaving behind a London where the valorous earl was about to raise his troops in rebellion, there can be no doubt that the two young men would have discussed the nature of active ambition and court success, and the chivalric heroism Essex represented. The conversation, as Manningham's diary suggests, would have been pursued too at Middle Temple. The earl's discourse of aristocratic supremacy may have opposed Elizabethan social mobility, but, at the same time, he was a champion of those ambitious young men who were keen for the opportunity for military valour and courtly patronage, and frustrated by the limited opportunities presented at the court of the aged queen.[8]

Webster was of an age to have been one of those young men in the Middle Temple, aware of the impact of the Earl of Essex, whether or not he was a follower himself. He wrote *The Duchess of Malfi* in the immediate aftermath of the death of Prince Henry, the inheritor of many of Essex's ideals and joined in his satellite court by many who had been in the earl's circle. Webster's *A Monumental Column*, an elegy for the prince, would have brought ideas of valour in an ideal prince to the top of the playwright's mind as he wrote *The Duchess*.[9] In this way the quasi-martial opening to his play, with a homosocial court lauding the champion of their chivalric sports, places Antonio in a more active, more three-dimensional light; there is no doubt that he is a successful

[8] Webster's own attitude to social mobility can perhaps be inferred from a section of his dedication of the 1623 quarto of *Malfi* to The Right Honourable George Harding, Baron Berkeley of Berkeley Castle: 'I do not altogether look vp at your title: The ancien'st Nobility, being but a rellique of times past, and the truest Honor indeede beeing for a man to conferre Honor on himself which your Learning strives to propagate, and shall make you arriue at the Dignity of a great Example' (*The tragedy of the Dutchesse of Malfy As it was presented priuatly, at the Black-Friers; and publiquely at the Globe, by the Kings Maiesties Seruants. The perfect and exact coppy, with diuerse things printed, that the length of the play would not beare in the presentment. Written by Iohn Webster* (London: Nicholas Oakes, 1623).
[9] The poem, *A monumental columne, erected to the liuing memory of the euer-glorious Henry, late Prince of Wales* (London: N. Oakes for William Welby, 1613), was entered into the Stationers' Register on Christmas Day 1612 and is dedicated to Robert Carr. Robert B. Bennett, in his article 'John Webster's Strange Dedication: An Inquiry into Literary Patronage and Jacobean Court Intrigue' (*English Literary Renaissance*, Vol. 7, No. 3 (Autumn 1977), pp. 352–67), argues that this dedication is ironic, inspired by Webster's belief that Carr may have been implicated in the prince's death by poisoning; that the prince was poisoned was a rumour believed by many at the time, including apparently the queen.

courtier or of the combination of education and homosocial ease that has enabled that.

Antonio's position in this wider court and his friendship with Delio is another factor demonstrating his skills to navigate a homosocial court. The friendship and parity between the two men are clear, as Delio asks Antonio's advice and adds to that information he knows. One might imagine them as akin to Wotton and Edmund Bacon, or Chamberlain and Carleton, exchanging court gossip and clearly in each other's trust. This friendship, and the framing it allows to the opening events, is a creation of Webster's. Delio is developed out of a minor figure in the source story, in a brief scene late in Painter's tale, where, in Milan, and not knowing his wife and children to be dead, Antonio is warned by a gentleman not to trust the Aragonese brethren. Painter's Delio admits that, though he has never seen Antonio before, 'vertue hath sutch force, & maketh gentle myndes so amorous of their like, as when they doe beholde ech other, they feele themselves coupled as it were in a bande of minds, & impossible it is to divide the same' (U4^r). The force of *amicitia* is obvious behind such a statement: the virtue of Antonio's mind is akin to that of Delio. He sees an *alter idem*, unlike the asymmetrical homosocial relationship in *The Winter's Tale*, or that, equally unbalanced, between Bosola and Ferdinand in *The Duchess of Malfi*. It is this parity that Webster expands into a friendship that runs through the play and that enhances Antonio's part in a wider homosocial network.

Returning intermittently throughout the play, 'most trusty Delio' (2.1.163) reinforces Antonio's virtue for the audience and acts as his loving friend; indeed, together with the heterosexual love of Antonio and the duchess, the affection between the men forms a contrast to the poison of court. If action and open valour are characteristics of the virtuous courtier, then it is no coincidence that Delio compares these qualities with male friendship; as he departs for Rome, he gives Antonio his weapon and asks that he 'lay this unto your breast: / Old friends, like old swords, still are trusted best' (2.2.79–80). The masculine camaraderie shown in their shared classical allusions and military language allows Antonio and Delio to form an antithesis to the corruption, lack of trust and *realpolitik* of the duke and the cardinal. Yet, importantly, Delio is realistic about the modern basis of power and influence, and less naïve than Antonio; he recognises courtiers' flexible morality where his friend sees their goodness. Thus, within this friendship Webster constructs a contrast that alerts his audience to the vulnerability of Antonio. This contrast perhaps explains too the otherwise rather odd use of Delio in Act 2, Scene 4 as the 'old suitor[]' of Julia who visits her in Rome and declares, 'I would wish you / At such time as you are non-resident / With your husband, my mistress' (ll. 72–4).[10] Delio's ability to thrive within the corruption of a modern court makes him more ambivalent than his unequivocally noble friend.

The use of Delio as a means of amplifying Antonio's goodness, and offering some contrast to it, encourages Webster's audience to debate whether or not the latter has any moral flexibility of his own if asked to do any act he does not believe honest. The secretary is virtuous; Antonio is barely tempted to act corruptly at any point in the play, and, indeed, on the rare occasion he does 'seem', and actively deceive as a necessary protection for his wife, it is, tellingly, at Delio's suggestion. He is 'lost in amazement' when Delio presents a practical, but deceptive, solution to his dilemma as the duchess goes into labour, suggesting Antonio should 'give out that Bosola hath poisoned her / With these apricots' (2.1.170–1). Antonio's difficulty in acting this role is shown bodily as he falls victim to a stress-induced nosebleed when facing subsequent questions from Bosola. As the friends meet after Antonio's flight from Ancona, and Delio tries again to help, his parting exclamation – 'Your own virtue save you!' (5.3.49) – verbalises for the audience the futility of such a hope.

We can see from Antonio and Delio's opening discussion on comparative monarchy that Antonio is a champion of honest counsel for rulers. They engage with the issues surrounding absolutism we saw Thomas discussing in his 1609 letters to Cecil, and in his published comments on the absolutism of the French monarchy in *Observations in his Travailes upon the State of the XVII Provinces as they stood Anno Dom. 1609*, and it is even possible that Webster discussed these ideas with Thomas at the time. A key point here is that, as Thomas had done in his published text, Antonio advocates for counsellors to advise the king and 'freely / Inform him the corruption of the times' (1.1.17–18). As in the previous chapter on *The Winter's Tale*, we can see that the audience is asked to question whether courtiers can give good counsel under an absolutist monarch. Arguing, as Thomas had before his own promotion to power, that these men have a 'noble duty' to 'inform [monarchs] / What they ought to foresee' (ll. 21–2), Antonio, of course, is set up in opposition to an autocratic ruler such as Ferdinand. The latter demands his courtiers

---

[10] John Russell Brown's note on this scene, I think, misses the structural value of the contrast it implies between Delio and Antonio. He is surely right that 'Webster [. . .] used [this incident] to aggravate the audience's sense of a growing web of intrigue and an increasing complexity of character' but the choice of Delio specifically (above the other minor courtiers who could have easily been given the task) creates a doubt over Delio's openness and accentuates still further the isolation of Antonio. See Revels Plays edition (London: Methuen, 1964), p. 62.

not to be advisors but flatterers, and, in illustration of this, quickly after this dialogue between Antonio and Delio he reprimands the assembled court for laughing without his permission: 'Methinks you that are courtiers should be my touchwood, take first when I give fire, that is, laugh when I laugh, were the subject never so witty' (ll. 120–2).

Antonio's innocence and honour are apparent throughout to the audience, yet ultimately it is that honesty that causes his downfall. Pretending to be merely the duchess's secretary, when he should be able to reveal to the light of day his legal and virtuous marriage with her, is a deception forced upon him as a result of court life. Those surrounding him suppose that, as a successful courtier, his honour must be assumed and that he must be as self-seeking as they are themselves. Being forced to hide his real relationship with his wife, he tells Delio, has led courtiers around him to assume he 'grow[s] to infinite purchase / The left-hand way' (3.1.28–9) and that the poor duchess can do nothing to prevent the supposedly scheming and acquisitive courtier:

> For, say they,
> Great princes, though they grudge their officers
> Should have such large and unconfined means
> To get wealth under them, will not complain
> Lest thereby they should make them odious
> Unto the people.
>
> (ll. 30–5)

Antonio is intelligent enough to grasp the ways of the court, but he is simply unable to deceive in order to manipulate his knowledge to his own advantage. Ultimately, he is left to lament that he cannot reveal the truth, and must become victim to the regime he opposes. Such a court as that in Malfi cannot cope with the virtuous counsellor Antonio admired in France. Virtue, honesty and openness make Antonio unable to thrive as a courtier where he is expected to be morally flexible, and to conform to the prerogative of those with power.

This, then, demonstrates why Antonio inevitably falls in this tragedy. Webster positions his character as a virtuous man who falls prey to the corruption of Ferdinand and the cardinal. He can be seen to reflect the honour code of late Elizabethan courtly debate, where Essexian sympathisers valorised military prowess, and he is able to navigate successfully the homosocial environment of the Malfi court. But his success is problematised by his honesty, and by others' attitudes to his social mobility. Early in the play, as Ferdinand comments that Antonio would have been a far better intelligencer at the Malfi court than Bosola, the cardinal replies that '[h]is nature is too honest for such business' (1.1.223). This is an indication of how little Antonio is willing to bend to the desires of an aristocratic patron; his sense of moral justice is clear, and he is not considered flexible enough to submit to his masters' personal power. Equally, for a court valorising martial endeavour, this is ideally combined with aristocratic origin, and Antonio is not merely not high born, he also challenges the aristocratic elite by marrying the duchess against her brothers' will. Ferdinand shows his distaste of his background, commenting that Antonio smells of 'ink and counters' and 'ne'er in's life look'd like a gentleman / But in the audit time' (3.3.70–2). By the Jacobean regime, a character such as Antonio can simultaneously benefit from the opportunities available to those with intellect, be opposed by the high-born for not being a gentleman, yet still embody the traditional values his rise appears to be challenging. As a courtier with echoes of Essexian ideals, he ironically falls victim to villainous noblemen who are supremely conscious of their high birth.

Malfi and a Vogue for Roman History

The play offers comment on a court that has much in common with the London of James I, though events ostensibly take place in Italy.[11] Webster depicts the inevitability of the abuse of courtly power in 1614, as Robert Carr held sway in London as the Earl of Somerset, now married to Frances Howard and without the problem presented by his former friend. Highly successful in the homosocial milieu of James's court, Carr's status is drawn from his influence over the king. Though Webster's stage representation is of an apparently Italian court, thus marked as safely 'different' to that in London, the audience becomes dangerously close to judging the power structures in the current English regime.

One of the catalysts for the shifting perception of courtiership in the later years of Elizabeth's reign and into that of James lay in the interest of the circle surrounding the second Earl of Essex in what has come to be known as politic history.[12] Works by Tacitus, Cassius Dio and Suetonius were widely read amongst the university-educated, and had

---

[11] Ann Rosalind Jones argues that Webster's use of Italian stereotypes, and stereotypical characters, frees him from the restrictions he would otherwise face in his exposure of corruption: 'the foreign other can be denounced as a source of corruption at the same time that s/he frees [. . .] the tragedian from strict obedience to the didactic assignments built into English [. . .] tragedy'; see 'The Italians and Others', in *Staging the Renaissance*, ed. by David Scott Kastan and Peter Stallybrass (Abingdon: Routledge, 1991), pp. 251–62 (p. 259).
[12] The Essex circle consisted of many who had, before his death, previously surrounded Sir Philip Sidney.

much to say on ambition and the abuse of power in Rome after the decline of the Republic. Courtiers such as Sidney and Essex encouraged the dissemination of the work of Roman historians, and under their patronage Sir Henry Savile translated most of Tacitus' *Historiae* and *Agricola* in 1591. Published as it was just before Richard Greneway's translation of *Annales* in 1598, this demonstrates the contemporary interest. As Colin Burrow notes, discussion of Tacitus 'frequently brought together reflections on the passions with arguments about how citizens should respond to tyrannical rule'.[13] Savile, for instance, in a section he writes between his translations, in Tacitean style, shows how the overthrow of the tyrannous Nero threatens being replaced by a tyranny even greater, and encourages debate on autocracy and the mob:

> Aponius an accuser, they ouerthrew, and drew cartes laden with stones ouer his bodie, beside manie other outraged and slaine, and some, as it happeneth where the reine is let loose to the furious multitude, innocently: insomuch that in Senate a graue & honourable counseller openlie protested, that in short time there would be great cause to wish Nero againe, as beeing more tolerable one tiranne then manie, and better to liue where nothing then there where all things were lawful.[14]

Early modern translations of Tacitus' exploration of the relationship between senate, emperor and people, his account of regime change, and the response of Rome to absolutism, opened up discussion of the mechanisms of political power, and gave analogues for the workings of the Jacobean court. So, from their time at university and the Inns of Court, Thomas and contemporaries such as Webster were surrounded by influential works showing an increasing awareness of the corruption of power and examining how citizens and courtiers could react when faced with it. Plays such as *The Duchess of Malfi* represent on stage the corruption and personal power exemplified in imperial Rome, and explore exactly those questions in their representation of characters such as Antonio and Bosola.

The translations of Tacitus at the end of Elizabeth's reign accompanied the work on the continent of Justus Lipsius, and encouraged a growing English interest in Neostoicism. Creator of the standard editions of Tacitus and Seneca, Lipsius, according to Blair Worden, 'saw in Tacitus's account of imperial Rome a close and dark parallel to the tyrannies and persecutions of his own time, the time of late Renaissance

---

[13] Burrow, *Shakespeare and Classical Antiquity*, p. 186.
[14] Cornelius Tacitus, *The Ende of Nero and Beginning of Galba: Fower Bookes of the Histories of Cornelius Tacitus*, trans. by Henry Savile (London, 1591), p. 13.

monarchy and of the wars of religion'.[15] Worden argues that reflecting Roman historians 'had become a habit of mind' by then. He cites the 1603 tribute on Elizabeth's death delivered by the Speaker of the House of Commons, who defined the virtues of the present age by contrasting them with imperial Rome: 'Virtue is now no treason, nor no man wisheth the reign of Augustus, nor speaketh of the first times of Tiberius.'[16] Grenewey, translator of the *Annales*, also showed his sense of the efficacy of reading Tacitus. In his preface, dedicated to the Earl of Essex and noting the earl's proven liking for the Roman historian, he notes that history is both 'a treasure of times past as well as a guide' and comments of Tacitus, 'In iudgement there is none sounder, for instruction of life, for al times, to those which oft read him iudiciously'.[17] The adverb allows protection for the author; one might not read Tacitus 'iudiciously', and this could lead to misjudgement.

The need for such protection was clear; the use of Tacitean accounts of imperial Rome as an analogy to the contemporary court was potentially subversive, and such a use is to be found well beyond the writings of those immediately connected to the Essex circle. From his early days at Westminster School, Ben Jonson relied upon Lipsius's standard edition, and his tutor there, admired historian William Camden, uses Tacitus in his *Annals* of the time of Elizabeth, commissioned by Burghley before his death. 'I have', he tells his reader, 'learned of Tacitus that the principal business of Annals is to preserve virtuous actions from being buried in oblivion, and to deter men from either speaking or doing what is amiss, for fear of after-infamy with posterity.'[18] Camden here argues traditionally, as does Jonson, that one of the purposes of writing history is to improve the actions of those who read it. That is, he gives such writing a moral purpose. Yet, Camden's familiarity with Tacitus and his concern over contemporary politics came at a time when history began to be used increasingly for a less didactic purpose. Thomas's university years and Inns of Court life in the 1590s thus took place against a backdrop of political dissatisfaction, which the reading of Roman history helped to articulate. It could lead to trouble for those who articulated it.

---

[15] Blair Worden, 'Ben Jonson among the Historians', in *Culture and Politics in Early Stuart England*, ed. by Kevin Sharpe and Peter Lake (London: Macmillan, 1994), pp. 67–89 (p. 76).
[16] *Journal of the House of Commons*, I. 148, cited in Worden's 'Ben Jonson', p. 69.
[17] Richard Grenewey, *The Annales of Cornelius Tacitus* (London, 1598); the first page of unnumbered prefatory material is his letter to the Earl of Essex.
[18] William Camden, *The History of the Most Renowned and Victorious Princess Elizabeth, Late Queen of England*, ed. by Wallace T. MacCaffrey (Chicago: University of Chicago Press, 1970), p. 7.

One example of the perception of such history as potentially subversive lies in events surrounding the Essex Rebellion. Part of Essex's circle of intellectuals and writers was Sir John Hayward, whose prose work *The First Part of the Life and Raigne of King Henrie IIII* was to be, in 1599, one of the first published examples of the application of politic history.[19] According to S. L. Goldberg, politic history involved a new way of reading historical events. Rather than a retelling of the past to effect moral improvement:

> The factual was separated from the moral: 'ought' and 'is' were seen to be different. Instead of discussing what princes ought to do in moral terms, the advocates of the new history sought to understand what they did in fact, how and why they did it, how effective their measures were.[20]

Malcolm Smuts adds that it was a 'style of "analytic" history, influenced by the model of Tacitus and other ancient historians, which sought to expose the underlying causes of political events and the secret counsels of rulers'.[21] It is often interpreted as counter-cultural, as we can clearly see in the treatment of Hayward. As Grenewey had done his translation of Tacitus, Hayward dedicated to Essex his work on the removal of Richard II and the success of Henry IV. In 1601, in the aftermath of Essex's abortive rebellion, he was accused of writing a work which had inspired the nobleman's course. Indeed, his description of Richard's reign does on the surface seem similar to that of Elizabeth: both monarchs are childless; both face revolt in Ireland; both levy unpopular forced loans; and in Richard's loss of the throne to a noble rebel with great military reputation, Hayward appeared to his accusers to be making another parallel between the two. Just as the authorities saw as a call to arms the staging of *Richard II* (perhaps Shakespeare's play) at the Globe on the eve of the Essex Rebellion, they saw Hayward's writing as encouragement to revolution.[22]

---

[19] The concept of analytic or politic history is discussed by S. L. Goldberg in 'John Hayward, Politic Historian', where he notes of Hayward that '[h]e is always concerned to probe beneath the surface of events, to show how the past illustrates the permanent realities of human nature and politics, and to draw conclusions about them' (p. 235). It is further explored by Alan T. Bradford in 'Stuart Absolutism'. He discusses historians who explored the human causes of historical events and 'who seem to have moved largely in the orbit of the Earl of Essex' (p. 132).

[20] Goldberg, 'John Hayward, Politic Historian', p. 234.

[21] Smuts, 'Court-Centred Politics', p. 22.

[22] Janet Dickinson reinterprets the usual links made between the figures of Richard II and Elizabeth, and between Bolingbroke and Essex. In her reading, the play shows the fear of the monarch having poor counsel and thus enables the Essex Rebellion to be seen as a misguided and histrionic attempt to reach the queen and to regain her favour. See *Court Politics and the Earl of Essex, 1589–1601* (London: Pickering & Chatto, 2012), p. 65.

The link is clear, therefore, between the Neostoicism founded by Lipsius, which so clearly influenced politic history, and the Sidney and Essex circles.[23] After the death of Elizabeth, Lipsius's ideas travelled with key members to the circle of Prince Henry, and to the Protestant faction led at the beginning of James's reign by Southampton and Pembroke: the men with whom, as we have seen, Thomas was close at the Jacobean court.[24] Thomas's willingness to read his court contemporaries in the light of classical history is shown in the letters he wrote to Carr from the Tower, explored in the last chapter. The nicknames used form evidence of the allusive and playful mode of the quotidian communication between the men, who had been such close friends while gaining power. These letters show them to be on the verge of a counter-cultural, Tacitean judgement of autocratic rule. But now that they were part of the ruling elite, the question was whether they would retain their moral code and advise the rulers they worked for as honest counsellors? Or whether they would be flatterers, with a moral flexibility that enabled autocracy? These very real questions for those aspiring to be a key part in James's court were examined on stage through the play written by Thomas's contemporary, perhaps his friend, John Webster.

In the manner of politic history, the play does not demand judgement to teach a better way; rather, it represents the evils of the time as an inevitable consequence of the mechanisms of court power and encourages its audience to reflect on the parallels between imperial Rome, Malfi and London. One of the key characters in exploring this counter-cultural opposition to the kind of power that he, ironically, facilitates is Bosola, and the remainder of this chapter will look more closely at his representation, again in the light of our three key issues: social mobility and education; homosocial ease; and a flexible morality enabling personal power.

The Corruption and Redemption of Bosola

Bosola is born of non-aristocratic stock, and even the term 'courtier' seems initially a little above him. Unlike Antonio, he is not a long-standing post-holder at a court, and he is described variously as 'intelligencer',

---

[23] J. H. M. Salmon, 'Stoicism and Roman Example: Seneca and Tacitus in Jacobean England', *Journal of the History of Ideas*, Vol. 50, No. 2 (April–June 1989), pp. 199–225 (pp. 205–7).
[24] It is worth remembering that Pembroke also often worked alongside Cecil – particularly at the Jacobean court. See Pauline Croft, *King James* (Basingstoke: Palgrave, 2003), p. 92.

'gentleman', 'fellow', 'court-gall' and Duke Ferdinand's 'creature'.[25] The audience can infer the *fabula* as elements of his 'backstory' emerge and as the play opens he appears to have just emerged from the galleys. The crimes of which he was accused were apparently undertaken at the cardinal's behest, and he is now looking for preferment to a court position. Unlike that of the more diplomatic Antonio or Delio, both clearly travelled and, one assumes, fluent in languages, Bosola's position seems unlikely to use the skills of a humanist education. Yet Bosola is also, Delio tells the assembled courtiers, 'a fantastical scholar' whom the speaker knew 'in Padua' (3.3.40): 'he hath studied himself half blear-eyed to know the true symmetry of Caesar's nose by a shoeing horn; and this he did to gain the name of a speculative man' (ll. 43–6). This description, though mocking, emphasises Bosola's intelligence and his imagination – perhaps fanciful ideas are implied in 'fantastical'. His desire to be known as a 'speculative man' is glossed by one editor as indicative of his courtly ambition, making him akin to Gabriel Harvey and, interestingly, Thomas Overbury.[26] Bosola's aspiration for social mobility would not be held back, therefore, we discover, by his education.

Bosola is not merely hired covertly as the underhand operative of great men; at Ferdinand's suit, he is given the 'provisorship o'th'horse' (1.1.211). That is, he has the position which sounds suspiciously like that at the Jacobean court for which the Earl of Pembroke and Robert Carr were notorious rivals in 1612: a position which, at the court of the huntsman King James, meant a great deal of influence. Bosola in this way has access to the duchess, makes her gifts in courtly fashion, and has the run of the court. Ferdinand's preferment gives him courtly status and the means of achieving social mobility.

Bosola's preferment, and his consequent role in court, thus gives him a position which might be expected to tempt a man into corrupt practice. Even Antonio believes

>   his railing
> Is not for simple love of piety,
> Indeed he rails at those things which he wants,
> Would be as lecherous, covetous, or proud,
> Bloody, or envious, as any man,
> If he had means to be so.   (1.1.23–8)

Bosola's association with 'railing' here suggests his ambiguous morality from the play's opening. Antonio's comment that in Bosola's case it

---

[25] Labels applied by himself and others in the first scene: l. 254, l. 208, l. 210, l. 23 and l. 280.

[26] See John Russell Brown's Revels Plays edition of *The Duchess of Malfi*, p. 94.

'[i]s not for simple love of piety' suggests that railing against something could be the desire to eradicate something immoral, fitting thereby into a malcontent's role, but he does not believe it is in this case. In a theatrical context, the term was often applied to the boys' companies' acerbic repertory that targeted contemporary abuses, and thus allied the work of these playing companies with the vogue for satire originating at the Inns in the late Elizabethan period.[27] As Michael Shapiro points out in an early perceptive account of the relationship between the child actors and their Inns of Court audiences, in order to mock societal targets playwrights often relied upon the presumption that children could not be blamed for speaking the truth. He cites Thomas Heywood who, in his 1612 treatise, attacks those children's troupes who suppose 'their juniority to be a priviledge for any rayling, be it never so violent'.[28] The Queen's Revels company in particular had such a reputation, which, Shapiro tells us, 'was never more violent than it was in Day's *Isle of Gulls*, acted at Blackfriars about 1606; the parallels in this play satirized James and his favorites audaciously enough to provoke government reprisal'.[29] Yet playwrights who wrote satire often justified their work on the grounds that it pointed out the follies of the world, and allowed audience members seeing it to learn from the portrayal. Antonio's accusation of 'railing', too, fits with Bosola's role as a 'gall' (or scourge) of the court, drawing the attention of those who would hear him to the immoralities and corruptions around him.[30] Thus, his aim seems akin to those who would apply Tacitean history to their own centres of power; very early in the play there is a suggestion of Bosola's role as a character who outlines abuses to eradicate them, as satirists did, and this makes his immorality seem less clear-cut.

As well as his education, in fact, Bosola, above all other aspirant courtiers in the play, has a second trait likely to enable his success: the moral flexibility to enable personal rule and prerogative decision making even when it is directly against the law. The brothers' choice of Bosola as their

[27] Even the style of the Roman historians was influential on contemporary writers with which Thomas's generation would have been familiar. Their engagement with the style of Tacitus and other imperial writers is summarised thus: 'Tacitean prose, the close, epigrammatic prose of the Empire, was better suited to modern times, when power was once more passing from the floors of representative assemblies to the secret consultations of court and cabinets'; see Worden, 'Ben Jonson', p. 77.
[28] Thomas Heywood, *Apology for Actors* (London: Nicholas Oakes, 1612), G3ᵛ.
[29] Michael Shapiro, 'Towards a Reappraisal of the Children's Troupes', *Theatre Survey*, Vol. 13, No. 2 (November 1972), pp. 1–19 (pp. 8–9).
[30] The word has several relevant associations: *OED*, n.2., 3a), 'A person or thing that harasses or distresses'; 4a), 'A place rubbed bare', implying constant scouring. It is undoubtedly related, too, to usage n.1, with associations to the liver and the bitterness therein. The term has similarity to that used by Marston in his *The Scourge of Villainy*.

intelligencer shows that they understand this quality, and contrast his willingness to behave illegally and immorally with Antonio's honesty. Bosola conforms in many ways to the stereotype of a corrupt instrument, coming from a tradition of intelligent and verbally dextrous vice characters and deceptive revengers. Metatheatrical soliloquies or asides make clear the contrast between the villainous actions of such a man, and his perceptive grasp of political necessity. In an echo of the martial courtier discussed above, he describes himself as 'a soldier that hazards his limbs in a battle' (1.1.58–9), and as he laments his poor treatment from those he fought for on his return, we might expect him to be desirous of revenge. His military service is important, but, in Bosola, valour is not a desire to prove himself virtuous and honourable in a homosocial court. Instead, he emphasises his greed and his acceptance of corruption, as well as his political acumen, in telling Delio and Antonio:

> [The cardinal] and his brother are like plum trees that grow crooked over standing pools: they are rich, and o'erladen with fruit, and none but crows, pies and caterpillars feed on them. Could I be one of their flatt'ring panders, I would hang on their ears like a horse-leech till I were full, and then drop off.
> (ll. 48–53)

Bosola may be a malcontent, but he is a political realist and recognises that to succeed in gaining preferment at a court such as that of the cardinal or Duke Ferdinand, he must appear to be something he is not. He must be a 'flatt'ring pander[]' and *not* berate them with how they had mistreated him. The initial characterisation of Bosola is thus of one who conforms to the corruption of the regime he must follow in a particularly conscious way. He adapts himself, like a passive 'horse-leech', to their decisions, however far those decisions are from legality. From the sidelines, he makes his own judgement of the court, which shows an awareness of the law and of what is moral action; yet he also shows clearly his understanding of the false appearance and flexible morality required for courtly success, and – in contrast to Antonio – his willingness to adopt such a position.

In the first part of Webster's play, though, audience understanding of Bosola's *fabula* does not come through use of soliloquy and aside – techniques which often create moral ambiguity in an antagonist. Instead, here, Webster leads his audience to infer the motivations behind the man (who works for preferment in a court he despises) through a mixture of verbalised malcontentedness and the comments of others. Antonio, who tells Delio that he has heard Bosola is 'very valiant' (l. 74), is informed by his less naïve friend that the man's 'seven years in the galleys' were the result of 'a notorious murder', which ''twas thought the Cardinal suborned' (ll. 68–70). Though Bosola has claimed himself willing to be a 'flatt'ring pander[]', he consistently refuses to flatter. Duke Ferdinand, who clearly admires his unusual verbal 'honesty', calls upon him to

> Give me thy hand, I thank thee.
> I never gave pension but to flatterers
> Till I entertained thee.   (3.1.89–91)

Bosola is thus self-aware from the start, but the full ambiguity of his characterisation emerges gradually. It is only after he has acceded to the most illegal and immoral orders of his political masters, and murdered the duchess on their behalf, that he is able to articulate his full condemnation of a system that he has understood from the outset:

>   a guilty conscience
> Is a black register, wherein is writ
> All our good deeds and bad, a perspective
> That shows us hell! That we cannot be suffer'd
> To do good when we have a mind to it!   (4.2.346–50)

The ambiguity of Bosola is not a new idea. C. G. Thayer responded in the 1950s to the metatheatricality of the play, and proposed that, depicted as an actor, Bosola was deliberately constructed by Webster to confuse the audience. Thayer comments on references to theatrical performance in the text and sees this metatheatricality combined with the change in Bosola's attitudes and actions in the final section of the play.[31] He concludes that shifts in characterisation are evidence of the character consciously playing a role:

> The idea of Bosola as an actor, with a counterfeit face and a disguise, with his and Ferdinand's references to himself as an actor, is entirely consistent with the ambiguous preliminary presentation of the character in the words of Antonio and Delio at the beginning of the play.[32]

Rather than seeing these conflicting initial assessments reflecting different levels of naïveté in Antonio and Delio, Thayer sees ambiguity embedded in Bosola from the opening. Yet, it is equally possible to see the development in Bosola as being a progression to a realisation of the full consequences of the political system he has previously accepted, and his reaction against that. Bosola's characterisation thus engages the

---

[31] Such as Ferdinand's address to Bosola after the murder of the duchess: 'we observe in tragedies / That a good actor many times is cursed / For playing a villain's part' (4.2.278–80).

[32] C. G. Thayer, 'The Ambiguity of Bosola', *Studies in Philology*, Vol. 54, No. 2 (April 1957), pp. 162–71 (p. 171).

audience in the wider debate surrounding the morality of courtiership which this book argues has become a key issue in the Jacobean period. Aspirant audience members from the legal sector are made conscious of the moral dependency they will have on their ruler's prerogative decision making, and they see that an intelligent man's awareness of the vicious path he is required to travel often only increases his suffering. In the manner of politic history, the play does not necessarily demand judgement to teach a better way; it may equally represent the evils of the time, in Tacitean terms, as an inevitable consequence of the mechanisms of autocracy and prerogative power.

Bosola's ambiguity reveals the difficulty of judging virtue and villainy in a court environment which demanded the unquestioning performance of the ruler's wishes in return for preferment: in other words, the tension between the law and political life that is a fundamental of early modern writing in this area. Any assessment of dramatic villainy must consider the issues of appearance and reality raised, as judgements of virtue in both the Elizabethan and the Jacobean theatre appear to rely on the belief that a man should seem to be what he genuinely was. Important to Elizabethan plays as much as to later plays like *The Duchess of Malfi*, false appearance and pretence remain signs of potential villainy. In the Jacobean theatre, though, the audience are presented with the courtier's increasing realisation that he is unable to resist his king's demand to behave deceptively. Such a courtier may understand, as Bosola does, that the demands made of him are immoral, but in tragedy his only way of resisting them is through the killing of his ruler – that is, through further immoral action. *The Duchess of Malfi* implies throughout the powerlessness of the courtier. In a court that cannot sustain virtue, even a pragmatist such as Bosola cannot survive. He is educated and able because of that to access social mobility, and he is morally flexible enough to commit acts he is commanded to undertake, however little he wishes to do so. But he lacks the third element necessary to court success – homosocial ease and an established social place in the masculine court environment.

Bosola is ultimately unable to succeed because from the opening court scene we see him isolated from other men; he has no Delio, no *alter idem*. He is 'the only court-gall' (1.1.23), astringent and acerbic: unique in the play. He 'rails' (l. 25) acidly from the sidelines, and his position as royal spy ensures that the audience always see him as alien and threatening to others around him. The importance of being part of a group in a homosocial court is even shown to apply to Ferdinand; even he is potentially threatened by the laughter of the pack around him, and secures his place as leader of that pack by reprimanding them immediately. The duke's active manipulation of the courtly group to isolate his opponents would have been reminiscent to many in Webster's audiences. In a homosocial environment, *amicitia* is quickly perverted into both bullying and misogyny, and it is accompanied by the kind of flyting wit familiar to those such as Innsmen who lived and throve in such an environment.[33] The targeting of individuals, and their disempowerment through mockery of their masculinity, plays by the same rules as the late Elizabethan epigrams and satires of Sir John Davies and John Marston, or the witticisms in Manningham's *Diary*.

However, for a monarch with the power of promotion and rejection, and even of life and death, the potential for the abuse of this power is clear. The motivation for railing, too, has shifted when undertaken by a ruler. Epigrams and satires ostensibly aimed at cleansing an environment of the kinds of moral deviations depicted, just as Bosola is initially treated as if he is scourging the court. But the mockery offered by one in power such as Ferdinand embeds and reinforces deviance. Against such male confederacy, a woman – even a duchess in her own court – has no power. A lesser-ranking character such as Bosola, though a man, is equally unable to resist the immoral demands made of him. The male pack led by Ferdinand aims to isolate both the duchess and Bosola in different ways to disempower them. The duchess acts subversively to secure her own group (Cariola and Antonio), though ultimately this proves ineffective. Bosola, through most of the play, has no one he works alongside or anyone else whose well-being is important to him. The moment where he first decides to put his affection and respect for another man above self-seeking, when he regrets his actions in killing the duchess and swears to support Antonio, ironically, he kills him. Bosola is forced into isolation throughout the play, and his lack of homosocial support ultimately means his own destruction. His isolation, and his shifting response to the instructions he is given by the cardinal and Ferdinand, both contribute to a change in audience response to the 'court-gall' as the play goes on.

As we might expect from a legally trained playwright, how the audience judge the behaviour of the rulers and courtiers they see on stage is

---

[33] An essay by Lynne Magnusson on a play clearly influenced by Shakespeare's knowledge of the Inns of Court, *Love's Labour's Lost*, explores Innsmen's use of flyting and verbal aggression. Using a version of a paradigm for identifying a speech community, originally developed by linguist Dell Hymes, to examine the shared characteristics of members of the Inns of Court, she analyses the impact of such a background on the language of Innsmen, and proposes what she terms 'scoff power' as a key linguistic feature both at the Inns and in Shakespeare's play. See 'Scoff Power in *Love's Labour's Lost* and the Inns of Court', *Shakespeare Survey*, Vol. 57 (2004), pp. 196–208 (p. 205).

driven in part by their relationship with the law. In conclusion to this chapter on *The Duchess of Malfi*, it is interesting to explore how legal ideas and process are used to guide response to the power structure that these two courtiers navigate in Amalfi. In an early discussion of the Aragonian brothers, Antonio illustrates Ferdinand's dishonesty in the manner of his hearing a legal case:

> He speaks with others' tongues, and hears men's suits
> With others' ears: will seem to sleep o'th'bench
> Only to entrap offenders in their answers;
> Dooms men to death, by information,
> Rewards, by hearsay.   (1.1.168–72)

In terms anyone familiar with the law would understand immediately, Ferdinand is damned by his manipulation of defendants, and his willingness to accept evidence that is not built on artificial or inartificial proofs, but is simply 'hearsay'. The condemnation is a lawyer's one, and it reflects the duke as unfit to rule. Delio's response continues the legal condemnation, and offers an evocative image which warns the audience of the danger the duke represents:

> Then the law to him
> Is like a foul black cobweb to a spider,
> He makes it his dwelling, and a prison
> To entangle those shall feed him.   (1.1.172–5)

Shakespeare's Leontes may have drunk and seen the spider; Ferdinand *is* the spider. Delio's characterisation is a powerful indication of his villainy for the legal audience segment, and issues a warning against those in authority who would put prerogative power above the common law.

Webster shows the irony of the courtier's position in legal terms too, in the aftermath of the supreme act of courtly submission to royal prerogative in the play. The order to kill the duchess is an autocratic one. If Bosola is to sustain his position at court, relying as that does on personal preferment, he has no choice but to do as he is commanded, however little he wishes to undertake the immoral act. Having overcome his aversion and showing the flexibility an aspiring courtier must demonstrate to succeed, Bosola faces the ultimate betrayal from a ruler that Delio has characterised as the spider embedded in the law, and he is challenged by a mad Ferdinand to reflect on the proper legal practice that should have been followed to condemn a woman to death:

> Was I her judge?
> Did any ceremonial form of law
> Doom her to not being? Did a complete jury

Deliver her conviction up i'th'court ?
Where shall you find this judgement registered [. . .]   (4.2.289–93)

Bosola's response shows his realisation that the 'office of justice' has been 'perverted quite' by the autocratic actions of the ruler he has hung from 'like a horse-leech' through the play: a ruler whose position in the social hierarchy has been diminished by his own prerogative commands, until he is reduced to the status of 'one thief hang[ing] another' (1.1.296–7). The reminder of an English court of law, with its jury and its systems of equity, is the turning point for the courtier who has been conscious of what he should do throughout, but has chosen advancement over honour. For the final section of the play, he chooses the route of honour, and his overall ambiguity as an antagonist is demonstrated in his claim, before killing the cardinal, that '[t]he weakest arm is strong enough that strikes / With the sword of justice' (5.2.336–7). His revenge, when it comes, will be 'just' and would, he implies, though they are in Italy, satisfy that English common law of which so many in his audience are the champions.

So, this chapter ends on the image of a Jacobean audience watching *The Duchess of Malfi* at Blackfriars shortly after Thomas's death. Those from the nearby Middle Temple who knew him before his success, or those who had known him from his court position, as until recently the powerful right hand of the new Earl of Somerset, might have made a connection between events in the play and the fall of the well-known Jacobean courtier. As Antonio utters the memorable line 'let my son fly the courts of princes' (5.5.72), those men may have reflected that the desire for worldly riches and success at the court of James I of England led to the death of Thomas Overbury. If social mobility, homosociality and adherence to the king's personal decision making enabled a courtier's success, watching *The Duchess of Malfi* may have led them to question whether the betrayal of his friend or the opposition of a ruler led to his downfall.

Chapter 6

Chapman's Changing Worlds: From *Bussy D'Ambois* to *The Revenge*

For when loue kindles any knowing spirit,
It ends in vertue and effects diuine;
And is in friendship chaste, and masculine [. . .]

Bussy D'Ambois, 5.1.186–8[1]

So far in the second half of the book, Chapter 4 has shown the importance of the relative powers of common and prerogative law, and legal perceptions of sovereignty, to the representation of honest counsel in *The Winter's Tale*. In Chapter 5, too, I showed the need for a combination of humanist learning, homosocial efficacy and flexible morality to be a successful, socially mobile courtier in *The Duchess of Malfi*. Both plays were written within the five-year period this book focuses on – that of Thomas Overbury's sudden rise, his courtly influence and his death. For this final chapter, I shall adopt a different method, and compare two plays to illustrate what the book as a whole argues: that there was a shift in perceptions of court and courtiership during the rule of James VI and I.

It is through two plays by George Chapman, *The Tragedy of Bussy D'Ambois* and *The Revenge of Bussy D'Ambois*, that I shall explore this changing representation of courtiership. I shall outline differences between the two plays in the first section of the chapter, before looking at how the plays present key ideas this book as a whole has focused on. The chapter will therefore look in the second section at the repre-

---

[1] Quotations from both plays are taken from *The Plays of George Chapman: The Tragedies with Sir Gyles Goosecappe*, general editor Allan Holaday (Cambridge: D. S. Brewer, 1987). *The Tragedy of Bussy D'Ambois*, edited by John H. Smith, has parallel texts A (the 1604 Quarto) and B (printed in 1641, and argued by Smith to be the revised text shown on stage in 1610–11). I shall quote from Text A, except where specified. *The Revenge of Bussy D'Ambois* is edited by Robert J. Lordi. References will be made within the text.

sentation of power and legality, using, in addition to Tacitus, a further Roman model in the writing of Seneca. Then, thirdly, it will move on to explore how social mobility is differently handled, and finally it will return to the shifting presentation of *amicitia* in these plays. This introduction shows a little about what lies ahead.

To compare the plays, it is worth explaining their particular usefulness, with a word about stage and publishing history. The very successful *Bussy D'Ambois* was first staged by the second Paul's company around 1604, the year that James, newly acceded to the English crown, entered London, and it was first published in 1607. At the closure of Paul's playhouse, it was adopted by the Children of the Queen's Revels and the text was probably adapted for performance in 1610 at the Whitefriars alongside its sequel, *The Revenge of Bussy D'Ambois*.[2] The latter play was written about six years after the original, therefore, and is thus contemporary with *The Winter's Tale*, though it was first published in 1613. Looking at the relationship between the earlier play and its sequel, as I shall in the next section of this chapter, is thus particularly suggestive of the development of key ideas across this early period of James's reign. Chapman has developed the text of *Bussy* for a more firmly Jacobean audience and there are important differences between the two plays.

George Chapman was connected to the satellite court of Henry, Prince of Wales, and, in that context, showed his interest in the legality and mechanics of power. He became sewer-in-ordinary to the prince around the time of the writing of *Bussy D'Ambois*, very early in James's reign. The prince's circle, as I suggested in the last chapter, showed great interest in Neostoicism and in imperial Roman history as an analogy for English monarchical power, and Chapman's classical learning makes him likely to have appealed to the members of that circle. Clearly, he had a wide knowledge of Greek texts as well as Latin, famously translating Homer and dedicating some of that to Prince Henry, but the second part of this chapter will centre in particular on his reading of Tacitus and Seneca. I have already demonstrated the use of ideas and concepts in the recently translated work of Tacitus, the imperial historian, as a means of exposing the corruption of contemporary court culture. Here,

---

[2] See Peter Ure, 'The Date of the Revision of Chapman's *The Tragedy of Bussy D'Ambois*', *Notes and Queries*, Vol. 197 (1952), pp. 1–2, for discussion of revisions and playing history. He suggests that the second text of *Bussy* may have been written at the same time as *Revenge*, even though printed much later. Munro (*Queen's Revels*, p. 160) discusses the possibility that Nathan Field played both Bussy in the original play and Clermont in *The Revenge*; he is also proposed as the possible reworker of the play into its later form.

although I will make a case for an interest in the effect of autocratic rule similar to that explored in previous chapters, I will draw a clearer line between the characterisation of types of rule and their legal frameworks in republican and imperial Rome: two classical models of power used paradigmatically by Chapman to suggest fear of an increasingly corrupt and secretive courtiership in Jacobean England.

Contemporary with, though somewhat older than, Tacitus, Lucius Annaeus Seneca, referred to as Seneca the Younger, was tutor and advisor to the Emperor Nero and his political career is often seen as influential on his philosophy and his dramatic work. Certainly, for a writer such as Chapman who explored the moral decisions demanded in early modern court life, considering the work of Seneca could only be productive. Both of the plays under discussion here owe debts both to Senecan tragedy and to his philosophical writings, and the later *Revenge of Bussy D'Ambois* marks out its protagonist, Clermont, explicitly as a 'Senecall man' (4.4.42). Through him, Chapman explores ideas of Stoicism in the face of absolutism and the second section of this chapter will explore how the prince's circle saw contemporary resonances in imperial rather than republican Roman values. Both Bussy plays are explicitly concerned with recent French politics at the court of Henri III, and the focus on recent French history enabled Chapman to raise issues of sovereignty, legal jurisdiction and the morality of courts, and to represent courtiership in a way that scraped past the English censors. He was to be imprisoned for his satirical comedy in 1605 and reprimanded for a political tragedy in 1608, but he managed to see *Bussy D'Ambois* and *The Revenge of Bussy D'Ambois* to the stage without any problem with the authorities for which we have evidence.[3]

The third section of the chapter will return to develop another issue this book has considered already: social mobility. As we have already seen, rising courtiers of more lowly or middling background are often set in antithesis to a martial nobility at court, with the power of the latter often creating a kind of Elizabethan nostalgia for a golden age of benevolent aristocratic counsel for a monarch. The second Earl of Essex personified this ideal in the Jacobean memory, particularly in the circle surrounding Prince Henry, and the patrician role in the king's court is debated further in the Bussy plays as Chapman depicts contrasting members of the French aristocracy. The social rising of the D'Ambois

---

[3] Mark Thornton Burnett's article on Chapman for the *ODNB* suggests that objections from French authorities may have led to the closure of the second Paul's boys: 'The company that staged the play, the second Paul's Children, closed soon afterwards, probably because there had been official objections to its French political content.'

brothers, by contrast, is important to both plays, but it has a different significance in each.[4] I shall thus bring to a close this section of the chapter by returning to the debate in Jacobean literature between the relative exemplarity of the idealised military noble courtier and the low-born but learned counsellor.

From this exploration of the wider classical and historical contexts of the plays, the chapter will finally return to a focus on the Jacobean version of classical *amicitia*, vital to courtiership at this period and inherent in depictions of male courtiership on stage, as we have seen in previous chapters. I will argue that the two Bussy plays illustrate the changing attitude to homosociality and male friendship in general across the first decade of James's rule: a change that I established in Chapter 2. I will also argue that these two plays show a comparable shift in perception of men's courtly relationships. As well as reiteration of the key idea that effective performance in a homosocial environment is vital for courtly success – shown clearly in my discussion of *The Duchess of Malfi* – the Bussy plays go on to show how such relationships are problematised over the six years between the two due to the different kind of favouritism perceived to be common at the court of the new monarch. The dramatic representation of increasingly important courtly *amicitia* echoes the notorious relationship between Thomas Overbury and the king's favourite; contemporaries called Overbury Carr's 'minion', a word with powerful connotations in discussions of recent French history and especially the notorious court of Henri III.[5]

Bussy D'Ambois and its Sequel: The Deliberate Confusion of Virtue and Vice

The presentation of the D'Ambois brothers in Chapman's plays demands that his audience consider what makes a dramatic hero. From 1604

---

[4] In making Bussy begin the play in such a low social position, Chapman manipulates French history. Jonathan Patterson notes that 'by introducing Bussy without prospects or heritage, Chapman deliberately goes against historical circumstance. Chapman makes Bussy poor to furnish him (and thereby the audience) with a vantage point from which to experience the relative worthlessness of the social order, and, simultaneously, his dependence on it' (*Villainy in France (1463–1610): A Transcultural Study of Law and Literature* (Oxford: Oxford University Press, 2022), p. 259).

[5] For more discussion of the pervasive sexual immorality of the court of Henri III, see Joseph Cady, 'The "Masculine Love" of the "Princes of Sodom" "Practicing the Art of Ganymede" at Henri III's Court: The Homosexuality of Henri III and His Mignons in Pierre de L'Estoile's *Mémoires-Journaux*', in *Desire and Discipline: Sex and Sexuality in the Premodern West*, ed. by Jacqueline Murray and Konrad Eisenbichler (Toronto: University of Toronto Press, 1996), pp. 123–54.

when the dramatic vogue for revengers and their tragedies was at its apogee, to the more nuanced moral questions asked of power six years later, the question of heroism in the early modern playhouse is a focus of both plays. Chapman modifies several characters from his first tragedy in writing his second, and his changes are suggestive of a blurring of the boundary between virtue and villainy. An audience familiar with the original *Bussy* would undoubtedly have wondered what to make of some of these changes. The king, rather ineffectual in *Bussy D'Ambois*, becomes a tyrannous Machiavel in *The Revenge*. Monsieur, Bussy's main antagonist, is initially an example of the perversion of *amicitia* which allows him to plot the death of his 'sweet-heart' and to be labelled one of 'Fates ministers' by the summoned spirit, Behemoth. In the sequel, he becomes less and less relevant; after several acts missing from the action, and reported dead in passing, he appears finally in the surreal dance of ghosts as Montsurry dies. Even Montsurry himself, Bussy's murderer and the object of Clermont's revenge, is changed from the hated agent of Monsieur and Guise's plot, and the torturer of Tamyra, into a passive, ridiculous figure who initially refuses to fight Clermont and lies instead on the ground, and then forgives his murderer as he dies.[6] The final and greatest example of the confusion of villainy and virtue, though, lies in the changing depiction of the Duke of Guise. The Guise of *Bussy D'Ambois* is the second of Fate's ministers, co-plotter of Bussy's death and Bussy's sworn opponent.[7] The Guise of *The Revenge* is the man whose murder causes Bussy's brother not to celebrate, but to commit suicide. Chapman writes against expectation in this second play in making the man, hated in Protestant England as the instigator of the St Bartholomew's Day Massacre, sympathetic and full of virtue. The changes are deliberate if Chapman was working on the revisions of *Bussy D'Ambois* as he wrote *The Revenge*; by 1610, he seems to have seen this blurring of moral boundaries as more indicative of contemporary court mores.[8] Part of this blurring seems to

[6] Jonathan Patterson also discusses the shift in characterisation from the play to its sequel, noting of the king that Guise's 'erstwhile thuggish sidekick during the St Bartholomew slaughter [. . .] has since become the superficially "milde and calm" Henry III' (*Villainy in France*, p. 216).

[7] In his earlier incarnation, Guise is an example of the type of villainous character described by Patterson: 'Operating on a transcultural scale, appearing in many places and in countless texts, these villain personae seemed grossly in excess of any individual's judgement and control' (*Villainy in France*, p. 219).

[8] One explanation for the shift in characterisation is given by Shona McIntosh, in 'The Massacre of St Bartholomew on the English Stage: Chapman, Marlowe, and the Duke of Guise', *Renaissance Studies*, Vol. 26, No. 3 (2011), pp. 325–44. She argues that in giving to a Catholic character with the history of Guise politically challenging views, certainly opposing absolutism and verging in places on republicanism, Chapman is enabled to

reflect new ideas about genre, and an increasing distrust of traditional tragedy in particular. As Lucy Munro argues, 'Towards the end of the first decade of the seventeenth century, there seems to have been a wide-spread anxiety surrounding the tragic form. This discomfiture centred on tragedy's teleological narrative structure and on the supposed need for it to follow a factual narrative.'[9] The changes in attitude to genre are connected with classical reception and the growth of politic history, and the changes that Chapman makes in his sequel to *Bussy* reflect this.

Initially it seems to be the first of the two plays that shows a tarnished hero. Despite his valour and clear-sighted opposition to tyranny, Bussy shows hypocrisy in accepting Monsieur's preferment and enters into court veniality, with an adulterous affair that leads to his own murder. Chapman's evocation of pervasive court immorality makes it very difficult to distinguish between qualities in the brothers which are to be admired and those which are to be condemned. Although established at court under the patronage of the king's brother, Monsieur, and thus in a position of dependency upon him, both Bussy and Clermont show their virtue when they declare their absolute refusal to kill a king.[10] But the fact that, in both cases, the protagonists tell their patron that this is the case without being asked explicitly to carry out any such act is evidence of the immorality of the French court. An aspirant younger brother is assumed to wish the removal of his ruling sibling, and he will achieve this by asking someone he has preferred at court to commit the deed for him. Monsieur's comment that '[t]here's but a Thred betwixt me and a Croune' (1.1.1.41) is unheard by Bussy as it is in soliloquy, but, despite his immediate caveat that 'I would not wish it cut, vnlesse by Nature' (l. 42), it is sufficient to suggest to the audience that Bussy's assump-

---

explore these issues without retribution: 'Key to Chapman's protection of himself from the consequences of this debate is his portrayal of the Duke of Guise in a deeply paradoxical manner' (p. 334).

[9] Munro, *Queen's Revels*, p. 148. On the reasons for the generic shift, she cites Rosalyn L. Knutson, who explains that plays 'grew old, not in an aesthetic but in a generic sense', and as they were reworked for a later period writers added 'new parts that exploited currently fashionable motifs in the genres to which the revived plays belonged' ('Influence of the Repertory System on the Revival and Revision of *The Spanish Tragedy* and *Dr Faustus*', *English Literary Renaissance*, Vol. 18, No. 2 (1988), pp. 257–74 (p. 274).

[10] Asked by Monsieur, 'Wilt thou doe one thing for me then syncerelie?', Bussy's response is immediate: 'I, any thing, but killing of the King [. . .]' (3.2.311–12). In Text B, this refusal is repeated, along with an assurance of his loyalty to Monsieur: 'Then doe not doubt, / That there is any act within my nerves, / But killing of the King that is not yours' (B: 3.2.392–4). Clermont's repetition of this sole exclusion from what he is willing to do, also for Monsieur, comes in the first scene of *The Revenge* (1.1.278) and sounds like a deliberate allusion to his brother's line(s). Munro (*Queen's Revels*, p. 160) gives this as one of the pieces of textual evidence to show Chapman was revising the first play as he was writing the second.

tion is based on Monsieur's desire. As in *The Duchess of Malfi* and *The Winter's Tale*, therefore, the plays depend on an audience's established perception of court life: on the acceptance that the ambition of courtiers to secure more power inevitably leads to immoral behaviour.

Plotting elements as well as characters in *The Revenge* echo the original Bussy play; for instance, Chapman uses duels in both plays, but he uses them to very different ends. In the original play, we witness Bussy's decision to challenge the three 'perfum'd muske-Cats' (Barrisor, L'Anou and Pyrhot) who taunt him in the second scene, and the decision of Brisac and Melynell to join him.[11] The actual events of the duel take place off stage and we hear them recounted to the king by a 'Nuncius', in the vein of Greek tragedy. Lasting over 100 lines in both textual versions, the detailed account gives rhetorical proof of Bussy's valour; he kills his own opponent, then revenges the deaths of the two who fight alongside him, and, the only one of the six to remain alive, he is described in the final line of the Nuncius's account as 'the brauest man the French earth beares' (2.1.137). Comparing the 'stern fight' (l. 32) to that in Troy, where Barrisor is Hector and presumably Bussy and his allies the Greeks, the Nuncius appears to be well travelled as well as well read; he tells the king, 'in Arden I haue seen an Oke / Long shooke with tempests' (ll. 94–5) and compares this tree to mighty Barrisor, and a little later in the account recalls his 'young trauels through Armenia' where he 'once did see [. . .] An angry Vnicorne' charge at a man (ll. 117–19). Bussy is, it appears, deadly as this unicorn and nails the unfortunate L'Anou to the earth, not with his horn, but with his sword. The highly entertaining account is full of the circumstances we might expect in such *diegesis* to produce audience excitement as the waging of the battle is recounted. The audience is driven to admire the valour of first one nobleman, then another, as Chapman's choice of detail creates *enargeia*: the emotion at each twist of the narrative, that Quintilian taught his readers would be the outcome of such rhetoric. The battle is followed by the king's judge-

---

[11] McIntosh presents this duel, and the subsequent royal pardon, as a sign of the weakness of kingship and as a section of the play linking it to Marlowe's *Massacre at Paris*: 'In *The Massacre*, Henry's coronation is interrupted when one of his favourites cuts off the ear of a servant, prompting the Guise to order his arrest. However, Henry intervenes, saying "I will be his bail / For this offence". This has a parallel in *Bussy* when [. . .] the Guise is pivotal in demanding retribution, calling it "a pitious and horrid murther!" but the king, after the intervention of his brother, pardons Bussy' ('The Massacre of St Bartholomew on the English Stage', p. 335). For Patterson, when Bussy expects the king to pardon his behaviour and defend his right to uphold his honour even if the law does not allow it: '[a] tragic irony accompanies this self-interested distortion of Bodinian doctrines of absolute sovereignty, by which Bussy secures an extrajudicial exoneration from the king' (*Villainy in France*, p. 260).

ment and sentencing of a man who has killed three of his noble courtiers and the sentence appears to contravene legal justice. Bussy may be brave, but the Nuncius's account focuses on the epic nature of the men's military ventures rather than providing any mitigating circumstances or motivation to enable the king to judge the equity of the case. Monsieur's defence of Bussy is to plead his own family connection to the king ('for your brothers loue', l. 146) to which the king, properly, replies that 'these wilfull murthers / Are euer past our pardon' (ll. 149–50). Yet, after Monsieur's eloquent defence of Bussy as a 'iust reuenger[]' rather than a 'murtherous mind[]' (ll. 168–9), the king does indeed pardon him. The audience may have been just as impressed by Bussy's martial valour as the on-stage auditors of the Nuncius's account, but the events they hear recounted cannot convince them of his innocence. The defence of Bussy by the enamoured Monsieur is based on partiality and in legal terms does not affect the king's, or the audience's, judgement of his guilt. As Bernadette Meyler argues, in the staging of royal pardoning,

> the play's judgment of the character is not altered by the pardon, but the consequences of judgment are instead suspended. Likewise, to the extent that equity involves relaxing what would otherwise be a negative judgment about the effects of a perpetrator's actions in light of his or her less than culpable intent, theaters of pardoning often stage the opposite scenario.[12]

In other words, the audience know that Bussy is guilty – the actual judgement is the same whether he is punished or pardoned, and the king refers to his 'merited death' (l. 182); but the king's pardoning of him has the effect of consolidating royal power. As Katherine Rowe comments, 'That pardon effectively makes Bussy's liberty a matter of royal prerogative.'[13] There is no sense in which Henri III relies on the equity of the case; we may or may not consider Bussy's intentions or motives and lessen our sense of his guilt, but the king does not do that. He considers Bussy guilty but, allowing himself to be persuaded by his brother, still pardons him.

To continue our exploration of the changes Chapman makes between the plays, the parallel duel in *The Revenge* is the challenge Clermont makes to Montsurry, the murderer of his brother, and which leads to his killing of the nobleman in the final scene – but this duel requires no royal pardon as he shortly after takes his own life. The appearance of the ghost of Bussy urging revenge, and the audience having witnessed the

---

[12] Bernadette Meyler, *Theaters of Pardoning* (Ithaca: Cornell University Press, 2019), p. 25.
[13] Katherine Rowe, 'Memory and Revision in Chapman's Bussy Plays', *Renaissance Drama*, n.s., Vol. 31, 'Performing Affect' (2002), pp. 125–52 (p. 132).

role Montsurry played in the earlier death, justify Clermont's actions to a greater degree than anyone could have justified Bussy's slaughter of the three noblemen, and could have led to a judgement involving equity. But Chapman contrasts the brothers in the two plays, as Clermont doesn't plead for pardon or allow a courtier-patron to do so on his behalf. Instead, he seeks his own death willingly in Stoic fashion and renders the king's judgement of the case irrelevant. The second play thus changes the focus from the exercise of royal power in response to a duel, and the audience's judgement of the personal power Henri III demonstrates, to the philosophical response of the protagonist. Clermont's survival or his death are not in the hands of his royal master, but in his own.

Legal students and practising lawyers in the audiences, for the boy players at Paul's playhouse for the first play's earlier production and at Whitefriars for both plays a few years later, were in a position to assess the parallels between the staged court and the court of King James. They could judge the veracity of the depiction of court life and royal justice within the discourse of corruption the plays established. As I noted earlier, indoor theatre audiences contained a larger proportion of Inns of Court men than the amphitheatres, due to higher ticket prices, geographical proximity and a similarity of age between many law students and the boy players. It was also due to the playhouses' choice of repertoire. Writers were often connected to the Inns, and their entrepreneurial theatre managers would have tried to ensure that their output appealed to their paying customers.[14] Munro argues that there is no direct link between the output of the playing companies and the interests of customers:

> There is, however, little evidence that audiences viewed dramatists and their plays as representing their interests. The audiences in the Blackfriars and Whitefriars theatres may have been richer than average but, judging by the many comments on failed plays, they were not especially discerning or cooperative. In many accounts the relationship between spectator and play is combative to say the least.[15]

Yet playhouses were businesses and had to appeal to their most influential customer base, even if they sometimes failed to achieve this. If one considers the way plays explore social mobility and ways of gaining court preferment; the debate between common law and the royal prerogative; or the development of a classically allusive stage language which assumes a humanist education, this connection can be argued to be a strong one. Often, clear reasons can be adduced as to why specific

---

[14] See, for example, Munro, *Queen's Revels*, p. 63.
[15] Munro, *Queen's Revels*, p. 65.

plays failed, and perhaps, despite these, the repertoire generally does represent audience interests.

Munro is surely right, though, that the relationship between audience and theatrical work is 'combative'. Boy company audiences were not undiscriminating – far from it – and several plays presented by the boy players were not wholly successful on stage: including, it seems, *The Revenge of Bussy D'Ambois*.[16] But in the climate of the Inns, with the popularity of satire and the performance of revels, not to mention the combative debate and mooting which lay at the heart of legal training, this combative quality does not necessarily mean a lack of common interest. By the season of 1610–11, following the closure of Paul's, the collapse of the short-lived Children of the King's Revels, and Burbage's reclamation of Blackfriars for adult players, the Queen's Revels company at Whitefriars was the only boys' company in London and it would be keen to keep its clientele engaged. Writing a sequel to a play that had been very successful was clearly a way to do that. The kind of sequel Chapman wrote engaged differently with some of the issues in the original play, and also, as the next section shows, built on the wider cultural and literary interests of the Blackfriars audience.

Royal Prerogative and the Fear of Absolute Power: Republican vs Imperial Roman Analogues

As I established in Chapter 5, the histories of Tacitus gained in popularity from the 1580s onwards. The Roman historian presented political life in imperial Rome and its mechanisms, and this was of increasing interest through the latter years of Elizabeth's reign, especially to those in the circles of Sidney and Essex. It continued to be of interest to many in Jacobean England, centring now on those around Prince Henry, some of whom had been in the previous groups and others of whom shared their political and religious views. The group had key things in common: they were Protestants who were largely supportive of a monarchy advised by a well-informed, aristocratic counsel, and unafraid of

---

[16] The dedicatory epistle in the first printed text of *The Revenge*, dated 1613, is to the Lord Chamberlain, Thomas Howard. Chapman admits that 'in the Scaenicall presentation, it might meet with some maligners', but is keen to say that 'euen therein, it past with approbation of more worthy iudgements' (A3ᵛ), and the play is advertised on the title page as 'often presented at the priuate Play-house in the White-Fryers', which must imply some level of success on stage. The playwright contrasts Howard's 'Iudicaiall Ingenuitie' with the assessment of 'those Ignoble and sowre-brow'd Worldlings' (A4ʳ) who he implies disliked the play. However, it is clear that the play did not reach the level of popularity enjoyed by the first Bussy play.

military engagement when defence of religion depended on that. One might overstate the counter-cultural role of the 'satellite court' of Prince Henry in this period, but it did include men of a certain set of beliefs, many of which were slightly different to those of the pacific king whose writings as King of Scotland had suggested his belief in his divine right. My argument here is that, whether or not James could be described as an autocratic monarch or was in favour of absolutism, elements of his court, and writers around them, showed a fear of increasing royal power.

Many around Prince Henry were influenced in this by wider continental political theory, and these writers' reception of classical texts. As Chapman's focus is on recent French history, it is informative to look at writing emerging from France in the years leading up to his time of writing *Bussy* and *The Revenge*, for instance a Huguenot tract emerging in Latin in Edinburgh in 1579, *Vindiciae Contra Tyrannos*. Anonymous, though often attributed to Philippe du Plessis-Mornay, the tract is typical of many in this period that argue those at court with power and influence, as well as the king himself, have a responsibility for the people:

> Let the magnates remember, rather, that if the role they receive brings honor, it carries many burdens also. The commonwealth has no doubt been committed and entrusted to the king as its supreme and principal protector, and yet to them also, as its co-protectors [. . .] The magnates [. . .] share the prince's guilt if they fail to suppress tyranny or to prevent it, or to compensate the prince's negligence with energetic activity of their own.[17]

The parallels between the early modern French monarchy and imperial Rome seem clear: 'From an early seventeenth-century standpoint, Henri III strongly recalled Rome's most villainous and profligate emperors, Caligula and Nero, yet he appeared to have surpassed both in his failure to maintain law and order, and discipline in public finances.'[18] In his discussion of the influence on Chapman's Byron plays of *Vindiciae Contra Tyrannos*, and of other texts similar to it emerging from France, Glen Mynott argues that part of the playwright's interest perhaps lay in the similarities between England and France at the beginning of the seventeenth century: for instance, both countries were led by new dynasties, where kings had been king of a smaller kingdom first, and both kings were making a peace with Spain that was unpopular with their nobili-

[17] *Constitutionalism and Resistance in the Sixteenth Century: Three Treatises by Hotman, Beza and Mornay*, ed. and trans. by Julian H. Franklin (New York: Pegasus, 1969), p. 192.
[18] Patterson, *Villainy in France*, p. 226.

ty.[19] Mynott cites J. P. Sommerville in arguing that, although absolutist ideas were in existence in England under Elizabeth, it was the arrival of James that 'brought them to prominence'.[20] He uses James's own words to parliament to illustrate his belief in absolutism, and how fear of the king's manipulation of the law lay at its heart:

> Fears about the imposition of absolute government in England were inten-
> sified by James's speech to Parliament in 1607 [. . .] While urging union
> between England and Scotland, which would incorporate the two legal
> systems, James complained of the arbitrary nature of a common law based
> on 'cases and presidents [precedents]' and suggested that all law should be
> clearly written down. James also claimed that the king was the final arbiter
> in any dispute over the interpretation of the law: 'In such a question wherein
> no positive Law is resolute, *Rex est Judex* for he is *Lex loquens* and is to
> supply the Law, where the Law wants.' This was a challenge to the heart of
> constitutional theology.[21]

James's ideas of the king being above the law could have opened the door to absolutism in future, even if he himself wasn't a tyrant; they would have removed the traditional protections of the commonwealth provided by the common law.

The fear of absolutism and tyranny was seen to have an analogue in Tacitean history, but also in the work of a second Roman writer increasingly influential on the group surrounding the prince – a writer personally involved in the politics of imperial Rome: Seneca. Recent work by Curtis Perry reviews ideas about the relationship between dramatists and Seneca, in the light of a re-evaluation of the latter's work. The influence of Seneca on early modern dramatists has, Perry argues, been seen to be stylistically negative but he aims to reassess this influence following recent revisions of Seneca's reception.[22] One of the major arguments in his book is that 'in Seneca's writings across genres [there is] an imperial-era recasting of a republican ethos in which elite identity was construed

[19] Glen Mynott, '"We must not be more true to kings / Than Kings are to their sub-jects": France and the Politics of the Ancient Constitution in Chapman's Byron Plays', *Renaissance Studies*, Vol. 9, No. 4 (1995), pp. 477–93 (p. 486).

[20] Mynott, '"We must not be more true to kings"', p. 486, citing J. P. Sommerville's *Politics and Ideology in England, 1603–1640* (London: Longman, 1986), p. 47.

[21] Mynott, '"We must not be more true to kings"', p. 487. The quotations are from King James I's speech to parliament, 31 March 1607, in *The Political Works of James I*, ed. by Charles Howard Mcilwain (Cambridge, MA: Harvard University Press, 1918; repr. New York: Russell and Russell, 1965), pp. 290–305 (pp. 293 and 299).

[22] Curtis Perry, *Shakespeare and Senecan Tragedy* (Cambridge: Cambridge University Press, 2020). He gives as examples Gordon Braden's *Renaissance Tragedy and the Senecan Tradition: Anger's Privilege* (New Haven: Yale University Press, 1985) and Robert Miola, *Shakespeare and Classical Tragedy: The Influence of Seneca* (Oxford: Clarendon Press, 1992).

in public terms and confirmed by mutual, reciprocal approbation among men'.[23] The French political context in *The Revenge* seems to demonstrate this 'recasting', as the 'mutual, reciprocal approbation' between Clermont and Guise contrasts actively with the prevailing climate of distrust and deception. In the original play, on the other hand, there is no sign on stage of an antithetical republican ethos of masculine support, and the nature of power in France, with the king determining preferment from the top, is established from the play's opening.[24]

In *Bussy D'Ambois*, Bussy, alone on stage at the play's opening, outlines why he despises court life. As one excluded from it, he notes how 'Fortune, not Reason, rules the state of things' (1.1.1); 'Who is not poore, is monstrous' (l. 3), he famously declares, making monsters of the courtiers whom he characterises with 'their affected grauitie of voice, / Sowerness of countenance, maners crueltie, / Authoritie, wealth, and all the spawne of Fortune' (ll. 11–13). Yet, like that of Bosola, Bussy's commentary is from the sidelines. He sets the political context with views that oppose the current regime, but he is set apart from the main stream of court opinion. Bussy has the scale and tenor of a Senecan protagonist and these 'are too absolute in their self-determination to be easily dissolved back into any socially structured political or providential allegory'.[25] Perry argues that Ciceronian, republican Rome is outward looking and demands that men play their part in this wider world, where Seneca reflects imperial Rome, internalised and focused on the self. Though Bussy opposes the world in which he finds himself, he is no more outward looking than the rest of the corrupt and self-centred court.

Seeing the source of the ahistorical play *The Revenge of Bussy D'Ambois* in the character of the stoical Count D'Auvergne in Grimeston's French history (the source of the Byron plays), E. E. Wilson Jr comments that '[i]n *The Revenge* Chapman wanted, above all else, to present a dramatic hero exemplifying the stoic philosophy in which he had become absorbed'.[26] In this play, opposition to the prevailing political ethos is more general than in *Bussy*, and the play opens with two separate dialogues outlining courtiers' disapproval of political life

---

[23] Perry, *Shakespeare and Senecan Tragedy*, p. 7. He cites Shadi Bartsch's *The Mirror of the Self: Sexuality, Self-Knowledge, and the Gaze in the Early Roman Empire* (Bristol: University of Chicago Press, 2006) as influential on this thinking.

[24] The only hint of this perhaps lies off stage in Bussy's reported slaughter of noble opponents in the duel, revenging the killing of the two men who supported him. But if this is a demonstration of Ciceronian ideals, it is a parody of them.

[25] Perry, *Shakespeare and Senecan Tragedy*, p. 114.

[26] E. E. Wilson Jr, 'The Genesis of Chapman's *The Revenge of Bussy D'Ambois*', *Modern Language Notes*, Vol. 71, No. 8 (December 1956), pp. 567–9 (p. 569).

in France. Malcontentedness appears rife, not simply to be the personal view of one character, as in *Bussy*, and it plays on a nostalgia reminiscent of republican ideals. This opposition is also associated with legal process. Renel comments that

> things most lawfull
> Were once most royall; Kings sought common good,
> Mens manly liberties, though ne'er so meane,
> And had their owne swindge so: more free, and more [. . .]   (1.1.19–22)

He does not oppose monarchy, but autocracy. Forming his argument around issues of law and justice, he contrasts 'th'inordinate swindge of downe-right power' (l. 15), which causes justice to be 'gag'd and tongue-tide' (l. 18), with the freedom an independent legal system should have. He tells the apparently supportive royal intelligencer, Baligny, that though previous generations in France enjoyed 'manly liberties', after the change to autocratic rule, 'no man could be good but he was punisht: / Tyrants being still more fearefull of the good / Then of the bad' (ll. 27–9). This opposition to the king's unfettered use of his prerogative continues throughout the play.

These attitudes are, of course, not quite as they appear. This is not a play about the removal of a bad king, despite the widespread acceptance that the regime is flawed. Instead, it is a play which focuses on the effect of pervasive courtly villainy on those who work within it. The play is concerned to explore the morality of the clash between those who oppose the regime, and those pragmatic politicians (with all the contemporary negative connotations of that noun) who work within and support it. Baligny is a master of the deceptive *habitus* which so often characterises courtly success on stage. Although he is married to Clermont's sister and one might expect a natural family loyalty, his priority is to draw out the radicalism of other courtiers and to report it to the king: 'hauing sworne my seruice in the search / Of all such Malecontents, and their designes, / By seeming one, affected with their faction' (ll. 123–5). He demonstrates all attributes of a villain: deceptive, quick witted, verbally dextrous, and putting ambition before all other ties, including those to his family. Similarly to Bosola, Baligny, despite a clear understanding of the immorality of power, goes on to be the king's 'creature', working for Henry to ensure the downfall and eventual death of Clermont. Eventually realising the betrayal of his brother-in-law, Clermont explains to Guise the effect of the man's deceptive appearance, that seemingly necessary tool of courtly success:

> O Baligny, who would beleeue there were
> A man, that (onely since his lookes are rais'd

Vpwards, and haue but sacred heauen in sight)
Could beare a minde so more then diuellish [. . .]   (5.1.121–4)

Baligny is indicative of the moral turpitude and pervasive corruption of the French court, and this is characterised by Clermont in terms of his lack of constancy. His face and his mind, his appearance and his actions, conflict in a way which appears to be a court norm. Yet Baligny, although a typical representation of the deceptive courtier, is not a revenger, and one might expect that a revenger would have some of those deceptive attributes too.

The Revenge challenges the audience's expectations of the revenge genre, and the way Chapman chooses to do this enables conclusions to be drawn about the ambiguity of Clermont. In her recent edition of the play, Katharine Eisaman Maus calls it an 'anti-revenge play[]', and notes that it 'attempts to domesticate some of the genre's disruptive energies'.[27] Indeed, another possible reason the play failed to capture many in its original audience could thus have been its generic experimentation. Albert H. Tricomi argues that Chapman's deliberate contrast between the two Bussy plays explains his 'refusal to write an orthodox Senecan revenge tragedy – to have Clermont play the melodramatic revenger, to bring the Ghost's customary call for vengeance upon the stage, to exploit the conventional blood and madness of revenge, and to allow his hero any death other than a composed one'.[28] Whether or not Chapman's decision to adapt the genre resided in this desire (and Tricomi's thesis is a convincing one on the whole), it is perhaps understandable that the taking out of the more sensational aspects of revenge tragedy, in a play which had a title encouraging its audience to expect them, might have led to disappointment in the playhouse. Tricomi argues that 'Clermont's even Stoic disposition must have provided an unexpected and ingenious dramatic turn for audiences expecting a swashbuckling sequel', but not seeing what they expected would not have been guaranteed to please. Of course, there is a debt to *Hamlet*, and both protagonists are notably reluctant revengers, but the two characters' reasons for deferral of action are different; it is in the differences between them that we see what makes Clermont so ambivalent a court figure.

While Hamlet considers whether there is sufficient motivation for revenge, whether he is able to act bravely enough, or even whether the

---

[27] Katharine Eisaman Maus, ed., *Four Revenge Tragedies* (Oxford: Oxford University Press, 1995), p. xxiii.
[28] Albert H. Tricomi, 'The Revised *Bussy D'Ambois* and *The Revenge of Bussy D'Ambois*: Joint Performance in Thematic Counterpoint', *English Language Notes*, Vol. 9, No. 4 (1972), pp. 253–62 (p. 261).

Ghost is a voice from the devil, Clermont is clear in his attitudes to such retributive action. Berated by his sister, Charlotte, for taking so long over the matter, he asks reasonably, 'Shall we reuenge a villainie with villainie?' (3.2.96). He positions himself as the virtuous antithesis to passionate revengers and replies calmly to Charlotte, 'Shall wee equal be / With villaines?' (ll. 97–8). He challenges his sister's reasoning, and explains his reservations in political and legal terms, arguing that 'Neuer priuate cause / Should take on it the part of publicke Lawes' (ll. 115–16). In terms of a Roman analogy, he here argues a republican case in an imperial, absolutist context. There is an obvious appeal to an audience of lawyers in rehearsing the debate around the relationship between law and revenge, and as elsewhere Clermont speaks as if mooting. He develops his ideas fully and with rhetorical skill, although he is notably unsuccessful in persuading the pragmatic Charlotte. His fundamentally undramatic style and passionless conclusion, in some ways the triumph of his Stoic philosophy, lie at the root of the difficulty an audience has assessing virtue and villainy in *The Revenge*.[29]

Clermont's Stoicism is part of the Senecan context of *The Revenge*, and the extent to which he can be seen as successfully Stoic is important. Several twentieth-century critics of the play, including some of its first editors, saw Clermont as the ideal and rational 'Senecall' man, his arguments perhaps representing those of the playwright himself.[30] Clermont's learning is established and consolidated through his rhetorical skill and his detailed use of Epictetus and Aristotle, as well as Seneca. But as later critics have argued, his suicide and his reasons for it show the limitations of his Stoicism. In her reassessment of the play, Suzanne Kistler argues persuasively that Clermont is actually a failing Stoic, and she sets the play alongside contemporary philosophical attitudes

---

[29] The audience have not seen the ghost of Bussy on stage and they do not see Clermont engaging in a debate with a revenant. Contrasting the sequel with the initial play, it is as if Chapman had decided to move any action off stage or replace movement in *Bussy* with a parallel stasis in *The Revenge*. The enacted torture, seduction and summoning of spirits of the first play is replaced by debate and inaction: the appearance of Bussy's ghost is not until Act 5, and when it does appear on stage, Clermont is so caught up in his discussion with Guise that he initially overlooks it.

[30] Fredson Bowers, for example, notes, 'the conception of Clermont's revenge and his methods corresponds entirely to the ideals of the best English thought of the period, so that in the person of Clermont we have for the first time a stage-revenger who could be an English gentleman' (*Elizabethan Revenge Tragedy, 1587–1642* (Gloucester, MA: Peter Smith, 1959), p. 145). See also John W. Wieler, *George Chapman: The Effect of Stoicism upon his Tragedies* (New York: King's Crown Press, 1949); Michael Higgins, 'Chapman's "Senecal Man": A Study in Jacobean Psychology', *The Review of English Studies*, Vol. 21, No. 83 (1945), pp. 183–91, and 'The Development of the "Senecal Man"', *The Review of English Studies*, Vol. 23, No. 89 (1947), pp. 24–33.

to argue that 'Chapman, an acknowledged intellectual, must have been as familiar with the [more popular] arguments against Stoicism as he was with Epictetus, Seneca, and the versions of Lipsius and Du Vair'.[31] She proposes that the contemporary Whitefriars audience would have known, as much as Chapman, that revenge was 'morally unacceptable', and in killing Montsurry, instead of being the image of virtue, Clermont 'has left behind his own world and entered theirs' – that of those characters who 'belonged to the world of conspiracy and policy'.[32] He has, in his own terms, 'reuenge[d] a villainie with villainie'. In her conclusion, though, Kistler ignores Seneca's *De Ira* which explores the concept of the Stoic revenger. Seneca gives exempla: 'My father being murdered – I will defend him; he is slain – I will avenge him, not because I grieve, but because it is my duty.'[33] Clermont in this way demonstrates that revenge can be carried out judicially, and does not need to be an emotive business. However, Kistler's argument that Clermont's portrayal is considerably more ambiguous than has been thought is overall a persuasive one.

This ambiguity speaks to the complexity of early Jacobean politics, and contemporary debates about absolutism, Curtis Perry argues, explain the shift from a fascination with republican to imperial literature:

> people ceased to have the same level of confidence in ideas about the efficacy of ethical community associated with Cicero and republican Rome. Seneca and Tacitus, because they write for a post-republican Roman world, offer perspectives felt to be valuable in a world of political and sectarian instability.[34]

There is a contrast set up between the modern, imperial court, where the freedom of men is limited by kings' tolerance of flattering courtiers, and the noble court of the past, where men grew more free and the commonwealth more virtuous, supported by their noble monarch. This is, of course, a contrast between a nostalgic view of Elizabethan mores, evocative in the Jacobean imaginary of the ideals of republican Rome, and the current court, analogous to the corruption of empire. We have already seen Renel comment in the opening scene on this paradigmatic shift:

> things most lawfull
> Were once most royall; Kings sought common good,

---

[31] Suzanne F. Kistler, '"Strange and Far-Removed Shores": A Reconsideration of *The Revenge of Bussy D'Ambois*', *Studies in Philology*, Vol. 77, No. 2 (Spring 1980), pp. 128–44 (p. 130).

[32] Kistler, '"Strange and Far-Removed Shores"', pp. 137–8.

[33] Perry, *Shakespeare and Senecan Tragedy*, p. 8, citing 1.12.1–2.

[34] Perry, *Shakespeare and Senecan Tragedy*, p. 156.

Mens manly liberties [. . .]
  [. . .] more free, and more,
But when pride enter'd them, and Rule by power,
All browes that smil'd beneath them, frown'd; hearts grieu'd,
By imitation; vertue quite was vanisht,
And all men studi'd selfe-loue, fraud, and vice [. . .]   (1.1.19–26)

The development of more autocratic government, seen in, or feared in, the rule of James VI and I, is thus characterised in Renel's speech. The play may ostensibly be about France, but the political message and the Elizabethan nostalgia in which it is framed certainly have resonance for court life in Jacobean London.

Social Mobility: Mushroom Courtiers and Martial Aristocrats

Elizabethan nostalgia can often be a cue to consider the morality of social mobility. As previous chapters have demonstrated, success at court is seen, from the 1580s onwards, in the context of an antithesis set up between two groups of men: those who saw themselves as born to rule, aristocratic counsellors, often with military experience, and those who, through humanist learning and through their wits, had been raised to power by the king or other key nobles. The Earl of Essex is often seen as a representative of the former. The latter, though – the men rising in society from more lowly beginnings – were seen as either praiseworthy, because they had been preferred for their talents, or culpable, because they had been raised by their ability to flatter and deceive.[35]

The Revenge begins with a direct address to this idea of a man's value being inherent in those of noble birth. Monsieur may be 'a Kings sonne borne' (l. 280), but, Clermont tells him clearly:

You did no Princely deedes
Ere you're borne (I take it) to deserue it;
Nor did you any since that I haue heard;
Nor will doe euer any, as all thinke.   (ll. 287–90)

---

[35] Jonathan Patterson argues that the play interrogates the contemporary debate over the possibility of a classically inspired nobility in modern political culture, a question as key in Jacobean England as in contemporary France. *Bussy*, Patterson suggests, 'is a mature humanist tragedy: one that draws from the wellspring of Antiquity (and, some would say, from a new-found radicalism) to ponder how a traditional culture of nobility shaped by frank ideals of martial valour could not adapt to the "mutable" environment of the Valois royal court' (*Villainy in France*, p. 258).

This radical refusal to acknowledge the authority of birthright continues in the ensuing dialogue with Guise, and the men clearly believe that
power should reside in those who have merit. Guise comments sneeringly
of 'the insolence / Of [Monsieur']s high birth and greatnesse (which were
neuer / Effects of his deserts, but of his fortune)' (ll. 294–6). The friends
are unified in their political radicalism and, as these are the characters
with whom the audience seem expected to have sympathy throughout the play, their beliefs have weight. The audience at Whitefriars in
1610–11 would have consisted of many who had benefited, or were
benefiting, from the social mobility possible in contemporary London.
Scholars such as Jean Howard and Janette Dillon, who explore the
impact of London settings on stage, do not see them as simply mimetic,
reflective of actual lived experience in London, but rather they inter-
rogate the representational qualities of place in contemporary drama,
and explore the impact on an audience of narratives which built associations around specific, known locations. Though Chapman avoids these
associations by setting his play ostensibly in France, the work of topographical critics helps us to see how playwrights show the economic and
social development of early modern London as well as an interpretation
of place; their work contributes also to an analysis of attitudes to social
hierarchy and ambition. Social mobility is, of course, also linked to
increasing trade and the demands for social participation from the newly
rich merchant classes. Dillon makes the connection between economics
and societal shift, summarising the difficulty London's inhabitants had
in making sense of the world around them: 'A rising population was
putting pressure on the boundaries of the city [. . .] greater social mobility was putting traditional social divisions under pressure.'[36]

Similarly, Howard's claim that '[w]riting about London, as many
dramatists did, was one way [. . .] discursively to manage change and
to provide interpretations and conceptualizations of both new and
old aspects of the city' could equally lead scholars to see the drama of
the period enabling audiences to understand the changing *social* landscape of early modern London, which is itself so intrinsically linked
to geographical shifts.[37] Monsieur reminds both Bussy and Clermont
that they have been plucked from obscurity to shine at court. In their
social mobility they are comparable with Camillo, Bosola and Antonio.
Discovered by Monsieur, as his would-be patron notes, 'discontent with
his neglected worth' (1.1.47), Bussy overcomes his initial malcontent

---

[36] Dillon, *Theatre, Court and City*, p. 32.
[37] Jean Howard, *Theater of a City: The Places of London Comedy, 1598–1642*
(Philadelphia: University of Pennsylvania Press, 2007), p. 3.

railing against the court and allows himself to be taken to 'the well-head' (l. 84): source of all plenty. Bussy covers his *volte-face* with a sophistic argument which suggests that pragmatism is a greater feature than idealism in his make-up. In soliloquy, he argues cogently that those who allude to Original Sin and propose that 'Mans first houres rise, is first steppe to his fall' (l. 136) are perhaps simply cynical. After all, he concludes, 'men that fall low must die, / As well as men cast headlong from the skie' (ll. 138–9). Despite his evident wit and verbal dexterity, as Monsieur sends him money it is difficult to see his actions as much more than hypocritical. His opening condemnation of the court suggests a clear-sighted recognition of its superficiality and its moral turpitude. His rejection of this position in favour of status and personal gain and sexual gratification is not the action of an unambiguously virtuous man.

The audience is told of Clermont's social mobility, too, through dialogue with Monsieur. As the courtier is proving less malleable than the Lord had hoped, he provokes Clermont, telling him he has 'rak'd thee / Out of the dung-hill? cast my cast Ward-robe on thee?' (1.1.256–7), suggesting that he has provided a suitable appearance for Clermont's rising fortunes, and enabled him to adopt the *habitus* of a courtier.[38] He says he made both brothers 'my sawcy bon companions' (l. 259), and taught them to call noblemen '[b]y the corruption of their names; Iack, Tom' (l. 261).[39] The implication of male camaraderie here, suggestive of the homosocial court environment and overcoming social difference, is to prove a pale shadow of the genuine *amicitia* between Clermont and Guise.

These verbal challenges to Clermont's social status from Monsieur also contrast with another admirable feature the brothers share; like

---

[38] The possible humour underlying parts of *The Revenge* is perhaps suggested by the similarity of these lines with those of another 1610 play, *The Alchemist*, where in a comparable situation, Face reminds Subtle that he was no one until the servant found him:

> You had raked and pick'd from dunghills, before day;
> Your feet in mouldy slippers, for your kibes;
> A felt of rug, and a thin threaden cloke,
> That scarce would cover your no buttocks –
>
> (1.1.33–7; *Cambridge Jonson*, Vol. III, p. 565)

Whereas Subtle was raking from dunghills, Clermont was raked out of one. Interestingly, apart from the lexical similarity, Face discusses clothing Subtle, as Monsieur does Clermont: a sign, perhaps, of asserting control, as it resembles making the other man their lackey or apprentice, obliged to wear the clothes provided by his employer. For a discussion of the equipping of servants with livery, see Robert I. Lublin, *Costuming the Shakespearean Stage* (Farnham: Ashgate, 2011), p. 68.

[39] As we saw in Chapter 3, the naming of individuals at court was an important way of asserting both intimacy and superiority; Overbury's use of code names, for example, as the Innsmen's use of Latinate nicknames in satirical work, seems related to the camaraderie implied in the D'Ambois brothers' use of affectionate abbreviations.

Bussy, Clermont has military credentials and is physically brave, not knowing the fear of death which, in contrast, threatens Guise. Both brothers have the martial qualities that, in other contexts, might mark out an aristocratic status and suggest heroism. Gilles Bertheau, in his essay on *The Revenge*, comments 'celle de restaurer les modes de l'action aristocratique corrompus par le vice et l'oisiveté des courtisans de la Cour du dernier Valois: Henri III', seeing the representation of Clermont as championing the aristocratic valour corrupted by the vice and idleness of the Valois court.[40] The social status of Clermont is thus problematised. Unlike the action heroics of the earlier representation of Bussy, in his brother this valour is symbolic of nobility: for Bertheau, more noble than the actual aristocrats. It echoes the heroism and martial quality of Essex and Sidney, and in their cases too it was combined with Neostoicism, but, in Clermont's case, it is not a product of high birth. The play suggests a natural nobility of character that is not connected to aristocratic birth, challenging key social assumptions underlying Jacobean nostalgia for the virtuous noble counsel of Elizabeth's reign.

Homosociality and the Triumph of *amicitia*

In his essay on 'worldly stoicism' in the play, Allen Bergson argues that Clermont's lack of heroism and the character's relationship with Guise reveal the site of the protagonist's ambiguity. His analysis of Clermont's language in the final act makes a convincing argument that Clermont's love for Guise proves more of an influence on the supposedly passionless Stoic than earlier critics have considered. As Bergson argues, there is a deep irony in Chapman's portrayal of a character whose anti-court stance is forged within the court itself, and whose rational Stoicism is not able to combat his emotional drives and his political being. As Bergson explains:

> it is Clermont's paradoxical, all too worldly love for the Guise – possible only within the court – that constitutes the most powerful threat to his Stoic otherworldliness. Although Clermont's suicide seems to manifest a Stoic contempt of the world [. . .] the figurative language he employs transforms that act into an expression of worldly love and dependence charged with both amorous and political connotations.[41]

---

[40] Gilles Bertheau, 'Passion et néostoïcisme dans *The Revenge of Bussy D'Ambois* (1613) de George Chapman (1559?–1634)', *Études Épistémè* [Online], 1, 2002, http://journals.openedition.org/episteme/8437 (accessed 24 August 2021).
[41] Allen Bergson, 'The Worldly Stoicism of George Chapman's *The Revenge of Bussy*

Alike in many of their attitudes and sympathies, Clermont and Guise form a pair of male friends in the humanist tradition. Their friendship is one of the mind, evocative of Ciceronian *amicitia* and its humanist echoes. Clermont clearly positions their relationship in antithesis to romantic heterosexual love, and even denies that the word 'love' can be used of a bond with women, relying – as this latter must – on instinctive animal impulses:

> I denie that any man doth loue,
> Affecting wiues, maides, widowes, any women:
> For neither Flies loue milke, although they drowne
> In greedy search thereof; nor doth the Bee
> Loue honey, though the labour of her life
> Is spent in gathering it [. . .]   (5.1.170–5)

Rather, their relationship, he argues, is based on masculine reason. It is the product of learning and religion, and provokes not passion, but virtue:

> [. . .] when humanitie rules men and women,
> Tis for societie confined in reason.
> But what excites the beds desire in bloud,
> By no meanes iustly can be construed loue;
> For when loue kindles any knowing spirit,
> It ends in vertue and effects diuine;
> And is in friendship chaste, and masculine.   (ll. 182–8)

The logic of the argument is reminiscent of classical and humanist writers on male friendship. Guise's response to Clermont's rational examination of their friendship, though, is considerably more erotic, and it is his 'bloud', not his mind, which is overwhelmed by his love for Clermont: 'Thou shalt my Mistresse be; me thinkes my bloud / Is taken vp to all loue with thy vertues' (ll. 189–90). The addition of 'vertues' appears almost an afterthought after the labelling of his friend as his mistress.[42] Guise finds the pursuit of Stoicism less easy in many ways. Faced with death, he has to wrestle with his fear, and only overcomes it through calling upon Clermont to 'chide / This softnesse from my flesh' (5.4.20–1). He appears throughout to indicate the potential for a more physical desire than Clermont.

Even for Clermont a 'chaste, and masculine' relationship is not the whole story. An entirely reasonable antithesis to the kind of passion

---

D'Ambois and *The Tragedy of Chabot, Admiral of France'*, *Philological Quarterly*, Vol. 55, No. 1 (Winter 1976), pp. 43–64 (p. 50).

[42] It is, of course, reminiscent of the recently published 'Master-Mistress' of Shakespeare's Sonnet 20, where the man addressed, 'the master-mistress of my passion', is demonstrated to be superior to a woman in his constancy.

which drives men to sex with women would not have produced the intensely emotional response which leads to his suicide. Suicide is the honourable exit for a Stoic and, in Stoic fashion, he controls the fear with which Guise struggles. Yet Clermont's suicide is prompted by his friend's death and the inability to contemplate life without him. It is not – as it perhaps should be – the outcome of his eventual, rather tame, revenge on Montsurry. The guiding impulse of Clermont's emotions at this vital point reveals how much he is a part of the court he appears to despise. As Bergson argues, 'Clermont's language reflects, as through habit, the political dependencies which so troubled him when a courtier; what is more, his language evokes the larger political world which he so inexplicably (and, for the audience, ironically) inhabited.'[43]

In the climax of *The Revenge* – the suicide of Clermont – the boundary between virtue and worldly corruption is not clear-cut. Learning of Guise's death, with a final message to his friend on his lips, Clermont first describes in Neoplatonic terms the impossibility of his surviving:

> But Friendship is the Sement of two mindes,
> As of one man the soule and body is,
> Of which one cannot seuer, but the other
> Suffers a needful separation.   (5.5.157–60)

Once again, they are two minds, but encompassed in one being. Bergson argues that his subsequent extended image of unclothing, though explicitly the removal of worldliness from his soul to prepare it for heaven, is transformed by his speech into a physical disrobing of lovers:

> The garment or the couer of the minde,
> The humane soule is; of the soule, the spirit
> The proper robe is; of the spirit, the bloud;
> And of the bloud, the body is the shrowd.
> With that must I beginne then to vnclothe,
> And come at th'other.   (ll. 170–5)

'Th'other' becomes a confused indicator simultaneously of God and Guise: a confusion continued in the ensuing ambiguity of 'my master cals', when his master, his Lord, again could be his friend or his deity, and actually appears to be a combination of the two:

>   my master cals [. . .]
> [. . .]
> Rather than here liue, readie euery houre
> To feede theeues, beasts, and be the slaue of power?
> I come my Lord, Clermont thy creature comes.   (ll. 183–93)[44]

---

[43] Bergson, 'Worldly Stoicism', p. 44.

[44] Clermont's speech as he decides on death is capable of being read in several ways.

In the final moments of his life, the courtier and the Stoic, the worldly lover and the otherworldly, combine to reveal the multivalence of Clermont. He is, in his aspiration for a philosophical and honourable existence, the product of an earthly, political world. By his lights, he has killed a man and – as he told his sister of a man who commits such an act – he is 'equal [. . .] / With villaines' (3.2.97–8). His all too human love for his friend becomes enmeshed with his love for God. His avowed desire for a classical purity is impossible in the face of the pervasive corruption of court life. As Suzanne Kistler argues, 'the final irony' of *The Revenge* is that Clermont, like Bussy before him, 'has no impact whatsoever on political reality. The corrupt court system continues unaffected by their lives or deaths.'[45]

The continuation of the regime is conveyed in the final irony of a fundamentally ironic play, as King Henry takes on the role conventionally given to the character in a tragedy who looks forward to the new, reformed regime. In *The Duchess of Malfi*, even though Delio's optimism seems unlikely, he is at least attempting a reform of the state. The revised version of *Bussy D'Ambois* has Tamyra and Montsurry going their separate ways after Bussy's death, and its reworked tragicomic ending is clearly necessary to lead into the sequel. Yet, as Munro comments, 'this version of *Bussy*, with its final image of eternal separation, also resists any consolation that tragedy might bring, and any sense that society can be rebuilt in its aftermath'.[46] The end is even less consoling in *The Revenge*, where the king who has presided over a court of deception, self-seeking and murder offers a brief regret at Clermont's death and ordains that the 'fatall roome' where he died should be 'shut vp', cut off from the court so the possibility of the D'Ambois brothers' influence

---

Where Bergson sees his final words of undressing as suggestive of *amicitia* and physical desire, Suzanne Kistler sees the extended metaphor of the ship as a perversion of Epictetus' image of the ship at anchorage and thus the speech as a rejection of Stoicism (see '"Strange and Far-Removed Shores"', p. 143). It is also possible to read the speech as a judgement of the slavish entrapment of acquisitive courtiers by their greed, and it can be seen in the light of recent work on colonialism linked to the Inns of Court, from which many of Chapman's audience would have been drawn (see, for example, Lauren Working, *The Making of an Imperial Polity: Civility and America in the Jacobean Metropolis* (Cambridge: Cambridge University Press, 2020). Clermont's speech talks of a ship reaching a foreign land and the acquisitive travellers going ashore for 'Fresh water, victuals, precious stones, and pearle', but fearing to be captured. In this context, Clermont is rushing back aboard at the call of the ship's master to avoid being left behind, and the court becomes the enslaver that a virtuous man must flee from, despite the exotic attractions laid out to lure men in.

45 Kistler, '"Strange and Far-Removed Shores"', p. 143.
46 Munro, *Queen's Revels*, p. 162.

is denied for ever. The ending of *Revenge* shows the bleakest and least comforting of tragic endings.

It is clear at the end of *The Revenge* that the power of individuals to effect change on their courtly environment is much less than suggested in *The Winter's Tale*, or even in *The Duchess of Malfi*, where Webster produces no real conviction that Bosola's removal of the corrupt individual at the 'well-head' will lead to long-term change. The plays discussed in this second half of the book, suggesting the inevitability of court corruption, have shown the impact that has on men, such as Thomas, who would be courtiers. As Clermont argues as he decides upon suicide, the alternative to following Guise to heaven is to remain at court, 'readie euery houre / To feede theeues, beasts, and be the slaue of power' (5.5.191–2). He would have to be one of Bosola's 'flatt'ring panders', surviving amongst those powerful at court by 'hang[ing] on their ears like a horse-leech'. Yet, despite the consistent portrayal of moral turpitude and the acceptance of pervasive corruption implied in a court position, it remains clear that audience members, as Thomas had, actively sought such preferment. Both Webster's and Chapman's plays show death to be the outcome of such a Tacitean environment, where deception enables absolutist rule and neither the common law, honest counsel nor true *amicitia* is able to resist the force acting against them. *The Winter's Tale* too, though its outcome is not ultimately tragic, threatens death as punishment for opposing absolutism and suggests that only a magical remedy can prevent this. The presentation on stage of the political world in which Thomas Overbury lived and died would, reasonably, have led audience members to believe by the time of the famous murder trials of 1615 that his death had been the result of Jacobean court corruption.

Afterword

As I write this final section of the book, news comes in of the searching of Donald Trump's Mar-a-Lago home to find hidden papers containing 'state secrets'. I remember the regular disagreements during his presidency about the use of executive powers and think of the Jacobean fear of the potential excesses of royal prerogative. In the UK, the press has enjoyed the stories about Prime Minister Boris Johnson's redecoration of his Downing Street home with 'hangings, pictures, and household stuff' from John Lewis and the financial drain on the state from political extravagance. Johnson's education at a school, Eton, with its roots in the Tudor humanist system, and the desire for social mobility in UK politics, remain current issues. His degree in Classics, at an Oxford college just down the road from the Queen's of Thomas Overbury, has informed his public persona, though few would accuse him of absorbing Ciceronian style or engaging in *imitatio*. However, in the case of both leaders, a key topic has been the nature of their speech making, and the role of rhetoric (or the lack of what we think of as statesman-like oratory) in the persuasion of voters. It is hardly worth commenting on the ongoing debate over political truth telling and deception in power. In other words, the issues of this book have never seemed so resonant.

So, what do we conclude about Thomas Overbury? He was, in the words of Chamberlain just after his death, 'a very unfortunat man, for nobody almost pities him, and his very frends speake but indifferently of him'.[1] Wotton's *Schadenfreude* at his rapid decline and imprisonment accompanies the dislike of the courtier conveyed in his letters to Edmund Bacon. Certainly, in the trials for his murder two years after this, both Edward Coke and Francis Bacon were to present him as an unsympathetic figure, insolent, as we have seen, and even guilty of treason.

---

[1] Letter 82, p. 173.

But Thomas had not always been disliked and distrusted. The first reference to him in print was an epigram in the *Affaniae* by his Oxford contemporary Charles Fitzgeoffrey, written in 1601, the year the subject travelled to Edinburgh.[2] The epigram is a complimentary, if hyperbolic and rather sentimental, evocation both of the writer's passion for Thomas, and of the esteem in which he holds his friend. Describing him as 'made from pure honey and pure affection, and the liquors of Juno's breast', Fitzgeoffrey goes on to explain how his fellow student heals the 'blind, bleary little eyes' of Cupid and suggests that, as the 'god of health', he only can heal the writer 'whose heart is stricken by a burning flame'. The evocation of Fitzgeoffrey's passion for Thomas is expressed in typically classical terms, as 'the furies of the fire' burning the poet's heart 'damaged by Diones wound' can only be extinguished by 'the honeyed stream' of Thomas's 'Muse'. The source of his friend's efficacy as a healer is, it seems, 'the nectar of [his] mouth and the balsam of [his] tongue', suggesting perhaps that, at this early stage, as his appearances in Manningham's *Diary* suggest, Thomas's articulate verbal dexterity is impressive. It is also clear that Thomas, even at this stage, could inspire the strong affections of young men; even if we do not see in Fitzgeoffrey's desire to 'perish wholly drowned and overwhelmed in the honeyed stream of his Muse' thinly veiled allusions to the little death of orgasm, the excess of his tribute to the younger man demonstrates the latter's power to enrapture those with whom he was close.

Ben Jonson, too, knew Thomas well, and over many years. References in Manningham suggest their relationship began before 1602, and they apparently had a dispute over the patronage of the Countess of Rutland after the writing of Thomas's poem *A Wife*. Jonson's talk to William Drummond of Hawthornden led the latter to recount an anecdote concerning the poem and the reading of it to the Countess of Rutland, daughter of Sir Philip Sidney, and wife to the fifth earl. According to Drummond:

> The Countess of Rutland was nothing inferior to her Father Sir P. Sidney in poesie. Sir Th: Overburie was in love with her, and caused Ben to read his wyffe to her, which he, with ane excellent grace did & praised the Author. that the Morne Thereafter he discorded with Overburie, who could have him to intend a sute that was unlawful.[3]

---

[2] Charles Fitzgeoffrey, *Affaniae I* (Oxford, 1601). Accessed at http://www.philological.bham.ac.uk/affaniae/1eng.html (31 August 2022), with English translation by Dana F. Sutton.

[3] *Ben Jonson*, ed. by C. H. Herford and Percy Simpson, 11 vols. (Oxford: Clarendon Press, 1925–52), Vol. I, p. 138.

The countess's supposed liking for the line 'He comes too *neere*, that comes *to be denide*' might, indeed, be surmised to be a warning to either of the men, if they, indeed, competed for her affections. Her marriage at fourteen to the older Roger Manners was supposedly an unhappy one, but her father's revered status, as well as her literary reputation and patronage, ensured that she became a magnet for those with literary aspirations, even without her personal charms.[4]

After the conclusion of the murder trials, Jonson wrote an epigram complimenting Thomas on raising the moral tone of the court.[5] He also complimented him in classical terms, if not quite so emotionally as Fitzgeoffrey. His esteem of the former courtier is also based on his wit, but he goes further, to explain 'where thou liv'st thou mak'st life understood', suggestive of a perception which could be expressed through his speech, but may also indicate insightful writings. This poem, published in 1616, shows, perhaps, a more positive reputation of the courtier after his untimely death, and, coming as it does from someone close to the man, it also gives some evidence of the terms in which he was valued by those who knew him. Jonson reformulates Thomas's lack of circumspection, and turns his perceptive but reckless comments on the court into a tribute, suggesting that they improve it: 'that wit there and manners might be saved'. Published after the conclusion of the murder trial, this could suggest more popular sympathy with the man that people had, by that point, forgotten was considered difficult and insolent.

It is easy to take on Francis Bacon's dislike of the murder victim, accompanied as it is by the acerbic comments of Wotton and Chamberlain, and assume that this was the wider view. Though the afterlife of Thomas Overbury is a bigger project than this Afterword can encompass, I'd like to finish with some suggestions that his contemporaries viewed him, and his political career, in slightly different terms.

---

[4] Drummond also offers another intriguing link between Overbury, Jonson and the countess, as all are named as having performed in one of Jonson's court masques, *The May Lord*, with Overbury playing Mogibell, while Jonson's name was Alkin (*Ben Jonson*, Vol. I, p. 143).

[5] *Ben Jonson*, Vol. VIII, p. 73. See David Wykes' essay on Jonson's epigrams ('Ben Jonson's *Chaste Booke* – The Epigrammes', *Culture, Theory and Critique*, Vol. 13, No. 1 (1969), pp. 76–87), which talks of Jonson's reinventing the eulogistic epigram. He notes: 'Certain elements here will be found to occur again and again in this type of poem. The title name is thought of as being full of meaning in itself; here Overbury's very name is praise. He is also a social hero, in this case in the context of the court, where his coming has saved wit and manners and put to flight ignorance and pride—two cardinal sins for Jonson. In line 4 the poet makes a distinction between the "great" and the "good". "Greatness" is conferred by the world, in titles and honours; "goodness" can only be earned and is incorruptible.'

It is worth remembering, firstly, that a man who knew Thomas well at the end of his life, and, indeed, was executed for his part in the murder, spoke of a different kind of man as he faced that execution. Gervase Elwes, Lieutenant of the Tower, talks of his 'bloody and enormous act against a kind gentleman, who deserved not ill at my hands, not at any man's else for aught I know' as he speaks at the scaffold, running counter to the narrative established by the prosecutors in court.[6] Publications following the trials suggest a more sympathetic popular memory, but they had obviously begun before this point; perhaps indeed the months of gossip caused by the trials themselves led to this. Francis Bacon, never letting slip by the chance to blame Thomas, comments on the immorality of the courtier who 'was wholly possessed with ambition and vain-glory' and 'was loth to have any partners in the favour of my lord of Somerset'. In his antipathetic summary at this point, though, Bacon reveals that contrasting popular sympathy: 'Overbury was naught and corrupt; the ballads must be mended for that point.' Clearly there are already, by the time of the trials in 1616, publications of ballads that show a different view of the murder victim to that Bacon is pushing.

The fact that these are ballads leads me to my final thoughts about the reception of Thomas by his contemporaries, and what he came to represent after his death. Ballads are a non-elite form of literature. Thomas Overbury, aspiring to rise in the Jacobean political world, is not an obvious subject for popular sympathy amongst those who were not part of the world of the royal court, but he perhaps became a touchstone for many arguing against autocratic power and the very elite that he had aspired to join. These nameless 'ballads' mentioned by Bacon are part of the evidence of an opposition to the perceived corruption of the Jacobean court, discussed at more length by Alastair Bellany:

> In newsletters, separates, broadsides, pamphlets and libels, on the streets, in the courtroom, at Paul's, on the Exchange and around the gallows, narratives linked Overbury's death to clusters of transgressions that had profoundly corrupted the Jacobean court, compromising its idealised status as moral educator of the country.[7]

Bellany presents the scandal as being used with some limited effect by the group of court 'patriots', opposed to pro-Spanish policies and the power of the Howards, in the immediate aftermath of the trials. However, he underplays how much the image of Thomas Overbury

---

[6] Howell, *State Trials*, p. 943.
[7] Bellany, *The Politics of Court Scandal*, p. 250.

presented in the popular literature of 1615–16 is based on features of the real Thomas that we have seen bubbling underneath much of his court career. Protestantism is a factor in the Howards' distrust of the courtier: a feature of his life in Oxford, represented in Manningham's diary, lying behind his association with Southampton and Pembroke in the factions of the Jacobean court, and apparent in his communications with one of those 'patriots', William Trumbull.[8] To take one text as an example of the promotion of Thomas's virtues, we might look at Richard Niccols' pamphlet poem, *Sir Thomas Overburies Vision*, published in 1616.[9]

The poem has the ghost of Thomas appearing to the poet in a dream, and taking him on a midnight visit to the Tower of London to hear from the ghosts of those who have, by now, been executed for participating in his murder. Apart from the clearly moral purpose of the poem, written by Niccols shortly after his re-editing of *A Mirror for Magistrates*, and showing much of the same tone, the poem also gives the character of Thomas a chance to lament, not his sins, as the others do, but his foolishness in being so trusting of his friend. He tells the poet:

> I was, (aye me, that I was ever so)
> Belov'd in court, first step to all my woe
> There did I gain the grace of Prince and Peeres,
> Knowne old in judgement, though but young in yeeres

Written only three years after Overbury's death, and by a writer who had some knowledge of the court, it would simply not be credible that his poem did not reflect some of the feelings of onlookers there. Niccols' early sympathy for the Earl of Essex (he sailed, for instance, as a young man as part of the fleet on the Cadiz expedition) would make him naturally look for the best in a man whose politics, and religion, he perhaps shared; but it does also give the lie to Chamberlain's condemnatory view of Thomas's friends. Indeed, the voice of his ghost in Niccols' poem addresses that very point, how slander of the courtier by his enemies after his death in 1613 was intended to destroy his image:

> Such monsters were my tiger-hearted foes,
> Who unremorsefull of my forepast woes,
> When from their cruell hands my soule was fled,
> Did with their tongues pursue me beeing dead.

---

[8] See, for instance, the exchange in Letters 25 (p. 86) and 27 (p. 88).
[9] Richard Niccols, *Sir Thomas Overburies Vision: With the ghoasts of Weston, Mrs. Turner, the late Lieftenant of the Tower, and Franklin* (London, 1616).

And he continues:

> Now when false rumours breath throughout the court
> And citty both, had blowne this false report,
> Many, that oft before approv'd my name
> With praise for virtue, blusht, as if the shame
> Of my supposed vice, thus given forth,
> Did argue their weak judgement of my worth [. . .]

Establishing the validity of the perception of politicians when they are alive is a difficult thing. Who can say whether Donald Trump aims to undermine the democratic system, or Boris Johnson is more misunderstood than the press would suggest? It is even more difficult over 400 years after a Jacobean courtier's death. Evidence for the complexity of the man lies in both the life of Thomas Overbury, and the afterlife of his reputation in 1615–16. As well as the literary texts that present him as more sinned against than sinning, one might look also at the posthumous reception of his most famous writing: the long poem entitled *A Wife*.

The poem's literary merits are not the subject of this book, but the genre Thomas chose to write is further evidence of his religious inclinations. *A Wife* fits into a Protestant tradition of writing treatises to encourage marriage but to discourage inappropriate marriage. Sid Ray, in her essay on such tracts, argues that this is a Puritan desire to encourage marriage in opposition to Catholic celibacy, and, as such, is a powerful demonstration of Reformation ideas.[10] There is some dispute about when Thomas's poem was written, though it is possible that it was a (perhaps ill-considered) gift for Robert Carr to help prevent him from making the mistake of marrying Frances Howard. Both the death in 1612 of Frances Manners (who was said, as we have seen, to have enjoyed the poem), and a reference to it in another epigram on Thomas Overbury which was published in that year, prove the poem's genesis must have been before the final fateful year of the writer's life.[11] Other

---

[10] Sid Ray, '"Those Whom God Hath Joined Together": Bondage Metaphors and Marital Advice in Early Modern England', in *Domestic Arrangements in Early Modern England*, ed. by Kari Boyd McBride (Pittsburgh, PA: Duquesne University Press, 2002), pp. 34–5.

[11] See Book V of John Owen's *Epigrammata*, no. 48, 'Sir Thomas Overbury's Ingenious Poeme of a Compleat Wife':

> Thou dost describe a Wife in such a dress
> As *Tully* doth an Orator express:
> And if to such a wife thou wedded wert,
> She would be farr to short of thy desert.

Accessed at http://www.philological.bham.ac.uk/owen/5eng.html (28 August 2022), translated from Latin into English by Dana F. Sutton.

scholars, such as Mark Bland, argue that it is in fact a much earlier work and not actually written in the context of Carr's love for Howard at all.[12] But, regardless of when it was written, the poem's posthumous publication history gives more evidence of the popularity Thomas enjoyed after death. *A Wife* was first published by Lawrence Lisle in 1614, having been entered into the Stationers' Register at the end of the year before.[13] The first edition published the poem alone, and the second edition in 1614 had it accompanied by the first three Characters ('A Good Woman', 'A Very Woman' and 'Her Next Part'). Many scholars no longer think the characters, written in a Theophrastian vein, were the work of Thomas Overbury, and indeed subsequent editions saw more and more characters added, by further hands. Presumably ghoulish curiosity was a contributing factor in the large number of editions of this volume that emerged on the heels of these, and Bruce McIver demonstrates how different dates of publication echoed new stages, initially, in the trials of those accused of involvement in Thomas's death. There are several publications, too, written in response to *A Wife*, some directly satirising its style and content. From the anonymous *The Husband; a poem expressed in a Compleat Man*, also brought out by Lawrence Lisle in 1614, to the 1616 satirical response of John Davies of Hereford (*A Select Second Husband for Sir Thomas Overburie's Wife, Now a Matchless Widow*), early responses were quick to appear and showed a desire to capitalise on the popularity of Thomas's poem.

In addition to literary evidence of his afterlife, one might also look at portraiture. There is, of course, the much-reproduced Renold Elstracke engraving, where the slightly puritanical Thomas wears a thoughtful, melancholy expression, and is writing a poem on his own death. But there is also a clutch of portraits that are likely to be images of the man who gained a special status after his murder as a Protestant champion of court morals. The undisputed portrait on the cover of this book is that currently owned by the Bodleian Library, and given to the library by the Overbury family. Its provenance is clear. Others, with a very great resemblance to this portrait, have more recently been claimed to be of Shakespeare, such as that usually referred to as the Cobbe portrait due to its ownership by the eighteenth-century clergyman Charles Cobbe. Part of the argument for this, proposed by Stanley Wells and other

---

[12] Mark Bland, in *A Guide to Early Printed Books and Manuscripts* (Oxford: Wiley Blackwell, 2010), p. 125, argues that *A Wife* dates from 1601–2 and was written while Thomas was still at Middle Temple.

[13] See Bruce McIver, '*A Wife Now the Widdow*: Lawrence Lisle and the Popularity of the Overburian Characters', *South Atlantic Review*, Vol. 59, No. 1 (January 1994), pp. 27–44, for more detail on the publication history.

contributors to a 2009 collection, is that the provenance of the painting is from the estate of the Earl of Southampton, Shakespeare's patron, and it is argued that he is likely to wish to possess a portrait of the famous playwright.[14] Whatever the rights and wrongs of the debate on the Cobbe portrait, it appears to me that the earl, one of the court patriots and a strong Protestant voice at James's court, was also very likely to wish to possess a portrait of the man who, after his death, became a symbol of anti-Catholicism and, perhaps rather ironically, an image of opposition to court corruption.

Henry Wotton was, as we have seen, no fan of Thomas Overbury, but he, like Thomas, spent much of his life trying to gain patronage and to thrive at a Jacobean court that this book has argued to be significantly different to its Elizabethan precursor. His description for his friend, Edmund Bacon, of courtiership, of the process he and Thomas undertook, seems a good place to end:

> So as I can yet but cast toward you a longing, and in truth an envious look, from this place of such servility in the getting, and such uncertainty in the holding of fortunes, where methinks we are all overclouded with that sleep of Jacob, when he saw some ascending, and some descending, but that those were angels, and these are men; for in both, what is it but a dream?[15]

[14] See *Shakespeare Found! A Life Portrait at Last: Portraits, Poet, Patron, Poems*, ed. by Stanley Wells (Stratford-upon-Avon: The Cobbe Foundation and the Shakespeare Birthplace Trust, 2009). Many of the conclusions in this text are challenged by Robert Bearman in his review of Wells' book, in *Shakespeare Quarterly*, Vol. 60, No. 4 (2009), pp. 483–7, and he explores the alternative theory that the portrait is indeed of Thomas Overbury.

[15] Letter 38, p. 129.

References

Primary Texts

Manuscripts

BL Add. MS 4106, fol. 91
Add. MS 4160, fol. 3
Add. MS 4160, fol. 332
Add. MS 31922, fol. 14
Add. MS 15476, fol. 92
Cotton Titus B, vii, fol. 483
Cotton Titus B, vv, fol. 464
Harley 7002, fols. 280–91

NA SP 14/15/105
14/50/20
14/72/67
14/72/257
14/81/32
14/82/29
14/82/31
14/82/33
14/82/35
77/10/231
77/10/286
78/55/94
78/55/99
78/55/101
78/55/126–7
78/55/144
84/68/303

Printed manuscript collections

Buccleuch Whitehall I: *Report on the Manuscripts of the Duke of Buccleuch and Queensberry, K. G., K. T., preserved at Montagu House, Whitehall*, Vol. I (London: Her Majesty's Stationery Office, 1899)

Calendar of State Papers, Domestic Series, of the Reign of James I, 1611–1618, preserved in the State Paper Department of Her Majesty's Public Record Office, ed. by Mary Anne Everett Green (London: Longman, Brown, Green, Longmans, & Roberts, 1858)

Calendar of State Papers and Manuscripts Relating to English Affairs, existing in the archives and collections of Venice and in other Libraries of Northern Italy, Vol. XII, 1610–1613, ed. by Horatio F. Brown (London: His Majesty's Stationery Office, 1905)

Downshire: *Report on the Manuscripts of the Marquess of Downshire, preserved at Easthampstead Park, Berks*, Vols. II and III (London: His Majesty's Stationery Office, 1936)

Mar and Kellie: *Report on the Manuscripts of the Earl of Mar and Kellie, preserved at Alloa House, N. B.* (London: His Majesty's Stationery Office, 1904)

Other printed primary material

Bacon, Francis, *The essayes or counsels, ciuill and morall, of Francis Lo. Verulam, Viscount St. Alban* (London: John Haviland, 1625)

——, *The Letters and the Life of Francis Bacon*, ed. by James Spedding, 7 vols. (London: Longmans, Green, Reader, and Dyer, 1861–74)

——, *The Works of Francis Bacon*, ed. by James Spedding, Robert Leslie Ellis and Douglas Denon Heath, 14 vols. (London: Longmans, Green, Reader, and Dyer, 1857)

Birch, Thomas, *The Court and Times of James I: Illustrated by Authentic and Confidential Letters from Various Public and Private Collections*, 2 vols. (London: Henry Colburn, 1849)

Camden, William, *The History of the Most Renowned and Victorious Princess Elizabeth, Late Queen of England*, ed. by Wallace T. MacCaffrey (Chicago: University of Chicago Press, 1970)

Cavendish, William, Earl of Newcastle, *Ideology and Politics on the Eve of the Restoration: Newcastle's Advice to Charles II*, ed. by Thomas P. Slaughter (Philadelphia: American Philosophical Society, 1984)

Chamberlain, John, *The Letters of John Chamberlain*, ed. by Norman Egbert McClure, 2 vols. (Philadelphia: American Philosophical Society, 1939)

Chapman, George, *The Revenge of Bussy D'Ambois: A Tragedie*, ed. by Robert J. Lordi, in *The Plays of George Chapman: The Tragedies with Sir Gyles Goosecappe*, gen. ed. Allan Holaday (Cambridge: D. S. Brewer, 1987)

Cicero, Marcus Tullius, *De Amicitia*, from *De Senectute, De Amicitia, De Divinatione*, trans. by William Armistead Falconer for Loeb Classical Library, Vol. XX (Cambridge, MA: Harvard University Press, 1923)

Cornwallis, William, *Essayes, by Sir William Corne-walys, the younger, knight* (London, 1600)

D'Ewes, Sir Simonds, *The Autobiography and Correspondence of Sir Simonds D'Ewes*, ed. by James Orchard Halliwell, 2 vols. (London: Richard Bentley, 1845)

Dugdale, William, *The Histories and Antiquities of the Four Inns of Court* (London, 1780)

Elliott, John R., et al., eds, *Records of Early English Drama: Oxford*, 2 vols. (Toronto: University of Toronto Press, 2004)

Fitzgeoffrey, Charles, *Affaniae I* (Oxford, 1601)

Fortescue, Sir John, *De laudibus legum Angliae*, ed. by S. B. Chrimes (Cambridge: Cambridge University Press, 1942)

Franklin, Julian H., ed. and trans., *Constitutionalism and Resistance in the Sixteenth Century: Three Treatises by Hotman, Beza and Mornay* (New York: Pegasus, 1969)

Goodman, Godfrey, *The Court of King James the First; by Dr. Godfrey Goodman, Bishop of Gloucester; to Which Are Added, Letters Illustrative of the Personal History of the Most Distinguished Characters in the Court of That Monarch and His Predecessors. Now First Published from the Original Manuscripts*, ed. by John S. Brewer, Vol. I (London: Richard Bentley, 1839)

Greene, Robert, *Pandosto. The Triumph of Time* (1588), in *The Winter's Tale*, ed. by Stephen Orgel (Oxford: Oxford University Press, 1996)

Guazzo, Stefano, *Civile Conversation*, Books 1–3, trans. by George Pettie (London: Richard Watkins, 1581); reproduced in *The Tudor Translations*, 2 vols. (London: Constable, 1925)

Harington, Sir John, *Nugae Antiquae: Being a Miscellaneous Collection of Original Papers in Prose and Verse*, Vol. I (London: J. Wright, 1804)

Harrison, William, *An Historical Description of the Iland of Britaine*, in Ralph Holinshed's *Chronicles* (London, 1587)

Heywood, Thomas, *Apology for Actors* (London: Nicholas Oakes, 1612)

Howell, T. B., *A Complete Collection of State Trials and Proceedings for High Treason and Other Crimes and Misdemeanours from the Earliest Period to the Year 1783, with Notes and Other Illustrations, Compiled by T. B. Howell, Esq.*, Vol. II (London: T. C. Hansard, 1816)

Ingpen, Arthur Robert, KC, *The Middle Temple Bench Book* (London: Chiswick Press, 1912)

Jonson, Ben, *Ben Jonson*, ed. by C. H. Herford and Percy Simpson, 11 vols. (Oxford: Clarendon Press, 1925–52)

——, *The Cambridge Edition of the Works of Ben Jonson*, ed. by David M. Bevington, Martin Butler and Ian Donaldson, 7 vols. (Cambridge: Cambridge University Press, 2012)

Manningham, John, *Diary of John Manningham of the Middle Temple and of Bradbourne, Kent, Barrister-at-Law, 1602–3*, ed. by John Bruce, Esq. (London: J. B. Nichols and Sons, 1868)

Martin, C. T., *Minutes of parliament of the Middle temple, tr. and ed. by C. T. Martin, with an inquiry into the origin and early history of the inn, by J. Hutchinson*, Vol. I (London: Middle Temple, 1904)

Montaigne, Michel de, *The Essayes or Morall, Politike and Millitarie Discourses of Lo: Michaell de Montaigne, Knight of the noble Order of St Michaell, and one of the Gentlemen in Ordinary of the French king, Henry the third his Chamber*, trans. by John Florio (London: Valentine Sims, 1603)

Niccols, Richard, *Sir Thomas Overburies Vision: With the ghoasts of Weston, Mrs. Turner, the late Lieftenant of the Tower, and Franklin* (London, 1616)

Nichols, John, *The Progresses, Processions, and Magnificent Festivities, of King James the First, His Royal Consort, Family, and Court: Collected from Original Manuscripts, Scarce Pamphlets, Corporation Records, Parochial Registers, &c., &c. Comprising Forty Masques and Entertainments; Ten*

Civic Pageants; Numerous Original Letters; and Annotated Lists of the Peers, Baronets, and Knights, Who Received Those Honours during the Reign of King James. Illustrated with Notes, Historical, Topographical, Biographical and Bibliographical, 4 vols. (London: Printed by and for J. B. Nichols, 1828)

Overbury, Thomas, *The Miscellaneous Works in Prose and Verse of Sir Thomas Overbury, Knt*, ed. by Edward F. Rimbault (London: John Russell Smith, 1856)

——, *Overbury's Characters*, ed. by Donald Beecher (Ottawa: Dovehouse Editions, 2003)

——, *Sir Thomas Overbury His Observations in his Travailes upon the State of the XVII Provinces as they stood Anno Dom. 1609, the Treatie of Peace being then on foot* (London: Bernard Alsop for John Parker, 1626)

Owen, John, *Epigrammata* (available online at www.philological.bham.ac.uk /owen/5eng.html)

Painter, William, *The second tome of the Palace of pleasure contayning store of goodlye histories, tragical matters, & other morall argumentes, very requisite for delight and profyte. Chose and selected out of diuers good and commendable authors, and now once agayn corrected and encreased. By VVilliam Painter, clerke of the ordinance and armarie* (London: Thomas Marshe, 1580)

Plowden, Edmund, *The Commentaries, or reports of Edmund Plowden, Of the Middle-Temple, Esq; An Apprentice of the Common Law, containing divers cases upon matters of Law, argued and adjudged in the several Reigns of King Edward VI, Queen Mary, King and Queen Philip and Mary, and Queen Elizabeth. Originally written in French, And now faithfully translated into English, and considerably improved by many marginal Notes and References to all the books of the Common Law, both ancient and modern* (London: In the Savoy, Printed by Catharine Lintot, and Samuel Richardson, Law Printers to the King's Most Excellent Majesty, for the Translator, and to Be Sold by the sellers in London and Westminster, 1761)

Quintilianus, Marcus Fabius, *Institutio oratoria (The Orator's Education)*, ed. and trans. by Donald A. Russell for Loeb Classical Library, 5 vols. (Cambridge, MA: Harvard University Press, 2001)

Rudyerd, Benjamin, *Le Prince D'Amour* (London: William Leake, 1660)

Shakespeare, William, *The Winter's Tale*, Arden 3, ed. by John Pitcher (London: Methuen, 2010)

Snagg, Robert, *The antiquity and original of the Court of Chancery and authority of the Lord Chancellor of England. Being a branch of Sergeant Snagg's Reading, upon the 28 Chapter of Magna Charta* (London, 1654)

Sparke, Michael, *Truth Brought to Light and Discouered by Time or a Discourse and Historicall Narration of the first XIIII Yeares of King Iames Reigne* (London: Richard Cotes for Michael Sparke, 1651)

Stuart, James, *Basilikon Doron of King James VI*, ed. by J. Craigie (Edinburgh and London: Printed for the Scottish Text Society by W. Blackwood & Sons Ltd, 1944)

——, *The Political Works of James I*, ed. by Charles Howard Mcilwain (Cambridge, MA: Harvard University Press, 1918; repr. New York: Russell and Russell, 1965)

Sturgess, H. A. C., *Register of admissions to the Honourable Society of the*

Middle Temple, from the fifteenth century to the year 1944, 3 vols. (London: Published for the Honourable Society of the Middle Temple by Butterworth, 1949)

Sully, Maximilien De Béthune, Duc De., *Memoirs of Maximilien de Bethune, Duke of Sully, Prime Minister of Henry the Great: Newly Translated from the French Edition of M. de L'Ecluse de Loges*, 5 vols. (Edinburgh: Alex Lowrie, 1805)

Tacitus, Cornelius, *The Annales of Cornelius Tacitus*, trans. by Richard Grenewey (London, 1598)

——, *The Ende of Nero and Beginning of Galba: Fower Bookes of the Histories of Cornelius Tacitus*, trans. by Henry Savile (London, 1591)

Webster, John, *The Duchess of Malfi*, New Mermaid, ed. by Brian Gibbons (London: A&C Black, 2001)

——, *The Duchess of Malfi*, Revels Plays, ed. by John Russell Brown (London: Methuen, 1964)

——, *A monumental columne, erected to the liuing memory of the euer-glorious Henry, late Prince of Wales* (London: N. Oakes for William Welby, 1613)

——, *The tragedy of the Dutchesse of Malfy As it was presented priuatly, at the Black-Friers; and publiquely at the Globe, by the Kings Maiesties Seruants. The perfect and exact coppy, with diuerse things printed, that the length of the play would not beare in the presentment. Written by Iohn Webster* (London: Nicholas Oakes, 1623)

Wilbraham, Roger, *The Journal of Sir Roger Wilbraham, Solicitor-General in Ireland and Master of Requests, For the Years 1593–1616*, in *The Camden Miscellany*, Vol. X (London: Royal Historical Society, 1902)

Wilson, Arthur, *History of Great Britain: being the life and reign of King James the first, relating to what passed from his first access to the crown, till his death* (London: Richard Lownds, 1653)

Wilson, Thomas, *The State of England Anno Dom. 1600 by Thomas Wilson*, ed. by F. J. Fisher, in *The Camden Miscellany*, Vol. XVI (London: Royal Historical Society, 1936)

Winwood, Ralph, *Memorials of Affairs of State in the Reigns of Q. Elizabeth and K. James, Collected (chiefly) from the Original Papers of the Right Honourable Sir Ralph Winwood, Kt.* (London: W.B. for T. Ward, 1725) – known, and referred to in the notes, as the *Winwood Memorials*

Wotton, Henry, *The Life and Letters of Sir Henry Wotton*, ed. by Logan Pearsall Smith, 2 vols. (Oxford: Clarendon Press, 1907)

Secondary Texts

Anderson, Sonia P., 'The Elder William Trumbull: A Biographical Sketch', *The Electronic British Library Journal* (1993), http://www.bl.uk/eblj/1993articles/article9.html (accessed 9 August 2017)

Arlidge, Anthony, *Shakespeare and the Prince of Love: The Feast of Misrule in the Middle Temple* (London: Giles de la Mare, 2000)

Aylmer, G. E., *The King's Servants* (London: Routledge & Kegan Paul, 1961)

Baker, John H., *An Introduction to English Legal History*, 5th edition (Oxford: Oxford University Press, 2019)

Barroll, Leeds, *Anna of Denmark, Queen of England: A Cultural Biography* (Philadelphia: University of Pennsylvania Press, 2001)

Bartsch, Shadi, *The Mirror of the Self: Sexuality, Self-Knowledge, and the Gaze in the Early Roman Empire* (Bristol: University of Chicago Press, 2006)

Bearman, Robert, review of *Shakespeare Found! A Life Portrait at Last: Portraits, Poet, Patron, Poems*, in *Shakespeare Quarterly*, Vol. 60, No. 4 (2009), pp. 483–7

Bellany, Alastair, *The Politics of Court Scandal: News Culture and the Overbury Affair* (Cambridge: Cambridge University Press, 2002)

Bennett, Robert B., 'John Webster's Strange Dedication: An Inquiry into Literary Patronage and Jacobean Court Intrigue', *English Literary Renaissance*, Vol. 7, No. 3 (Autumn 1977), pp. 352–67

Bergson, Allen, 'The Worldly Stoicism of George Chapman's *The Revenge of Bussy D'Ambois* and *The Tragedy of Chabot, Admiral of France*', *Philological Quarterly*, Vol. 55, No. 1 (Winter 1976), pp. 43–64

Bertheau, Gilles, 'Passion et néostoïcisme dans *The Revenge of Bussy D'Ambois* (1613) de George Chapman (1559?–1634)', *Études Épistémè* [Online], 1, 2002, http://journals.openedition.org/episteme/8437 (accessed 24 August 2021)

Bland, Mark, *A Guide to Early Printed Books and Manuscripts* (Oxford: Wiley Blackwell, 2010)

Bourdieu, Pierre, *Ce que parler veut dire: l'économie des échanges linguistiques*, trans. by Gino Raymond and Matthew Adamson, ed. by John B. Thompson, as *Language and Symbolic Power* (Cambridge: Polity, 1991)

——, *The Field of Cultural Production: Essays on Art and Literature*, ed. by Randal Johnson (New York: Columbia University Press, 1993)

Bowers, Fredson, *Elizabethan Revenge Tragedy, 1587–1642* (Gloucester, MA: Peter Smith, 1959)

Braden, Gordon, *Renaissance Tragedy and the Senecan Tradition: Anger's Privilege* (New Haven: Yale University Press, 1985)

Bradford, Alan T., 'Stuart Absolutism and the "Utility" of Tacitus', *Huntington Library Quarterly*, Vol. 46, No. 2 (Spring 1983), pp. 127–55

Bray, Alan, *The Friend* (Chicago: University of Chicago Press, 2003)

——, 'Homosexuality and the Signs of Male Friendship in Elizabethan England', *History Workshop*, No. 29 (Spring 1990), pp. 1–19; reprinted as 'Homosexuality and Male Friendship', in *Queering the Renaissance*, ed. by Jonathan Goldberg (Durham, NC: Duke University Press, 1994), pp. 40–61

——, *Homosexuality in Renaissance England* (London: Gay Men's Press, 1982)

Burrow, Colin, *Imitating Authors: Plato to Futurity* (Oxford: Oxford University Press, 2019)

——, *Shakespeare and Classical Antiquity* (Oxford: Oxford University Press, 2013)

Cady, Joseph, 'The "Masculine Love" of the "Princes of Sodom" "Practicing the Art of Ganymede" at Henri III's Court: The Homosexuality of Henri III and His Mignons in Pierre de L'Estoile's *Mémoires-Journaux*', in *Desire and Discipline: Sex and Sexuality in the Premodern West*, ed. by Jacqueline Murray and Konrad Eisenbichler (Toronto: University of Toronto Press, 1996), pp. 123–54

Croft, Pauline, 'Can a Bureaucrat Be a Favourite? Robert Cecil and the Strategies of Power', in *The World of the Favourite*, ed. by J. H. Elliott and L. W. B. Brockliss (New Haven: Yale University Press, 1999), pp. 81–95

——, *King James* (Basingstoke: Palgrave, 2003)

——, 'The Reputation of Robert Cecil: Libels, Political Opinion and Popular Awareness in the Early Seventeenth Century', *Transactions of the Royal Historical Society*, 6th series, No. 1 (1991), pp. 43–69

Cromartie, Alan, *The Constitutionalist Revolution: An Essay on the History of England, 1450–1642* (Cambridge: Cambridge University Press, 2006)

Cuddy, Neil, 'The Revival of the Entourage: The Bedchamber of James I, 1603–1625', in *The English Court: From the Wars of the Roses to the Civil War*, ed. by David Starkey et al. (London: Longman, 1987), pp. 173–225

D'Addario, Chris, 'The Texture of the Everyday in John Manningham's *Diary* (1602–1603)', *English Literary Renaissance*, Vol. 42, No. 2 (Spring 2012), pp. 203–22

Daybell, James, *The Material Letter in Early Modern England: Manuscript Letters and the Culture and Practices of Letter-Writing, 1512–1635* (London: Palgrave Macmillan, 2012)

Dickinson, Janet, *Court Politics and the Earl of Essex, 1589–1601* (London: Pickering & Chatto, 2012)

DiGangi, Mario, *Sexual Types: Embodiment, Agency, and Dramatic Character from Shakespeare to Shirley* (Philadelphia: University of Pennsylvania Press, 2011)

Dillon, Janette, *Theatre, Court and City, 1595–1610: Drama and Social Space in London* (Cambridge: Cambridge University Press, 2000)

Dunning, Chester, 'The Fall of Sir Thomas Overbury and the Embassy to Russia in 1613', *Sixteenth Century Journal*, Vol. 22, No. 4 (Winter 1991), pp. 695–704

Eden, Kathy, *Poetic and Legal Fiction in the Aristotelian Tradition* (Princeton: Princeton University Press, 1986)

——, *Rhetorical Renaissance: The Mistress Art and Her Masterworks* (Chicago: University of Chicago Press, 2022)

Elam, Keir, *Semiotics of Theatre and Drama* (New York: Methuen, 2002)

Enterline, Lynn, *Shakespeare's Schoolroom: Rhetoric, Discipline, Emotion* (Philadelphia: University of Pennsylvania Press, 2012)

Finkelpearl, Philip J., *John Marston of the Middle Temple: An Elizabethan Dramatist in His Social Setting* (Cambridge, MA: Harvard University Press, 1969)

——, 'Sir John Davies and the Prince D'Amour', *Notes and Queries*, Vol. 10, No. 8 (1963), pp. 300–2

Forker, Charles R., *Skull Beneath the Skin: The Achievement of John Webster* (Carbondale, IL: Southern Illinois University Press, 1986)

Fox, Adam, *Oral and Literate Culture in England, 1500–1700* (Oxford: Oxford University Press, 2000)

Fraser, Sara, *The Prince Who Would Be King: The Life and Death of Henry Stuart* (London: William Collins, 2018)

Geng, Penelope, *Communal Justice in Shakespeare's England: Drama, Law and Emotion* (Toronto: University of Toronto Press, 2021)

Gennep, Arnold van, *Les rites de passage*, trans. by Monika B. Vizedom and

Gabrielle L. Caffee as *The Rites of Passage* (Chicago: University of Chicago Press, 1960)

Goldberg, S. L., 'John Hayward, Politic Historian', *The Review of English Studies*, n.s., Vol. 6, No. 23 (July 1955), pp. 233–44

Gurr, Andrew, *Playgoing in Shakespeare's London* (Cambridge: Cambridge University Press, 1987; 3rd edition, 2004)

Guy, John, 'The Rhetoric of Counsel in Early Modern England', in *Tudor Political Culture*, ed. by Dale Hoak (Cambridge: Cambridge University Press, 1995), pp. 292–310

Hasler, P. W., ed., *The House of Commons 1558–1603*, Vol. I (London: Her Majesty's Stationery Office, 1981)

Higgins, Michael, 'Chapman's "Senecal Man": A Study in Jacobean Psychology', *The Review of English Studies*, Vol. 21, No. 83 (1945), pp. 183–91

——, 'The Development of the "Senecal Man"', *The Review of English Studies*, Vol. 23, No. 89 (1947), pp. 24–33

Howard, Jean, *Theater of a City: The Places of London Comedy, 1598–1642* (Philadelphia: University of Pennsylvania Press, 2007)

Hudson, Judith, *Crime and Consequence in Early Modern Literature and Law* (Edinburgh: Edinburgh University Press, 2022)

Hutson, Lorna, *Circumstantial Shakespeare* (Oxford: Oxford University Press, 2015)

——, *The Invention of Suspicion* (Oxford: Oxford University Press, 2007)

——, 'Not the King's Two Bodies: Reading the "Body Politic" in Shakespeare's *Henry IV, Part 1* and *2*', in *Rhetoric and Law in Early Modern Europe*, ed. by Victoria Khan and Lorna Hutson (New Haven: Yale University Press, 2001), pp. 166–98

Jones, Ann Rosalind, 'The Italians and Others', in *Staging the Renaissance*, ed. by David Scott Kastan and Peter Stallybrass (Abingdon: Routledge, 1991), pp. 251–62

Kantorowicz, Ernst H., *The King's Two Bodies* (Princeton: Princeton University Press, 1957)

Kistler, Suzanne F., '"Strange and Far-Removed Shores": A Reconsideration of *The Revenge of Bussy D'Ambois*', *Studies in Philology*, Vol. 77, No. 2 (Spring 1980), pp. 128–44

Knutson, Rosalyn L., 'Influence of the Repertory System on the Revival and Revision of *The Spanish Tragedy* and *Dr Faustus*', *English Literary Renaissance*, Vol. 18, No. 2 (1988), pp. 257–74

Kurland, Stuart, '"We Need No More of Your Advice": Political Realism in *The Winter's Tale*', *Studies in English Literature 1500–1900*, Vol. 31, No. 2 (Spring 1991), pp. 365–86

Levy, Fritz, 'The Decorum of News', in *News, Newspapers, and Society in Early Modern Britain*, ed. by Joad Raymond (London: Frank Cass, 1999), pp. 12–38

Lindley, David, *The Trials of Frances Howard: Fact and Fiction at the Court of King James* (London: Routledge, 1993)

Lublin, Robert I., *Costuming the Shakespearean Stage* (Farnham: Ashgate, 2011)

McElwee, William, *The Murder of Sir Thomas Overbury* (Oxford: Oxford University Press, 1952)

McIntosh, Shona, 'The Massacre of St Bartholomew on the English Stage: Chapman, Marlowe, and the Duke of Guise', *Renaissance Studies*, Vol. 26, No. 3 (2011), pp. 325–44

McIver, Bruce, '*A Wife Now the Widdow*: Lawrence Lisle and the Popularity of the Overburian Characters', *South Atlantic Review*, Vol. 59, No. 1 (January 1994), pp. 27–44

Magnusson, Lynne, 'Scoff Power in *Love's Labour's Lost* and the Inns of Court', *Shakespeare Survey*, Vol. 57 (2004), pp. 196–208

Magrath, J. R., *The Queen's College* (Oxford: Clarendon Press, 1921)

Maus, Katharine Eisaman, ed., *Four Revenge Tragedies* (Oxford: Oxford University Press, 1995)

Meyler, Bernadette, *Theaters of Pardoning* (Ithaca: Cornell University Press, 2019)

Miola, Robert, *Shakespeare and Classical Tragedy: The Influence of Seneca* (Oxford: Clarendon Press, 1992)

Munro, Lucy, *Children of the Queen's Revels* (Cambridge: Cambridge University Press, 2005)

Mynott, Glen, '"We must not be more true to kings / Than Kings are to their subjects": France and the Politics of the Ancient Constitution in Chapman's Byron Plays', *Renaissance Studies*, Vol. 9, No. 4 (1995), pp. 477–93

O'Callaghan, Michelle, *The English Wits: Literature and Sociability in Early Modern England* (Cambridge: Cambridge University Press, 2007)

Patterson, Jonathan, *Villainy in France (1463–1610): A Transcultural Study of Law and Literature* (Oxford: Oxford University Press, 2022)

Perry, Curtis, *Literature and Favoritism in Early Modern England* (Cambridge: Cambridge University Press, 2006)

——, *Shakespeare and Senecan Tragedy* (Cambridge: Cambridge University Press, 2020)

Ray, Sid, '"Those Whom God Hath Joined Together": Bondage Metaphors and Marital Advice in Early Modern England', in *Domestic Arrangements in Early Modern England*, ed. by Kari Boyd McBride (Pittsburgh, PA: Duquesne University Press, 2002), pp. 34–5

Rowe, Katherine, 'Memory and Revision in Chapman's Bussy Plays', *Renaissance Drama*, n.s., Vol. 31, 'Performing Affect' (2002), pp. 125–52

Salmon, J. H. M., 'Stoicism and Roman Example: Seneca and Tacitus in Jacobean England', *Journal of the History of Ideas*, Vol. 50, No. 2 (April–June 1989), pp. 199–225

Schneider, Gary, *The Culture of Epistolarity: Vernacular Letters and Letter Writing in Early Modern England, 1500–1700* (Newark: University of Delaware Press, 2005)

Sedgwick, Eve Kosofsky, *Between Men: English Literature and Male Homosocial Desire* (New York: Columbia University Press, 1985)

Shapiro, Michael, 'Towards a Reappraisal of the Children's Troupes', *Theatre Survey*, Vol. 13, No. 2 (November 1972), pp. 1–19

Simkin, Stevie, *Cultural Constructions of the Femme Fatale: From Pandora's Box to Amanda Knox* (New York: Palgrave Macmillan, 2014)

Smuts, Malcolm, 'Court-Centred Politics and the Uses of Roman Historians, c.1590–1630', in *Culture and Politics in Early Stuart England*, ed. by Kevin Sharpe and Peter Lake (London: Macmillan, 1994), pp. 21–43

Sommerville, J. P., *Politics and Ideology in England, 1603–1640* (London: Longman, 1986)

Stewart, Alan, *Close Readers: Humanism and Sodomy in Early Modern England* (Princeton: Princeton University Press, 1997)

Stone Peters, Julie, *Law as Performance: Theatricality, Spectatorship, and the Making of Law in Ancient, Medieval, and Early Modern Europe* (Oxford: Oxford University Press, 2022)

Stubbs, John, *Donne: The Reformed Soul* (London: Penguin, 2007)

Thayer, C. G., 'The Ambiguity of Bosola', *Studies in Philology*, Vol. 54, No. 2 (April 1957), pp. 162–71

Thomas, Courtney Erin, 'Politics and Culture at the Jacobean Court: The Role of Queen Anna of Denmark', *Quidditas: The Journal of the Rocky Mountain Medieval and Renaissance Association*, Vol. 29 (2009), pp. 64–107

Tosh, Will, *Male Friendship and Testimonies of Love in Shakespeare's England* (Basingstoke: Palgrave Macmillan, 2016)

Tricomi, Albert H., 'The Revised *Bussy D'Ambois* and *The Revenge of Bussy D'Ambois*: Joint Performance in Thematic Counterpoint', *English Language Notes*, Vol. 9, No. 4 (1972), pp. 253–62

Ure, Peter, 'The Date of the Revision of Chapman's *The Tragedy of Bussy D'Ambois*', *Notes and Queries*, Vol. 197 (1952), pp. 1–2

Van Elk, Martine, '"Our praises are our wages": Courtly Exchange, Social Mobility, and Female Speech in *The Winter's Tale*', *Philological Quarterly*, Vol. 79, No. 4 (Fall 2000), pp. 429–57

Watson, Jackie, '"My lodging is so near the Star Chamber that my pens shake in my hand": Letters, Truth and Lawyers' Fears', in *Forum for Modern Language Studies* special issue, 'In Pursuit of Truth: Law and Emotion in Early Modern Europe' (January 2018), pp. 46–59

Wells, Stanley, ed., *Shakespeare Found! A Life Portrait at Last: Portraits, Poet, Patron, Poems* (Stratford-upon-Avon: The Cobbe Foundation and the Shakespeare Birthplace Trust, 2009)

White, Beatrice, *The Cast of Ravens: The Strange Case of Sir Thomas Overbury* (London: John Murray, 1965)

Whitney, Charles, *Early Responses to Renaissance Drama* (Cambridge: Cambridge University Press, 2006)

Wieler, John W., *George Chapman: The Effect of Stoicism upon his Tragedies* (New York: King's Crown Press, 1949)

Wilson, E. E., Jr, 'The Genesis of Chapman's *The Revenge of Bussy D'Ambois*', *Modern Language Notes*, Vol. 71, No. 8 (December 1956), pp. 567–9

Worden, Blair, 'Ben Jonson among the Historians', in *Culture and Politics in Early Stuart England*, ed. by Kevin Sharpe and Peter Lake (London: Macmillan, 1994), pp. 67–89

Working, Lauren, *The Making of an Imperial Polity: Civility and America in the Jacobean Metropolis* (Cambridge: Cambridge University Press, 2020)

Wykes, David, 'Ben Jonson's *Chaste Booke* – The Epigrammes', *Culture, Theory and Critique*, Vol. 13, No. 1 (1969), pp. 76–87

Index

EU representative:
Easy Access System Europe
Mustamäe tee 50, 10621 Tallinn, Estonia
Gpsr.requests@easproject.com

www.ingramcontent.com/pod-product-compliance
Lightning Source LLC
Chambersburg PA
CBHW051103030726
47504CB00006B/1761